AREA HANDBOOK

for

BURMA

Co-Authors

John W. Henderson

Judith M. Heimann

Kenneth W. Martindale

Rinn-Sup Shinn

John O. Weaver

Eston T. White

American University Washington D.C. Foreign Area Studies

Research and writing were completed April 1971

Published 1971

(This pamphlet supersedes DA Pam 550-61, June 1968)

36490

DA Pam 550-61

Library of Congress Catalog Card Number: 75-612066

For sale by the Superintendent of Documents, U.S. Government Printing Office
Washington, D.C. 20402—Price $3.00

FOREWORD

This volume is one of a series of handbooks prepared by Foreign Area Studies (FAS) of The American University, designed to be useful to military and other personnel who need a convenient compilation of basic facts about the social, economic, political, and military institutions and practices of various countries. The emphasis is on objective description of the nation's present society and the kinds of possible or probable changes that might be expected in the future. The handbook seeks to present as full and as balanced an integrated exposition as limitations on space and research time permit. It was compiled from information available in openly published material. An extensive bibliography is provided to permit recourse to other published sources for more detailed information. There has been no attempt to express any specific point of view or to make policy recommendations. The contents of the handbook represent the work of the authors and FAS and do not represent the official view of the United States government.

An effort has been made to make the handbook as comprehensive as possible. It can be expected, however, that the material, interpretations, and conclusions are subject to modification in the light of new information and developments. Such corrections, additions, and suggestions for factual, interpretive, or other change as readers may have will be welcomed for use in future revisions. Comments may be addressed to:

The Director
Foreign Area Studies
The American University
5010 Wisconsin Avenue, N.W.
Washington, D.C. 20016

PREFACE

Since publication of the *Area Handbook for Burma* in 1968 the shape and direction of the Revolutionary Government of the Union of Burma's new Marxist-oriented program have become clearer, making desirable a revision to take into account new developments and new information. Much of the research that is the basis for the 1968 volume was conducted in 1966 and reflected developments that had come to public knowledge somewhat earlier, in some cases predating the forcible seizure of power in 1962 by a military group headed by General Ne Win.

Although access to Burmese sources has continued to be somewhat limited and official statistics have remained unavailable in many fields, the Ne Win government's plans for socializing the economy and revamping the society to a degree have been made public, although the total program still is not known. This is in part because the government has severely limited the ability of outside research workers, journalists, and others to enter the country. There has been some recent evidence, however, that these strictures are being lightened to some extent.

The 1968 handbook was prepared by a team headed by T.D. Roberts and including Jan M. Matthews, David S. McMorris, Kathryn E. Parachini, William N. Raiford, and Charles Townsend. This revision is intended to make the handbook current, as nearly as possible, with 1971.

The handbook's purpose is to provide in a compact, convenient, balanced, and objective form an integrated exposition and analysis of the dominant social, political, and economic aspects of Burmese society. It is designed to give readers an understanding of the dynamics of the component elements of the society as well as an insight into the ideas and feelings of its people and the role of the country in the world around it.

Readers may find some inconsistency in the spelling of Burmese place names compared with usage to be found on some widely used maps and in various publications. Spelling of most place names has followed official United States government maps and *Burma: Official Standard Names Gazetteer No. 96* of the United States Board on Geographic Names, published in March 1966. In some instances differing official Burmese usage or general international use by English publications is followed when it seemed likely that such spellings would more readily be recognized by the reader.

Burmese practice in the use of personal names has been followed in the bibliography and index of this volume. Those who are unfamiliar with Burmese practice should note that there are no Burmese surnames, family names, or married names. Burmese have names of one, two, or three syllables, and these do not necessarily bear any relation to the name of father, husband, sibling, or any other relative. They are preceded by titles that indicate sex and that also take account of age and social position relative to the speaker. The most common adult title used to address or refer to men of superior age or social status is "U." A man, however, would never refer to himself as "U" but would instead employ the more modest title "Maung." The female equivalent to "U" is "Daw," and to "Maung," "Ma."

English usage in this edition of the handbook follows *Webster's Third New International Dictionary* (unabridged). English weights and measures are used except that all tons are metric tons unless otherwise noted.

COUNTRY SUMMARY

1. COUNTRY: The Union of Burma. Independent state after 1948. Burmese empire embracing most of modern nation first appeared in eleventh century. Partially under British colonial rule, 1826 to 1886; fully until 1947.

2. GOVERNMENT: Revolutionary Council composed of the military elite heads the Revolutionary Government of the Union of Burma. Its chairman, governing through a hierarchy of appointed security and administrative committees, rules by decree. The only authorized party—the Burma Socialist Program Party—is dominated by the military. Its declared mission is to provide leadership and gain mass support for the government. Provisions for governmental system in 1947 Constitution largely ignored after 1962.

3. SIZE AND LOCATION: Area, 262,000 square miles. Extends 800 miles from southern to northern extremities; 500 miles on longest east-west axis. Bordered on northeast by Communist China; on east, by Laos; on southeast, by Thailand; on the southwest, by the Andaman Sea; on the west, by the Bay of Bengal; and on the northwest, by East Pakistan and India.

4. ADMINISTRATIVE DIVISIONS: Major subdivisions: seven divisions of Burma proper; four constituent states; and one special division. Major units subdivided into districts, which are further divided into townships. Villages lowest element in country, and wards lowest in towns and cities. System of designations generally as established by British. *Military*. Army system of regional commands utilized for political control and for military administrative and tactical purposes.

5. TOPOGRAPHY: Four major features extend generally north and south. The Shan Plateau, average elevation 3,000 feet and deeply dissected, in the east; the valley region, in the center; the long mountain rib, much of which is 6,000 to 8,000 feet, in the west; and the narrow Arakan Coastal Strip.

6. CLIMATE: Predominantly tropical except in northern highlands. Strongly influenced by monsoon. Three seasons: rainy, end of May to October; cool, end of October to middle February; and hot, middle February to end of May. Annual rainfall by region varies from less than 25 to over 200 inches.

7. POPULATION: About 27 million estimated in 1970. Annual growth rate estimated at 2.2 percent. About 80 to 85 percent rural. Only Rangoon, Mandalay, and Moulmein have over 100,000 population. Approximately 70 percent ethnic Burmans. Other most

important ethnic elements: Karens, Shans, Kachins, Chins, Kayahs, Mons, Indians, Pakistanis, and Chinese.

8. LABOR FORCE: Estimated at 10.5 million in 1967-68 period. Approximately 67 percent in agriculture, 8 percent in trade, 7 percent in manufacturing; no other sector has more than 3 percent.

9. LANGUAGES: Burman is official language spoken by estimated 90 percent of population. Non-Burmans usually speak own tongue as first language. English used frequently by persons with higher education and in political circles.

10. RELIGION: Estimated 75 to 85 percent of population Theravada Buddhists. Other believers include Hindus, Muslims, animists, and Christians. All religions tolerated.

11. EDUCATION: Literacy officially estimated at 60 percent in 1970. Academic education under state control heavily oriented toward goals of the Burmese Way to Socialism. Compulsory eight years of education a rule but not enforced because of lack of facilities.

12. HEALTH: Many diseases common to Southeast Asia widespread. Medical services and facilities inadequate. Widespread use of folk medicine. Poor sanitation and lack of public information on causes of disease degrade health. Life expectancy estimated at 40.4 years for men and 43.8 for women.

13. JUSTICE: Civil and ordinary criminal courts operate under the Chief Court from national to local level. Special crimes courts, working in concert with security and administrative committees, litigate political offenses.

14. ECONOMY: Agrarian, with system of state monopolies and state-controlled cooperatives. Government priority to industrialization and production of import substitutes. Proclaimed ultimate objective is nationalization of all means of production, distribution, and exchange.

15. AGRICULTURE: Rice is the most important crop for domestic consumption and export. Two-thirds of total cultivated acreage in rice. Efforts to diversify only slightly successful. Productivity low considering resource base.

16. INDUSTRY: Poorly developed despite high priority accorded by government after 1952. Food processing, especially of rice, predominates.

17. FOREIGN TRADE: Government controlled through the Trade Council and conducted by its subsidiary Trade Corporation No. 22. Leading exports, rice and teak. Leading imports machinery and transport equipment.

18. FINANCE: *Currency.* The kyat is standard unit. Backed by foreign exchange and gold holdings. Official rate of exchange remained steady since independence at 4.76 kyat to US$1. Deficit

budgets 1966 to 1970, caused largely by emphasis on industrial development, more than halved reserves.

19. COMMUNICATIONS: Government owned and controlled. Internal mainly by wireless. External wireless largely through Ceylon and India. Most prevalent direct links with foreign countries are radiotelephone.

20. ROADS: Approximately 16,000 miles of highways, of which 4,200 miles paved. Animal transport predominates.

21. RAILROADS: State owned and operated. In 1971, 1,850 miles single track (meter-gauge) in use, with second track in 386-mile Rangoon to Mandalay section under construction.

22. WATER TRANSPORT: Approximately 5,000 miles of navigable rivers extremely important to economic life. Irrawaddy River the most important. Rangoon principal port handles about 85 percent of seaborne trade. Few natural harbors.

23. AIR TRANSPORT: Union of Burma Airways owns and operates all commercial aircraft, in 1970 numbering seventeen. About forty airfields, nearly all with short runways. In 1969 longest in Moulmein, 8,900 feet.

24. INTERNATIONAL AGREEMENTS AND TREATIES: Mutual nonaggression treaty of 1960 with Communist China stands alone. Burma followed strict nonalignment policy after 1948. Member United Nations after 1948 and in 1971 represented on many of its affiliated organizations. Member Colombo Plan after 1952.

25. AID: Received from regional and international organizations. Economic and technical assistance on both reimbursable and non-reimbursable basis received from countries of widely differing political orientation. Government-to-government agreements demanded. Is generally against foreign joint ventures, and private investment is prohibited.

26. SECURITY: Disaffection among minority ethnic groups, a constant source of disorder after 1948, continued in 1971. Communist insurgents, principally the White Flag faction, which in 1971 was the largest and strongest communist group, also limited government control in some areas. The National People's Police force in 1970 numbered about 40,000. Military played key role in maintaining law and order.

27. THE ARMED FORCES: The Ministry of Defense also serves as a triservice headquarters. Approximate strengths: army, about 120,000; navy, about 6,000; air force, 7,000. National Service Law of 1959 for compulsory training never implemented because requirements met by volunteers. Defense costs: approximately 35 percent of regular government expenditures in 1970-71 period.

BURMA

TABLE OF CONTENTS

TABLE OF CONTENTS (Continued)

Page

LIST OF TABLES

xii

LIST OF ILLUSTRATIONS

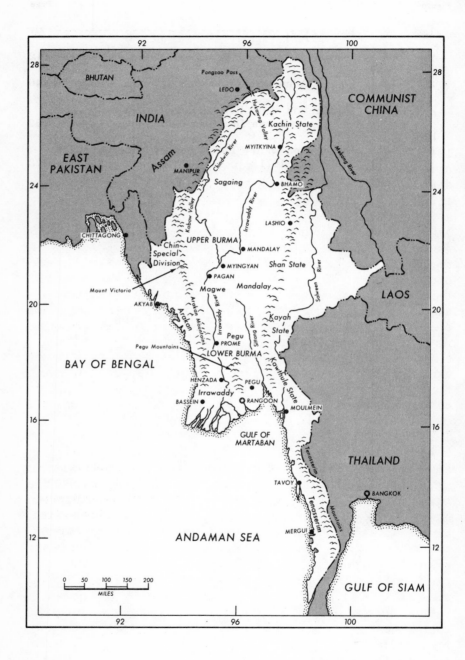

Figure 1. Burma

SECTION I. SOCIAL

CHAPTER 1

GENERAL CHARACTER OF THE SOCIETY

Burma joined the family of sovereign, independent states in 1948, after nearly a century of British colonial rule, with a dominantly Buddhist but multiethnic population, an agrarian and alien-dominated economy, and a fledgling parliamentary system of government in which cabinet ministers were responsible collectively to a popularly elected legislature. At independence, Prime Minister U Nu and his socialist colleagues dedicated themselves to the achievement of three major goals: national solidarity, especially between the majority Burmans and ethnic minority groups; economic development and diversification; and parliamentary democracy. In 1971 these goals remained elusive, although General Ne Win, after his assumption of power in 1962 in a military coup, followed a policy of accelerated national development based on different priorities. As of 1971 the country was, in effect, a unitary state with a highly centralized government supported by a one-party system. This was true despite the fact that under the Constitution, then in abeyance, the name of the country—"Union of Burma"—and provision for a constituent state structure were intended to apply to a federal form of government.

The country's population, estimated at about 27 million in 1970 is scattered over an area of 262,000 square miles located in Southeast Asia just east of the Indian subcontinent. The available land is sufficient to support the population, but before the end of the twentieth century it is expected that the population, increasing at an annual rate of 2.2 percent in the early 1970s, will double and that land scarcity could become a major problem. The government position heretofore has been that the country, which has traditionally enjoyed food surpluses, is underpopulated and that population control is not needed. In 1971 most of the people continued to live off the land. Money income remained low; the diet was modest in volume, low in protein, and high in starch content. The general contentment with the physical conditions of living, evident until the mid-1960s, was becoming less pronounced in the early 1970s because of a growing shortage in daily necessities and an inadequate distribution system.

About two-thirds of the country is located in the northern

tropical zone, from which a long, narrow strip extends southward for some 500 miles. This length, coupled with a mountain-broken terrain, gives the country a wide variation in climatic conditions. Virtually all of the long and tortuous land frontier, which is shared with five neighboring countries, passes through rugged mountains and heavily forested highlands that have served historically to isolate the country from its neighbors.

Of the various ethnic groups, the most numerous are the Burmans, who represent over 70 percent of the population. The language of the Burmans is the official one of the country and is spoken either as a principal or as a second language by most of the minority peoples who make up the remainder of the population. Burmans constitute nearly all of the indigenous population of the urban areas, which produce most of the leading figures in public life. Except in a few minority enclaves, Burmans are numerically predominant throughout the lowlands (commonly defined as Burma proper). Only a few Burmans have settled in the frontier highlands, where the most important ethnic groups are the Shans, Karens, Chins, and Kachins. Before the coming of the British no Burmese monarchy had managed to subjugate effectively all of the frontier peoples.

Nearly all Burmans and many members of minority groups—or an estimated 75 to 85 percent of the population—share the same faith, Buddhism. The remainder adhere to other religions, such as animism, Christianity, Hinduism, and Islam. Most of the non-Buddhist minority peoples are animists, worshipers of the spirits of nature. Observance of animist rituals does not preclude worship as a Buddhist, and Buddhist missionaries are actively proselytizing their faith in frontier areas. Christianity is comparatively strong among the Karens, the Kachins, and the Chins. The numbers of Hindus and Muslims have declined sharply since the early 1960s because of the mass exodus of Indians and Pakistanis from the country.

In the first decade after independence government leaders were able to steer the nation through one crisis after another, despite a formidable array of difficulties stemming from their lack of training and experience in government, the persistence of personal differences and ideological fissures within the leadership circle, and civil insurrections launched by both communist and ethnic minority rebels. They were able to weather the first decade in part because of the harmonious and cooperative relationships that existed between civilian and military leaders.

Ideologically, civilian and military leaders were for the most part socialist oriented, inspired in their political outlook as much by their leftist contemporaries in India and England as by their common participation in the Marxist-inclined nationalist-revolutionary movement of the World War II period. They adopted the rhetoric of socialism as a basis for the determination of national priorities and policies. They rejected the principles of capitalism, which they equated with foreign rule and exploitation.

Nevertheless, for pragmatic reasons, they did not seek to introduce any new political or social system different from that they had known under British rule. Rather, in an effort to realize what came to be known popularly as Burmanization of the country, the founding fathers of the new nation followed a policy of gradual modernization through parliamentary methods of moderation and legislative reconciliation. In this process, they appealed to the principles of democracy, nationalism, and socialism.

The Burmanization program entered a new era in 1962 when, upon supplanting the constitutional government of U Nu, General Ne Win formed an all-military, self-selecting supreme organ of power, the Revolutionary Council. Proclaiming that parliamentary democracy had failed in Burma, Ne Win inaugurated an authoritarian, military rule unencumbered by any constitutional restraint. Ensuring an administration responsive to the Revolutionary Council was effected by detaining temporarily most of the career party politicians active in the pre-1962 years, forcibly retiring a number of senior civil servants allegedly because of their conservative attitudes, and installing army officers in key positions throughout the governmental infrastructure.

In essence, General Ne Win's avowed intention was to shorten the timetable for the nation's political and economic development by minimizing conflicting and divisive sociopolitical forces. This intention was predicated on the explicit assumption that the application of a military-type discipline and control would result in a greater measure of unity, efficiency, productivity, and popular political participation.

In proclaiming the ultimate goal of establishing an exploitation-free "socialist democratic state," the Revolutionary Council set up a one-party political system based on a Marxist-colored ideology called the Burmese Way to Socialism. Under this political system the nation's only authorized political organization—the Burma Socialist Program Party (BSPP)—and the government are blended into an integrated instrument of persuasion and control. The council proclaimed that the armed forces would play the leading role in the operation of the new political setup. Efforts to strengthen internal cohesion have been intensified with much greater vigor than had been the case in the pre-1962 years.

Among other features of the Ne Win rule has been the policy of socializing nearly all sectors of the national economy. As a result, private enterprises, except those in agriculture, have been reduced to a marginal role, and the state has become increasingly burdened

3

with difficulties. These difficulties stem from the lack of an adequate incentive system and from an excess of bureaucratic planning and control. In its effort to induce popular acceptance of the new politicoeconomic system, the government has embarked on an extensive program of information and education. For example, the school system has been revised so that political indoctrination has become an officially acknowledged and basic part of the socialist educational process.

In foreign relations General Ne Win has continued his predecessor's policy of strict neutrality and nonalignment. Furthermore, he intensified efforts to reduce or eliminate foreign influences, political and economic, asserting that they interfered with his program of socialist construction.

The Revolutionary Government of the Union of Burma, as it is officially called, seeks to achieve its socialist aims and introduce what General Ne Win calls "direct participatory democracy" by mobilizing the people through its political arm, the Burma Socialist Program Party. The party's two major instruments of mass mobilization are what the government called people's peasants' councils and people's workers' councils, established in all areas but those troubled by insurgency.

The aim and role of the party as well as of the all-military Revolutionary Council were explained by General Ne Win in a statement made in 1966:

> The Revolutionary Council had to take over state power because of unavoidable circumstances. In fact, the state power belongs to the people. It must be restored to the people, its original owners. The way...to [transfer power] is first to reorganize a political party consisting of peasants, workers and the working people...and then build it up into a revolutionary party that will lead the people along revolutionary lines through the adoption of constitutional statutes and rules with common consent.

In 1971 the party remained the only legitimate channel of political expression and participation. The party leadership was military, as was the majority of party membership. Along with the armed forces and the military-dominated agencies of the central government, the party not only served as an instrument of political control and persuasion but also provided opportunities for social advancement to those willing to accept the Burmese Way to Socialism as a code of personal and public conduct.

In early 1971 the party was in the process of evolving into a broadly based "people's party," the formation of which is officially viewed as the beginning of the nation's march toward socialism. Membership was expanded sharply, and political indoctrination was intensified.

Of greater immediate concern to the public has been General Ne Win's policy of accelerated economic nationalization and its consequences. For example, to the once economically dominant minority of British, Indians, Pakistanis, and Chinese, nationalization brought the end of an era. The progress of Burmanization in the years before 1962 had been accompanied by a gradual decrease of the foreign control of business and the departure of a trickle of businessmen and skilled workers, but the momentum generated by the Enterprise Nationalization Law of 1963 saw the trickle become a flood. Within a few years of General Ne Win's takeover, the country's managerial and professional class had become virtually extinct. Gone with the businessmen and entrepreneurs were also the foreign medical personnel and educators who had staffed the foreign-operated hospitals and schools, for these too had been closed or nationalized.

The expanded role of the state has created difficulties in terms of planning, coordination, and implementation. Coupled with the absence of adequate price and material incentives, the absence of experienced managerial talent, and continuing insurgency, economic activity has tended to stagnate. State enterprises have operated to meet production quotas, with minimal attention to product quality or service to customers. The problem has been compounded by the poorly functioning distribution system, causing the shortage of consumer goods in many areas.

The government has acknowledged on many occasions that, during the transitional stage toward socialism, dislocations of production and distribution were to be expected. In this connection the *Working People's Daily,* an influential, progovernment English-language newspaper in Rangoon, commented in 1971 that the people could understand and overlook temporary inconveniences but that they could not be asked to be patient with trade personnel who deliberately caused damages, shortages, and the disappearance of goods.

Since 1962 the government policy has been focused, on the one hand, on increasing the output of primary goods, such as rice, teak, and minerals, so as to obtain surpluses for export to pay for imports and to permit a higher rate of capital investment and, on the other hand, on developing import-substitute industries. This policy has been dictated by the predominantly agrarian character of the economy.

In a major effort to improve the distribution system and in effect to nationalize the remaining segment of the economy that has not been nationalized, the government in 1970 started organizing a network of consumer, producer, and credit cooperatives as an intermediate stage of transition toward full socialism. The government was giving increased attention to measures to reverse the downward spiral of exports, which in 1970 had dropped to the lowest level since independence. The drop was attributable mainly to the depressed state of the rice market abroad. Among other major problems in 1970 were: the continuing balance of payments deficit; declining gold and foreign exchange reserves, which had reached the lowest level in fifteen years; and the state enterprises operating generally with a deficit.

According to the draft of the country's First Four-Year Plan (fiscal 1971/72 to 1974/75) announced in March 1971, the government seeks to increase the gross national product (GNP) by 10 percent during the plan period. The plan assigns top priority to: the development of agricultural, meat and fish, and forestry sectors for export purposes; the establishment of industries for manufacturing consumer goods and goods that can be substituted for imported items; the increased production of minerals to be processed and used internally; and the development of indigenous heavy industries. The plan calls for an increase in per capita income of 8 percent between fiscal 1970/71 and 1974/75.

In efforts to dramatize their grievances or press their demands for the fullest possible autonomy, many of Burma's minority groups had resorted to armed insurrection as early as 1948. The civil insurgency, once described by General Ne Win as "a twin brother of independence," remained in 1971 as a major internal security problem. It has forced the authorities to divert a sizable portion of government resources for purposes of internal pacification. The problem of insurgency has been compounded also by the participation of ideologically inspired communist rebels, who had taken to armed struggles even before independence. The Communists have acted independently of, but sometimes also in conjunction with, the ethnic insurgents. In 1971 the government continued to express the view that its counterinsurgency efforts were succeeding and that it would eventually be able to bring together all dissident groups into a mutually beneficial relationship. Such optimism was accompanied by an effort aimed at improving the levels of education and living conditions in the frontier regions.

In 1971 the government followed the policy of minimum involvement in religious matters on the grounds that a preferential treatment of any particular faith would have the effect of antagonizing followers of other religions, thus contributing to national disunity. This policy, essentially a continuation of the government position at the time of independence that religion and state should be separated, was discontinued briefly in 1961 when the government of Prime Minister U Nu declared Buddhism as "the State religion" in a constitutional amendment.

Buddhism exerts an all-pervasive influence as the principal source of social as well as political values and attitudes. Since independence governments have attempted to use Buddhism in their endeavors to foster a common awareness of national identity and to combat communist insurgents, who the authorities stated were

6

anti-Buddhist and thus anti-Burmese.

The people are not segmented into mutually exclusive groupings based on heredity. There are, however, flexible social, economic, cultural, and geographic criteria for social status. Burmese live for the most part in nuclear family units rather than as extended families. Nevertheless, close feelings of kinship with relatives outside the family prevail, influencing a wide range of individual and group relationships in the society. Women enjoy approximately the same rights as men both within and outside the family.

Most of the population depends, directly or indirectly, on agriculture for its livelihood and lives in small villages surrounded by farm plots. In Burma proper these villages have remained in place over generations, although there is some shifting of the surrounding tracts in order to allow land to lie fallow for a time or to bring new areas into cultivation. In the frontier highlands villages may be permanent or may be moved after varying numbers of years to new locations within a limited area. Some villagers are still seminomadic and continue to practice shifting cultivation by abandoning a village site and moving on as soon as the fertility of the land has been exhausted.

The urban population is still relatively small and, until the mid-1960s, included many Indians, Pakistanis, and Chinese who, together with the British, dominated the economic life of the country. Many Chinese remain, but Burmans have largely rejected the others. Many of the indigenous people, who spend all or most of their working lives in towns, were born in villages, and some return to their place of origin to spend their last years among relatives. Although few in number, urban dwellers exert powerful political and other influences on the society. Military officers, civil servants, party officials, professionals, and engineers are for the most part concentrated in Rangoon and Mandalay, as are the occasionally politically strident university students.

Burmans appear in historical accounts first in the ninth century, by which time peoples north of the Himalayan passes had completed their southward trek into Upper Burma and had established themselves as the dominant ethnic Burmans in the strategic central Irrawaddy lowland region. There ensued a long series of internal warfare, mainly with Mon people who had settled farther to the south in Lower Burma.

After three wars with British India, the first one starting in 1824 and the last ending in 1886, Burma was eliminated as an independent kingdom, and its territory was incorporated into the British Empire. By the early 1900s, however, a small but stridently vocal and nationalistic urban intellectual group had begun to develop. After World War I a wave of sentiment favoring self-determination led to the granting of limited self-government, and the occupation of most of the country by the Japanese during World War II destroyed the myth of Western invincibility. After the war British rule was reinstated but, because of mounting popular pressures for an end to colonialism, the British left the country peacefully.

The nationalist revolutionaries who assumed the leadership of the independent nation were without practical experience in government and had to rely on the British-trained senior civil servants. Moreover, the war had disrupted the economy and caused extensive material damage. Transition was painful, and even before independence the country was subject to insurrection.

The new nation was also beset by internal disagreements as to the manner in which various political segments could be brought together and religious tensions could be minimized to permit the emergence of an integrated multiracial and multireligious polity. Wranglings among career politicians over ideological, personal, and programmatic differences assumed serious proportions.

The nation's experiment with parliamentary democracy, undertaken under U Nu, came to an abrupt end in 1962 when General Ne Win seized control of the government. This led to the Burmese Way to Socialism, which rejected parliamentary democratic processes. This concept does not permit multiparty partisan competition, elections, or parliamentary representation as they were known and practiced in pre-1962 years. Group interests other than those of the peasants and workers are officially viewed as self-seeking and exploitive. Private enterprise is regarded as harmful to the cause of establishing a socialist welfare state.

CHAPTER 2

PHYSICAL ENVIRONMENT AND POPULATION

Burma has an area of approximately 262,000 square miles, sharing land boundaries with Pakistan and India in the west and northwest, with Communist China in the north and Northeast, and with Laos and Thailand in the east and southeast. In the south and southwest, the country faces the Bay of Bengal and the Andaman Sea, providing it with an extensive coastline running from Pakistan in the north to Thailand in the south. In outline, Burma can be compared to a diamond-shaped kite with a long tail. At points of maximum extent the kite's body stretches some 800 miles from north to south and 500 miles from east to west. The tail, protruding from the southeastern flank of the kite, shares the Malay Peninsula with Thailand for another 500 miles southward to the Isthmus of Kra (see fig. 1).

The land frontiers, with the exception of a few water features, consist of a ring of tortuous uplands that become ranges, defining most of the borders. These mountains make overland transportation between Burma and its neighbors very difficult and, as a consequence, most foreign trade must be seaborne. The long coastline provides for this purpose several good harbors associated with river mouths. Internally, the principal means of communication is the Irrawaddy River system which drains the greater part of the country in a generally north-to-south pattern.

A distinction is generally made between Upper Burma and Lower Burma. This distinction has considerable geographic justification but actually derives from history rather than from natural features. During the first half of the nineteenth century, Great Britain, in two wars, annexed Lower Burma, an area generally corresponding to the southern states of the nation. The remainder of the country, Upper Burma, was not annexed until late in the nineteenth century, after a third war. Although these terms have long been without political significance, they are still often used for convenience (see ch. 3, Historical Setting).

No complete census of the country has been made since 1931, but partial counts and samplings of representative urban and rural areas were carried out in 1941 and in the 1953-54 period. These surveys developed only partial information, but they contained sufficient basic data on which government agencies and individual experts have since been able to formulate population estimates periodically. Official estimates for 1970 and 1971 placed the total population of Burma at about 28 million.

Population density varies considerably by region, the heaviest concentration being found in the Irrawaddy Delta and in major river valleys. The scantiest settlement is in the mountainous areas of the frontier. The country's populated places tend to be strongly riverine, and their sites demonstrate the primary dependence of the people on waterways as lines of communication and as sources from which to draw water for irrigating rice fields. Practically all the larger towns and cities are situated on, or close to, major watercourses. In the Irrawaddy Delta, where the rural density is the highest and the land is most intensively farmed, there is a maze of waterways, some 1,700 miles of which are navigable by small craft.

Exploration and survey of mineral resources had been only partially completed by 1970, but already established mining activities and surveys during the 1960s revealed extensive ore deposits containing lead, silver, zinc, lignite coal, iron, tin, and tungsten. Many of the deposits have a low mineral content and are expensive to exploit. Remoteness and lack of transportation impose further handicaps.

PHYSICAL ENVIRONMENT

Boundaries and Administrative Divisions

Burma's perimeter includes approximately 3,170 miles of land borders with neighboring countries and a 1,200-mile seacoast. These boundaries, with the exception of a small undefined section along the Indian frontier, have been demarcated, and in 1970 there were no disputes over alignments.

The longest border, 1,358 miles, is with Communist China. Historically, it was a buffer area, and all of Burma above the 25th parallel was claimed by China. The question was settled, however, by the Sino-Burmese Boundary Treaty of 1960, which involved the transfer of minor disputed areas. Generally, the border is a natural one that follows Himalayan ridges, drainage divides, and the course of the Mekong River to the point where Burma, China, and Laos converge.

The 148-mile border with Laos continues to follow the Mekong River to the Burma-Thailand-Laos tripoint and has been fully demarcated since 1808. From this point the 1,118-mile border with Thailand sweeps southward to its southern terminus on the west coast of the Isthmus of Kra. The line coincides generally with natural features and has been demarcated since 1940.

In the west the forty-five-mile border with Pakistan has been recognized as corresponding with the course of the Naf River but until 1966 had been a problem because the river tends to change its course. In 1966 a protocol recognized the center of the channel as it existed at the time as the frontier. Subsequent changes in the river henceforth will not change the borderline.

Late in 1970 a small portion of the Indian border had not been fully demarcated, but no border disputes were current or anticipated. An India-Burma joint boundary commission was at work on the problem. The border, almost 800 miles in length, consists primarily of mountain and drainage features.

Both the Burmese and the peoples of neighboring states take an informal attitude toward border crossing, and it has long been traditional for traders, permanent and seasonal migrants, and practitioners of religiocultural observances to move freely back and forth without observing frontier markers. This movement has been controlled more by the physical difficulty of passage than by the official ban on motor vehicle crossings. The fact that the borders do not correspond to ethnic groupings, so that people of the same racial extraction live on both sides, perpetuates the practice.

For political and administrative purposes Burma is divided into Burma proper (comprising seven divisions) four contstituent states, and one special division. These elements form natural geographic regions whose borders are rooted in history. Some trace their history to ancient kingdoms and principalities; others correspond to jurisdictions established by the British. The seven divisions are Mandalay, Irrawaddy, Pegu, Magwe, Tenasserim, Arakan, and Sagaing. The five states are Shan, Kawthule, Kayah, Kachin, and the Chin Special Division.

Geographic Regions

Topographic features divide the country into four north-to-south belts. Reading westward from the borders with Communist China and Thailand, they are the Shan Plateau, the Central Belt, the Western Mountain Belt, and the Arakan Coastal Strip (see fig. 2)

The deeply dissected Shan Plateau rises to an average elevation of about 3,000 feet above sea level. Its western edge is clearly marked off from the Central Belt by a north-south cliff, or fault scarp, which often rises 2,000 feet in a single step. Much of the surface of this plateau is of a steeply rolling, hilly nature. In other portions mountain masses rise abruptly to heights of 6,000 feet or more.

Several of the shorter streams in this plateau flow sluggishly through broad valleys, but the largest river, the Salween, is deeply entrenched. It flows in a series of rapids and waterfalls through steep, narrow valleys, and little or no land is available for

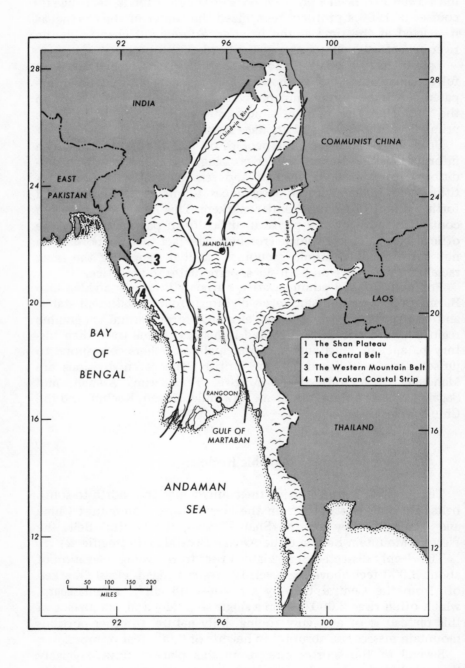

1 The Shan Plateau
2 The Central Belt
3 The Western Mountain Belt
4 The Arakan Coastal Strip

Figure 2. Geographic Regions of Burma

cultivation in the valley bottoms. It has, however, considerable, but little developed, potential as a source of hydroelectric power. The Shan Plateau area available for cultivation is accordingly restricted to rolling plateaus and a few small river valleys.

To the south toward the Isthmus of Kra, the ranges of the Malay Peninsula are repeated northward to merge with the plateau. This area, roughly corresponding to the tail of the kite, is sometimes treated as a separate region. It is, however, topographically associated with the Shan Plateau.

The major part of the Central Belt is composed of ancient river valleys that have been covered by deep, alluvial deposits through which the Irrawaddy, its tributary the Chindwin, and the Sittang rivers flow. The lower valleys of the Irrawaddy and Sittang rivers form a vast, low-lying delta area of about 10,000 square miles. The delta continues to move seaward at a rate of 3 miles per century because of the heavy silting brought by the rivers. It is the most intensively populated and farmed area in the country and is the heartland of the nation's rice economy. The northern portion of the Central Belt above the 25th parallel is a relief stemming from a mountain mass where the ridges of the Himalaya Mountains curve southward and become the mountain system of Burma's eastern frontier. These mountains are very high and rugged and contain Hkakabo Razi on the northern frontier, which rises to almost 20,000 feet and is the highest peak in the nation. Mount Saramati on the Indian border, at 12,500 feet, is the second highest.

The Western Mountain Belt is composed of ranges that originate in the northern mountain arc and continue southward to the extreme southwestern corner of the country. Here they disappear under the sea only to reappear some 200 miles offshore as India's Andaman Islands. These ranges are known by several names along the Burma-Assam border, but in the southern portion of the belt where they lie entirely within Burma they are known as the Arakan Mountains. As in the Shan Plateau, the landscape is dominated by a series of parallel ridges separated by streams flowing in restricted valleys. Here, however, the slopes are very steep, and the mountains are far more rugged than any in the Shan Plateau. Mount Victoria, for example, rising to about 10,000 feet, is the highest peak in the Arakan Mountains and the third highest in the nation. Passage across the Western Mountain Belt is possible only by precipitous trails through a few traverse gaps. The region is hard to reach and has a very small proportion of land level enough for more than the most rudimentary kind of agriculture.

The Arakan Coastal Strip is a narrow, predominantly alluvial belt lying between the Arakan Mountains and the Bay of Bengal. In its northern portion there is a broad area of level land formed by the flood plains of the several short streams that come down from the mountains. In the south the coastal strip narrows and is displaced in many places by hill spurs that reach the bay. Offshore there are many large islands and hundreds of smaller ones, a number of which are low lying and level enough to permit intensive rice cultivation. The region as a whole has a high percentage of rich farmland, but it suffers from a serious lack of communications with the rest of Burma. Surface travel to East Pakistan, for example, is far easier than travel to other parts of the mother country.

River Systems

Burma's primary drainage system consists of the Irrawaddy River complex. This river and its tributaries and other streams that make up its basin drain some two-thirds of the country. It rises near the northernmost tip of Burma and flows the entire length of the country to its enormous delta where nine mouths empty into the Andaman Sea. The Irrawaddy's most important tributary, the Chindwin River, drains the northwest and is fed by tributary streams from the mountains of the Indian frontier. The Irrawaddy is navigable for a distance of over 800 miles inland; and the Chindwin, for another 100 miles.

Also regarded as a portion of the Irrawaddy basin is the Sittang River, which rises just south of Mandalay and parallels the Irrawaddy on its eastern flank. The Sittang has suffered from excessive silting as a consequence of cultivation and forest clearing. Between 1910 and 1958 its depth at Toungoo, located about the midpoint of its 300-mile length, dropped from an average of eighteen feet to three feet, but its width doubled. The Sittang can be used by small boats for short distances between its shoals, gorges, and rapids.

The other large river, the Salween, rises in Communist China and parallels the Irrawaddy as it courses through the eastern part of Burma. Until it reaches the Shan Plateau it has no tributaries, but in that area it is fed by numerous streams, some of which are several hundreds of miles in length. The Salween has a narrow, ribbon-like drainage basin, and its course is so deeply incised and broken and suffers such enormous changes in level that it is perhaps the least useful of the major rivers for navigation purposes. In this river, too, there has been excessive silting, which has interfered with harborage around its mouth at Moulmein.

In Arakan Division there are four major rivers that flow from north to south and are separated by abrupt watersheds related to the Arakan Mountains fold structure. All empty into the Bay of Bengal. The courses of these rivers become trellis patterns near the coast, there is must silting, and all have deltaic extensions. Except for the Kaladan River, which is navigable upstream for about fifty-five miles, they are of little use for navigation but are important because of population clusters at their estuaries.

The remaining river system consists of short streams that run westward to the Andaman Sea in Tenasserim. They flow as torrents separated by ranges that are repeated seaward as a string of offshore islands. All of these rivers carry heavy silt loads, none is navigable, and they are important primarily as settlement points.

There are few lakes. The largest is Lake Inle, which covers about 100 square miles in a basin area of the Shan Plateau. It is the residue of a much larger body of water that is still shrinking. Drained by a tributary of the Salween River, it abounds in fish and is surrounded by very fertile paddies and a cluster of farm villages. It is also a much-favored recreation spot. Other lakes and ponds are for the most part either closed bodies in the courses of former rivers of Upper Burma or are formed by reclaiming marshes of the deltas.

Climate

The climate of the country is under the influence of the southwest monsoon, which blows off of the Indian Ocean and divides the year into three seasons; a rainy season, from the end of May to the end of October; a cool season, from the end of October to the middle of February; and a hot season, from the middle of February to the end of May. Except for the northern highlands and, to a lesser degree, parts of the Shan Plateau, temperatures are high all year, and the cool season is cool only by comparison with the hot season. The mean annual temperature for the country as a whole is about 80°F., but there is considerable variation between different parts of the country. In the lowlands during the wet season the humidity is constantly high, and the temperature may reach 100 degrees or more. Here also there is comparatively little noticeable change from day to day, even though the cool season does bring some relief. In the Shan Plateau temperatures range 10 to 15 degrees lower than those in the lowlands, making it the nation's most pleasant area for habitation. Many peaks in higher elevations of the northern mountains are snowcapped.

Although the country is under the influence of the monsoon, the amount of rainfall varies sharply by area. Along the Arakan and Tenasserim coasts, where the wet monsoon winds are forced to rise and cool, rainfall is very heavy, reaching as much as 200 inches a year. In the rain shadow of the Arakan Mountains, however, the precipitation in some places is less than 25 inches.

The winds that enter Burma through the Irrawaddy and Sittang river deltas meet level land and, although they bring some rain, it is only about one-half of that which drenches Arakan and Tenasserim. After passing over the Central Belt, these winds are forced to rise by the northern mountain complex and again begin to lose moisture. The annual fall is not as heavy as in the coastal regions but averages about seventy-two inches.

Soils

Most of the hilly and mountain regions were formerly forest covered and had large areas of good, fertile soils. Where clearings have been made, temporary cultivation has destroyed much of their virgin richness. In wetter regions the heavy rains often have washed away the top soil almost entirely. This circumstance is particularly notable in the Shan Plateau, where the limestone rock, originally covered by a thin, red soil, has suffered from extensive leaching. The richest soils are the alluvial coverings of the flat deltaic areas and the broad river valleys. Excellent loamy soil is also afforded by the mixed clays and sands derived from the rocks of Pegu. In Irrawaddy the rocks and other sandy formations give rise to extensive tracts of very thin soil.

Flora and Fauna

Forests cover an estimated 57 percent of the country. About one-fourth of forested areas in all regions includes stands of valuable teak, occurring not as homogenous forests but as individual trees associated with a variety of other forest cover. In general, vegetation in the northern mountain area is one of dense forests except where shifting agriculture has denuded the hillsides. In valleys and slopes up to 2,500 feet, it takes the form of tropical rain forest. Above this elevation lower temperatures result in a mixed growth of oak, laurel, rhododendron, and chestnut. Above 10,000 feet and extending to the snowline, the forest is composed essentially of conifers. In the highest reaches the trees become dwarfed, and an alpine coniferous shrub becomes prevalent.

Farther to the south vegetation becomes more complex. Shifting agriculture and burning forests to drive out game have removed much of the original tropical rain forest cover, which does not return. Instead, a second growth of scrub forest, which lacks the valuable hardwoods of the rain forest, makes it appearance. As in the north, temperate zone foliage is characteristic of the middle and upper slopes of mountains, and bamboo clumps and tropical undergrowth flourish in the valleys. In the extreme south the hill areas of Lower Burma consist of evergreen rain forest.

16

In central lowland areas there are expanses of open land interspersed with bracken and rough grasses. Where there is less than forty inches of rain per year, the forest becomes very poor and passes into scrub and semidesert at the lowest levels. True pastureland is rare and severely inhibits cattle raising. In Lower Burma there is a great variety of trees and shrubs that produce edible, medicinal, or poisonous fruits and berries. Coconut palms are commercially important along the coast and particularly on the offshore islands.

The fauna of Burma is quite varied and includes tigers, leopards, bears, wild dogs, and several varieties of deer. The deer are sometimes hunted as a useful food supplement for mountain dwellers. The predators are occasionally dangerous to human life but, more importantly, are such serious hazards to livestock that the animals are placed in stockades each night. Elephants, wild boar, and buffaloes sometimes cause damage to crops but are seldom otherwise dangerous. Freshwater fish are abundant in rivers and in lakes and ponds.

Poisonous snakes are numerous in the countryside and are sometimes encountered by city dwellers. The country has in fact the highest mortality rate in the world from snakebite; mortalities reach their peak during December in areas along rivers in the dry zone and in deltaic areas. Of the numerous venomous varieties of snakes, the most dangerous is the cobra. Other species include coral snakes, true and pit vipers, kraits, and at least fifteen kinds of sea snakes.

Among the rodent species, the little Burmese rat is noted as a host of fleas, and the prevalent bandicoot rat is known to be a vector of ratbite fever. Mosquitoes abound and are carriers of malaria, dengue, and filariasis. Various flies are dangerous as disease carriers, and such other insect pests as lice, fleas, mites, and ticks are abundant.

POPULATION

Firm demographic data for Burma were not available in early 1971, and virtually all figures on the size, composition, and distribution of the population must be estimated. Official estimates are based on values developed in the census of 1931 augmented and updated by a number of partial censuses, surveys of representative areas, and research studies carried out by the government at various intervals since 1941. It is from these activities that the conclusion was drawn that the total national population in 1971 was about 28 million, including 13,843,000 males and 14,358,000 females.

Population Structure

There is no significant difference in the number of males and females in the population. An unofficial estimate made in 1966, when the total population was set at 25.2 million, listed 12.3 million males and 12.9 million females. The same estimate also confirmed findings of population samplings made in 1953 and 1954 that the number of women was slightly higher than that of men in the countryside and that the reverse was true in the urban areas. Despite the fact that the total population has increased by about 1.9 million since then, there is no reason for assuming that these proportions have changed significantly.

The population density varied widely among different regions, but in 1970 the average was estimated to be about 102 persons per square mile. The heaviest concentration, more than 200 persons per square mile, was in the farming areas of the Irrawaddy basin and the lower delta region. Other heavy population concentrations were found in the lowlands of the Irrawaddy and Sittang rivers. At the other extreme were Tenasserim and the border regions where densities ranged from 11 to 30 persons per square mile.

There are more than 100 indigenous ethnic groups and subgroups in the country. There are nine ethnic groups that are numerous enough to be economically and politically important. They are the Burmans, the Karens, the Kayahs, the Shans, the Kachins, the Chins, the Indians, the Pakistanis, and the Chinese (see ch. 4, Social Systems and Values). The ethnic Burmans (see Glossary), who live almost entirely in Burma proper constitute about 70 percent of the population. The country derives its name from this group, and all ethnic groups living in Burma are known collectively as Burmese. Four of the groups are concentrated in frontier political jurisdictions that carry their names; namely the Kachins in Kachin State, the Shans in Shan State, the Kayahs (see Glossary) in Kayah State, and the Chins in the Chin Special Division. The Karens predominate in Kawthule State. The Chinese are found in the populous farming areas of Lower Burma, the frontiers of Shan State, and most urban settlements. The Indians and Pakistanis are mainly in Lower Burma.

Population Dynamics

The annual rate of population growth in 1970 was estimated at about 2.2 percent. Estimates substantially higher and lower than this figure have been made, but it is probable that the rate of increase has been accelerating progressively in recent years as a consequence of drastically reduced mortality among the very young. Recorded live-birth mortality of those under one year of age, for example, dropped from over 300 per 1,000 in the 1945-49 period to about 109 in 1965. In 1970 it was still showing a decline (see ch. 5, Living Conditions). Press estimates of the death rate in 1968 were 12.9 per 1,000 persons, compared with 39.3 in 1951.

The population, in fact, was growing at a rate faster than the rate of increase in food production; this has not yet created serious difficulties, however, and the country still is a food surplus region. Vacant land is plentiful, and population pressure is not a major problem except in the cities, which are growing at a rate substantially more rapid than that of the country as a whole.

The most significant internal migratory movement in the country's history began in the mid-nineteenth century, when Lower Burma came under British rule. At that time the center of population began a shift from the dry zone centering on Mandalay to the Irrawaddy Delta and the towns of Rangoon, Moulmein, and Bassein. In addition, during the years of independence there has been some movement of refugees from insurgent frontier areas. These displaced persons have gravitated largely to urban localities.

Migration into the country from abroad has had its principal source in congested east India. For many years Indian peoples, mostly from areas around Bombay and Madras, have filtered in as seasonal migrants or as settlers. Most entered by crossing the Naf River or the Arakan highlands, first in a trickle and then in a flood as the rich delta areas of the south opened up during the late nineteenth century. This migration was seasonal and occurred in response to a demand for laborers in the ricefields.

Much of the initial migration was temporary, but large numbers established themselves in urban occupations, such as shopkeeping and moneylending. More accustomed to British ways than the Burmese, more amenable to hard manual labor, and more frequently able to speak English, the Indian immigrants assumed important roles in the economy and in public administration. This provoked Burmese animosity, which flared into riots that by 1938 became very serious.

Accordingly, a ban was placed on Indian immigration after Burma achieved its independence, and life became increasingly difficult for people from India and Pakistan. An exodus commenced that was accelerated by the Enterprise Nationalization Law of 1963 which, although not directed specifically at Indians, was most severely felt by them. Only a few were deported, but about 90 percent of registered Indians and Pakistanis left voluntarily. All were required to leave behind not only their properties but also most of their personal possessions. There still remained by 1971 a sizable number of Indians and Pakistanis.

An entirely differnt kind of immigration from India began soon after World War II. It was the entrance of a few thousand Lushai Chins from the Chittagong Hills to join their ethnic kinsmen in the highlands of the Chin Special Division. The reasons for this movement are not clear, but they probably involved land hunger, famine, and wartime dislocation. There is no evidence that these people were disturbed by the events that caused the exodus of other Indians, and their informal immigration illustrates the ease with which peoples of related ethnic stock can move back and forth across the borders.

Immigration of the Chinese has been considerable, but it has been totally unlike that of the Indians. They came at a later date and in a trickle rather than a flood. The Chinese were also affected by the Enterprise Nationalization Law, but it is doubtful that their number has been greatly reduced by it. Unlike the Indians, the Chinese have interbred with, and adopted the ways and sometimes the names of, the indigenous population. In 1971 there was some evidence that limited illegal Chinese movement into Burma was continuing.

Patterns of Settlement

About 80 to 85 percent of the population can be classed as rural, and over two-thirds of all the people are directly dependent on agriculture for a livelihood. Farmers do not live on isolated farms but in farm villages, from which they go out to till the nearby fields. The larger villages support a few artisans, several shops, the civil administrators, teachers, and the monks of the pagoda.

The most sparsely settled areas are in the Shan Plateau, the Western Mountain Belt, and the rugged northern hill and mountain portions of the Central Belt. These districts occupy nearly half of the land area yet contain less than 15 percent of the population. At the other end of the scale are districts with a population density of well over 100 persons per square mile, most of which lie in the lower valleys and deltas of the Irrawaddy and Sittang rivers. These districts occupy little more than 15 percent of the land area but contain about 45 percent of the population. The basic population unit is the rural village, of which there were about 14,000 in 1970. The population thus shows a concentration in a few areas where natural and historical factors have led to the most intensive development of agriculture.

Patterns of village layout vary in accordance with location, topography, and ethnic character, but they all have in common a tendency to cluster in crowded groups of houses. In heavier populated areas houses are built close together on one or both banks of a stream or a road. Villages elsewhere are sometimes strung along a ridge or crowded at random in a bottomland. Almost invariably, however, the clustered pattern of houses is maintained. Villages are usually surrounded by a stockade and, within the village itself, the individual house or houses of a family group are further isolated by compound walls. These traditional devices were contrived as protection against dacoits, which are bands of armed robbers common to India and Burma, and against insurgent groups that have been active since the country's independence.

Even in mountain villages, where shifting agriculture is practiced, the village tends to remain fixed rather than move to a new site after the surrounding farming soil is exhausted. The villages are at least semipermanent, and people may venture four miles or more to farm their fields. In villages where the nearby fields are exhausted, the farmer may set up a temporary shelter, which he uses when work in the fields is heavy. In addition, temporary satellite villages are sometimes established in the vicinity of the parent village.

Although cultural, economic, and historical influence have helped to determine which areas should be most intensively cultivated and where farm villages should be located, geographic factors have most frequently been of decisive significance. The most important of these have been the river systems, which form the main lines of communication and provide water for the ricefields. The capital and largest city, Rangoon, is situated on the Rangoon River and is connected by a canal to the Irrawaddy River, on which the second largest city, Mandalay, is located. The third largest city, Moulmein, is at the mouth of the Salween River; and the fourth, Bassein, is a delta city situated on an Irrawaddy distributary. Most of the division and state capitals and about fifty of the largest population centers are situated on or close to streams. In 1971 only three cities were estimated to have populations of at least 100,000. The estimated population of Rangoon was about 1.8 million, including outlying suburbs. The population of Mandalay was estimated at about 200,000, and that of Moulmein, at about 160,000.

CHAPTER 3

HISTORICAL SETTING

For a thousand years the history of the country has been shaped by two major influences—external pressures, including intermittent warfare with neighboring states and British colonialism, and continual internal efforts of the Burmans (see Glossary) to gain and retain control over other ethnic groups in the country. Whereas the external factors had become less dominant, the domestic struggle was continuing in 1971, although the Burmans by then accounted for some 70 percent of the population.

At various times earlier the Mons were subjugated by the Burmans and, as frequently, rebelled. The Shans, the Arakanese, and the non-Buddhist peoples of the frontier hills have all had periods under Burman control and periods of independence. The tendency for the country to fractionate along ethno-geographic lines has continued.

Wedged between China and India, Burma has been greatly affected also by events taking place beyond its borders. From India came the two most significant influences—Buddhism and British colonialism. Since the time of ancient Rome, the proximity to China has attracted foreign traders to northern Burma en route to China. Invasions by China and Chinese wars that spilled over onto Burmese territory have occurred frequently in ancient and modern times. To that east, intermittent warfare with Thailand produced centuries of instability.

The appearance of Western traders in the port cities of Lower Burma beginning in the fifteenth century was, for the most part, unwelcome to the Burmese kings, partly because of the tendency of the Westerners to encourage separatism on the part of the Mons and other delta ethnic groups (see fig. 1). Several centuries of strained relations that ensued between the Burmese throne and the Western traders and their embassies culminated in the piecemeal annexation by force of arms of the entire country by Great Britain during the nineteenth century.

British colonial policies, most of them designed for use in British India to which Burma was administratively joined until 1937 and extended without modification to the newly acquired territory, proved destructive to the traditional economy, society, and government.

Beginning in the 1920s, and increasingly in the late 1930s, Western-educated Burmese were allowed to participate to some degree in government decision making. These concessions came in response to nationalist agitation. Popular elections to choose indigenous members for the legislature were introduced, and the colonial government embarked on a program designed to lead to eventual self-government for Burma.

The initial experiment with Western parliamentary institutions under British tutelage was cut short by World War II. Early Japanese victories expelled the British from the country. This encouraged Burmese nationalism, especially after 1943, when the Japanese established a nominally independent Burmese government. Within two years after the end of the war, Great Britain agreed to restore independence to Burma. The independent republic, the Union of Burma, came into being on January 4, 1948.

The nationalist leadership of independent Burma was determined to rid the country of foreign influences, a determination first expressed in the 1947 decision to take the country out of the British Commonwealth. Efforts were made also to rid the economy of foreign dominance and to set up a welfare state along Marxist lines. A political system of parliamentary democracy, however, was to be followed, and the monarchy was not revived.

Shortly before independence day, the new nation suffered the loss of some of its ablest leaders through assassination. Other critical problems faced the new government—the result of ethnic group friction, ideological differences among the politicized elite, and severe economic difficulties. Constitutional means were abandoned by the government's opposition, and civil war began. During its first two years, the survival of the Union of Burma was at issue. The nadir was reached in mid-1949. Although insurgencies and economic difficulties continued to trouble the country in the 1950s and 1960s, the threat to the continued existence of the nation from internal upheaval was never as serious as in the first two years of independence.

Parliamentary democracy did not survive, however. After a decade of civilian rule had failed to provide effective government, the armed forces under General Ne Win established first a temporary caretaker regime, at the invitation of Parliament; in March 1962, after a brief interval of civilian rule, Ne Win returned to power by means of a military coup. General Ne Win's regime, called the Revolutionary Government of the Union of Burma (RGUB), promptly dissolved Parliament and began to rule by decree. This government was still in power in early 1971.

PRECOLONIAL PERIOD

Early Settlement

There is general agreement among scholars that the indigenous peoples of Burma are descendants of immigrants from the north.

The southward drive of migrants from the Asian mainland did not halt at Burma but eventually spread to Indonesia and possibly to the islands beyond. The migrants all had in common a mongoloid physique and a cultural heritage distinct from that of China and India, notable especially for the comparatively high status of women.

The migrants are divisible into different language groups, however. The Mons were probably the earliest group to reach Burma. They came out of Central Asia and, approaching Burma from the east, they populated the area around the mouths of the Salween and Sittang rivers. From there they could exert control over the Irrawaddy Delta and the seaports of the Gulf of Martaban. The Mons belong to the Mon-Khmer language group, to be found also in parts of Thailand and in Cambodia. Soon after the Mon migration, or possibly earlier, groups of migrants from Central Asia reached Burma by way of Tibet. These included the speakers of Tibeto-Burman languages: Arakanese, Chins, Kachins, and several smaller groups, as well as the Pyus, who have disappeared from modern Burma but are widely believed to have been the vanguard of the Burman migration. By the eighth or ninth century A.D., the Burmans had entered the rice growing areas of Upper Burma.

Northeast of Burma, in Yunnan, China, a kingdom of the Tai (see Glossary) had been established at Nanchao in the seventh century. In the late eighth or early ninth century a raid by Nanchao Tai brought about the collapse of the last Pyu kingdom in Upper Burma, but it was not until the twelfth century that the Tai, called Shans in Burma, migrated in large numbers. During the twelfth and thirteenth centuries the Tai also migrated to Assam, Thailand, Laos, North Vietnam, and southeastern China. The Karens may also have migrated to Burma and Thailand at about this time.

Mon and Pyu Kingdoms

Burmese and Mon chronicles assert that, during the lifetime of the Buddha, the Mons built a shrine to enclose some of the Buddha's hair on the site where the Shwedagon pagoda now stands, in Rangoon. Although most historians regard this account as mere legend, it is certain that Mons have lived in the Burmese delta area since ancient times and were influential as transmitters of Buddhist religion and culture to later migrants to mainland Southeast Asia. From the seventh to ninth centuries A.D., Mon states dotted coastal Burma and the Chao Phraya valley of Thailand. There is considerable evidence to suggest that Suvarnabhumi, the "land of gold" mentioned in ancient Indian Buddhist literature, was a confederation of Mon city-states, with its port at Thaton on the Gulf of Martaban.

The Mons maintained close ties with India and Ceylon, the original centers of Buddhist literature and learning, and in the ninth century established Pegu as the capital of their kingdom in Burma. Pegu at that time was nearer the sea than it is now. Mon power was always centered in the delta area and never extended far into the north of Burma.

Upper Burma, however, also has archaeological sites that point to the existence of city-states, possibly built by the Pyus, 2,000 years ago. Somewhat later, during the first millennium A.D., the Pyus founded a great capital at Prome, on the Irrawaddy. Prome was the biggest city every built in Burma. A circular brick wall with moats and twelve gates enclosed it. Inside the walls were rice fields, so that the city could withstand a long siege.

Indian cultural influences were prominent at Prome. The religion of the people was Buddhist, although Brahmins from India were used by the king as royal astrologers, to enhance the king's prestige and to preside over ceremonial occasions. Prome was located farthest south of any Pyu city. By the eighth century the Pyus had abandoned their capital at Prome and had moved north, perhaps to Halingyi (north of Shwebo). The new capital was sacked by the invading Tai from Nanchao in the late eighth or early ninth century, and after that the Pyus receive scant mention in Burmese history.

Pagan: The First Burmese Empire, 1044-1257

The Burmans first appear in historical accounts in the ninth century. At that time they seized Kyaukse and other rice-producing areas in Upper Burma. From the time of their first appearance in Burma until the nineteenth century annexation of their kingdom by the British, the Burmans usually established their capital in Upper Burma, where it could control both of the two main river valleys— the Irrawaddy and the Sittang. Pagan, Sagaing, Ava, Amarapura, and Mandalay—almost all of the major Burman capitals—are located in this region, the Burman homeland. Before the days of modern communications, this area was a strategic center for the control of the river valleys and of overland trade between India and China via northern Burma.

In A.D. 849 the Burmans built a fortified city at Pagan. With the building of Pagan, the dating of Burmese history becomes less conjectural because of the wealth of inscriptions and other historical records beginning with the Pagan period.

Numerous dynastic struggles occurred during the first two centuries of Pagan's existence, but in A.D. 1044 Anawrahta, a Burman military leader, became king of Pagan. During a thirty-three year reign, he united all of modern Burma, with the exception of the

Shan Plateau, central and southern Arakan, and southern Tenasserim. A brilliant tactician, Anawrahta was the first to use war elephants on a large scale at the head of the infantry. After conquering the Mon city of Thaton, he brought its king, courtiers, clergy, sacred Buddhist scriptures, and the entire population of 30,000 persons back to Pagan with him.

The dynasty founded by Anawrahta lasted approximately 200 years. The Mons, although politically subjugated, were culturally dominant over the Burmans. The Mon language began to replace Sanskrit and Pali (see Glossary) in royal inscriptions, and the Mon form of Buddhism became Pagan's official religion. The Mons had maintained links with Ceylon after Buddhism faded in India, and their belief, although tinged with Hindu and Mahayana (see Glossary) features, was closer to pure Theravada (see Glossary) beliefs than the popular Buddhism then current in Upper Burma. The latter was a debased form of Buddhism led by blue-robed bearded holy men, known as *ari*, who claimed sacred and magical powers. Anawrahta, who regarded himself as a patron of Buddhism, was anxious to curb the power of the *ari* and purify Burmese Buddhism. He also commissioned the building of the great Shwezigon pagoda of Pagan.

Kyansittha (1084-1112), whose name means "soldier lord," came to the throne after having led troops to crush a Mon rebellion in which Anawrahta's son and heir was killed. During his twenty-eight-year reign the empire was at peace, and amicable relations were established with the Sung emperor of China, to whom he sent an embassy, and with Ceylon, which welcomed Burmese pilgrims and traders. The king's piety was as great as that of his predecessor, Anawrahta. The Ananda pagoda of Pagan, still in daily use in 1971 as a Buddhist temple, was built during this reign, and a ship loaded with treasure was sent to Bengal to cover the cost of repairing the great ancient Buddhist temple at Bodhgaya, near Benares, the site of Gautama's enlightenment in the sixth century B.C. The temple at the holy site had fallen into decay after the Muslim conquest of India. During Kyansittha's reign the Burmans' language, Burmese, was reduced to writing. An inscription with the text given in four languages—Pali, Pyu, Mon, and Burmese—has been found for this period.

The next king, Alaungsithu (1112-67), was so pious and devoted to building pagodas and going on pilgrimages that he was popularly believed to be a future Buddha. The pattern of life of the Pagan period remained, substantially unchanged, the pattern for Burma until the nineteenth century.

The cultivation of irrigated ricefields through the use of a highly developed network of irrigation canals maintained under the royal authority was the basis for the Pagan empire's prosperity. Artificial ponds were also constructed to raise food fish. Meat and dairy products were consumed in quantity. Betel nut was chewed and tea drunk. Commerce and trade were carried on through the barter of gold, silver, and precious stones. Thousands of temples were built at the expense of wealthy and pious citizens seeking to earn merit (see ch. 7, Religion).

Royal viceroys headed the provinces, but there was no hereditary nobility. Instead, there were officials appointed by the king who served at his pleasure. Upon the death of the king, unless he had named his heir, a few senior officials met in council to choose the new ruler from among the royal candidates. Local government was dominated by the *myothugyi* (headman for a group of villages or village clusters), who was usually chosen by the elders of his area. Officials at the capital and *myothugyis* tended to be members of families that had held these positions, but explicit inheritance requirements for office were not usual. There was also a custom of granting riceland to certain families in exchange for the requirement that these families provide certain specific services for the king, such as serving in the palace guards or providing food for the court. There was also a small group of hereditary slaves, but most slaves were nonhereditary debt slaves. Women had positions of prominence and responsibility in the arts, the professions, and business.

By the mid-thirteenth century the Pagan empire had been weakened. Heterodox Buddhist monks had gained much wealth from donations of land by pious laymen that the king could not tax. They held great public feasts, during which they engaged in magic and alchemy and ate and drank to excess. Efforts by the king to suppress clerical debauchery and deal with the spread of armed banditry in the kingdom failed. In addition, the kingdom was threatened by Shans, part of the Tai migration, who had by that time established small kingdoms in northern Burma and in the east, along the Salween River.

The Tai capital of Nanchao in Yunnan, China, was overrun by Kublai Khan's Mongol armies in 1253, and soon thereafter Kublai Khan, by then emperor of China, tried to exact tribute from Pagan. The demand was refused by Pagan's last king, who executed the Mongol envoy for refusing to remove his shoes in the royal presence. Before long, a Mongol army arrived to punish Pagan. In 1287 the Mongols destroyed the city, looting and burning the houses and stripping the temples of their gold and silver. For a short time the Mongols kept a garrison at Tagaung and declared Upper Burma a Chinese province. By 1303 the provincial claim was dropped, and the Mongols withdrew their garrison.

With the fall of Pagan to the Mongols, the Mons, with the assistance of a Shan adventurer named Wareru, declared their independence of the Burmese empire as did Arakan, a region along the Bay of Bengal inhabited by people related to the Burmans of the north but which had had a dynasty of its own as early as the fourth century A.D.

Ava, Pegu, and Arakan in the Fourteenth and Fifteenth Centuries

At approximately the same time as the Pagan-Mongol war, three Shan brothers, sons of a Shan chieftain of the plateau and his wealthy Burman wife, began to carve out kingdoms for themselves in Kyaukse and the surrounding area, land that had been the major source of Pagan's rice supplies. For a time there were Shan-headed kingdoms at Pinya and Sagaing in Upper Burma, but by 1364 they had been destroyed. Ava became the capital of Upper Burma.

During the fourteenth and fifteenth centuries Burma remained divided into several large and small states. At Ava, Shans usually held the throne and the senior positions in government, but the people and culture of the kingdom were Burman. In Lower Burma, at Pegu, the Mons had their own dynasty, founded by Wareru. In the mid-fourteenth century the Mons of Pegu fought off an invasion of armies of the new Tai kingdom of Ayuthia (in what is now Thailand). The kingdom of Pegu lost the whole region of Tenasserim to Ayuthia but retained the rest of its territory intact.

The third major kingdom of the period was Arakan which, after five decades of strong government under its own dynasty, in 1456 seized Chittagong, the neighboring coastal area to the west (in what is now East Pakistan). The Arakan dynasty cultivated close relations with the Muslim court at Bengal and grew wealthy by participating in the luxury trade between Europe and the Far East, the eastern half of which was being handled primarily by Muslim traders.

Beginning in 1385, for roughly forty years, the Burmans of Ava fought an interrupted war against the Mons of Pegu but, despite the wars, Burmese culture flouished during the fourteenth and fifteenth centuries. Poetry especially thrived, and the purification of Theravada Buddhism in Southeast Asia was instigated by a king of Pegu, who invited monks from all over Burma, Thailand, and Cambodia to be reordained at Pegu according to the orthodox Ceylonese rites. Trade also prospered in the delta. In 1435 Nicolo di Conti, a Venetian trader and the first known European to visit Burma, stayed four months at Pegu. He was followed by other Italian traders, one of whom left a vivid description of the splendor of Pegu court life, financed by the royal trade in shellac, sandalwood, textiles, and rubies.

During the period of almost constant warfare between Ava and Pegu, some Burmans found refuge out of the main path of the fighting in a walled town at Toungoo, on the upper Sittang River. When Ava was sacked and destroyed in 1527 by Maw Shan tribesmen from the North, the refugees flocked to Toungoo, which by then had gained control of the good riceland of the Kyaukse region. Within a few years a king came to the throne of Toungoo who was to initiate the reunification of Burma.

Second Burmese Empire, 1551-1752

King Tabinshwehti of Toungoo (1531-50) first reunited the Mon territories as far north as Prome and as far south as Tavoy into a single kingdom and established his court at Pegu in 1539. He soon won the support of the Mons for his rule.

The kingdom fell apart again upon his death, but by the following year his brother-in-law, King Bayinnaung of Toungoo (1550-81), had reconquered all of Tabinshwehti's domain and within twenty years had wrested Ava from the Shans, as well as Shan states to the north and east. He also conquered the Tai kingdoms of Chiengmai and Ayuthia to the east and won back Tenasserim. He received homage from Shan chieftains on the Burmese-Chinese border and tribute from the raja of Manipur, a small state northwest of Burma.

Pegu in Bayinnaung's time was a port on the route of trade to China via the Irrawaddy and northern Burma. It was also a convenient stopover for travelers to Southeast Asia via the Lower Burma ports of Syriam, Martaban, and Bassein. East-West trade had been taken out of Muslim hands by the Portuguese in the early sixteenth century. Portuguese traders and mercenaries were to be found at many of the port cities and capitals along the trade routes.

Within a few years of Bayinnaung's death, his empire began to disintegrate. Ayuthia and Chiengmai won back their independence. Ayuthia also won back Tanasserim and nearly captured all of Lower Burma as well, after having assisted the Mons in a rebellion against the Burman king. Fearing the Tai, the rulers of Arakan and Toungoo allied to take over the wealthy trading ports of Lower Burma. Arakan took Syriam and, together with Toungoo's army, the Arakanese captured and destroyed Pegu. Then the allies pushed back the invading Tai army. The Tai returned to Thailand, accompanied by thousands of Mon refugees who feared the conquering Arakanese soldiers.

The number of Westerners living and trading in the ports of Lower Burma increased during the seventeenth century. For a time a Portuguese mercenary, Philip de Brito y Nicote, who had been appointed Arakanese governor of Syriam, became, with the help of his Mon subjects and a small band of Portuguese soldiers, the de facto overlord of Lower Burma. In 1613 Bayinnaung's grandson, Anaukhpetlun (1605-28), who had gained control of Ava and some of the Shan states, defeated de Brito at Syriam and had him executed. He deported most of the Portuguese, their wives, children, and Eurasian followers to Shwebo, where he settled them in their own villages and made them hereditary gunners of the king.

King Anaukhpetlun restored Pegu as the capital of Burma, but the next king decided to move the capital to Ava in 1634. Rebellions of the Mons and the fact that Pegu harbor was silting up may have influenced him in this decision. Ava, or nearby sites in Upper Burma, thereafter remained the seat of the Burmese kings for the remainder of the monarchy.

The retreat of the court from the delta area to the traditional Burman homeland in Upper Burma greatly reduced the influence on the court of Western ideas and people. The coastal towns of Lower Burma, however, continued to attract traders. During the seventeenth century the Dutch, the British, and the French all established trading posts in the port towns.

During the next reign Upper Burma became a battlefield for clashes between Manchu forces and the last Ming emperor of China, who fled to Burma via Yunnan. The dynasty at Ava grew weaker. Raiders from Manipur nearly captured Ava in 1749, and the Mons, with French support, took advantage of the weakness of the empire to secede and reestablish their own dynasty at Pegu. In 1752 the Mons of Pegu took Ava and captured the king and his family. The second Burmese empire, begun by Bayinnaung in 1551, had collapsed.

Third Burmese Empire, 1752-1885

The Mons' attempt to unite Burma under their control was countered by a Burman warrior named Alaungpaya, who emerged from obscurity as the *myothugyi* of Shwebo, north of Ava, and during eight years of constant war reunited Burma and founded what was to be the last Burman royal dynasty.

To celebrate a victory over the Mons, Alaungpaya established a port at the little coastal town of Dagon (site of the Shwedagon pagoda) and gave it a new name, Rangoon, meaning end of strife. He destroyed the Mon fort at Syriam and deported the French soldiers he found there to the foreigners' villages at Shwebo. Believing the British to be implicated in a fresh Mon rebellion at Pegu, in 1759 Alaungpaya burned down the British trading post at Cape Negrais (established in 1753) and killed all the people there who had been in British employ. The British closed down their trading post at Bassein in 1761. After their defeat, the Mons of Burma gradually reduced in numbers. Many migrated to Thailand, and others became assimilated into the Burman majority.

Alaungpaya died in 1760 while campaigning in Thailand. His successor moved the capital of the empire back to Ava from

Shwebo and resumed the invasion of Thailand. His army captured and destroyed Ayuthia in 1767 and brought back to Burma many gifted Tai artists and artisans who helped to bring about a rebirth of Burmese art and literature. The victory also restored Tenasserim to Burma. The subjugation of the Tai by Burma was of short duration. In 1776 the Tai won back their independence and subsequently founded a new capital for their kingdom at Bangkok. Tenasserim, however, remained under Burmese control.

During the 1760s, alarmed at the expanding size of the Burmese empire, China sent its governor of Yunnan Province with an army into Upper Burma while the bulk of the Burmese army was engaged in the siege of Ayuthia. Four separate invasions of Burma took place in three years. In 1769 the Chinese were finally repulsed, and a peace treaty was signed between the Chinese and the commander of the victorious Burmese forces. Immediately after this victory, the Burmese army campaigned in Manipur, where they succeeded in placing a Burmese nominee on the throne.

A continuing problem for the third Burmese empire, as had been the case with earlier empires, was that there had never been instituted a method of ensuring the peaceful succession of a new king. With few exceptions, the death of a king was followed by assassinations and rebellions caused by rivalry for the throne. Upon succeeding to power, the new ruler often attempted to secure his throne by executing potential rivals.

In 1782 King Bodawpaya came to the throne after a bloody struggle. He then massacred all of his potential rivals and their followers, including the previous king's wives and all the royal children. He was equally ruthless in eliminating dissidents and potential dissidents in the army, the peasantry, and the *sangha* (see Glossary). Once having consolidated his power, Bodawpaya worked to improve the administration of the kingdom. He had the capital moved from Ava to a site a few miles away, Amarapura, which his astrologers regarded as more auspicious. He improved tax collection, communications, and the legal and educational systems and worked to restore unity and discipline to the *sangha* and to the civil administration. He also conquered Arakan, then in a state of anarchy. The annexation of Arakan in 1782 brought his empire alongside the expanding British Empire in the Indian subcontinent.

BRITISH EXPANSION INTO BURMA

Arakan and Tenasserim, 1826

The importance of Western trade and commerce in the coastal area grew during the eighteenth century. A shipbuilding industry became established in the ports. The British East India Company was the biggest customer for Burmese teak. The shipbuilding industry and the dockyards of the British at Rangoon and the French at Mergui were putting money into the hands of ordinary Burmese for the first time. Many Burmese were attracted to the ports by the opportunities to earn money.

The Westerners, however, were not content with the limited trading privileges granted them by the Burmese kings. In addition to wanting more generous trading privileges, the British also wanted to settle the Arakan border problem. There had been frontier incidents involving the pursuit by Burmese imperial forces of indigenous Arakanese conspirators and rebels who had fled to British India. The British were also concerned during the late eighteenth and early nineteenth centures with excluding France, then Great Britain's enemy, from the ports and shipbuilding facilities on the Burmese coast.

In 1795 a mission to Bodawpaya's capital, headed by Captain Michael Symes, was sent by the governor general of the British East India Company to deal with these matters. As a result, Captain Hiram Cox was stationed at Rangoon for a few years as the agent of the British East India Company. Captain Cox's arrogant behavior and his intemperate reports to the governor general in India contributed to worsening relations between the Burmese throne and the British.

In 1819 King Bagyidaw ascended the throne. At his coronation the raja of Manipur was absent, thereby signalizing refusal to continue tribute to the Burmese king. The Burmese sent a punitive expedition; the raja fled westward with his army into the neighboring state of Cachar, and soon the entire area between Burma and Bengal was embroiled.

In 1824, after twenty-five years of border incidents, the British sent forces from India to resolve the problem militarily. By 1826, after two years of war, British victory forced the Burmese king to cede his claims to Assam, Arakan, and Tenasserim to the British East India Company and to promise that Burmese would no longer interfere with Manipur and the other nearby states between Burma and British India. These arrangements were included in the Treaty of Yandabo of 1826. By this treaty the Burmese court was also obliged to accept a British resident. A commercial treaty, also signed in 1826, granted the British some trading concessions.

The Burmese empire lacked able leadership during this critical period in its relations with the Western powers, possibly as a result of the custom of massacring the families of royal rivals. Bagyidaw became insane and was deposed by his younger brother Tharrawaddy in 1837. The new king's antipathy to foreigners led to the closing of the British residency in 1840. Tharrawaddy, too, went insane before his death in 1846. His son, Pagan, upon his ascent to the throne, conducted a massacre of the royal kinsmen on a grand scale. This atrocity, committed in the presence of Western witnesses, contributed to the deep distrust with which the British East India Company regarded the Burmese government.

Although it was a poor age for the monarchy, the early nineteenth-century Burmese court produced much of permanent cultural value in music, poetry, drama, and scholarship. Perhaps the major contribution of King Bagyidaw's reign was the compilation of the *Glass Palace Chronicle of the Kings of Burma,* a major historical document assembled at court by monks and lay scholars.

Pegu and Martaban, 1853

A trivial incident arising out of complaints of two British ship captains of unfair treatment at the Burmese courts led to the dispatch in 1852 of an expeditionary force from India to enforce redress. In less than a year the successful campaign ended with the conquest of the delta provinces of Pegu and Martaban, which correspond approximately to the former Mon kingdom of Pegu.

By 1853 all of Lower Burma had been annexed and incorporated as a province of British India. The new conquest cut off the remainder of the Burmese kingdom from the sea.

By now various Western powers were exerting pressure on Burma from all sides, not because of its intrinsic value but as a means of reaching the interior of China. British manufacturers had been urging the potential importance of new markets in that region. The opening of the Suez Canal in 1869 gave a new stimulus to trade between Europe and Asia. The completion in the same year of a railroad across the United States encouraged increased United States commercial involvement on the seaboard of China. The French were exploring access to Yunnan. The Burmese court, hoping for a chance to escape the dominance of Great Britain, sent missions to France and other Western powers in a vain attempt to secure aid. Having avoided involvement with Western powers for centuries, Burma suddenly became a center of intrigue in world politics.

In domestic affairs King Mindon (1853-78), who had come to power during the second Anglo-Burmese war, did what he could toward equipping his people to meet the Western powers on terms of equality. He modernized the administration, improved communications, experimented in industrial development, and sent young men abroad for study. In 1857 he moved his capital from Amarapura to Mandalay. A boost to Burmese morale resulted from the holding in 1872 of the Fifth Great Synod of Buddhism by King

Mindon attended by Theravada Buddhists from all of Burma. A great synod for Theravada Buddhism had not been held for approximately 2,000 years.

King Mindon's throne was insecure, however, and in 1866 the heir apparent, the prince whom the king had selected to continue his reforms, was assassinated. Soon thereafter, the Karenni (see Glossary) people rebelled. To secure his throne and crush rebellion, Mindon needed a better and stronger army quickly. In 1867 he granted concessions to the British on condition that he be allowed to import arms, but the British government in Lower Burma refused to sanction the importation of any arms. In 1875, lacking the means to prevent it, Mindon was forced by the British to acquiesce to the independence of the Karenni states.

Upper Burma, 1886

Theebaw, an inexperienced youngster, was elevated to the throne by a palace conspiracy after Mindon's death. Great Britain was by then concerned over the possible expansion of French interests in Burma and took advantage of a dispute between the government of Upper Burma and a British timber firm to send an ultimatum demanding the immediate acceptance by the throne of terms amounting to a surrender of Burmese sovereignty. King Theebaw was unable to resist. After a brief and almost bloodless campaign late in 1885, he was taken captive and exiled to India, and his kingdom was annexed. On January 1, 1886, all of the Burmese empire became a province of the colony of British India. (The British East India Company had surrendered its possessions to the British crown in 1858.)

Having reached the border with China, the British, who were anxious to promote trade and good relations with that country, signed a treaty in 1886 with the Manchu emperor in which the emperor agreed to cede to Great Britain whatever claims to sovereignty or tribute China might have had in Upper Burma. In return, China would participate with Great Britain in determining the location of the borderline (see ch. 10, Foreign Relations).

Impact on Burma of British Rule

As a result of the annexation of Upper Burma in 1886 and the extension of British rule to the entire territory, ethnic particularism was encouraged. In the plains—where the majority of the Burmans, as well as the Mons (by then a small community) and some of the Karens lived—direct rule, with close supervision by British personnel down to the district level, was instituted as being necessary for the growth of trade and the development of economic resources. In the frontier hills inhabited by the Shans, Chins, Kachins, and others— where there was little prospect of trade or industry—direct rule was avoided as an unnecessary expense in favor of ruling the people indirectly through their own chieftains.

This policy had the effect of isolating the frontier peoples from each other and from the Burmans in the lowlands. The Karenni states (Kayah State), for example, whose independence from Burma had been forced upon Mindon by the British in 1875, did not become part of Burma until colonial rule ended in 1948. The sense of ethnic difference felt by the various Burmese peoples was strengthened by the colonial government's practice of recruiting Karens, Chins, and Kachins for the armed forces and excluding Burmese.

Ethnic diversity was increased during the colonial period as a result of the large-scale immigration of foreign Asians, especially Indians and Chinese, to fill some of the positions in government, commerce, and industry for which the Burmese were untrained or regarded by the colonial authorities as unsuited. Being then officially a province of British India, Burma was especially attractive to Indians. The use of Indian and Karen troops under British officers to put down Burman-led insurgencies in 1886 and afterwards contributed to the lasting animosity felt by the Burmans for these two ethnic groups.

Industry and commerce were developed during the colonial period. Timber and various mineral resources were exploited. Industries were mostly British owned. The petty shopkeepers and retail traders were usually Indian or Chinese. Indians also held a virtual monopoly on lower level positions in many government departments, and British, recruited in Great Britain, filled the senior government posts.

Communications were vastly improved, increasing the control of the central government over the people and the influence of the world market on the indigenous economy. A fleet of paddlewheel boats of the Irrawaddy Flotilla Company moved men and goods up and down the long river. Railroads, roads, and telegraph lines were also constructed in this period.

The indigenous Burmese sometimes found employment as judges, magistrates, and policemen, but their economic activities were largely confined to agriculture, chiefly the production of rice for export. The introduction of a monetized sector to the economy and the development of a brisk market for delta riceland led the inexperienced Burmese farmer into serious indebtedness, often resulting in the forfeiture of his land. Estimates are that approximately half the agricultural land of Lower Burma was alienated during the colonial period. Much of this land came to be owned by Chettyars, a South Indian caste of moneylenders (see ch. 12, Agriculture and Industry).

Burmese social institutions were also greatly affected by British rule. Anxious to avoid interfering with the religion of the Burmese, the British colonial government refused to patronize the Buddhist religion—the faith of the Burmans, Mons, and Shans—as the Burmese kings had done or to appoint a primate to have authority over the Buddhist clergy. The discipline and morale of the *sangha* rapidly declined.

Support for the monastic Buddhist school system was also lacking. Schools providing vernacular secular education or the rarer and more sought after English-language education that would equip the graduate for employment by the Westerners were attracting many ambitious Burmese and were reducing the appeal of monastic schools and the prestige of the *sangha,* formerly the most highly educated group. A few Burmese were able to acquire British educations. Among these were a number of ambitious young lawyers who pursued their legal education at institutions in England. The Western-educated, English-speaking Burmese became the modern elite of their country.

The chief political institution of the central government, the monarchy, was abolished at the time of the British takeover. Soon thereafter, as part of a policy designed to bring Burma into uniformity with the administrative system of the rest of British India, the government abolished the traditional Burmese institution of the *hkaing,* a regional grouping of villages and village clusters (sometimes called township unit), headed by a *myothugyi.* The *myothugyi,* typically a man of substance and prestige in his region, had been the backbone of Burmese local government and had acted as local magistrate, collector of revenue, and military commander in time of emergency. Unlike the more senior officials sent out by the king to the provincial capitals, the *myothugyi* was a local person and depended upon local support.

In place of this traditional Burmese institution, the colonial government established village-size units, each with a local headman. The job of the headman was to execute orders given him by the British official residing at the capital of one of the approximately forty districts into which the province of British Burma was divided.

Burmese Nationalism in the Colonial Period

For five years after the annexation of Upper Burma, resistance to foreign rule and to the abolition of the monarchy kept tens of thousands of British-officered Indian and Karen troops in the field subduing guerrilla bands led by *myothugyis*. This insurgency was subdued in 1890, but a generation after annexation the effects of the total disruption of society caused by the British colonial policies and by the economic revolution taking place in the country were mirrored in a sharp rise in the incidence of violent crime, especially robbery, dacoity (in India and Burma, robbery by murderous gangs), and murder.

The early twentieth century was a period of renewed Burmese nationalism. The Japanese victory in the Russo-Japanese war and the revolution taking place in China were contributory factors, as were the activities of the *sangha,* which, free of the control by the government that had in former times kept the *sangha* out of politics, had begun producing a generation of nationalist leaders. Buddhism also helped to unite nationalist laymen.

In 1906 the Young Men's Buddhist Association (YMBA), as it was called in English, was founded by Buddhist laymen, including some of the British-educated lawyers and students at English-language schools in Rangoon. Within a few years the YMBA was engaged in a nationwide campaign ostensibly against the British refusal to remove their shoes before entering pagodas. The campaign stimulated anti-British nationalist sentiment. The YMBA also set up schools throughout the country where Buddhism and Burmese nationalism were taught in addition to English and some of the modern subjects of the secular school curriculum.

Another important boost to Burmese nationalism, however, was provided by the British. In 1917 the secretary of state for India announced in the British Parliament:

> The policy of His Majesty's Government, with which the Government of India are in complete accord, is that of the increasing association of Indians in every branch of the administration, and the gradual development of self-governing institutions, with a view to the progressive realization of responsible government in India as an integral part of the British Empire.

This policy was enunciated in order to gain the cooperation of Indian nationalists during World War I. In 1919 the so-called dyarchy reforms were instituted in the government of British India, providing for control over certain departments by popularly elected legislators while other departments remained under the direct control of the British colonial governor or his appointees. The Burmese, who had looked forward to finally reaping an advantage out of their inclusion in British India, rose in protest when the British made known their decision to exclude Burma from these reforms on the grounds that Burma was different from the rest of British India and was at a different stage of political development.

Boycotts and demonstrations occurred throughout Burma. The YMBA joined with other Burmese organizations to form the General Council of Burmese Associations (GCBA) as a nationalist organization. The GCBA organized noncooperation activities against the colonial government. A students' strike at the new Rangoon University in December 1920 soon spread to other schools. The YMBA schools, renamed national schools, enrolled many of the striking students. Nationalist monks founded the General Council of Sangha Samaggis (GCSS) in 1922.

Acting in response to the strength of Burmese nationalist sentiment, the British extended the dyarchy reforms to Burma in 1923. These reforms called for a legislative council of 103 members, of whom 80 were popularly elected. The Legislative Council, through its chosen ministers could, in large measure, determine policy in certain "transferred subjects," such as education, public health, agriculture, forestry, and public works. Other subjects, such as law and order, finance and revenue, and justice and police, were "reserved"—that is, under the direct control of the British provincial governor of Burma. Still other subjects were under the control of the central government of British India, in which Burmese had virtually no representation. An additional and important restriction on the dyarchy reforms was that they were not applicable to any of the indirectly ruled territories—the Shan, Chin, and Kachin areas—or to the then independent Karenni states.

In choosing the legislature, the electorate was divided into four ethnicly determined voting rolls: Burmese (by which was meant indigenous Buddhists from Burma proper); Indians, Anglo-Indians (including Anglo-Burmese), and Karens. The Karens were regarded as needing separate representation from the other Burmese because they were non-Buddhist; a significant number of them, although not a majority, were Christians.

The Burmese could supply candidates for fifty-eight seats, but the remainder were reserved for elected legislators from the other three voting rolls. Many Burmese nationalists boycotted the elections. Only 12 percent of the electorate voted the first time, and by the third election, in 1928, only 20 percent of the electorate participated.

Nationalists continued to agitate against colonial rule after the dyarchy reforms had been instituted. In 1924 and 1925 there was a nonpayment-of-taxes campaign, and in 1930-32 an uprising, born of superstition and desperation, took place in the countryside of the Tharrawaddy region. It was led by a former monk and practitioner of Burmese folk medicine named Saya San, who claimed to be the Galon raja (Garuda king) of Burma. Saya San's adherents, called Galons, were convinced that they were magically invincible to the British bullets. The rebellion spread to other areas, gaining popularity among farmers who were suffering from a fall in rice prices resulting from worldwide economic depression. Before the rebellion was suppressed, the British had had to bring in two supplementary divisions from India. The rebels suffered 3,000 casualties and 9,000 captured or arrested. When the rebellion was over 350 of the rebels were convicted on criminal charges and 78 were hanged.

In the 1932 election for the Legislative Council, the chief issue was whether Burma should continue to be part of British India or be separated. Fearing that, as a separate colony, Burma would be left out of the movement toward increasing self-government in which India was engaged, two young British-educated Burmans—Ba Maw, a lawyer who had become famous as defense counsel for Galon rebels, and U Kyaw Myint—founded an antiseparationist party to fight the election. They were victorious, but Ba Maw and many other Burmese were soon persuaded that separation would be in the longrun interest of Burma. In 1935 the Government of Burma Act was passed. It provided that Burma should become a separate British colony in 1937. Burma was also granted a new constitution in 1937 that gave much more initiative and political power to Burmese legislators and ministers, although, like its predecessor, it was not applicable to the indirectly ruled frontier ethnic enclaves.

The new constitution was not satisfactory to a nationalist group that had established itself on the campus of the Rangoon University. A group of student leaders as a gesture of defiance had, in 1931, placed before their names the title *thakin* (master), a term of address that had been ordinarily reserved for Europeans, the Burmese equivalent of the Indian word *sahib*. In 1935 the Thakins organized a political party with the name Do-Bama Asi-ayon (We, the Burmese Confederation). In 1936 the Thakins supported a second university strike in Rangoon, led by Thakin Nu, a graduate law student, and Thakin Aung San, an undergraduate. In 1937 Thakin Nu, Thakin Aung San, and the Do-Bama Asi-ayon party boycotted the elections under the new constitution.

Ba Maw became prime minister of a coalition cabinet and for two years led his government through successive crises: a nationwide riot between Burmese and Indians, a religious riot between Burmese and Indian Muslims, riots by Burmese against Chinese, a labor strike, and a students' strike. When his government fell, in February 1939, there was a scramble for positions in the government, which resulted in U Saw and the newly formed Patriot's Party coming to power.

WORLD WAR II

When World War II broke out in Europe, rumors and unrest spread throughout Burma. The Burma Road, a hard-surfaced road built in the 1930s from Yunnan to Burma in order to supply China in its fight against the invading Japanese, seemed likely to embroil Burma in the fighting. The Flying Tigers of the Chinese Air Force under United States General Claire Chennault arrived to protect the Burma Road in late 1941.

Private armies began to be organized by the Thakins, by Ba Maw, and by U Saw, among others. Ba Maw, U Saw, and many others, including members of the Thakin group, were arrested. Thakin Aung San escaped arrest by fleeing to Amoy, where he was contacted by the Japanese. He returned to Rangoon in March 1941 in a Japanese cargo boat and selected members of the Thakin group, later to become famous as the Thirty Comrades, to receive overseas training in subversion and guerrilla warfare by the Japanese.

In December 1941 Japanese troops, together with the Thirty Comrades leading the Burma Independence Army (a force that had been assembled in Thailand), entered Lower Burma. The ranks of the Burma Independence Army, under the command of General Aung San, swelled as it became clear that the British were falling back toward India, pushed by the Japanese. Chinese troops in Lower Burma, commanded by United States General Joseph W. Stilwell, were also forced to retreat into India. In the colonial army, however, the Burmese—chiefly Karens, Kachins, Chins, and Eurasians—remained loyal to the Allies. In March 1942 the Burma Independence Army undertook to disarm members of disbanded Karen regiments. Within the next several months, incidents and bad faith on both sides led to widespread killing by Burmans of Karens and by Karens of Burmans throughout the delta region.

By May 1942 the Japanese had cut off the Burma Road and were masters of almost the entire country. The nucleus of the Burmese colonial government, including a few Burmese cabinet ministers and senior civil servants, was set up in Simla, India, for the duration of the war.

The Burmese had not been satisfied under British rule and, when the Japanese arrived with a promise of independence, they were generally welcomed. It soon became evident to the Burmese, however, that little had been gained besides a change of masters, although the Japanese made a show of ruling the people through their own leaders.

The last prewar prime minister, U Saw, had been interned in Africa by the British. Another prewar prime minister, Ba Maw, however, had been jailed in Burma on a charge of sedition and had escaped during the invasion. The Japanese immediately enlisted his support. In August 1942 Ba Maw was appointed head of the executive administration under the Japanese military government. The Burma Independence Army and the nationalist leaders grew impatient for independence. In mid-1942 the Japanese tried to suppress the Burmese army and reorganized it under a new name, the Burma Defense Army.

In August 1943, however, the Japanese declared Burma an independent country. Ba Maw was the ruler, with the title *adipati* (head of state). The minister of defense was Thakin Aung San, who had commanded the Burmese forces and been the leader of the Thirty Comrades. Thakin Nu (later known as U Nu) was first put in charge of foreign affairs and later was made minister of information. Another of the Thirty Comrades was Ne Win, then brigadier in the Burma Defense Army, who was destined to reach the top rung of power in 1962. He had also been in the Do-Bama Asi-ayon party before the war.

The real power remained in Japanese hands, however, and Thakin Aung San was determined to rid Burma of the Japanese. In this aim his most ardent support came from the Communists. Thakin Than Tun (who had been in charge of agriculture in the executive administration of 1942) and Thakin Soe were the most prominent of the Communist leaders. Thakin Soe went underground to organize the resistance; Aung San and Than Tun continued outwardly to support the Japanese while organizing the clandestine Anti-Fascist Organization. In December 1944 Aung San got word to the British that his forces were contemplating an armed rising against the Japanese and asked for Allied assistance. In March 1945 he surprised the Japanese by suddenly transferring all his forces to the Allied side. Aung San's forces, their name changed to the Patriotic Burmese Forces, gave valuable help in expediting the recapture of Rangoon in early May.

POSTWAR INDEPENDENCE ACHIEVED

By the end of World War II the prestige of the British had been greatly impaired within Burma by their inability to protect the country from conquest by the Japanese. The fruits of their enterprise had also been greatly damaged. Many towns had been reduced to rubble. Oil wells, silver and tungsten mines, harbor installations, and rolling stock had been blown up, in many instances by the British before departing. The currency system and the distributing system for goods had been destroyed. Approximately half of the 1 million Indians who had been residents in Burma in 1939 had fled to India during the war, suddenly reducing substantially the number of professional people, skilled laborers, and retail traders in Burma.

In addition to the loss of prestige by the British, the experience of nominal independence during the war years made the prospect of a return to the 1937 Constitution intolerable to Aung San and most of the Burmese people. Aung San converted his underground Anti-Fascist Organization into an overt nationalist federation of parties, factions, and individuals under the name Anti-Fascist People's Freedom League (AFPFL). Virtually the entire AFPFL membership subscribed to Marxist theories. Marxism had been popular at the British universities that many of the leading Burmese politicians had attended. It had also been the belief of the Indian nationalists with whom Burmese nationalists had maintained close contact. The ideology of the AFPFL was greatly influenced by the Socialist Party, a small constituent party of the AFPFL that was founded in 1945 and that included some of the most influential British-educated leaders, many of whom had belonged to the prewar Do-Bama Asi-ayon party. The Burma Communist Party also joined the AFPFL.

The British not only resisted demands for independence but also were not prepared to return Burma to the degree of self-government granted by the 1937 Constitution. Instead, the returning governor, Sir Reginald Dorman-Smith, announced the British decision to have a temporary reversion to direct rule as it had functioned before the dyarchy reforms of the 1920s. While Burma was under direct British rule, which was to last for a period of three years or possibly less, economic reconstruction was to be entrusted to officials of the colonial government working in cooperation with the European-owned companies that had dominated the Burmese economy before the war.

The AFPFL went into opposition, led by Aung San, who was also the chief of a new military-style organization called the Patriotic Volunteer Organization (PVO). The PVO had begun in 1945 as an organization of those former Patriotic Burmese Forces personnel who had not been absorbed after the return of the British into the Burma Army. The PVO also attracted new recruits throughout lowland Burma so that, by 1946, it was estimated that the organization had over 100,000 members.

A contemporary Burmese observer described the PVO as "in effect, the unarmed private army of the AFPFL." It was also, to some degree, a personal instrument of Aung San. The PVO drilled publicly in uniform, carrying dummy weapons. It also organized nationalist demonstrations and strikes.

Factionalism soon appeared among the nationalists of the AFPFL. In February 1946 one group of Communists, under Thakin Soe, split off from the Burma Communist Party to begin armed insurrection against the colonial government. The insurrectionists called themselves the Communist Party of Burma, and they became known as the Red Flags or the Trotskyites. The remainder of the party, known as the Burma Communist Party, often called the White Flag party, was led by Thakin Than Tun. In October 1946 the White Flags were expelled from the AFPFL.

Banditry and insurgency in the countryside; rumors and demonstrations in Rangoon; and violent clashes involving Red Flag, White Flag, and PVO forces characterized the immediate postwar years. At the same time, Burma had severe inflation and inadequate distribution of essential goods. Finally, strikes of government servants, postal workers, railwaymen, and police made imminent the danger of total collapse of the government. The governor took leave on grounds of ill health. Shortly thereafter, Sir Hubert Rance, who had established cordial relations with Aung San in the last year of the war, took over as governor and inaugurated a more liberal regime. Aung San and his associates were promptly admitted to the governor's executive council, and shortly thereafter, in December 1946, the new British Labour government announced that Burma would be allowed to decide its own destiny. The British prime minister, Clement Atlee, summoned Aung San and other leaders to a conference in London.

In January 1947 the London conference resulted in an agreement that Burma was to become independent within the year and could exercise free choice whether or not to remain within the British Commonwealth; that a constituent assembly was to be elected in April 1947; that, for the interim period, Aung San and the other Burmese on the governor's Executive Council would function as an interim Burmese government; and that it was the agreed objective of the British government and the members of the Burmese delegation "to achieve the early unification of the Frontier Areas and Ministerial Burma with the free consent of the inhabitants of those areas."

The issue of the frontier peoples was a delicate one since the British felt an obligation to the Karens, Kachins, Chins, and others, many of whom had loyally served the British as soldiers before and during World War II and who had considerable autonomy under the colonial regime. At the same time Great Britain was unwilling to insist on guarantees for the minority peoples that would antagonize the AFPFL, which was determined that all of Burma, including the frontier areas, must be united and independent of Great Britain.

In February 1947 a meeting was held in Panglong in the Shan Plateau at which the representatives from the minority peoples were asked to "express their views upon the form of association with the Government of Burma which they consider acceptable during the transition period." Aung San personally led the Interim Burmese Government delegation to Panglong. On February 12, 1947, a unanimous resolution declared that "freedom will be more speedily achieved by the Shans, the Kachins, and the Chins by their immediate cooperation with the Interim Burmese Government."

In commemoration of the date of the Panglong resolution, February 12 is celebrated as Union Day, a Burmese national holiday. The Karens—who did not have a frontier state of their own but were settled among the Burmans, Mons, and other ethnic groups of Lower Burma—sent observers to Panglong but did not vote. A delegation of Karens went to London to seek autonomy for Karens in their own state within the British Commonwealth but received no encouragement.

In April the elections for constituent assemblymen gave a large majority to the AFPFL, headed by Aung San, who had by then been given the title *bogyoke* (great general), an honorific not previously accorded to anyone in modern times. Among the frontier tribes there was no machinery for holding elections, but representatives were sent to sit with the other Burmese when the Constituent Assembly met.

The constitution that emerged provided some measure of autonomy for the frontier states and also contained a provision permitting the secession after ten years under certain specified conditions of some of the frontier states. The Shan and Wa states were joined together to become the Shan State, and the Karenni states, whose people agreed to relinquish their independence, came into the Union of Burma as the Karenni State (see ch. 8, Political System and Values).

While the drafting of the constitution was still taking place, on July 19, 1947, gunmen broke into a meeting of the Executive Council, the interim government's cabinet, and murdered Aung San, six other executive councillors, and two bystanders. Once again, assassination had deprived the country of some of its limited supply of established leaders. U Saw, the ambitious last prewar prime minister, was subsequently convicted of having instigated the murders and was hanged. Thakin Nu, then speaker of the Constituent Assembly, was invited by the British governor to take Aung San's place. A constitution creating the Union of Burma, an independent republic outside the Commonwealth, was approved in September 1947. In October the Nu-Atlee agreement granting Burma its independence was signed. On January 4, 1948, the independent Union of Burma came into existence, with U Nu (who had dropped the title *thakin*) as prime minister and the Constituent Assembly serving as a provisional parliament until general elections could be held.

TROUBLED TIMES FOR THE YOUNG REPUBLIC

By independence day the Union of Burma was already under attack from several insurgent groups. The Red Flags, although few in number, were extremely intransigent, as were the Mujahids, a small Muslim group of terrorists in the north of Arakan who wanted their own separate Muslim state. In February 1948 the White Flags, who had been opposing the AFPFL since their expulsion from it in October 1946, adopted a policy of promoting the violent overthrow of the AFPFL government. Despite repeated invitations from U Nu to reenter the AFPFL and offers to meet with White Flag leaders, the White Flags went underground in March and called out their clandestinely organized armed forces of approximately 25,000 men. Burmese historians date the beginning of the civil war from the revolt of the White Flag Communists.

Civil War

The PVO, leaderless since Aung San's death, soon broke into two factions. The White Band PVO joined the Communists in their revolt, and the Yellow Band PVO remained loyal to U Nu's government. The next group to desert the government consisted of battalions of the Burma Army composed of former members of Aung San's wartime forces.

The Karens, too, soon became a threat. The Karens were not satisfied with their position in the new Union of Burma. The Constitution provided for a Karen state to be created out of the Karenni State, the Salween District, and other areas with Karen populations "if the majority of the people of these areas and of the Karens living in Burma outside these areas so desire." The state had not yet been created nor had the proposed boundaries been defined because, unlike most other minority groups in Burma, the Karens were settled in various parts of Lower Burma, intermingled with the Burmans rather than being concentrated primarily in one enclave.

Until a state could be formed for them, the Karens were granted a special region, which was named Kaw-thu-lay and included the Salween District and some adjacent Karen areas. The Kaw-thu-lay Special Region was given a small measure of local autonomy. This was not enough for a group of Karen separatists who had tried in vain before independence was granted to Burma to gain British support for a Karen state, within the British Commonwealth and apart from Burma.

The Karenni people, for their part, deeply resented any plan of the government of the Union of Burma to grant the Karens, a different ethnic group, a portion of the Karenni territory, with its politically separate existence dating back to 1875. At Karenni insistence their state was given another name, Kayah State, and the Constitution was amended to remove it from the territory earmarked for the Karens.

In addition to dissatisfaction over not having their own state, the Karens were also troubled by the spread of insurgency. As in the past, the breakdown of law and order was accompanied by assaults by Burman armed bands against Karens. The Karen National Defense Organization (KNDO) was formed, and by January 1949 the Karens were in open rebellion. A Karen battalion in the Burma Army mutinied and joined the KNDO.

The rebellion of the Karens temporarily brought together Burmans of different factions to crush them. Many Burman mutineers returned to the army to take part in the campaign against the Karens, and in some areas members of the White Band PVO observed a truce with the government forces in order to attack Karens.

The Karen rebellion greatly accelerated the process of Burman domination of the armed forces. From 1887 until the end of British rule, Burmans had been excluded from the armed forces. Instead, minority peoples, especially Karens, had been recruited for the Burma Army. Troops from Aung San's army were absorbed into the Burma Army after World War II, but the forces remained primarily non-Burman. On February 1, 1949, because of the Karen revolt, U Nu relieved from duty all Karens in the government forces, including the commander in chief.

Lieutenant General Ne Win, one of the Thirty Comrades and a brigadier in Aung San's Burma Defense Army, became chief of general staff and supreme commander of the armed forces, including the police and military police. The government forces remained predominantly members of minority groups—Chins, Kachins, Anglo-Burmese, and others—but the leadership was now Burman.

The organizational cohesion of the AFPFL had never been great, and the civil war further weakened it. In March 1949 members of the Socialist Party (by then the largest single party in the AFPFL) resigned from the cabinet, and General Ne Win was chosen by U Nu to be deputy prime minister in charge of home affairs and defense, in addition to continuing as supreme commander of the armed forces. Ne Win had a large personal following in the armed forces and was usually addressed as *bogyoke,* the honorific previously reserved for the late Aung San.

During the first half of 1949 rebel bands gained much territory. The KNDO and the various Communist groups held most of Lower Burma. In March 1949 Karens and Communists formed a brief and limited alliance to take and hold Mandalay. For the most part, however, the different rebel factions kept apart. Largely because of the failure of the rebels to cooperate with each other, the government of the Union of Burma was able to regain the initiative in the latter half of 1949.

Within a year most of the country along the main roads was under government control, at least in daylight hours. The threat to the continued existence of the Union of Burma posed by the civil war had been overcome, although the insurgents continued to dominate much of the countryside. A general amnesty was offered and received a good response. General Ne Win left the cabinet and returned to the army. In 1951 a separate Karen state, Kawthule State, was established along the Salween valley by constitutional amendment, and the support by Karens for the KNDO's insurgency was reduced, although it did not cease altogether.

General Elections, 1951-52

Elections, due within eighteen months after independence, had been delayed by the civil war. By 1951, however, the government was able to begin holding elections in cleared constituencies. As the insurrections receded over the next year, elections were held in various parts of the country. The AFPFL won a large majority of the seats in both chambers of the legislature, and U Nu continued as prime minister. Factionalism soon began to attack the AFPFL parliamentary group, however.

Nonetheless, the political problems were less pressing in the middle 1950s than were the problems of the deteriorating economy and the continuing insurgencies. Insurgent groups began to revive in this period, largely because the central government was distracted from its campaign against the rebels by a new threat to security caused by the presence in northern Burma of several thousand troops of the armed forces of Nationalist China (see ch. 10, Foreign Relations).

Plans and Problems

The first decade of the independent Union of Burma was a period of economic disorder and disappointment. On the eve of independence Burmese nationalists were all in favor of one or another form of socialism. They shared a suspicion of foreign investors and a dislike of laissez-faire capitalism. Expectations among the Burmese were that the removal of foreign rule and foreign control of business and its replacement with an indigenous socialist regime would produce abundance for every family within a short time. In 1947, when moving the adoption of the draft constitution, U Nu said:

> The foundations laid for New Burma are those of a leftist country. . .In a leftist country, there will be no such thing as a handful of people holding the monopoly over the inexhaustible wealth of the land while the poor and starving grow more and more numerous. . .In a leftist country, there

will be no distinction between the employer class and the
employed class, or to put it simply, there will be no such
thing as the master-class and the governed class.

Nationalization and increased activity by the government in part-
nership with private businesses were utilized in an effort to realize
these aims. The Land Nationalization Act was passed in 1948, designed to redistribute all agricultural land so that each family would
receive a maximum of 50 acres. The act was applied to one township only, where it was a failure. Another land nationalization act
was passed in 1953. (By 1958, when the law was suspended by Ne
Win's caretaker regime, slightly under 3.5 million acres of land had
been nationalized.)

The marketing and export of rice, which had been controlled by
a few private British firms before World War II, were taken over by
the British military authorities after the Japanese had been expelled. In 1946, as a concession to Burmese sentiment not to restore rice marketing to the foreign firms, the colonial government
had established the State Agricultural Marketing Board as a permanent government organization to be responsible for the whole
marketing process. The board was retained after independence was
achieved (see ch. 12, Agriculture and Industry).

Public utilities and some of the big companies engaged in providing communication facilities were nationalized in 1948, as was
the teak industry. Soon thereafter, joint ventures were established
involving the government and the large foreign firms that had
operated oil and mining enterprises before the war. Efforts were
also made to encourage private foreign investment, but many
foreign businessmen felt reluctant to invest in a country in which
civil war endangered their investments and their personal safety.
The government also made clear that preferential treatment would
be granted to Burmese nationals and that foreign companies would
be obliged to employ Burmese and not Indians, Gurkhas, Chinese,
or Eurasians, the chief sources of labor for industry before the war.

In addition to ridding the economy of foreign dominance and
providing for an equitable distribution of resources through
nationalization, the government was determined to promote the
industrialization of the country. A two-year plan for economic development, including detailed plans for the setting up of factories
and mills to process rubber, sugar, timber, textiles, and steel, was
published by the AFPFL in April 1948.

The civil war prevented implementation of much of this plan,
but by 1952, a time when the insurrections were diminishing in
force, the economy appeared to be recovering. Rice production,
although not up to prewar figures, was improving and, with the
outbreak of the Korean conflict in June 1950, the demand for
Burmese rice had increased substantially, resulting in the doubling
of rice prices between mid-1950 and 1952.

At this point the Pyidawtha (Happy Land) plan, an ambitious eight-year economic development plan, was announced for the years 1953 to 1960. The Pyidawtha plan reflected the recommendations of a private United States engineering firm that had been hired by the Burmese government to make an economic survey and proposals for economic development.

By 1953, however, the economic situation was less encouraging than it had been the year before. The Korean war boom was over, and the rice price had dropped. Burma terminated further United States aid in conjunction with its campaign to remove the Nationalist Chinese troops from northern Burma (see ch. 10, Foreign Relations). Loans from the British and Commonwealth countries had been granted to the young republic, but they had been spent with little to show for them. The civil war had used up much of the government's funds and had prevented the collection of taxes from landowners, formerly an important source of government revenue. Free education for all, initiated in 1951, and numerous other expensive social welfare programs had been begun in an effort to maintain and increase the loyalty of the Burmese people to their government. U Nu also held the Sixth Great Synod of Buddhism in Rangoon beginning in 1953. The holding of the synod promoted the government's prestige at home and in other Theravada Buddhist countries—Ceylon, Thailand, Laos, and Cambodia—but involved considerable expense.

The Pyidawtha plan, which was dependent for its success upon far greater resources of capital, skilled labor, and managerial experience than Burma possessed at that time, was abandoned in 1955, when foreign exchange reserves had fallen to half the 1953 figure. Shorter term plans that followed in the middle 1950s also failed to improve the economic situation.

BREAKDOWN OF PARLIAMENTARY DEMOCRACY

The 1951 elections had given the government party, the AFPFL, a large victory, partly because the opposing groups were in rebellion and did not participate. In Parliament government proposals were endorsed almost automatically. Government programs for economic and social development, hastily enacted and inadequately supervised, fell seriously short of their goals, and their failure contributed to a growing loss of public esteem for the AFPFL.

The AFPFL parliamentary group began to break apart. The Socialist Party, the largest constituent party of the AFPFL, split into two factions. The left wing of the Socialist Party, dissatisfied with the government decision to remain neutral concerning the Korean conflict, quit the AFPFL and formed a new opposition party, the Burma Workers and Peasants Party (BWPP), also known as the Red Socialist Party. Parlimentarians of the BWPP, although too few to outvote the AFPFL majority, made use of the sitdown strike and the walkout to call attention to their demands. Another small party, the Justice Party, also appeared in the opposition. It was organized and led by a supreme court justice who had quarreled with U Nu.

General Elections, 1956

The BWPP and the Justice Party allied to form the National United Front (NUF) to appose the AFPFL in the elections of 1956. Although the NUF won only 45 seats in the Chamber of Deputies (the lower house), as against 250 seats for the AFPFL., it received nearly 45 percent of the popular vote, the AFPFL getting under 48 percent. Soon after the election, U Nu stepped down from the prime minister-ship for a year in order to devote his attention to an attempt to revitalize and reunify the AFPFL. U Nu had often threatened to retire premanently from politics, and three of his ministers—U Ba Swe, U Kyaw Nyein, and Thakin Tin—each took the opportunity offered by U Nu's temporary retirement to mobilize personal support for himself as eventual heir to U Nu's primacy.

When U Nu resumed the prime ministership in June 1957, the AFPFL was less unified than ever before. In March 1958 the AFPFL split in two: the "Clean" AFPFL, as U Nu called the fac-tion headed by himself and Thakin Tin, and the "Stable" AFPFL, as it was called by its Socialist Party leaders, U Ba Swe and U Kyaw Nyein. The Stable AFPFL was the larger faction and, when it moved into the opposition, U Nu had to win votes of parliamentary members from the NUF and from minority communities in order to stay in office.

In addition to the competition between AFPFL factions for power within Parliament, growth of politicomilitary organizations that supported rival leaders and parties encouraged factionalism. For example, the Stable AFPFL had the backing of the Auxiliary Union Military Police, whereas Thakin Tin had the support of the so-called peace guerrillas of the All-Burma Peasants' Organization. In Rangoon a violent clash occurred between the newly established Union Labor Organization of the Clean AFPFL and U Ba Swe's Trade Union Congress, Burma. The split in the AFPFL also led to armed struggles between political rivals in the rural villages, each side seeking to gain control of the village defense forces that had been set up by the central government to help loyal villagers repel insurgents. Motivated in part by the fear that the insurgent forces, which had been losing ground throughout the mid-1950s, would be likely to benefit from renewed insecurity in the country unless a strong government took charge, on October 28, 1958, U Nu moved in the Chamber of Deputies that General Ne Win be offered the prime ministership of a caretaker government.

Caretaker Government, 1958-60

In his acceptance speech before Parliament, General Ne Win promised to "do my best to hold fair and free elections within six months if the insurgency and crimes are brought to an end within the period." His cabinet was composed of former civil servants. Party politicians were excluded.

The primary task undertaken by the caretaker regime was the establishment of law and order. The various small armed organizations that had grown up under the patronage of political leaders and parties were disbanded. Several hundred politicians were arrested. Thousands of rebels were killed or captured or surrendered. Town and village defense was reorganized and removed from the control of civilian politicians.

Ne Win saw as the next most pressing need the restoration of order to the administration of government offices, enterprises, and services. To achieve this, the general inserted military men into many of the government departments and turned over control of the state-owned industrial and commercial enterprises to the Defense Services Institute, under the direction of his subordinate Brigadier Aung Gyi. Within a short time the Defense Services Institute was operating a large economic complex, including banking, factories, and shipping as well as numerous commercial enterprises. Some had been taken over from private control, and others were newly established by the Defense Services Institute. Government services were substantially improved. Soldiers led a cleanup campaign in the streets of Rangoon. Garbage was collected regularly. Approximately 200,000 squatters, many of them refugees from the insurrections in the countryside who had crowded into Rangoon, were resettled in satellite towns on the outskirts of the city.

The administration of the semiautonomous states was brought into closer conformity with that of the rest of the union. The hereditary chiefs of the Shan and Kayah states were induced to surrender substantial political and revenue powers—powers that they held according to the customary law of their peoples and that had long been regarded by the leaders of the government of the Union of Burma as incompatible with a modern democracy as well as potentially threatening to the integrity of the union.

In foreign affairs Ne Win continued the policy of strict neutrality of the preceding regime and in January 1960, as the caretaker government prepared to surrender its power, an agreement was reached with Communist China concerning the border with Burma. The border had been a source of dispute between the two countries for many years (see ch. 10, Foreign Relations).

By the start of 1960 the cost-of-living had declined, the foreign exchange reserve had risen, crime and insurgency had been reduced, and the entire government bureaucracy was evincing a higher level of efficiency than before the caretaker regime took office.

Politically, the caretaker regime had avoided labels, although government spokesmen frequently found occasion to attack members of U Nu's Clean AFPFL. No army political party was created, but the armed forces established national solidarity associations in towns and villages throughout Burma that involved the cooperation of military and civilian personnel in security and social welfare projects and in demonstrations of loyalty to the Union of Burma. These associations were continued by the armed forces after the civilian government was restored.

U Nu Returns to Power

In February 1960 General Ne Win began the return to civilian government by holding elections for parliament. U Nu, at the head of the Clean AFPFL, fought an effective campaign on the issue of democracy versus fascism and on a promise to establish Buddhism as the state religion if he became prime minister. For the first time in Burma's history more than half the electorate (59 percent) turned out to vote, and U Nu won a massive victory. After taking office on April 4, 1960, U Nu reorganized his party and renamed it the Pyidaungsu (Union League) Party. The Stable AFPFL was the major opposition party, and after the election it dropped the prefix from its name. The NUF, although it contested many seats, won none.

Upon taking office, U Nu was faced with the task of carrying out various campaign promises he had made to special interest groups. The promise of establishing Buddhism as the state religion had won him support in the Burman rural districts and in the *sangha*, but when the Constitution was amended to that end there were protests and demonstrations by the Kachins, Chins, and Karens. A second amendment, guaranteeing government protection of other religions, was opposed by Buddhist monks in Rangoon, who seized a Muslim mosque and had to be removed by the city's riot squads.

U Nu had also made campaign promises of establishing separate semiautonomous Mon and Arakanese states. Ethnic separatism was reviving. Several small revolts had flared up in the Shan State in 1959 after the *sawbwas* (hereditary chiefs) had relinquished their authority and, now that ten years had elapsed since the Constitution had come into effect, it was legally possible for the Shans to consider seceding from the Union of Burma. In February 1962 leaders of the constituent states met in Rangoon to discuss minority problems. There was discussion of the possibility of replacing the present constitution with one that provided for "pure federalism."

In addition to threats to the country's integrity, there were internal divisions within U Nu's Pyidaungsu Party that became severe during the national congress of the party in January 1962. Following this U Nu resigned for tactical reasons his position as party president. The economy was sluggish, and the efficiency of the government had been eroded. In addition, the business community of Rangoon was disaffected by the announced decision of the government to nationalize all foreign trade as of March 1, 1962.

MILITARY COUP

On March 2, 1962, General Ne Win announced over the radio that "the armed forces have taken over the responsibility and the task of keeping the country's safety, owing to the greatly deteriorating conditions in the Union."

The coup, which was almost bloodless, had been accomplished in the early morning hours of March 2, and by the afternoon the Revolutionary Council had been formed; General Ne Win became chairman, and all of the councillors and ministers were drawn from the armed forces. The Constitution was suspended, and Parliament was dissolved. U Nu, some of his cabinet ministers, and a number of ethnic minority group leaders were imprisoned. The Revolutionary Council, consisting of fifteen army officers and one each from the navy and air force, began to rule by decree (see ch. 9, Political Dynamics).

On April 30 the Revolutionary Council promulgated a manifesto entitled *The Burmese Way to Socialism.* This manifesto, which became a basic political document of the Revolutionary Government of the Union of Burma, explicitly rejects parliamentary democracy on the grounds that during its existence in Burma it "failed to serve. . .socialist development. . .and deviated from socialist aims." Some nine years later, General Ne Win and his government were still in power.

CHAPTER 4

SOCIAL SYSTEMS AND VALUES

As one of its major explicit goals, General Ne Win's Revolutionary Government was engaged in 1971 in an attempt to transform Burmese social arrangements and values and to reallocate prestige and power among the various social groups in the country. The government's aim has been to instill "Burmese Socialist" behavior and values in the armed forces; the small number of Westernized government workers, politicians, professional people, and students; the business community; the industrial labor force; and, above all, the peasantry.

The criteria for social status before the March 1962 military takeover had included many diverse factors. Among them were ethnic origin and religious affiliation. The amount of land owned and the extent of contribution to Buddhist institutions and community festivities played a part. The degree of Westernization and level of education were added in more modern times. Kin connection to persons of high status, type of employment, and personal qualities of leadership, judgment, astuteness, and piety also were important. Efforts were being made by the Revolutionary Government to either eliminate or greatly modify these criteria.

It is not clear to what extent the Revolutionary Government had succeeded by 1971. The elimination of popularly elected government at both the national and village levels, the banning of all social organizations except those sponsored by the only legal political party—the Burma Socialist Program Party (BSPP), the redistribution of agricultural land, and the nationalization of most nonagricultural enterprises could not have been achieved without profound social effects. The disestablishment of Buddhism as the state religion and its reduced influence on the political leadership were also factors.

Efforts have been made by the Revolutionary Government to promote the integration of all Burmese into the national society. The national society has at all times lacked unity and has been divided into loosely affiliated subsocieties—rural Burman, urban, and minority group enclaves. Burmese society for the most part has lacked formal inherited classes or commonly agreed upon status hierarchies. There are a few positions, such as that of village headman, that tend to be passed down within a given family, from father to son, son-in-law, or nephew, and there are inherited chieftainships in some of the minority hill tribes. For most Burmese, however, inheritance is of less significance than achievement in determining social status. Although possession of wealth is one element in achieving social prestige, it is not the determining factor; nor do people tend to categorize themselves or others as belonging to a certain economic class. Political power is of more importance than wealth in achieving social prestige.

An important concern of a Burmese is to use the correct titles and forms of deference toward persons with whom he has face-to-face contact. In so doing, he must determine his social status relative to the person. In reaching this determination, the age and sex of each party to the interaction are the chief guides.

After the Revolutionary Government came to power, the armed forces became the unifying superstructure tying together the entire country administratively, politically, economically, and socially. (see ch. 8, Political System and Values). In addition, the ruling BSPP, as an instrument of the Revolutionary Council, has worked to eliminate social divisions and to produce a unified, multiracial national Burmese society. Participation in the BSPP—which was in early 1971 in the process of becoming a mass party—or in its subsidiary social organizations, what the government called "people's workers' councils" and "people's peasants' councils," were the most common means being employed to break down social barriers based on ethnicity, home locality, or other social distinctions. The methods used included mass demonstrations, seminars for rural delegates, and ideological training at schools, such as the Central School of Political Science, which graduate a few thousand each year. Indoctrination in the BSPP official ideology is the chief activity of these various government-sponsored seminars and training schools. The eventual goal invisioned by the Revolutionary Government is that the Burmese will become a united people, composed of workers and peasants, loyal to the ideology and to the leadership of the BSPP (see ch. 9, Political Dynamics).

HISTORICAL INFLUENCES

Burmese society has undergone several major upheavals since the middle of the nineteenth century. The first of these was the destruction of traditional Burmese social arrangements and institutions by the conquering colonial power, Great Britain, and their partial replacement by social arrangements and institutions in which foreign ideas and foreign personnel were preeminent (see ch. 3, Historical Setting). The second upheaval was the destruction of the colonial social arrangements during and after World War II. The third upheaval, still in progress in 1971, was the destruction of the postcolonial social institutions and patterns that had evolved in the two decades preceding 1962. In each case the disruption has led to less social cohesion and less clear-cut social patterns. The disrupting agent—whether the British colonial government, the Japanese army, the Burmese nationalists, or Ne Win's Revolutionary Government—has been more successful in destroying previously existing social arrangements than in establishing new ones.

Nonetheless, a persistent feature of Burmese society from the time of the monarchy has been its division into several loosely connected subsocieties: the traditional Burman Buddhist rural society, which was by far the largest and least dynamic subsociety; the small urban subsociety, the leaders of which aspired to national power and prestige; and the minority enclaves, each having its own distinctive social arrangements and culture.

During the period of the monarchy, Burmese urban society was built around the royal court. Urban society was highly stratified, with persons in the upper ranks almost totally dependent upon the king's patronage for their positions. Unlike the king, the high-ranking officials did not inherit their positions. These royal favorites were engaged in rivalry among themselves, a competition that often evolved into conspiracy and revolt. The villages were essentially egalitarian and were at pains to perpetuate the great social distance between the countryside and the court. A traditional Burmese prayer, still in use in the 1960s, includes the phrase "spare me the five evils," by which is meant flood, fire, kings, thieves, and enemies.

Although the urban and rural societies of Burma proper (see Glossary) were in many ways distinct from one another, they shared a common religion, Buddhism, and many other cultural features. There were also present, in the hill areas that bordered Burma proper, enclaves of non-Burmese-speaking peoples, many of whom were not Buddhist and who had social arrangements markedly different from those of Burma proper. These elements formed the groundwork for the emergence of a disunited society.

During the British colonial period the social distance between the people of Burma proper and those of the frontier hills was widened. The lowland Burmese were ruled directly by colonial officials from their headquarters in Rangoon, whereas the people of the hills were governed loosely and indirectly through their own traditional leaders. The colonial development of the economy of Burma proper—which led to much of its agricultural land being alienated—did not affect the hills nor were their social arrangements disrupted to the same extent as were those of the Burmese in the lowlands. The British colonial policy of barring Burmese Buddhists from the armed forces and recruiting in their stead Karens, Chins, and Kachins contributed to ethnic animosities.

Upon assuming control over Burma, the British also introduced several new elements into the country's society. In place of the indigenous monarchy, there was established a government headed by foreigners and operating in accordance with laws and institutions that had evolved in Great Britain. Gradually some Burmans were coopted into the colonial regime. This group, with its Western education and style of life and its dependence upon British patronage, began to establish itself as a separate self-perpetuating class in Burmese society, indigenous racially but alien in its values and its source of power.

In addition to the small group of high-status Westernized Burmese, there also grew up during the colonial period a large foreign community, concentrated in the urban centers, that contained some British and other Western businessmen, missionaries, and professional people but also included hundreds of thousands of foreign Asians (primarily Indians, but also many Chinese) who took over the intermediary roles that were by then required by the economic development and expanded bureaucracy of the colonial period. Indians and Eurasians predominated in many branches of the government, especially in clerical and menial positions. Indians and Chinese filled the intermediary positions in the newly monetized economy, such as moneylender, mortgage holder, retail trader, and rice miller.

By the end of the colonial period Rangoon and the other urban centers were to a considerable extent organized into social strata, membership of which was partly contingent upon ethnic origin. At the top were the Westerners—senior government officials, businessmen, and professional people. Just below them were the Westernized Asians (including some Burmese) and Eurasians. There was a small middle income group composed primarily of foreign Asians who held middle-ranking government positions and handled retail commerce and trade. The urban mass was composed of manual laborers, all Asian—Burmese, Indians, Pakistanis, and Chinese.

LINES OF DIVISION WITHIN SOCIETY

Despite the lack of formal classes, there are within Burmese society numerous cleavages, some of which have been activated or intensified by three decades of war and civil insurgency. The dividing lines demarcate social groups, the members of which share a common social status, behavior patterns, or values. These demarcations separate urbanites from rural people, Burmans from minority ethnic groups, Buddhists from non-Buddhists, monks from laymen, military personnel from civilians, government officials from private citizens, Westernized from non-Westernized persons, traditionally oriented people from modernizers, Communists from non-Communists, and insurgents from loyal citizens.

These dividing lines shape social groups that are not cohesive nor necessarily mutually exclusive but overlap each other. For example, an urbanite can be a member of the *sangha* (see Glossary); a modernizer can be a Burman or a member of a minority ethnic group. The group identification assigned an individual varies with the context of relationship. These dividing lines are not for the most part insuperable social barriers, and there is fairly free movement across some of them. An example is the fact that any Buddhist male can become part of the *sangha* for as long as he is willing to abide by its rules. In some cases a person can even change his ethnic identity by adopting the language and culture of a different ethnic group. These lines of demarcation also do not define groups necessarily of equal size or importance. These lines are, nonetheless, significant because it is the position on one side or another that helps define for a Burmese his relationship to others. It also helps him determine in a given situation where his interests and loyalties lie.

The absence of unity of Burmese society was reflected to some extent in the presence of insurgencies of long duration. In 1971 insurgent groups were active in much of the northern and western frontier areas and in other sections as well (see ch. 9, Political Dynamics). Although cleavages within Burma's noninsurgent society were numerous and often deep, they were minor compared with divisions among the insurgents. These divisions were not only social but often political and military as well. Some groups had foreign backing; for example, that furnished by the Chinese. There were also, Mon, Arakanese, Karen, Kayah, Kachin, and Shan insurgent separatist groups, but these have seldom been able to cooperate.

Urban and Rural

Urban residents, although they numbered fewer than 20 percent of Burma's population in 1971, included virtually all leaders of national importance and provided examples of the modern style of living that many rural villagers, especially those of the younger generation, wished to emulate. The urban centers also included a high proportion of the nation's government employees. Government employment had been prestigious since the time of the Burmese monarchy and had become since the mid-1960s virtually the sole means of achieving secular power and prestige of more than villagewide importance. In general, urbanites of middle or upper income levels in the early 1970s were deferred to by the rural people regardless of the latter's local social importance or economic position.

Ethnic and Religious Minorities

As in the case of urban residents, the influence of minority peoples on the nation is disproportionate to their numbers. Although members of minority ethnic groups constituted approximately 30 percent of the nation's population in early 1971, the minority groups have been the major suppliers of troops to insurgent forces that have plagued the country since 1947. Some of the minority peoples, such as the Shans, Palaungs, Mons, Arakanese, and perhaps 85 percent of the Karens, are Buddhist, but the non-Buddhist Burmese, roughly 15 percent of the population, were in the early 1960s so violently opposed to the attempt of the government to officially impose Buddhist religious and cultural values on the country that Buddhism became a divisive rather than a unifying force for the nation, in spite of the high proportion of adherents among the citizens (see ch. 3, Historical Setting). A contributing factor to religious friction has been the tendency of Burmese Buddhists to regard as less civilized those persons who adhere to traditional animist beliefs and to view indigenous Christians and Muslims as culturally foreign and thus inferior.

The Sangha and the Laity

Although the *sangha* is a comparatively small group, limited by a lack of centralized organization or hierarchy, divided into two competing orders of monks, and obliged by monastic rules to be removed from worldly affairs, it commands the highest forms of deference of any group in Burmese society and has been the prime defender of traditional Burmese values against Western, communist, or other modern secular values. Because of the opposition of the *sangha* to the modern secular values contained in the official ideology and policies of the Revolutionary Government, the *sangha* has enjoyed less influence with the government since 1962 than at any time since independence. Nevertheless, at the village level, the prestige and influence of the *sangha* were still great in early 1971, according to the limited information available.

The *sangha* membership was estimated in 1964 as numbering about 800,000 monks. A survey in a rural Burmese district conducted in the early 1960s showed that approximately 2.5 to 3 percent of the Buddhist male population were members of the *sangha* at any given time, more than half of them for a short period—generally less than a year. Nevertheless, virtually all male Burmese Buddhists spend some time in the *sangha* and, during that time, adhere to its stringent rules of conduct and receive in exchange the highest social status in Burmese Buddhist society. On those few occasions when the *sangha* has operated as a pressure group and engaged in demonstrations, as it did, for example, during Burma's struggle for independence, its influence on public opinion has been great.

The Armed Forces

By 1971 the armed forces had become the most powerful organization in Burmese society. This was a relatively recent development. During the colonial period the army had been led by British officers and manned by members of the minority ethnic groups. Burmese Buddhists had been explicitly excluded. During World War II, beginning with a nucleus of the Thirty Comrades, the nationalist leader Aung San had forged a Burman-dominated force to fight for Burmese independence. Some of Aung San's forces were merged into the colonial army after the war, and gradually, during the first decade of independence, the armed forces under the leadership of General Ne Win became a Burman-dominated nationalist organization. During the period of the Ne Win caretaker regime from 1958 to 1960, the army gained the reputation for being the most efficient modernizing organization in the country (see ch. 3, Historical Setting). This view of the armed forces was the one being promulgated in the government-owned press in 1971.

Since the mid-1960s almost all of the senior positions in government and industry have been manned by members of the armed services, whereas before 1962 these positions had been almost entirely in civilian hands. The network of political, social, and administrative units throughout the country, extending from Rangoon to the village level, was connected by a military chain of command (see ch. 8, Political System and Values). Because of their dominant position, the military in 1971 received deference from the civilian population.

Modernizers and Traditionalists

Although most Burmese are traditionally oriented, the national leadership has been primarily nontraditional in its orientation since the time of independence. The leaders have attempted to modernize Burma rather than to restore it. Within the modernizing group, however, there were variations in commitment to British, Marxist, or nationalist ideas and institutions. During the colonial period the most powerful Burmese were the officials employed by the British to fill positions in the colonial administration. These Burmese government officials spoke English among themselves, had Western educations, lived in their own separate Western-style neighborhoods, and adopted Western dress and behavior. To many of the Burmese nationalist politicians and intellectuals who were active in the last years of the colonial regime, the position of the government officials as agents of a foreign power and their rejection of Burmese values in favor of Western ones were offensive.

The political leaders of the nationalist movement who came to power after independence ousted many of the officials from the government service and denigrated their wholesale allegiance to British values. The dominant political group attempted to strike a balance between Burmese nationalism, rooted in traditional non-dynamic values, such as Buddhism and the wearing of Burmese dress, and modern institutions and values borrowed from Great Britain, such as equality before the law and parliamentary democracy. All political leaders were committed to socialist economic ideas, and an important minority in the political leadership was in favor of communist concepts and institutions. Profound ideological rifts in the civilian political elite, deepened by personal rivalries, disastrously weakened the group's hold on government.

After the removal of the civilian political elite from power in March 1962, the influence of Western, especially British, values and institutions on the ruling group was greatly reduced, as was the influence of Buddhism. In other respects, the ruling group has continued, as had the civilian government that preceded it, to promote a nationalist, socialist orientation that was dynamic and modern but rooted in traditional indigenous values.

URBAN SOCIAL STRUCTURE

Burma has few large urban centers. Rangoon was the only city with a population over 1 million in 1971. Mandalay and Moulmein were the only others exceeding 100,000 (see ch. 2, Physical Environment and Population). There are about 280 towns but only a handful of urban centers with populations exceeding 50,000. Whereas during the colonial period the urban centers had been primarily the centers of foreign influence and only secondarily the foci of national sentiment, since independence these cities, especially Rangoon, have gradually shed much of their alien character and have become the centers from which national institutions seek to disseminate their ideas concerning a dynamic national culture and society.

Although the social distance between the urban and rural people has remained great, the influence of urban life upon rural society has increased with improved communications and with government sponsorship of mass demonstrations, seminars, and conferences that have brought hundreds of thousands of rural villagers to the cities each year and exposed them to members of the national, urban-based political leadership. Contrariwise, the allegiances to family, ethnic group, and religion, bonds that were forged in the traditional rural setting, have been maintained by the urban population insofar as urban conditions permit.

Elite Group

Most of the members of the country's urban-based ruling group are army officers assigned to civilian duties, sometimes in addition to their military functions. Many of the older military officers are veterans of the Burma Independence Army and share a sense of pride in having contributed to the achievement of Burmese independence. The role played by the senior military officers in the independence struggle is widely publicized and provides a measure of nationalist legitimacy to the 1962 assumption of power by a military coup.

The armed forces, made up of volunteers, enjoy above-average salaries and housing. Some members have opportunities to learn a profession, such as engineering or accounting, and for some there are opportunities to manage government enterprises and to fill positions of influence in the government administration. Membership in the armed forces is a means to achieve upward social mobility.

Social leadership in the urban areas has become a government monopoly. All mass social organizations not under the sponsorship of the government or its party, the BSPP, have been illegal since 1964, and all but a few urban enterprises were nationalized in the 1960s. Articles and editorials appearing in the government press in the late 1960s and early 1970s indicated that, for civilians, entry and promotion in government service were tied to acceptance and understanding of the official BSPP ideology (see ch. 8, Political System and Values). Selection for ideological training at institutions established for the purpose has, therefore, become the chief channel for civilians seeking higher status.

Below the ruling group, urban society is not readily divisible into explicit social classes. Official terminology describes all wage earners as workers. The differentials in income between the highest paid and lowest paid wage earners were reduced after the nationalization of urban private enterprise. The pay of the lowest paid laborer was raised to the minimum government wage, whereas managerial personnel were reduced to the salary granted government workers of comparable rank.

Efforts have been made by Burmese leaders since independence, and especially since 1962, to blur status differences, real or potential, and to emphasize educational and ideological means of achieving upward mobility. Close supervision by government "security and administrative committees" or their representatives in all urban neighborhoods is one of the means used by the government to ensure conformity of the people to the approved social pattern.

Students and Youth

In the first decade after independence modern secular education drew young people to the cities, where the secular schools were located. Modern secular education, along British lines, was then, as it had been during the colonial period, the chief means for achieving entry into the officer class of the government bureaucracy or the professions. The highest status went to the Burmese who had a degree from a British university. Education in itself was not highly valued. The status of academicians was not high, and it diminished in the postindependence period, but Western-style education was the means to achieve prestigious employment with the government or as a highly paid professional person.

The belief that higher education was the way to qualify for prestigious employment has carried over from the colonial period in motivating Burmese since 1962 but with less justification than formerly. Job openings have failed to keep pace with educational opportunities (see ch. 9, Political Dynamics). The disruptive potential of unemployed students and youth has been recognized by the government, and in early 1971 there was discussion in the Burmese press of the need to establish a youth organization similar to those that had been established by the BSPP for workers and peasants.

The government's concern has been not only to alleviate the social problem caused by the presence of a discontented idle urban group but also to reorient the values of students and youth away from colonial values and toward Burmese socialist values. Youth work camps were opened in mid-1970 for volunteers to do work in agriculture, industry, and rural development. These work camps were supposed to provide employment for idle students and also were aimed at reorienting student values so that educated youths would cease deprecating manual labor and become instead, in the words of a 1970 Burmese newspaper editorial, "educated revolutionary workers."

Another government program, begun in the mid-1960s to inculcate new values among youth, has been the *luyechun* program. Under this program, outstanding students, ranging from the upper primary grades through college, are awarded the honor of being a *luyechun* (person of high distinction). During April and May the *luyechun* are brought to one of two holiday camps—on the Inle Lake in the Shan State or at Ngapali, a seaside resort in Arakan Division. There they receive social service and citizenship training and participate in an active sports and recreation program.

Aliens and Alien Values

The urban areas have always been the centers from which national and foreign attitudes were disseminated to the Burmese public. Until the 1960s urban areas in Burma were primarily areas of foreign dominance. The decline in the number of aliens in the cities during the 1960s and the tight restrictions on visits by foreigners still largely in effect in early 1971 have greatly reduced the impact of the outside world on Burmese urban life and have virtually eliminated foreign influences on rural life.

In 1960 there were an unofficially estimated 500,000 Indians and 300,000 Chinese in Burma out of a total population estimated at 20 million. The land tenancy policies and the nationalization of the nonagricultural sector of the economy undertaken during the 1960s led to a mass exodus of foreigners, especially Indians. Since September 1966 emigration of foreigners has continued at a rapid pace. The Chinese began to accelerate their emigration rate in response to an anti-Chinese riot in June 1967 in Rangoon. The riot was touched off by Chinese students demonstrating their allegiance to Mao Tse-tung and the Communist Chinese Cultural Revolution (see ch. 10, Foreign Relations).

The alien population in Burma in 1971 was small and primarily urban. Unofficial estimates in early 1971 showed 100,000 Indians, 20,000 Pakistanis, and 400,000 Chinese. These figures included some who had recently acquired Burmese citizenship. A small and in many ways exceptional group of Chinese in Burma are the Panthay, Chinese Muslims from Yunnan, who began migrating to the towns of Upper Burma and the Shan State in the late nineteenth century. The 1931 census listed only 1,100 Panthay, mostly in towns in the Shan State. By 1961, however, they were estimated at about 10,000, many of them new refugees from the communist regime in China. A few could be found in most towns of Upper Burma. Many have married outside their group, and the younger generation is being drawn into Burmese culture. Panthay elders interviewed in the early 1960s anticipated that the community would soon be assimilated and disappear.

The repatriation of Indians and Pakistanis was continuing with the support of the governments involved in 1971. Burmese citizenship for Indians, who had always been the largest nonindigenous group in Burma, had been comparatively easy to obtain at the time of independence, but by 1961 only 6,700 had applied for it. During the 1960s citizenship became more difficult to obtain, but in late 1970 the Burmese press contained reports that efforts were being made to speed up the processing of 60,000 applications for Burmese citizenship that had been received.

Eurasians had numbered about 25,000 before World War II and had been primarily urban residents. In 1931 there had been just under 10,000 Eurasians in Rangoon alone. Most automatically qualified for Burmese citizenship, and many were also able to remain British subjects, in which case they could be dual nationals or divest themselves of one or the other nationality. By the early 1960s it was estimated that about 10,000 had emigrated to one of the British Commonwealth countries, about 10,000 had either never had, or had renounced, British citizenship and were Burmese citizens only; and the remainder had retained British citizenship and stayed in Burma. Most of the urban Eurasians were Christian and spoke English. Some changed to Burman-style names during and after World War II.

There also still existed in 1971 a small Eurasian rural community in Upper Burma. These were Burmese citizens and were culturally Burmese except in their religion, Roman Catholicism. They were the descendants of Portuguese and French soldiers and their Burmese wives, who had been exiled by Burman kings to villages in Shwebo District in the early seventeenth century and the mid-eighteenth century. There they were settled on farmland in exchange for the hereditary obligation to serve in the royal army (see ch. 3, Historical Setting).

Other than diplomats or persons having official business with the Burmese government, foreigners were normally limited to a stay in Burma of not longer than one week, as of early 1971. This represented a liberalization of earlier regulations that had restricted the stay of foreigners throughout much of the 1960s to twenty-four hours. The immigration policy was most easily enforced at the ports of entry, but efforts were also being made in the early 1970s to prevent illicit crossing of the border at places where control could be exerted. Members of hill tribes and other persons found entering Burma were repatriated to their side of the frontier.

As part of the Revolutionary Government's policy of instilling Burmese socialist values and eliminating conflicting values, efforts have been made, especially in urban areas, to purge Burmese life of what the government spokesmen regard as undesirable foreign influences on social patterns. Newspaper editorials periodically attack Westernized dress and dating patterns among the urban youth as immodest and unsuitable for Burmese. Ballroom dancing is deplored in the press. Dance halls and nightclubs have been closed. Foreign films are censored.

The reduction of Western cultural influences on the urban elite was accelerating in 1971, in large measure as a result of the government's educational policies. Before 1962 the senior ranks of the bureaucracy and of the political parties contained many persons who had received university and graduate training at foreign universities, chiefly at British schools. Since 1962 few persons have been sent for further studies overseas. There were 580 students abroad in 1969.

THE BURMAN FAMILY

Although the process of urbanization, which until 1971 had proceeded at a relatively slow pace compared with other sections of the world, has weakened the status of the family in cities to some extent, the family has remained the basic social unit. In rural society it could be said to be the only secular unit to command the wholehearted support of young and old. In both urban and rural societies it maintained much of the same general outlines.

In rural areas a household compound contains one or more houses sheltering either a nuclear family, composed of parents and dependent children, or an extended family, often including a set of grandparents or sometimes adult siblings and their children. In the case of extended family households, it is somewhat more common for the kinship link to be through women—a mother living with her married daughter or two sisters and their husbands—than through men. Richer families, especially those with more than the average amount of land, are more likely to have extended family households than are poorer families. Land is owned by the household head, but all of the children of the landowner, male and female, have equal inheritance rights.

During the 1950s and 1960s legislation came into effect designed to limit the maximum size of landholdings, to give land to the landless, and to prohibit the collection of rent on agricultural land. By the late 1960s hundreds of thousands of formerly landless farm laborers had acquired small holdings, and many formerly well-to-do landowners had become comparatively poor. In 1969 and 1970 there were reports in the Burmese press of complaints by farmers at meetings of the people's peasants' councils (the farmer organizations established by the government under the guidance of the BSPP in the late 1960s) concerning evasion of land redistribution and tenancy regulations in the villages. Information on the effects of the new land redistribution on family household size and inheritance arrangements was not available in early 1971.

The people of a household cooperate with each other and are able to substitute for each other in household or agricultural chores and in caring for children. Deference is paid by youth to elders, children to parents, younger siblings to older siblings, and females to males.

The relationship between mother and daughter is usually very close and lasts for life. Wives and mothers run the house, keeping control of the household money and often holding the family's savings, stored in the form of gold jewelry, which can be sold if necessary for family needs but not without the woman's consent.

All members of the household fall under the authority of the senior father-mother pair. This authority is rarely explicitly invoked, and those who oppose it usually have the option of quitting the household for that of another relative or, in the case of males, entering the *sangha*.

The kin connections between persons of different households are many, since the Burmans' bilateral descent system acknowledges as kin all persons connected by blood through all four grandparents. Since most marriages take place between fellow village residents or between persons of neighboring villages, villagers can usually claim a kin connection with any of their neighbors. The kin tie, however, is only as important as both parties choose to make it. The Burmans do not revere dead ancestors nor does the kin tie of itself obligate cousins to greater loyalty than that accorded to other fellow villagers. It is often difficult for outsiders to distinguish a neighbor from a relative since the terms of address in use in village society are kin terms. for example, uncles and males of one's father's generation are addressed by the title U; senior males of the same generation as oneself are addressed by the title used for one's elder brother, Ko; nephews and all boys of his generation are addressed by the title Maung.

RURAL BURMAN SOCIETY

The Burmans, like all other indigenous ethnic groups in the Union of Burma, are more than 80-percent rural in residence and engaged in small-holder farming. They live in villages enclosed by palisades, the maintenance of each section of the palisade being the responsibility of one of the village households. Within the village are located the various households, each set off in its own fenced compound.

A typical Burman village in the Mandalay Division of Upper Burma studied in 1960 had approximately 550 people, evenly divided between the sexes, living in 116 houses within 94 household compounds. The population had been very stable for four generations and, aside from marriage and participation in marketing and religious observances with persons in the five or six neighboring villages, few had ever left their village of birth or been greatly influenced by external factors. With the exception of one sewing machine, a loudspeaker-amplifier system run on batteries, a few shotguns, some radios, and a truck, the technology of the village was what it had been centuries earlier. Bullocks for plowing were the major capital investment. The monastery-school and two pagodas located beyond the village, a short distance from the village palisade, were the main foci for community life. The entire village professed Buddhism.

Village Social Relations

Village society is essentially classless. As in the household, deference is given by juniors to seniors and, although women defer to men, the concern with relative age is by far the most important regulator of social behavior. There are several times in the year when it is customary for formal obeisance to be made by younger persons to all persons of the parental generation or above. The titles by which persons are addressed reflect age in relation to the speaker; except for great differences in education, position, or wealth and in relations between laymen and monks, age is the crucial factor in determining who shows deference to whom.

A number of factors are involved in determining who has exceptional prestige other than that accorded to seniority. Even though members of the *sangha* receive the highest forms of respect, this is not necessarily a reflection of personal admiration. It is rather a ritual deference given for providing models of the ideal Buddhist way of life—detached from worldly concerns and devoted exclusively to earning merit. In addition, the act of making obeisance to a monk or showing him respect earns merit for a layman and thus allegedly improves his own chances of acquiring superior status in his next incarnation.

A certain amount of prestige accrues to the village headman. In the past this office tended to be passed down within a single village family either to a son, nephew, or son-in-law of the incumbent. He did not inherit the office automatically but was chosen by the consensus of village elders or by formal election of the villagers. In the case of formal elections, the recognized heir was often elected unanimously. Such unanimity was not universal, however.

By 1971 the chief qualification for village headman was the endorsement of the local Security and Administrative Committee. Such endorsement tended to be granted to a man thought to be politically and ideologically loyal to the BSPP and its policies and who met the approval of the military commander in the area (see ch. 9, Political Dynamics).

The attitude of the village population toward the headman has often been ambivalent. Some of the headman's duties—collecting taxes and serving as a channel for the transmission of government regulations and policies to the village people—come into confrontation with the Burman dislike of compulsion by authorities. The headman is said to govern by virtue of *arnar,* a term that means authority that is backed by the government or other compelling power. The term has some unpleasant connotations as opposed to the term *awza,* which means authority that comes from exceptional personal attributes and qualities of leadership.

Each community usually has at least one man with *awza.* Such a man has certain specific personal attributes. His chief attribute, according to village belief, is the possession of extraordinarily powerful *pon,* the mystical male power. *Pon* is invisible, but the possession of it is evidenced in a man's character, behavior, and luck. The man with strong *pon* is successful, by which is meant that he is not in want and is not obliged to toil continually for his livelihood; he is industrious; he is alert in mind and manner; his movements are lively; and his speech is pithy. He is shrewd at making long-term evaluations and judgments and has a feeling for the less obvious significance of things. He is also compassionate, never pushing his power to the limit.

In a typical rural Burman village in 1960 there was a single universally recognized man with *awza,* a well-to-do (in village terms) landowner and speculator in cash crops. He served on the village council as one of the four elders who assisted the headman in hearing minor criminal cases and exacting fines, organizing secular projects, and administering village public works. Although he was not the headman, the man with *awza* was usually the first person to be called upon by government officials or other persons having business in the village. Most formal and informal village gatherings, except household celebrations and religious observances, were held in front of his house. In many other ways also, his status as the man of authority in the village was made explicit.

Studies of other villages in the early 1960s, however, revealed that in some villages, especially ones with relatively unstable populations and ones that had been drawn into involvement in insurgencies or national political feuds, there were often anarchic conditions. In such villages there was no person of authority, either because there was no man who could lay claim to superior *pon* or because there were several contenders for power who led competing factions. In both cases the headman had little control over the villagers, who disobeyed him at will.

Factionalism was reported as being endemic to rural Burman society by an anthropologist who did fieldwork in Upper Burma in 1961 and 1962. This factionalism seldom erupted into physical violence. Competition and animosity between factions were usually conducted in such a way as to avoid any direct personal confrontation.

Factions are unstable, and their memberships tend to shift as the result of changes in the short-term goals of the individual members. The leader of a faction is a man thought to have superior *pon,* and the other members of his group are usually persons who have a personal relationship with the leader or with someone else in the group who has such a relationship with the leader. If the leader's power fails him, if he dies, or if he leaves the community, his followers may seek another leader, or the faction may dissolve.

Anyone not entitled by virtue of superior *pon* or official position to assert his will over others and who attempts to do so is disliked. The ideal Burman leader is a man of charismatic qualities and Buddhist virtue who does not push his authority too hard. Below him are the ordinary Burman villagers who show their good manners and careful upbringing by behaving with proper deference to superiors and tactfully avoiding any inconvenience to them or disturbance of decorous behavior by a show of deep feeling or strong emotion. The avoidance of conflict or any highly charged interaction with all but one's most intimate associates is a value instilled in Burmans from childhood.

Interpersonal behavior is therefore usually maintained at a level of superficial courtesy. Should this surface courtesy be ruptured, however, because of loss of emotional control by one or another of the participants, there is likely to be physical violence.

Relations Between the Sexes

There are certain acts of deference required by women and restrictions placed upon them that reflect a belief in the superiority of the male to the female. A male is believed to have *pon,* which is regarded as a male birthright. This reflects the Burmese belief that a man has higher status on the wheel of rebirth as the result of his having acquired, in previous incarnations, a more favorable balance of merit and demerit than that of a woman (see ch. 7, Religion). The male's *pon,* upon which the welfare of his household is thought to depend, can be threatened or diminished by certain acts of his wife. She must not allow her lower garments to touch her husband's bed or personal belongings. She must not touch his head or pass articles of hers over his head. These injunctions are easily followed and are not violated deliberately except as an act of malice. Monastic regulations also forbid women to have any physical contact with members of the *sangha.*

In other respects, women are the equals of men. Their rights to property are equal to those of men in inheritance and marriage and in the event of divorce. Women are dominant in the running of the household economy. Upon marriage, they retain their own names; and upon divorce, which is easily obtained, a wife is almost always welcome to return to her parents' house.

Individual Life Cycle

Birth and Infancy

Pregnancy is a time for pampering and indulging the prospective mother. Women find it a happy time. Babies are always welcome, and to be childless is thought to be an affliction. When the time for delivery approaches, a room is set aside for the delivery, and a fire is prepared there by the men of the household. Usually a woman's mother, grandmother, or aunt, as well as a midwife—often a professional government midwife—assist at the birth.

At birth, part of the baby's umbilical cord is cut off with a bamboo or metal knife and is carefully buried under the eaves of the house and at right angles to it. If the cord is buried incorrectly, the belief is that the baby will be a great crier. The baby sleeps in a cradle made by the father; for seven days the mother and child are secluded in the delivery room and, for an additional ten days, they must stay in the house.

The child is introduced to society at his naming feast, to which invitations are sent out to relatives and friends announcing the child's name. Names consist of one, two or three monosyllables. The choice of the name often depends partly on the date of birth and partly on efforts to associate the child with desirable attributes. There are no surnames. A child is never given the identical name as his parent, and the names of deceased relatives are avoided. A name often has certain supernatural associations for its owner and may be changed by the individual to improve his luck or when he embarks on an important venture.

Childhood

Weaning is very gradual, beginning at one year or under and continuing until age two or three. Any woman of the household with breast milk will suckle a child if the mother is absent. Children are closely watched but greatly indulged until approximately the age of six. Relatives and neighbors attempt to satisfy every demand of young children and try to placate them.

Although children imitate the behavior of their elders, from whom they are never separated, they are not consciously instructed, reprimanded, or disciplined until school age when, for the first time, strict demands for conformity are made upon them by either the local monk-teacher (*sayadaw*) at the village monastery-school or the secular teacher at the government school. At this age proper behavior is also demanded at home, and corporal punishment is sometimes administered.

The sudden break in the pattern of discipline of the child that occurs at about age six has been held accountable by numerous social scientists working in Burma for a lifelong concern of Burmans with achieving personal autonomy. The often-noted Burman tendency to evade or defy the demands of superiors who try to compel obedience rather than seek consent, the strong individualism that upon occasion hinders cooperative activity among Burmans, and the tendency in some for rage to be unrestrained and to lead to violence are all attributed by these social scientists to Burman child-rearing practices.

As children grow older, they are able to participate in the work of the household. Daughters help to care for younger children from a very young age, and by age nine or ten sons and daughters bring firewood and take over some agricultural chores. Their contributions to the household's labor pool is highly valued. Children are also regarded as a form of social insurance, since it is anticipated that they will care for their aged parents.

No special ceremonies mark puberty, but there are two ceremonies for children that often take place at approximately the time of puberty: the *shinbyu* (initiation into the *sangha*) for boys and the *natwin* (ear-piercing) for girls (see ch. 7, Religion). The *shinbyu* is regarded by parents as virtually obligatory for the boy's spiritual welfare. It also brings merit to the parents of the novice and other sponsors of the initiation ceremony and feast.

Details of the *shinbyu* vary in different parts of the country and according to the funds available to the participants, but the basic features are usually the same. The initiates are elaborately dressed and are taken to the monastery grounds, where the monks are fed by the laymen, and then a large feast is shared by occasionally as many as 300 invited guests and relatives. The central part of the ceremony is the ritual acceptance of the initiates into the *sangha* as novices by the officiating monk. After this, the boys allow their heads to be shaved, and they are invested in the yellow robes that are the Buddhist monk's uniform. Most boys initiated in this manner spend only a token period of a few days in the monastery, but some villagers still follow the traditional practice of spending the whole of a three-month *sangha* retreat period in the monastery, where they are required to maintain rigid conformity to monastic rules of dress, posture, speech, and behavior (see ch. 7, Religion). The chief hardships the novices undergo are thought to be conformity to the *sangha* rule that no food be consumed after noon until the next day and separation from the closely knit family household.

Traditional Burmese culture makes no provision for the religious initiation of girls, but the *natwin* is held for girls who are teenagers or slightly younger. It is not as widely practiced as the *shinbyu*; when it is held, it is often as an adjunct of the *shinbyu* of a brother or cousin, for the sake of economy and convenience. For the same reasons, it is common for several youths to have their *shinbyus* simultaneously at a single ceremony.

Courtship and Marriage

Girls do not customarily go out alone after their early teens. There are, however, many opportunities at religious festivals, at harvests, and at family parties for girls and boys to meet. Boys may go together in a group of two or three to pay calls on one or more houses where young girls live. If a girl shows a preference for one, the others will stay away on subsequent calls.

Among the wealthier people, parents of marriageable children are concerned that their prospective children-in-law are from approximately the same social and economic background as their own. Arranged marriages are common, but there are also many exceptions.

Burmese Buddhism does not contain any ceremony endorsing or sanctifying marriage. Marriage is a civil contract based on mutual consent, and the only necessary evidence of a lawful union is that the partners live and eat together. There is often a marriage ceremony, however, presided over by an astrologer called a brahman—whose role, like that of the court brahmans of ancient Burma's Hindu court, is to choose an auspicious day and hour for ceremonies and to recite magic formulas. Divorce is relatively easy to obtain but is rare. Usually the quarreling spouses come together again after a brief separation unless the marriage is childless.

Old Age

Whereas the years of raising a family are regarded as productive, materially oriented years, once the children are grown, the Burmans consider it proper for a person to devote most of his attention to spiritual effort, especially to the acquiring of merit that will be important in determining status in the next incarnation. The elderly assume most of the responsibility for the family altar, for seeing that the daily offering of food to the monks is properly made, and for organizing religious festivals and fund-raising efforts for the *sangha* of the monastery or for pagodas. As evidence of their detachment from worldly affairs, the aged are expected to be retiring and unobtrusive in behavior toward others and should not indulge in conspicuous display of wealth or appetite. The elderly are cared for by their children and often have an intimate relationship as teachers and allies of their grandchildren.

Death and Funeral Observances

The decline of the human body is seen as inevitable. As death approaches, the articles of value a person wears are removed and given to the *sangha*. A relative may chant from the sacred Buddhist literature in order to divert the mind of the dying person from his mortal concerns. When death comes, it is said that the butterfly spirit, the symbol of life, has left the body. Relatives bathe the corpse and watch over it in groups at night until burial. Occasionally a *pwe* (see Glossary), an outdoor theatrical presentation, is held, and the body in its wooden coffin is placed near the scene of the *pwe* to ease its alleged loneliness.

Except for monks, who are cremated, corpses are buried within a few days of death, whenever it is convenient for the relatives to gather together. On the sixth day after death, the grave is visited by a family member who calls on the spirit of the deceased to attend a ceremony on the following day. The next morning monks are invited to come to the house of the deceased, where they chant prayers and are fed and given offerings. The spirit of the dead person is thought of as being seated on a mat prepared for him and as gaining merit from this ceremony. The religious part of the ceremony ends; the lay people are fed, and the monks depart. The graves are not visited, tidied, or maintained. Meritorious acts on behalf of the dead, such as feeding the monks in his name, are means of honoring the dead and are believed to contribute to a better life for the dead person in his next incarnation.

INDIGENOUS MINORITIES

The ethnic policy of the Revolutionary Government of the Union of Burma has been to deemphasize ethnic differences and to eliminate where possible the causes of ethnic friction and national disunity. The disestablishment of Buddhism as the national religion was an early act to implement this policy. Such terms as "racial minorities" and "nationalities" have also disappeared from official usage. In addition, since 1964 official lists of the indigenous ethnic groups of Burma have been organized by Burmese alphabetical order rather than, as formerly, listed in descending order of population strength.

The most comprehensive statement of the government's policy toward the indigenous minorities was issued in a speech by

Revolutionary Council Chairman General Ne Win on February 12 (Union Day), 1964. The essence of the statement was that it was essential that all nationalities be committed to national solidarity of the Union of Burma; that all nationalities, irrespective of race or religion, should act together in all tasks to preserve the union; and that all nationalities have the right to work for the preservation and development of cherished culture, religion, and customs, but that any action that would adversely affect national unity should be avoided.

Various projects for the improvement of economic and social conditions in the constituent states where minority groups predominate were begun in the middle and late 1960s. Subsidiary cash crops were introduced to diversify the economy; breeding of hogs and poultry was begun; dams, embankments, and irrigation canals were constructed; education and health facilities were greatly expanded; and communications facilities were improved. Rangoon University students were assigned to do field studies on minority group customs and social systems in order to improve national understanding of these peoples and to preserve the nation's multiethnic heritage.

At the Academy for Development of National Groups, located at Ywathitgyi in Sagaing Division, the government was training 425 students of forty-seven nationalities of Burma to be "architects of the future for building up the edifice of unity and solidarity in the Union of Burma," according to an October 1970 article in the Burmese press. The academy, which offers a four-year course of study, was founded in 1964 to provide training for selected members of the various nationalities so that they could implement the national ethnic policy.

Mons and Arakanese

The persistence of a sense of ethnic distinctiveness felt by Mons and Arakanese is more the result of historical factors than the result of significant differences in culture from the Burmans. Both the Mons and the Arakanese take pride in the history of their ancient kingdoms, which substantially predate the first Burman kingdom (see ch. 3, Historical Setting).

The Mons (whom the Burmans call Talaing) were once the dominant ethnic group of Lower Burma, but during the last half of the eighteenth century, after their kingdom had been conquered and destroyed by King Alaungpaya, many thousand Mons took refuge in Thailand. Some of the Mons remaining in the delta assisted the British in the first Anglo-Burmese war of 1824-26 and, upon its conclusion, fled to British-annexed Tenasserim. According to an unofficial estimate made in 1970, there were 350,000 Mon speakers in Burma, most of them living on the Tenasserim coast (see ch. 6, Education, Cultural Activities, and Public Information).

The influence of Mon culture on Burman culture has been great since early times; Burmese Buddhism is derived chiefly from Mon beliefs and practices. Other than language, there are no significant differences in culture or living patterns between modern Burmans and Mons. Nonetheless, the desire for ethnic separation has been expressed by insurgent groups from time to time (see ch. 9, Political Dynamics).

There is evidence of a kingdom in Arakan dating back to the fourth century A.D. Whether the people of this kingdom were Indians, as has been suggested by many, or Arakanese—one of the earliest groups of Tibeto-Burmans to reach Burma—is not known. From the fifteenth to seventeenth centuries the Arakanese had close ties with Muslim India and controlled Chittagong (in what is now East Pakistan). Islam spread to Arakan, although Buddhism remained the dominant religion. In the eighteenth century some 50,000 Arakanese refugees fled to Chittagong during a prolonged rebellion against the Burmese throne.

Many Arakanese have retained feelings of separate identity in spite of the close similarity in language and culture with the Burmans, and in the early 1960s they exerted pressure upon the central government to grant them their own state. A draft constitution for Arakan State had been submitted to a government preparatory committee in early 1962. The plans for Arakanese statehood were canceled by the Revolutionary Government upon its coming to power.

There are no census figures or estimates for the Arakanese population. The total population of Arakan Division, which includes members of various indigenous ethnic groups as well as a substantial number of Pakistanis, was 1,847,000 at the start of 1969. As in the past, Arakan Division had the highest concentration of Muslim inhabitants in Burma. The 1931 census (the last complete Burmese census) showed Muslims as constituting 4 percent of the total population; 41 percent lived in Arakan Division, and most of the others lived in the delta and central districts of Burma. At that time 68 percent of the Muslims in Burma were Indians (now Pakistanis), and only 30 percent were indigenous Muslims, A student of the Muslim community in Burma has suggested that these proportions were probably still approximately the same in 1962.

Indigenous Muslims in Arakan Division have attempted to identify themselves socially and culturally with the Buddhist majority and avoid being labeled as *kala* (foreigners or Indians), a derogatory term. In this attempt they have not been wholly successful.

During World War II the Japanese arrived first in southern Arakan, and the invasion sparked Buddhist-Muslim violence. Muslims from the south fled to northern Arakan, where they began retaliating against Buddhists. By the end of the war the Muslim population was concentrated in the north, and the inhabitants of the south were almost all Buddhists.

After the war northern Arakanese protested against the reintroduction of Arakanese Buddhist officials into the north and against the failure of the British to fulfill a wartime promise to create a Muslim national area. Pakistani Muslims began immigrating illegally to Arakan from Chittagong, and many Muslim armed bands were formed that engaged in looting and in smuggling rice into Pakistan.

Shortly before independence was granted to Burma, an army of Muslim separatists called the Mujahids, their Muslim nationalism having been aroused by the creation of the Muslim state of Pakistan, began to mount large-scale military actions against the Burmese government forces. The Burma Army campaigned against the Mujahids in the 1950s and broke the rebel army into small units. By 1961 the rebellion had virtually collapsed.

Shans

The Shan people are closely connected by language and culture to the major indigenous ethnic group of Thailand. The Shans call themselves Tai and speak a Tai dialect. Unlike their cousins in Thailand, however, their language is written in an adaptation of the Burmese script. Shans are the second largest minority group in Burma, after the Karens.

Although the Shans live primarily in the Shan State, with a secondary concentration in the Upper Irrawaddy basin area of Kachin State, they are not hill people. They live in the river valleys and pockets of level land of the hill regions, growing irrigated rice, like the Burmans and other lowland peoples. Their religion, Theravada Buddhism, and their culture are as advanced as those of the people of Burma proper. After the fall of Pagan to the Mongols in 1287, the Shans dominated lowland Burma politically until the sixteenth century.

Before and during the British colonial period the Shan State (then known as the Shan states) was fragmented into approximately three dozen states of varying size, each ruled by a hereditary prince. In the nineteenth century the princes paid tribute to the Burmese kings in exchange for noninterference in Shan affairs. In the colonial period a similar arrangement was worked out with the British. The princes owned large tracts of land. Many sent their children to school in Rangoon and on to British universities. By the time of independence there was an elite group composed of Shan aristocrats who were equally at home in British, Burmese, and Shan languages and cultures.

When the Constitution of 1947 was drafted, provision was made for the princes to choose among themselves twenty-five representatives to sit in the Chamber of Nationalities, the upper house of Parliament. In 1959, however, during the Ne Win caretaker regime, the princes were induced to relinquish their hereditary powers both in and out of Parliament. At the time of the 1962 coup, many of the princes were temporarily jailed. In the mid-1960s the Revolutionary Government's actions on behalf of cultivators of small plots broke up the big estates. An unofficial source in the late 1960s reported that some princes had successfully evaded these regulations by making paper transfers of land to family members.

Shans have a distinctive costume. Men wear jackets like those of Burmans, but instead of the *longyi* (wraparound skirt) they wear loose-fitting trousers. Many men also wear turbans, and some ornament their bodies with tattoos. Women wear tight-fitting, long-sleeved jackets and skirts woven of light colored silk. Although almost all Shans are Buddhists, they have kept their religious institutions separate from those of the Burmans, Mons, and Arakanese. When Prime Minister U Nu attempted to establish Buddhism as the state religion of the Union of Burma, Shan Buddhists objected, fearing the extension of the authority of the Burmese *sangha* over Shan monks.

The Constitution of 1947 of the Union of Burma contained a provision allowing for the secession of the Shan State from the union after a ten-year period of union membership had elapsed. The right to secession has since been disallowed by the central government, but there has been insurgency and separatist agitation in the Shan State since 1959.

Karens

The Karens are Burma's largest minority group, totaling an estimated 10 percent of the total population. The Padaungs, another hill people who live in the Shan State, are classified by some scholars as Karens and by others as related to the Palaungs and the Was, Mon-Khmer-speaking hill groups. The Kayahs (formerly called the Karennis or Red Karens) are held by some to be related to the hill Karens. Historical and political factors, however, have led the Kayahs to maintain their identity separate from that of other Karens.

The Karens began as a hill people, but during the nineteenth century many moved to the plains area of the Tenasserim coast and also to the predominantly Burman Irrawaddy Delta and peripheral areas. Kawthule State was created for the Karens in 1951 and is predominantly Karen in population. In the Irrawaddy Delta and adjacent areas live the Sgaw Karens, sometimes called Burmese Karens. Another important Karen population cluster, consisting primarily of Pwo Karens (also known as Talaing Karens), lives in an area northwest of Bassein.

The Karens of Lower Burma during the time of the Burmese monarchy were governed indirectly through their own chiefs and were not obliged to provide labor for Burmese public works or for the government militias. Instead they paid a tax to the king's appointed representative at the township level. They avoided contact with their Burman and Mon neighbors and had a reputation for timorousness and honesty. The plains Karens tended to locate their villages inland away from the rivers. Headmanship of the village was hereditary, passing from father to son or nephew. Village administration and government were conducted by the headman with the cooperation of village elders. Occasionally a headman of strong character would head several villages simultaneously, but there was little political or social cohesion among Karens beyond the village. The two main groups of Karens in the plains, the Sgaw and the Pwo, were significantly different in language and customs from each other.

Many of the plains-dwelling Karens accepted Christianity, primarily as a result of American Baptist missionary efforts begun in the nineteenth century. It was estimated in 1970 that 15 percent of the Karen population had been converted to Christianity. The missionaries also put the Karen language into written form by adapting Burmese script. During the colonial period Christian Karens received a substantially superior education to that of the Burman majority. At one time Christian Karens numbered 22 percent of the student body at Rangoon University, although they only numbered about 2 percent of the population.

The approximately 85 percent of the Karen population that has converted to Buddhism includes most of the plains Karens as well as almost all of the hill Karens, of whom the major group are the Bwe Karens who live in the rugged hill area between the Sittang and the lower Salween rivers. Political institutions among the hill Karens are more rudimentary and less cohesive than among the Karens of the plains. The hill Karens still sometimes wear the Karen national costume, largely abandoned by the plains Karens, consisting of short black trousers and a tunic. The women wear a similar tunic, more elaborately woven, over a petticoat. The plains Karens are now fluent in Burmese and, their farming techniques, appearance, and behavior are virtually indistinguishable from those of their lowland neighbors.

Burman-Karen animosities were fanned by the policies of the colonial government, which granted Karens of the plains a separate voting roll in national elections and recruited Christian Karens into the Burma Army to put down Burman-led rebellions. These animosities were further intensified when Karen troops and Burmese nationalist troops were temporarily aligned on opposing sides during World War II. Kawthule State was created in 1951 by the central government as a constituent state to satisfy Karen demands for autonomy but, because of the scattered residence pattern of the Karens, it was not possible to include all Karens in their own state. Kawthule State in early 1969 had an estimated population of under 800,000, whereas contemporary estimates of the total Karen population placed it at between 2 million and 3 million.

The Hill Tribes

General Social Characteristics

Although the hills along the Burmese frontier contain many different ethnic groups and subgroups, each with its own language or dialect, its own customary law, and its own political, economic, and social arrangements, some generalizations about the hill peoples are applicable. All the hill people live by small-holding agriculture. Politically the largest effective unit is usually the village community, led by a hereditary headman in cooperation with the members of the village council. Headmen in a given area may give allegiance in turn to a tribal chief, who is usually the scion of the senior family of the clan or tribe. Membership in the village council may be granted to elders, or, among some groups, such as the Chins and the Nagas who live along Burma's eastern border, it may be achieved through holding a sequence of ritual feasts, the holding of each feast entitling the host to a higher grade in the community social scale.

Among the hill peoples, traditional land tenure arrangements are concerned less with ownership than with use rights. Land is thought of as belonging to the tribe and is held in trust by the chiefs; each headman is the trustee of the village land. The village, however, is a tribal unit rather than a territorial unit; if, in the course of twenty years or so, the land in the original village area becomes exhausted as a result of the slash-and-burn agricultural methods employed by the hill people, the village as a whole may move to new land. The government land tenure policies in effect in 1971 were in conflict with the traditional land tenure arrangements of the hill peoples.

Social values differ among the hill peoples, but some are commonly held. One of the reasons why few hill tribesman accumulate great wealth is that hoarding is deprecated, and a premium is placed on conspicuous spending, especially the giving of feasts. Although many of the hill tribesmen, especially hill Karens, are Buddhist and many others are Christian, the majority are still faithful to their traditional religions. Most of these beliefs combine elements of ancestor worship with animism, the worship of spirits in all natural phenomena. The belief is general that spirits must be propitiated or they will cause harm. Acts regarded as likely to anger the spirits entail formal sacrifices to appease them. The offender is usually fined in accordance with the cost of holding the ritual thought to be necessary to propitiate the angry spirits. Fines, awarded as compensation to the injured party, are the chief means of rectifying wrongs and punishing criminals in traditionally oriented hill communities.

Chins

Unofficial estimates placed the total Chin population in 1971 at 500,000, roughly half of them in the Chin Special Division. Estimates vary in part because of disagreement among scholars as to which small hill groups to classify as Chin. Persons of different dialect groups show significant differences in custom. The major dividing line within the Chin group separates the Northern Chins (also called Mar) from the Southern Chins (also known as Pawi). Chin traditional clothing is minimal. Women wear a skirt and no blouse, and men wear a loincloth. About 70 percent are animists, and Christians and Buddhists together make up about 30 percent of the Chin population. Christian missionary activity began in the Chin area in the nineteenth century, and Buddhist missionaries have been active in the period since World War II.

The Northern Chins have hereditary chiefs and an aristocracy. They have also evolved a more elaborate economy and a more permanent type of settlement than have the Southern Chins. Some have moved into the lowlands, where they farm irrigated ricefields and live interspersed among the Burmans. The Southern Chins, by contrast, have a more democratic form of traditional village government and a less evolved agricultural system and economy.

Improved communications, participation in the army from the time of the colonial regime, and the introduction of a monetized sector to the economy have encouraged Chins to seek higher education and improved living conditions. An anthropologist doing fieldwork in the Chin Hills region in 1958 reported that innovation had so far produced little strain to Chin society and that educated young people, older, illiterate traditional leaders, Christians, and animists were able to live as neighbors with little friction.

Originally known as the Jinghpaw or Singhpo, the Kachins reached northern Burma in the first millennium A.D. and upon their arrival pushed the earlier inhabitants, the Chins and the Palaungs, westward and southward, respectively. They also attacked and destroyed the Tai-speaking Ahom kingdom in Assam. The Kachins bear a physical resemblance to the Gurkhas of Nepal and, like them, are famous for being fierce fighters and able mercenaries. For many years Kachins formed an important part of the colonial Burma Army. Kachins numbered approximately 350,000 as of 1970; most lived in Kachin State, and some lived in the Shan State.

Preliterate and animist before the nineteenth century, the Kachins, like the Karens, were the object of missionary activity of the American Baptists. The missionaries put the Kachin language into the roman alphabet. Although Christianity was reported as spreading among the Kachins in the early 1960s and Buddhist missionaries were also working among them, the Kachins have remained mostly animist. A writer estimated in 1970 that nearly 90 percent of the Kachins were animists.

As with most of Burma's hill people, the Kachin form of agriculture is shifting cultivation of unirrigated hill slopes by the slash-and-burn method, with fallow periods of from eight to ten years for each plot. Since World War II Kachins have begun moving down into the valleys, where they cultivate irrigated rice like the Shans and the Burmese of Burma proper. Kachins who have done this in the Shan State have begun to accept Buddhism and to be absorbed into the Shan population. A source of conflict between the Kachin hill farmers and the central government at Rangoon has been the dependence of Kachin hill people on opium poppies as a cash crop. According to a Burmese newspaper article of December 1970, no less than 20,000 acres of poppies were being grown in Kachin State. Opium cultivation is permitted by Kachin State law under license but is strongly depreciated by the central government, which has attempted to induce Kachins and other hill people to plant other cash crops instead.

Kachin culture is deeply concerned with veneration of ancestors and with genealogy. The Kachins believe that they are all descended from a single progenitor, who had five sons. The chiefs can generally trace their genealogy all the way back to one of these sons, whereas commoners can record their ancestry back only a few generations. The chief's title and position as village leader are inherited by his youngest son. Sometimes an older son will found his own small village rather than remain in his home area subservient to his younger brother. There are, in addition, villages that lack an aristocratic headman and are governed by a democratically chosen leader. These traditional arrangements may have been affected or modified by the installation of security and administrative committees after 1962. Kachin traditional dress for women includes mantles of silver tassles and disks.

In 1960 a Kachin insurrection against the Union of Burma began with the formation of the Kachin Independence Army in the northern part of the state. The control of the central government over much of Kachin State was reported in 1970 to be weak.

Kayahs

The Kayahs (formerly known as the Karennis or Red Karens) live in Kayah State, a territory which was independent of Burma from 1875 to 1948. In 1875 the hereditary princes of the three Karenni states (as they were than called) forsook their longstanding tributary relationship to the Burmese throne in favor of a similar relationship to the British crown. At the time of Burmese independence the Karenni states became the single Karenni State and a constituent state of the Union of Burma with the same rights for its hereditary rulers and for secession as were granted the Shan State. In 1951 the name was changed to Kayah State. In 1959 the princes, like those of the Shans, renounced their hereditary privileges.

The population of Kayah State in early 1969 was estimated at 193,000, of whom perhaps 75,000 were Kayahs. The state also contains numerous other ethnic groups, including Black Karens, Striped Karens, and Bwe Karens. The Kayahs have remained animists and slash-and-burn hill rice farmers, although they have political and social arrangements similar to those of the Shans and believed to have been acquired from the Shans.

The Kayahs have been anxious to maintain their identity separate from that of the Karens of Kawthule State and elsewhere. In 1962 the Kayah leadership supported a movement to divide Burma into a federal union of sovereign states.

Other Hill Peoples

The Pa-o or Thaungthu peoples, who numbered perhaps 200,000 in 1970, live in the south of the Shan State, around Taunggyi. The costume of Pa-o women consists of black clothing and turbans. Linguistically they are connected to the Karens. Unlike other Karens, they have an ancient written language. They are Buddhists, as are also many of the Palaungs, another group of hill farmers in the Shan State, who speak a Mon-Khmer language. The Palaungs, who were believed to number about 60,000 in 1970, have a distinctive costume for their women consisting of blue jackets with red collars and skirts with cane hoops around the waist.

84

Other small groups living in the Shan State include the Ithas, who live on Inle Lake; the Padaungs, who live in the hills along the Kayah border and whose women wear brass rings that give them elongated necks; the Akha, who are tea growers; the Lahu and Lisu peoples, who live high up in the mountains and grow rice, maize (corn), and opium poppies; and the Kaws or Ekaws, who live on the mountaintops and are reputed to be the most warlike people on the eastern border.

The Wa people, who live on the frontier between the Shan State and Yunnan, are the most primitive people in eastern Burma. Reports of headhunting, as part of the fertility rites at plowing time, were made by reputable scholars as late as the 1940s. Others of the Wa group, known as tame Was, have settled in Kengtung and Manglun and have abandoned headhunting.

The Kachin Hills have many of the same groups as the Shan State and, in addition, several other groups, including the Shan-Chinese (called Shan Tayok), who have migrated from the east and are more allied to the Chinese than to the other Burmese people. In the western part of Kachin State and north of the Chin Hills region are the Naga Hills, inhabited by the Nagas. Although their language is related to the Chin dialects, their political structure relates to that of the Kachins. In earlier days headhunting was commonly practiced by them. Nagas on the Indian side of the border have been engaged in insurrection against the central government in New Delhi for many years, but by early 1971 there were no reports of insurrections against the Burmese government by Burmese Nagas.

Virtually all of Burma's lesser hill groups have ties to groups speaking the same language and sharing the same culture who live across Burma's frontiers. Pockets of different groups of hill tribesmen have been found scattered through the upper elevations of all mainland southeast Asia, south China, and northeast India. Relations between Burmese hill people and the people of the plains are uneasy for the most part, as the result of great differences in culture and values.

CHAPTER 5

LIVING CONDITIONS

Burmese living conditions in 1971 reflected the transitional nature of the society. While persistently holding to certain traditional values, the society strove at the same time to adapt to the new socialist philosophy expressed by the leadership as the Burmese Way to Socialism. Direct foreign influences had been minimized, and the country's political and economic systems were being radically altered by a revolutionary government that held virtually absolute power. Much of the older way of life remained the same, however.

The health situation throughout both rural and urban areas continued to be far short of government goals. Medical services had been well established by 1940 but then collapsed during World War II and the Japanese occupation. After the war serious political disturbances prevented restoration, much less the expansion and improvement, of health services. Despite some intervening progress there was still in 1971 a great lack of facilities; professional staff, sanitation, and public hygiene were inadequate by modern standards; and there was a correspondingly high incidence of disease and mortality.

Statistics published in 1969 estimated that in 1963 Burmese average life expectancy was 43.6 years for males and 45.9 years for females Only Laos and South Vietnam (both 35 years) were lower among the countries of East Asia. At the same time the number of people served by each physician was also relatively low at 1 per 11,900. In East Asia only Cambodia, Indonesia, and Laos had less favorable ratios.

The concept of a welfare state had been alien to the traditional political and economic patterns of the country. The leaders who guided Burma to independence in 1948, however, were familiar with the state socialism and welfare programs of Europe and wanted to adapt them to the needs of their own country. Since then all the governments of Burma have considered the state primarily responsible for the welfare of its people. This thinking was given practical expression in 1952, when wide public support of comprehensive social and economic development programs was solicited through adoption of the Pyidawtha Plan, designed to give Burma a modern industrial economy in a welfare state (see ch. 11, Character and Structure of the Economy).

The need for social reform and development to promote the public welfare was further stressed and became a key plank in the new regime of General Ne Win when it took over the reins of government in 1962. It proclaimed its commitment to building a "society of affluence and social justice free from haunting anxieties for food, clothing and shelter." Although handicapped by a lack of funds and by inexperience, the government in 1971 was still engaged in a number of public health, housing, and community development programs.

DIET AND NUTRITION

In most of the country the basic diet consists of boiled rice and a bland curry sauce containing various condiments. The composition of the sauce differs in accordance with locality and economic circumstances. Among country people of average means the usual base of the sauce is one or more of the common garden vegetables stewed with spices. Garlic, onions, peppers, and leaves of the tamarind and mango trees are used to give the concoction added taste and flavoring. Depending on their availability and the economic ability of the consumer, seafood or meat curry is also enjoyed. Almost as essential to a meal as rice and curry is *ngapi*, a salted paste of fish or shrimp, which is used as a curry condiment or as a seasoning with other foods. *Ngapi* derives its importance not only from the frequency with which it appears on the table but also because it is the cherished national dish. Generally, an average meal also includes a clear soup and a green salad or a cooked vegetable.

The standard menu varies somewhat in different regions of the country and in line with purchasing power. In some of the hilly frontier areas corn may take the place of rice as a staple. In time of extreme want countrypeople occasionally subsist almost entirely on boiled rice and salt, the latter being regarded as the one indispensable seasoning. Usually, however, there is not much difference, except perhaps in quantity, between the diet of the rich and that of the poor. When served other than as an ingredient of the curry sauce, fish or meat usually appears as a garnish rather than as a main dish. Beef and mutton are generally disliked and, on the few occasions when meat is eaten as a main dish, it is usually pork. Freshwater fish is abundant and is consumed more frequently than fish from the sea except in coastal areas.

Beverages are seldom taken at mealtimes, but tea is frequently drunk between meals. Coffee is fairly popular but expensive, and villagers often look on it as a Western affectation. Even pasteurized milk is of doubtful purity and is generally disliked in its fresh form. Condensed cow's milk, most of it imported, is popular for use in tea and, particularly in urban areas, for feeding babies.

The customary practice is to have two meals a day—one eaten in midmorning and the other in the late afternoon. The meals are usually the same in composition. Sometimes a light breakfast is added as a third meal. The regular meals are supplemented by frequent between-meal snacks. In addition to tea, snacks most often consist of sweets and fruits. The people like all fruits and are especially fond of sweets. Perhaps the most favored sweet is the whirlwind cake, a pancake made of sweetened rice flour.

There is evidence of widespread nutritional defects among the population, but these stem from dietary practices rather than from a shortage of food. The highly polished rice that is preferred and is a mainstay of the daily fare loses most of its vitamin and mineral content in the milling process. Although most curries contain some meat, fish, or eggs, the individual portion does not supply adequate quantities, and there is a marked deficiency in protein intake of most people. Much of this lack has a monetary basis, but much is caused also by the Buddhist aversion to taking life of any kind. This is reflected in the unpopularity of beef and mutton. Seafood is an essential ingredient of *ngapi,* but professional fishermen are usually non-Buddhists and are looked down upon because they destroy life. Fresh fruits and vegetables are important dietary elements, but they cannot make up for other deficiencies. The few analyses of the diet that have been made indicate that a large proportion of the people are undernourished, the major nutritional problems relating to deficiencies in iron, iodine, thiamine, and riboflavin.

The Burmese Buddhist faith regards drunkenness as a violation of right conduct, but excessive drinking occurs occasionally in the villages. Nevertheless, among the poor peasants drinking of palm toddy or rice liquor is not uncommon. In the cities among the affluent imported liquors are consumed. Laborers and other people of lesser means many use locally distilled liquors.

Tobacco is used extensively by both sexes. The cheroot, a barrel-shaped type of cigar, is the favored tobacco form, but the Shans and some other frontier residents prefer to smoke pipes. Cigarettes are manufactured but are not in great demand. Opium is grown legally in some portions of the Shan State, but there is little addiction to it, and the government has cut back on the legalized cultivation of poppies. As in other parts of Southeast Asia the betel nut is commonly chewed.

CLOTHING AND HOUSING

Clothing

The traditional, and still the most popular, outfit worn by the Burmese consists of a *longyi* (wraparound skirt) and a *eingyi* (long-sleeved jacket). These garments are worn by both sexes and differ only in that the man's *longyi* is knotted in front and the woman's is secured at the side. women also wear a white bodice fastened with colorful, decorative buttons under their *eingyis*. Men wear headcloths of vivid colors; women may wear silk or muslin scarves. In addition women often carry parasols.

Flat sandals are the common form of footwear for all. Most women have at least a few pieces of jewelry for social occasions, as there is a tendency to put any surplus cash into jewelry, which gives status and serves as a store of wealth. The basic style of dress is common to all classes, the clothing of the rich differing from that of the poor only in its quality and in the quantity possessed.

Western-style clothing has grown in popularity. In particular, the use of simple Western garments by children in both town and country was becoming common in 1971. Even in Rangoon, however, the colorful national costume still was being worn extensively. Men appear in Western clothing more often than women, but sometimes they are criticized for doing so on the ground that they are abandoning their national identity.

The traditional costumes of most of the minority ethnic groups of the frontier regions are versions of the *longyi* and the *eingyi*. There is a great diversity, however, in the colors and styles, the kinds of headgear, and the types of jewelry, belts, and other adornments. A complete description of the ceremonial costumes of the Shan tribes alone, for example, could fill several volumes.

Housing

The typical dwelling in a Burmese village has walls of woven bamboo, wooden flooring, a thatched roof and, usually, a veranda extending along its front. The interior is divided into several rooms for sleeping, and a space for cooking is situated at one side or in the rear. Sanitation facilities are either separate from the house or nonexistent. Windows have hinged shutters of plaited bamboo, which may be closed during times of heavy wind or rain. Most dwellings in rural areas have only one story but are raised above ground level on wooden posts. Because of the thatched roofs and inflammable building material, houses are very vulnerable to fire.

Some of the tribesmen in the hill areas of the frontier live in clusters of bamboo longhouses in which a number of families occupy separate quarters opening into a central corridor. Where sawed boards, usually teak, are readily available, wooden houses are often built. In the Shan State some houses have thatched or corrugated iron roofs and walls of overlapping teak slats, which can be opened or closed like venetian blinds. In the northern part of the

Chin Special Division many of the houses are made of teak and are so constructed that they can be dismantled and reconstructed in a new place when the occupants move. In towns and cities of Burma proper (see Glossary) many homes of the well-to-do and official buildings are constructed along Western lines.

Home furnishings tend to be simple. Thin mats woven from grass are used for sleeping. Meals are served on low tables at which the diners sit on the floor. Chairs are not customarily used, and rugs and pictures are rare. For clothing storage there is a wooden box or occasionally a wooden chest of drawers. Kitchens are equipped with china dishes and teapots, a large water storage jar, and metal cooking pots of various sizes. Serving spoons are used, but the traditional way to eat is with the fingers.

In the cities the household furnishings of prosperous families tend to be more abundant and varied. Many urban people own radios, and an occasional family may have a kerosine stove, although cooking is usually done over charcoal. Only a few of the more wealthy and Westernized people have refrigerators, air conditioners, and other electric appliances. Their use, however, is severely limited in many areas by the absence of electric power.

HEALTH AND SANITATION

Vital statistics available in 1971 were based on figures published in 1968, and even these were predicated on incomplete coverage. Reports and registrations of births, deaths, and diseases were recorded only in larger towns and cities representing less than 10 percent of the population so summary conclusions drawn from them are, at best, only well-informed estimates. The recorded crude death rate was 12.9 per 1,000, and infant mortality was 114.5 per 1,000 births. By 1971 these figures were probably somewhat more favorable because of more available and improved medical service.

Common Medical Beliefs and Practices

Belief is widespread among the less educated that many physical ailments and deaths are caused by supernatural forces. The protection of charms and amulets is valued, and some of the hill people regard cabalistic tattooing as a safeguard to health. When such devices fail to ward off disease or injury, the sufferer may resort to traditional therapy, much of which is rational and effective. Home remedies made from local materials are commonly used for minor conditions recognized as requiring medication or treatment.

In more serious cases the people may go to a traditional medical practitioner, either by preference or because modern medical care is not available. The traditional healers have varied procedures, including casting a patient's horoscope to assist in the diagnosis. There are also treatments involving massage and the internal and external use of medicinal preparations derived from roots, herbs, and minerals. Those who specialize in massage and herbal remedies are required to be registered with the government.

Sanitation

Sanitation throughout the nation is the main environmental factor affecting public health. Its effects are made worse by a climate that favors insect and waterborne vectors of disease and by the capacity of disease organisms to survive outside the human host. Improper disposal of human waste is a major pollutant of water supplies. The virtual absence of modern food sanitation also spreads disease and infection.

Bad sanitary conditions do not stem from any general uncleanliness of the people but from the failure of the general population to recognize causative factors related to the spread of disease and from the conflict between traditional or religious and modern scientific concepts. Public opinion, for example, is generally hostile to the idea of preventive sanitation when it involves the destruction of living creatures, including such disease carriers as insects and rats.

Diseases

Malaria, respiratory diseases, leprosy, venereal diseases, intestinal disorders, cholera, and plague, although not necessarily in that order of frequency, are the most prominent diseases in the country. Malaria was long considered the most serious because of its high incidence and the debilitating effect it has on many people. Eradication programs dating from the mid-1950s have been only partially successful but have provided a measure of control and reduced the rate of transmission in some areas. High rates tend to recur if control measures are slackened. Incidence of the disease is greatest in the Shan Plateau, and Chin Hills, and other hilly regions. Along the coast the infection rates are generally lower. Control measures in the central plains have been most effective. Other diseases transmitted by mosquitoes include dengue fever and filariasis. No yellow fever has been reported.

Acute respiratory diseases are common, and their incidence increases seasonally with the onset of cool weather in October.

Influenza and pneumonia, in particular are major causes of death. Pulmonary tuberculosis is a great problem although it seldom proves fatal. There are tuberculosis clinics in Rangoon and Mandalay, but more hospital facilities for the isolation of patients are needed. In 1971 the government was carrying out a five-year plan to combat the disease.

Leprosy was a major threat and was greatly feared by the people. The overall incidence was believed to be about 10 per 1,000 persons, but the disease is more prevalent in the drier regions and among children. There were some twenty leprosy treatment centers with a capacity of over 3,500 patients. The largest was Leprosy Village at Kengtun in the Shan State.

Syphilis and gonorrhea are the principal venereal diseases, but other types occur in considerable number, especially in urban areas. Smallpox is prevalent, but it is not a major killer. It last reached epidemic proportions in 1960. Since the acceleration of a country-wide vaccination program in 1966, it has been largely kept under control.

Water pollution and an abundance of houseflies contribute to a heavy incidence of enteric diseases, including typhoid fever, amoebic and bacillary dysentery, and diarrhea. There are frequent epidemics of cholera, usually beginning at the start of the monsoon and spreading northward from endemic foci in the Irrawaddy Delta and the mouth of the Salween River. Each year several hundred thousand vaccinations are given in an attempt to control cholera.

Plague occurs as an endemic product of the rat flea vector, but the incidence has been declining in recent years. Rickettsial bush or scrub fever is widely distributed and is the most common form of typhus encountered. Yaws occurs in several regions, including the vicinity of Mandalay, and trachoma is quite prevalent, especially in towns of the Irrawaddy Delta. Animal diseases, such as rabies, anthrax, and brucellosis, may infect humans and sometimes may be fatal to them.

Health Services

During the colonial period and the early years of independence public health services and facilities were administered by the local authorities. These agencies operated local hospitals in which the services were free, although payment was required for private rooms. In addition, Christian missionary groups operated a number of hospitals throughout the country, and the Hindu Ramakrishna Mission had a large facility in Rangoon.

In 1953 the public health administration was reorganized, and all facilities and services were centralized in the Ministry of Health.

The hospitals managed by local authorities were put under direct control of the ministry, and in 1965 all missionary hospitals were also taken over and absorbed into the public health system. Thus in 1971 the Ministry of Health administered, and had exclusive responsibility for, all government health services and programs.

Under the minister, a director of health services planned and operated the system. The director was assisted by four deputy directors in charge of public health, hospitals and dispensaries, maternal and child health, and laboratories. Below cabinet level the organization of health services paralleled the country's administrative divisions, and medical officers in each component were responsible for activities in the villages and hamlets.

Latest available statistics (1969) indicated that Burma had 315 hospitals having a combined total of 21,600 beds, or about 1 bed per each 1,750 persons. Many of the hospitals were in need of maintenance and modernization, and some were housed in rented buildings constructed for other purposes. There were also about 60 clinics in the main cities and towns that furnished specialized outpatient care. Rangoon General Hospital, with about 1,000 beds, was the largest and best-equipped hospital in the country. In addition to medical and surgical wards, it had tuberculosis, pediatric, orthopedic, cobalt radiation, and other specialized units. Other important installations in Rangoon included the modern and newly nationalized Hindu Ramakrishna Mission Hospital; the Dufferin Hospital, which specialized in obstetrics and gynecology; the 400-bed Contagious Disease Hospital; and the 200-bed Worker's Hospital. There was also a hospital for mental patients, which was partially supported by the World Health Organization.

Mandalay, Moulmein, Bassein, and Taunggyi each had hospitals of 200 beds or more. Taunggyi was the site of an older civil hospital and the new, well-equipped Sao San Htun Hospital, which was a gift from the Soviet Union. The American Medical Center, as it was formerly named, with a 250-bed hospital at Namkhan in the Shan State, was established by Doctor Gordon Seagrave, who gained fame as the Burma Surgeon. It was nationalized in 1965 and was one of the largest facilities serving rural people. Only a few of the larger, more modern hospitals had food service In most hospitals a patient's family provided his food.

In addition to hospitals, limited medical service on an outpatient basis only was available in urban and rural areas alike, through health centers of the ministry. Each center was headed by a doctor or, as was usual in rural areas where doctors were not available, by a public health assistant. Under him, the usual center staff consisted of another health assistant, a vaccinator, one or more visiting nurses, and several midwives.

In 1971 about sixty centers were operating in urban areas. In large cities and towns requiring more than one such facility, individual centers served a specified section or neighborhood. In smaller towns one center served the entire community.

In 1954 a project was begun to establish 800 health centers in the countryside, and by 1966 more than 600 were actually in operation. Each rural health center was responsible for providing medical service to an area covering about fifteen village tracts with a population ranging between 15,000 and 40,000. The senior staff member, if he was a public health assistant instead of a doctor, received quasi-medical training in Rangoon and was supplied with a kit containing drugs selected as the most needed in his region. He was expected to diagnose ordinary ailments, perform simple surgical operations, teach hygiene, and generally supervise the health and sanitary practices in his area. In addition to operating his village dispensary, the health assistant toured the countryside as time permitted. Treatment was given to villagers for the cost of the required medicine.

Medical research and all medical laboratory services were centralized in appropriate divisions of the Directorate of Health Services in the Ministry of Health. Its major elements include the Burma Medical Research Council, the National Health Laboratories, and the Union of Burma Applied Research Institute. The Burma Medical Research Council is charged with activities to improve the health of the people by advancing medical and allied sciences through research and by coordinating the work of individual scientists interested in medical research. The Burma Medical Research Institute, an independent agency within the Ministry of Health, has fifteen departments—bacteriology, experimental medicine, hematology, instrumentation, library, medical statistics, nutrition, parasitology, pharmacology, physiology, publications, virology, biochemistry, animal science, and radioisotopes—collects, coordinates, and collates data in each of these subjects. From its collected data it publishes the annual report of the council and special reports of medical interest as they develop.

The National Health Laboratories contains the operating facilities and does the actual scientific research that provides basic data for the institute and the council. It was founded in 1968 by amalgamating the Pasteur Institute, the Harcourt-Butler Institute of Public Health, the Pharmaceutical Institute, the Office of the Chemical Examiner, the Office of the Public Analyst, and certain activities of the Union of Burma Applied Research Institute. It has separate divisions for administration, public health, chemicals, food and drugs, and clinical research.

The Pasteur Institute, which began as a private agency in 1915, concerns itself with research on food and nutrition. The Harcourt-Butler Institute of Public Health is both a general health laboratory and a teaching center for all public health services in the country. The Pharmaceutical Institute is the nation's only producer of vaccines and biologicals. The Office of the Chemical Examiner and the Office of the Public Analyst collect and test samples of food and drugs and enforce laws regarding their purity. The Union of Burma Applied Research Institute has facilities for determining useful applications of new information developed in chemical, pharmaceutical, and food research.

Medical Personnel

The availability of trained medical personnel in Burma was a continuing problem of concern in 1971. There were then almost 3,000 physicians and surgeons who had recognized degrees from an accredited medical school. There were, however, several hundred licensed medical practitioners with ten years of general education and four years of vocational study. On this basis it was estimated that there was only 1 fully qualified or partially trained medical assistant for each 1,200 persons in the total population.

The principal sources of physicians and surgeons are the medical institutes of the Arts and Science University located at Rangoon and Mandalay and a new medical school at Mindalagon, a suburb of Rangoon. The institute at Rangoon had 178 teachers and a student body of 1,805; the institute at Mandalay had 92 teachers and 520 students. Together these institutes graduate about 400 to 500 new doctors a year and were doing much to reduce the critical shortage. The problem of providing these new doctors with facilities to undergo their necessary internships, however, remained a bottleneck limiting their availability for general practice among the public. The only recognized establishments for interns in 1971 were the general hospitals in Rangoon and Mandalay. Gradually, however, the hospitals at Bassein, Mandalay, and Moulmein are being upgraded for this purpose, and new ones in Maymyo and Taunggyi are prividing training for interns. When the full system is in operation, it is expected that the annual output of qualified doctors will approximate 500.

About half of the country's doctors were practicing in Rangoon and Mandalay, and a large proportion of the remainder were in the larger towns of Moulmein, Bassein, and Taunggyi. Most were employed as staff members in government hospitals, and only about 300 were in private practice. There were therefore very few physicians and surgeons available in rural areas. Villagers had to travel to urban centers for modern medical care or depend on the partially trained medical assistants at the rural health centers. Many, consequently, depended almost entirely on the ministrations of traditional medical men.

The situation with regard to dentists was equally, or even more, serious. In 1971 there were believed to be only twenty-six dentists in the entire country. The College of Dental Medicine had been added to the schools of the Arts and Science University, however, and its enrollment of 141 was expected to alleviate the problem in a few years.

Other medical personnel consisted of 296 pharmacists, about 3,000 nurses, approximately 4,500 midwives, and an unknown number of laboratory assistants and technicians. Only an estimated 12 of the pharmacists were career professionals trained in formal schools; the others were men who had received training in mixing drugs at various hospitals providing that service. Most of the nurses received their training at one of the state training schools or the six government and two nongovernment hospitals offering nurses's training programs. Laboratory assistants and technicians were trained by the Rangoon General Hospital or by facilities within the National Health Laboratories.

WELFARE

Until the British established their rule in Burma, social problems of the country were dealt with in an individual manner by the family or sometimes by the local community. In any case, social welfare seldom reached beyond the confines of the village. Economic development under the British resulted in profound social changes in which the village became much less important as a functional unit and the religious orders lost much of their organization and standing. Meanwhile, urban communities were growing and developing their own welfare problems.

The colonial authorities introduced new methods to cope with these conditions, especially those concerning health and education. As public awareness of welfare problems increased, particularly after 1900, private organizations, such as the Young Men's Buddhist Association (see Glossary), were formed to provide various services for the people. These activities, for the most part, still did not reach beyond the towns.

A change came after Burma achieved independence in 1948, and the country's leaders became aware of the role social welfare might play in the nation. Domestic unrest, however, prevented much from being done until the Pyidawtha conference was held in 1952. It resulted in the adoption of a social and economic development plan that, among other things, established a number of programs dealing with health, housing, and rural community development.

These programs were met with initial enthusiasm and some success, but they generally fell short of their stated goals because of political uncertainties and the inexperience of planners and administrators assigned to them. After 1962 these conditions forced the government to review all development plans. Many programs and targets for social welfare were retained, but integrated planning was shelved.

During the 1950s the government received considerable technical and financial aid from foreign sources for its social welfare programs. Since 1962, however, this had been progressively restricted in order to preserve a neutralist stance and to limit foreign influences in the country. Multilateral programs under the auspices of the United Nations Children's Fund and the International Labor Organization have been most active. The Burma Red Cross Society, which has some 200 local branches, is affiliated with the International Red Cross Society in Geneva.

One of the government's main instruments for public welfare has been the social security system, which was initiated in 1955 and is administered by the Social Security Board in the Ministry of Labor. It is applicable to employees of establishments in commerce and industry that have ten or more workers. In 1971 about 500,000 persons were covered. The board maintained offices in Rangoon, Mandalay, Moulmein, and four other cities and operated its own clinics and hospitals, the largest of which was the Workers' Hospital in Rangoon.

Social security benefits cover sickness, maternity cases, and work injuries. Workers are required to pay 1 percent of their earnings for sickness and maternity benefits, but work injuries are taken care of without charge. The benefits for work injuries include treatment of the injury, permanent and temporary disability payments, and widows' and orphans' pensions. Funeral grants are furnished under sickness insurance. There are no unemployment benefits, and old age pensions are available under a separate system for government employees only.

A public housing program is the responsibility of the National Town and Country Housing and Development Board. It is concerned mainly with residential construction on the outskirts of Rangoon and other cities. This housing has replaced squatters' shacks built by those whose homes were destroyed during World War II and by refugees from insurgent areas. The government provides minimum public utilities and services. Most of the actual construction was done by the relocated persons themselves with materials made available by the government at nominal prices. Sanitation in the new residential areas and the quality of the dwellings are more satisfactory than similar facilities in the older areas.

Country dwellers receive welfare assistance in the form of more and better public health facilities and schools; an inexpensive tractor rental service; and help in roadbuilding, irrigation ditch digging, and cleaning and drilling village wells. Much of the work is based on self-help programs, in which government officials demonstrate proper practices to the villagers. The whole rural welfare program was directed by social welfare officers responsible to the Department of Social Welfare.

PATTERNS OF LIVING AND LEISURE

Like feasting, which usually accompanies the celebration of a holiday, going to a *pwe* (see Glossary) is a favorite way of spending leisure time. There are several kinds of *pwes,* but essentially these are kaleidoscopic theatrical performances that begin early in the evening and often last all night. The content varies from slapstick comedy, including offcolor jokes, to religious drama. Monsters and spirits are represented along with human beings in the plays. *Pwes* invariably include dancing by girl entertainers, who are accompanied by traditional music. Clowns, jugglers, and magicians often take part (see ch. 6, Education, Cultural Activities, and Public Information).

There are *pwes* for every occasion. They are usually given free of charge by a family or group. People attend from miles around, carrying thin grass mats and soft quilts on which to sleep during breaks or uninteresting portions of the performance. Motion pictures are enjoyed and are fairly well attended, but there are few motion picture theaters in the hinterland. Serious films are not popular, and few people understand or appreciate the kind of humor expressed in Western-style comedies.

Sports are also very popular, and the country boasts of two games of local origin. One game is *chinlon,* a contest in which teams stand in a circle and kick, butt, or otherwise bat a light wicker ball back and forth in an effort to keep it in the air without touching it with hands or arms. The other sport, restricted to Lake Inle in the Shan State, consists of boat races in which the paddlers row with their legs. Rowers stand perilously on one leg on platforms set on the bows and sterns of shallow dugout canoes and, holding the handle of the oar in one hand, wrap the other leg around its shaft and propel the craft by sculling with a leg movement. Crews are dressed in brightly colored costumes, betting is traditionally heavy, and the contests attract large crowds.

More conventional sports are also popular, and participation is encouraged by the Union of Burma Sports and Physical Education Committee, a government organization. Track and field competition is lively. Soccer is a major team sport, and several times Burma's team has been coholder of the Asian Youth Soccer Challenge Gold Cup. Volleyball, tennis, boxing, judo, and karate are also popular diversions. Golf is becoming increasingly popular in urban areas.

CHAPTER 6

EDUCATION, CULTURAL ACTIVITIES, AND PUBLIC INFORMATION

Education and cultural activities, including the dissemination of public information, were all oriented in 1971 toward attaining the national goal referred to as the Burmese Way to Socialism (see ch. 8, Political System and Values). The motivating force was the national government which, since achieving independence in 1948, has assumed increasing authority and influence in all aspects of national development.

After succeeding the British colonial authorities, the government took jurisdiction over a society that was in a state of cultural flux. The educational establishment was small and not designed to produce indigenous leaders aware of Burma's future role as a sovereign state; traditional art forms had lost much of their vitality because of exposure and subordination to Western ideas; and the media of mass communications were generally weak, diversely oriented, and of limited influence. The government, therefore, was faced with the task of adapting this heritage and making it capable of serving modern Burma and the interests of socialism. The process proceeded slowly at first, then picked up momentum after General Ne Win took over the reins of government in 1962.

In the field of public education the Ne Win regime declared that the existing school system would have to be transformed into one based on socialist values. Thereafter, political indoctrination became an officially acknowledged and fundamental part of the educational process, and two important steps were taken to transform the system itself. One measure was the nationalization of all private high schools and many lower schools and their absorption into a unified public school system under the Ministry of Education. Previously, the private institutions, largely foreign operated, had served a substantial percentage of the student population and provided some of its best education. The second measure was the establishment of Burmese as the national language and as the only authorized language of instruction. Up to that time almost all schooling above the primary level had been conducted in English.

The imposition of these measures resulted in a temporary lowering of educational standards from which the country was still recovering in 1971. Specifically, most of the teachers who were foreign were eliminated, which left the schools understaffed, and the exclusive use of Burmese required a full range of Burmese-language textbooks, which simply did not exist. The number of teachers and books has steadily increased; but in 1971 many schools were still undermanned, and the quantity of books remained so limited that many teachers had to conduct classes with texts that were inadequate both in number and variety. Burmese literacy was officially estimated at 60 percent in 1970, a relatively high rate for Asia.

In the area of cultural activities, alien Western values had been superimposed on Burmese society and had engulfed native artistic and intellectual expression to the point where indigenous creativeness had become vitually moribund. Accordingly the regime embarked on a program of cultural revival to rekindle national group identification in terms of older Burmese cultural symbols. This program has been highly successful under the Ministry of Culture. In 1971 the ministries of information and culture were under a single cabinet minister, Brigadier Thaung Dan.

The Ministry of Information was given a centralized responsibility for releasing all information about government plans, programs, and activities. It founded new daily newspapers and nationalized most major independent ones to serve as government organs and to accelerate the process of Burmanization. The ministry also assumed ownership and operation of all radio stations; created both the only news service permitted to operate in the country and the only firm licensed to import printed materials; and controlled all films, books, and other matter by close and detailed censorship. The official policy, applicable to all media, has been to censor controversial or polemic materials and to forbid discussions of national policy that did not praise the development of a truly Burmese socialist state.

Rumor and gossip have become widespread, particularly in Rangoon. A reluctance on the part of the government leaders to give out information has meant that interested citizens often must guess about internal government activities. These subjects are bandied about in local markets and in teahouses despite the lack of real knowledge about them. Rumor is given added weight by the general tendency to accept speculation, partly because of a desire not to contradict or imply that another person does not know what is occurring.

LANGUAGES

The Burmese national language is the tongue originally spoken by the Burmans, the dominant ethnic group. It belongs to the

Tibeto-Burman language family and is related to other Tibeto-Burman languages spoken in Burma and other parts of Southeast Asia. Along with standard Burmese there are several different languages and dialects, all related to some degree, that are spoken by ethnic Bumans in different regions of the country. Some groups, such as those in Arakan and Tenasserim, are referred to as Burman because their culture is like that of standard Burmese speakers although, except for basic derivation, they show very little linguistic similarity. Several small groups of Burmans in southwestern Shan State appear to have accepted elements of Shan speech and culture.

The language of the Burmans is spoken with little apparent variation in the central areas of Burma—the valleys of the Irrawaddy and the Sittang rivers. The overwhelming majority of this area's inhabitants are native Burmese speakers regardless of their ethnic affiliations. The only possible exceptions are the Moulmein and Thaton districts, where Karen and Mon speakers may be in the majority. Even these people, however, learn Burmese as a second language. Burmese is the medium of education and of historic literature. It is also the second language among a large percentage of the non-Burman ethnic groups and is important for them as the language of contact with the modern world and contemporary affairs. In all, some 90 percent of the population speak Burmese at least as a second language.

Burmese is a monosyllabic, agglutinative, and highly tonal language closer to Chinese than to any of the Indian languages, with which it has, in fact, no kinship. A single syllable may have as many as four completely different meanings according to the tone or stress of its pronunciation. It has a written form derived from rock-cut scripts of southern India. Its alphabetical characters were originally rather square but acquired a softness and roundness after being written on palm leaves in Burma, and in 1970 they presented a mainly circular appearance. The written language tends to be florid and pretentious whereas the spoken word is pithy, idiomatic, and keen edged.

In spoken language the Burmans call themselves Bama, although in literary usage the term is Myanma. They are also known by a number of names among neighboring ethnic groups, including Mon among the Shans and Myen among the Kachins. The Chins use two words in referring to the Burmans: *vai* (civilized) is used to describe Burman society as a whole and a more derogatory term, *kawl*, to describe the Burman individual.

There are forty-four Chin-speaking peoples of western Burma and the Chin Special Division, each having less than 10 percent of the total number of Chins, estimated at 500,000 in 1970. The term *Chin* actually refers to a variety of groups whose languages are more closely related to each other than to any other group. Chin speakers do not identify themselves as a single entity, although many groups, such as the Laizo, Mizo, Hyou, and Asho, use varying forms of the word *zo* (such as *yo* and *sho*) as a term of self-identification. *Zo* has the connotation of "uncivilized" in contrast to *vai* and, by implication, to Burman. The Chin-speaking population extends across the Burmese national border into northeastern India and Pakistan, where the language is usually called Kuki, or Kuki-Chin. North of the Chins are the Nagas, with whom they merge linguistically and culturally. There is reported to be little difference between the two groups, and it is difficult to determine where one begins and the other ends.

There are relatively few speakers of Mon-Khmer languages in modern Burma, the major ones being the Mons and the Palaungs (see ch. 4, Social Systems and Values). They are linguistically affiliated with a number of minor forest and mountain people of Southeast Asia, as well as with several ethnic groups in North and South Vietnam. The Mons were very important in the history of Burma until the middle of the eighteenth century but are now one of the nation's least known peoples. Alternate names for these people and their language have been Peguan and Talaing. The Palaungs, hill people of northern Burma, have a distinct linguistic relationship with the Mons. They are identified by a number of names, most of which are simply dialectical variation of the same term. Most commonly they call themselves Ta-ang and are otherwise known by the Burman term *Palaung*.

The Shans, together with similar groups in Thailand, Laos, Communist China, North Vietnam, and South Vietnam, speak a language derived from the Tai-Chinese language family. Estimated in 1970 to number about 1.5 million, they are usually called Shans by the Burmans, but their name for themselves is Tai, frequently localized by adding the name of a local village. Shan speakers are found throughout Burma except in the Chin Hills, Arakan, and Tenasserim regions. They are concentrated in the Shan State, where they are relatively uniform with regard to culture; elsewhere in Burma they tend to be scattered and strongly Burmanized. Nevertheless, considerable uniformity of culture and language exists among all Shans, even those in the extreme north who are separated from the main group.

The Karen speakers totaled in 1971 an estimated 3 million if the Kayahs, or Red Karens, are included. These people, however, do not all share the same cultural traits. They are part of a larger linguistic family that extends across the border into Thailand. All Karen groups do not speak the same language although all versions are closely related. The four major Karen groups in Burma are the Sgaw, the Pwo, the Pa-o, and the Kayahs. The Burmans use the term *Kayin* in referring to the plains-dwelling Karens (largely Sgaw and Pwo) and *Thaungthu* for the more remote Karens (Pa-o).

Language diversity in peripheral areas tends to prolong traditional differences between groups. Among the Chins, for example, there are over a score of different languages and dialects. In its basic forms, Chin was reduced to writing by the missionaries, who developed an alphabet-making use of Latin characters.

Shan is even more strongly tonal than Burmese or any of the other minority languages. Shan also has an alphabet, a written language, and a literature of its own, all closely linked to the culture of Thailand. The Karens had no written language until early missionaries devised an alphabet adapted from that of Burmese. Kachin, like Chin, uses a Latin alphabet.

True bilingualism is highest in central Burma where almost all native speakers of Chin, Karen, Mon, and Shan are able also to use Burmese, which serves as a lingua franca. The only other indigenous language of significance in intergroup communications is Shan. In the Shan State over a fourth of the Kachins and about one-half of the Mon-Khmer-speaking Palaungs also use Shan.

There is little reliable information about the extent to which English, Indian dialects, and Chinese are used as secondary languages. The ratio of those literate in English is certainly higher in urban than in rural areas. It is taught in secondary schools and is permitted in official communications.

There are probably few Burmans who can speak Chinese or any of the languages of India or Pakistan, and almost none knows another language of Southeast Asia. East of the Salween River there are some Shans who know Thai from trading south into Thailand or from World War II when the Shan states of Mong Pan and Keng Tung were controlled by Thailand. Also as a result of World War II, a number of Burmese can speak Japanese to varying degrees, though few can read it.

Burmese is the only authorized language of instruction and is a compulsory subject in all primary schools. The literary form differs considerably from the spoken. Thus, the child who learns to read Burmese does not learn the same form he has been talking for the previous years of his life but is acquiring a new form of the language, which he will rarely use unless he is called upon to make a formal speech.

EDUCATION

Role in Society

The Burmese word *kyaung* means both monastery and monastery school, indicating the close traditional relationship between education and religion that has existed in the country for centuries. The Buddhist monastic schools that dominated the precolonial period placed their teaching emphasis on how to live, not on how to earn a living. Their role was to teach discipline, morality, and respect for elders as significant aspects of the Buddhist way of life. Education in this sense was a positive value in the culture, and the person lacking education was regarded not only as ignorant but also as irreverent. To this extent it became a criterion of social prestige.

During the colonial period, however, private schools under British government supervision were established, and the job-getting value of an education began to emerge. There was little industry; intermediate business jobs were filled largely by Indians and Chinese; and most managerial and professional positions were occupied by the British. Going to school, therefore, meant either gaining a limited literacy in the monastic schools or obtaining a British kind of education leading to a civil service assignment. Thus, in addition to imbuing an individual with traditional values, education became associated with work in an office. This fostered a prevailing view that an educated person should not perform manual labor of any kind, and a feeling developed that it was undignified to work outdoors.

The years since independence, and particularly since 1962, have seen a profound change in the role that education plays in society. Earlier there had been an insurmountable gap between the traditional learning available in the monastic schools and that required for the colonial civil service offered in the British schools. With independence it was necessary to close that gap because most of the foreigners who administered the country and operated its economy left Burma with the colonial regime or were driven out by official policies aimed at Burmanizing the nation. The educational system thus was faced with the heavy task of providing the education necessary to enable the Burmese to meet the new demands for managerial and other practical skills created by the departure of the aliens.

The government's response to the problem was to centralize all school authority and administration in the Ministry of Education, to revamp school curricula to qualify students for more than civil service employment, and to establish a number of vocational schools to teach crafts and industrial skills. A great many of the younger people desired to learn engineering or mechanical, electrical, or construction skills, but often they were unable or unwilling to obtain sufficient preliminary education to qualify them in these specialties. Others who were educationally qualified were unable to gain admittance to the overcrowded industrial schools. In addition, the demand for skilled industrial workers remained at first so limited, pending industrial development, that successful completion of training was by no means a guarantee of employment. There was little interest in trade even when jobs were available.

Despite these difficulties, the value of getting a good education is clearly understood by most Burmese and deeply appreciated by those who are able to attain it. Its job-getting importance has broader value and greater application than ever before. but those majoring in the arts continue to outnumber the science majors at the universities. A university degree and a profession or a desk job with the government remain the ideal goals of most intelligent and ambitious people, but technical and vocational training followed by a good job in industry has increased in popularity with economic development.

The Educational System

Schools for the indigenous population included those of the monasteries as well as those of the regular public school system provided by the state. Children began their schooling at the age of six years, and under the law attendance was compulsory through the first eight or elementary grades, although this rule could not be universally enforced because of a lack of facilities in some areas. No tuition or other charges were required for monastic, elementary, and vocational schools, but a small fee was imposed at high school (secondary) and postsecondary levels.

The school year ran from June through March and involved 210 school days with a minimum of five hours' instruction per day. All curricula, including much of that employed in the monastic schools, were established in detail by the Ministry of Education, which also prescribed the uniforms to be worn by teachers and students below college level.

Monastic Schools

The monastery school is an ancient Burmese institution that has been declining both in number and influence in recent years. Nevertheless, since nearly every village has a monastery, monastic schooling is still generally available throughout the country. These schools have traditionally been open to all Buddhist boys, and usually a boy is sent to one for at least one or two years.

There is little formal standardization of curricula or procedures. The pupils assemble in one room, seated on the floor in orderly rows with a monk-teacher at their head. Discipline is strict and the monk, as a man of religion and as an elder, is entitled to, and insists upon, the utmost respect. Pupils are required to pay strict attention at all times and to join enthusiastically in mass recitations. Academic progress is much less emphasized than is discipline.

The central core of the curriculum is ethical conduct as conceived by the Buddhist faith. The teacher recites tales of Gautama Buddha, illustrating Buddhist precepts, and the pupils are required to recite them aloud and in unison. Geography, largely cosmological rather than scientific, is taught; history is traditional and somewhat folkloric; simple reading in Burmese is learned; and lessons in arithmetic are rudimentary with a practical emphasis on measurement of land and grain and on counting money.

Monastic schools were in a state of transition as the government sought to bring them into closer alignment with the public school system. Their basic religious and ethical orientation remained unchanged, but most of the fundamental academic instruction was operated by the state, and monks no longer taught beyond the fourth grade.

Public Elementary Schools

In early 1966 the public schools were completely reorganized in accordance with the newly passed Fundamental Education Act. This legislation divided the overall system into three levels of schools: primary, middle, and high schools.

The elementary cycle was divided into kindergartens, primary, and middle schools. Kindergartens were established only where funds and facilities could be provided for them and, although they were an integral part of the system providing one year of preschool instruction, they were not made a prerequisite for entrance into the regular first grade. Primary schools were commissioned to teach grades one through four, inclusive. Middle schools completed the elementary cycle by teaching grades five through eight, inclusive. The number and size of kindergartens were not available, but an official source reported that for the 1968-69 school year, the latest for which figures were available in 1971, there were 14,359 state primary schools with 3,070,976 pupils, 903 state middle schools with 537,512 pupils, and 510 state high schools with 107,467 pupils. The total teaching staff was reported as 64,539.

Compulsory courses in the elementary cycle included Burmese, arithmetic, geography, history, and general science. In schools where teachers and facilities permitted, courses were offered also in religion, domestic science (for girls), gardening, drawing, and physical education. At the middle school level English was introduced as a compulsory subject beginning with grade five; some schools also were equipped to offer additional vocational courses. In urban areas these usually involved carpentry, commercial subjects, and basic technology; in rural areas they were appropriately concerned with agricultural and animal husbandry subjects.

Completion of middle school marked a decisive fork in the

educational road. At this point those best qualified for higher academic education, as indicated by their final examinations, were encouraged to matriculate in a general high school; others were offered vocational training as facilities permitted.

Secondary Schools

Those who desire to continue their education beyond middle school may do so in one of two ways. The best qualified students usually elect to attend one of the general high schools; less qualified graduates from middle schools may get a purely vocational education at one of several specialized agricultural or technical institutions.

For those interested in agriculture there are five agricultural high schools, located at Myaungmya, Myittha, Nansam, Shwebo, and Thegon; and two agricultural institutes, located at Pyinmana and Thaton. For those preferring technical training there are five technical high schools, located at Mandalay, Maymyo, Taunggyi, and two at Rangoon; and three technical institutes, located at Insein, Kalaw, and Mandalay. All these institutions offered some instruction in Burmese, English, mathematics, physics, chemistry, and drafting but emphasized courses pertaining to their specialized disciplines.

The agricultural high schools and the agricultural institutes teach scientific agriculture, animal husbandry, and practical work, differing only in that the high schools provide two years' instruction leading to an agricultural high school certificate, whereas the institutes provide three years' instruction leading to a diploma in agriculture. The technical high schools offer 2 1/2-year courses in building trades, sheet metal work, welding, machine shop practices, automobile and diesel engine maintenance, electricity, and radio mechanics. Graduates are prepared to be apprentices in industry or to work as semiskilled workmen elsewhere. The technical institutes offer three-year courses in civil, electrical, mechanical, and mining engineering and qualify technicians for jobs in those fields.

The regular high schools are conventional four-year liberal arts and sciences institutions. Students who complete their final examinations are awarded high school diplomas, which entitle them to matriculate in a university or college of their choice.

Universities and Colleges

All public higher education was consolidated into two large universities and their affiliated colleges. The Arts and Science University, Rangoon, had ten affiliated colleges, and the Arts and Science University, Mandalay, had five (see table 1).

Table 1. *Selected Burmese Universities and Colleges, 1969*

Institution and affiliated college	Number[1]	
	Teachers	Students
Arts and Science University, Rangoon[2]	424	7,198
Institute of Animal Husbandry and Veterinary Science	16	214
Bassein College	54	885
Moulmein College	64	654
Workers College	32 (426)[3]	5,725
Institute of Education	85	1,846
Institute of Economics	140 (37)[3]	1,964
Medical Institute	178 (37)[3]	1,805
Institute of Medicine (Mingaladon)	83	336
College of Dental Medicine	13	141
Institute of Technology	171	2,250
Arts and Science University, Mandalay[4]	187	3,593
Institute of Agriculture	58	523
Institute of Medicine	92	520
Myitkyina College	29	432
Magwe College	35	652
Taunggyi College	30	563

[1] Estimated.

[2] Colleges are in Rangoon unless name indicates another location.

[3] Part-time teachers.

[4] Colleges are in Mandalay unless name indicates another location.

Source: Adapted from *The Far East and Australasia, 1970: A Survey and Directory of Asia and the Pacific*, London, 1970.

All these institutions of higher learning have appropriate faculties in arts, sciences, social sciences, agriculture, medicine, forestry, law, engineering, and education and award degrees in these disciplines as authorized in their basic charters. The general pattern is for the first two university years to be devoted to basic studies, including an introduction to the student's major field. The bachelor of medicine and surgery degree customarily represents a seven-year program of premedical and medical studies beyond the first two years; the bachelor of science degree in engineering represents an additional six years; and one in forestry requires an additional five years.

Teachers and Teaching Methods

The teaching career does not appear to offer great inducements—schools are crowded; many are located in remote areas; and the pay is low. Recruitment of teachers to meet the increasing needs of the rapidly growing schools presents a serious problem for government authorities. Some concessions to the educational background required of teachers, especially those for elementary schools, therefore, must be made in order to staff the schools.

Persons who have had only one year of high school are eligible to apply for training at one of the seven teacher training institutes located at Bassein, Kyaukpyu, Meiktila, Myitkyina, Toungoo, Taunggyi, and Thegon. They undergo a one-year course that qualifies them to teach one of the first four grades in an elementary school. Many primary school teachers have training exceeding this, but the great bulk of them do not.

Middle school teachers are slightly better trained. They must be high school graduates and receive their teacher training at one of the three state teaching|teacher colleges. These institutions, located at Mandalay, Moulmein, and Rangoon, offer teacher training courses that last for two years. Successful completion of a course entitles the graduate to teach up to, but not beyond, the eighth grade in an elementary school. Many middle school teachers have more extensive educational backgrounds, but this represents the minimum required.

High school teachers are trained at the Institute of Education of Arts and Science University, Rangoon. The school offers several degree programs requiring from two to four years of study, depending on the field of qualification. In addition, some high school teachers of technical and vocational subjects are trained in teacher training courses offered by agricultural and technical secondary schools.

It was not clear in 1971 regarding the sources from which Burma drew its faculties for universities, colleges, and specialized schools at the postsecondary level. Some probably received degrees at foreign universities in Europe or the United States. Others, probably the majority, were graduates of these schools themselves.

Methods of instruction have been slow to change, and progressive ideas have not been easy to incorporate into the formal pattern of teaching. In primary schools memorization and unison recitation tend to persist. Formal study recitations have characterized the middle schools. At the university level lecturing at dictation speed with the students taking verbatim notes remains common procedure. This is owing in part to tradition, in part to a shortage of books, and in part to a critical shortage of teachers. The result at all levels has been heavy emphasis on memorization of facts and recall of these facts upon demand.

The system thus provokes the use of essay-type questions on examinations, which require factual recall, rather than of objective-type questions, which call for creative reasoning. Teaching methods have been under review, but the introduction of new and improved techniques has been difficult. More progress in this direction has been made in urban areas than in the villages, where tradition and superstition are strong and where there is more opposition to change.

ARTISTIC AND INTELLECTUAL EXPRESSION

Many of the country's writers on cultural subjects have complained that British conquest and colonial rule destroyed the vitality of Burma's traditional art forms and brought nothing of real value to replace them. At the middle of the nineteenth century the court at Mandalay was the cultural center, supporting the best of the country's artists, dancers, musicians, woodcarvers, and metalworkers. The British annexation ended this patronage and introduced a new set of artistic and intellectual values that submerged traditional standards. New forms were adopted or traditional ones were modified in the theater and, to a lesser extent, in music. Exclusively Western models were followed in literature and painting. As a result, traditional artistic and cultural expression withered and became largely dormant until after independence.

Burmese intellectual life was affected in much the same way. Some alien forms were adopted outright; others modified Burmese concepts. A Western educational system was introduced, but few of the intellectual attitudes basic to the model in the West were assimilated. The form was acquired but not the content.

An intellectual elite in the Western sense has been slow to emerge. Even those whose social status depended on Western education, such as university faculty members, did not feel themselves to be part of a distinct intellectual group.

Upon achieving independence in 1948, the government embarked on a campaign of cultural revival to regain native initiative in distinctive Burmese art and culture and to preserve and promote the development of indigenous traditions. Such a renascence was clearly recognized by the leadership as an important part of the process of national integration and viability.

In addition to aid to higher education and expansion of schools at all levels, the revival programs included: the establishment of state museums; the founding of new schools for music, drama, and art; annual cultural exhibitions; schools for the study of Buddhism; and the proliferation of many new learned societies and research institutions.

Architecture and Sculpture

Religious architecture and its associated arts, sculpture in particular, are the most important forms of artistic expression in Burma. The ubiquitous pagodas, whitewashed and occasionally covered with gilt, are evidence of the religious focus of society.

The Pagan period (named for the earliest Burman capital) of the ninth to the thirteenth centuries, known as the classic era in architecture, saw the synthesis of various foreign, especially Indian, architectural elements into a characteristically Burmese style. The best known pagoda of this period, the Ananda pagoda, was constructed according to tradition by Buddhist monks from India. Though its form is Indian, the ornate exterior decoration is typically Burmese.

With the exception of exuberant decoration, the most distinctive element of Burmese architecture of this classic period is the emphasis on verticality. The vertical is stressed by terraced recessions that culminate in the superstructure of the stupa, which tapers to a point. This emphasis came to characterize all Burmese pagoda construction. The typical pagoda is a structure of solid masonry, shaped roughly like an elongated bell, rising to a point topped by the Burmese umbrella.

The Shwedagon pagoda in Rangoon, built to entomb eight hairs of the buddha, epitomizes this tradition and has served as the model for many pagodas throughout the country. Probably the most famous Burmese shrine, the Shwedagon was not completed until the fifteenth century and has been continually added to ever since. It is set on a low hill surrounded by flat delta lands. Covered with goldleaf, it rises about 320 feet above its platform and is magnificent against its background of green tropical foliage.

Like architecture, Burmese sculpture was originally based on Indian models and then evolved its own styles. The most representative sculptures are numerous reliefs found on pagodas illustrating the life of the Buddha. These reliefs show distinctive qualities of animation and grace plus the characteristic Burmese liking for ornate decoration.

The classic period in Burmese architecture ended with the Mongol invasion and the Thai migrations (see ch. 3, Historical Setting). From the thirteenth century until the British occupation in the nineteenth century, development was cut off from foreign influences that had contributed to the original synthesis. What emerged was a sophisticated folk art that elaborated on classic forms in a typically Burmese flamboyant style. The wooden palaces and gilt pagodas of Mandalay show this development at its peak. It was into this tradition that Western forms were introduced by the British. Just as in other spheres of art, the result was that in part these forms were adopted outright and in part they were synthesized with the native Burmese tradition.

The British erected buildings throughout the country, but their main efforts were concentrated at Rangoon. Most of the main buildings were designed for the government or for Western business firms. The city that emerged was Western style, oriented toward the port, and crossed with broad, tree-lined avenues. Solid masonry predominated, and the erection of any other type of structure within the city proper was forbidden.

It was only in the twentieth century that an architecture evolved combining basic Western forms and construction methods with traditional Burmese styles. A British-trained architect, U Tin, was largely responsible for this development. His work is best exemplified in the city hall and the Myoma High School in Rangoon. In the city hall U Tin added nineteenth-century Burmese forms and decorative motifs to a basically European building. The principal additions were plaster decorations imitating the carved woodwork of the nineteenth century and towers with multiple, overlapping roofs like those of the Mandalay palace and the structures associated with pagoda entrances and shrines.

The nationalist outlook of the government after independence gave impetus to the attempt to evolve a truly Burmese architecture that would express the new state. Of the newer structures, the best example of the modern style, also created by U Tin, is the railroad depot in Rangoon. Much of the future Burmese architecture, however, will be influenced by Burmese now studying abroad, particularly in the United States.

Music, Dance, and Drama

A varied heritage of song, dance, and drama, sometimes inseparable one from the other, has persisted from precolonial times despite strong Western influences in the modern era. Since the late nineteenth century Burmese music especially has been affected, and certain Western instruments, such as the violin and the guitar, have become popular and are sometimes used to accompany traditional airs.

The earliest Burmese musical instruments include a drum with a cowhide head, a kind of high-pitched clarinet, a flute, and a small harp. The present-day composition of the Burmese musical troupe is traced back to about 1760 when many Thai artists (dancers, composers, musicians, woodcarvers, and metalworkers) were brought to Burma. Thereafter many Thai airs and songs were adopted.

Earlier Burmese forms of songs, music, and dancing are the *sidaw, bonshe, dobat,* and *ozi,* all named for the associated type of drum they feature. *Sidaw* music, song, and dance were intimately associated with the court; *bonshe,* largely folk dance music, was performed at plowing and harvest times. *Dobat* and *ozi* are ordinarily used by villagers for all sorts of occasions except funerals. *Ozi* is one of the most commonly encountered forms of Burmese music, for it accompanies the ceremony for Buddhist novitiates. *Dobat* often accompanies the chanting of the *thangyat,* a kind of poem recited in chorus alternately by two groups. It is most commonly heard at Burmese New Year celebrations.

In addition, there is an orchestra usually heard as an adjunct to dramatic performances. It ordinarily includes various drums and wind instruments; a "gong-circle"consisting of a circular low wooden frame within which the performer sits and plays a string of gongs arranged in a scale; a "drum-circle" similarly constructed and played; and a split-bamboo clapper struck to provide additional rhythmic accompaniment.

Burmese drama is intimately connected with music and dancing. The most common form is the *anyeint pwe,* a form of burlesque performed by an orchestra, two male actors, and one or more female dancers. The play is a series of alternating episodes beginning with an interchange between the two actors or clowns, toward the end of which the dancer enters and takes part. After some chaffing and joking the clowns yield the stage to the dancer who sings and dances for a brief period. The clowns then reappear and, after another bantering scene among the three, the dancer departs to be replaced by another. This may, and usually does, go on for hours. The *anyeint pwe* is perhaps the most widespread of all dramatic art forms in Burma. It is heard frequently on the radio and is produced throughout the year except in the rainy season. A simple stage with a minimum of stage property is all that is required.

The *zatpwe,* or Jataka show, is seen less often. It takes its name from the more than 500 Jataka stories that the Buddha told his disciples in answer to questions raised by them. Like the *anyeint pwe,* the *zatpwe* is presented outdoors on a very simple stage, and admission is usually free. It, too, is accompanied by an orchestra and may last many hours.

Other forms of drama, seldom seen nowadays, are the puppet show and the *yamazat.* The puppet shows are an intimate union of play and music, similar to the *zatpwe,* but in abbreviated form. The *yamazat* is based on the epic Indian poem, the *Ramayana,* about the trials and wanderings of Prince Rama, his wife, and his followers.

Since World War II another type of dramatic presentation has flourished on a limited scale in Rangoon. It is called the *pyazat* and resembles the musical comedy in the United States. It is performed in motion picture theaters at fixed prices.

The *pyazat* theater is a repertory theater in which each show is presented afternoons and evenings for a fortnight and then is replaced by a new one. The plays vary little. The main plot concerns a boy and girl who come together in the face of the disapproval of their elders. Several other couples are also involved. Alternating scenes are separated by interludes in which comedians banter in the fashion of the *anyeint pwe.* In the denouncement all whose love has been thwarted are united and live happily ever after. The orchestra uses Western instruments and alternates between wholly Western tunes and Westernized Burmese airs.

Handicrafts

Before the introduction of factory-made fabrics from abroad, it was customary for every Burmese household to have its own handloom operated by girls of the household. The products of these looms were for domestic consumption rather than for sale. The cloth was coarse but durable and was woven either from silk or from cotton.

There were also certain centers of weaving whose textiles were especially esteemed. Near Henzada there flourished a center for the manufacture of heavy silks resembling brocades. Characteristic products were shot silk in pieces eight yards by two-thirds of a yard, in reds, greens, and yellows, the woof colors generally being in lighter shades than the warp. Certain color combinations, such as two shades of green, were avoided as being unlucky, whereas rose and pink combinations were especially esteemed.

Modern weaving centers exist at Prome, Tavoy, Shwedaung, Mandalay, and Kindat. Cotton blankets in red, yellow, and black stripes are made in the Chin Hills region; thicker blankets, white with red stripe patterns and fringed edges, are a specialty of Pakokku. The so-called Shan bags in a wide variety of patterns and colors are the products of most of the hill peoples. Related to these are the sleeping and sitting mats that form an essential furniture item in every house. Of these the coarser types are woven from pandanus palm fibers or thin strips of bamboo. The finest quality mats are made from a species of reed and are unbelievably smooth and flexible.

The production of lacquer ware is a flourishing craft carried out in many areas but centered in modern times at Nyaungu near Pagan. The basis of lacquer is a grayish, gummy liquid obtained from trees by tapping. This liquid then hardens in moist air to a jet black solid. The liquid is mixed with clay or ash and applied in many successive layers to a framework of split bamboo or of bamboo and hair. Each separate coat is allowed to dry hard and is smoothed before the next coat is applied. When completed, the object is turned on a primitive lathe for polishing. Despite the dark color of the original lacquer, it may be colored by the addition of various dyes to give shades of red, orange, green, and yellow. Goldleaf is used for decorating the original piece. A first-class object may take as long as six months to produce.

Objects made from laquer are diverse in shape and purpose. They include begging bowls for monks, food carriers with matching plates and cups, drinking beakers, betel boxes, containers for toilet articles, combs, and other items of dress. Lacquer is also used locally to waterproof umbrellas, to fix goldleaf, to give tone and luster to glass mosaics, to make book covers and ornate religious texts written in black on a red and gold background, and to decorate wooden pillars in palaces and monasteries.

Burma is rich in timber suited to many uses. From these varied woods and using but a limited range of tools, Burmese woodcarvers have demonstrated what is probably their greatest skill. All wooden objects provide scope for their artistry. It is probable that in early times sumptuary laws confined such ornamentation to palaces and monasteries, where all available space is covered with carved figures of spirits, birds, and animals in wonderful settings of foliage, flowers, and ornamental scrollwork. The carving often seems crude, but the overall effect with its added lacquer and gilt embellished with mosaic in glass, is very pleasing.

Apart from these major work subjects the bulkheads of most rivercraft are richly carved, as are the panels of carts and shelves and stands in the home. To these major achievements must be added the host of smaller items that form part of every household and the miracles of ingenuity in bamboo and rattan in the use of which the Burmese are singularly skillful. Furniture, cooking utensils, combs toned a rich brown in sesame oil, umbrella frames, and boxes made of cane or of toddy-palm leaves are produced and decorated.

Pottery is also varied and attractive. The clays available are diverse but are generally rich in iron and turn red or orange on firing. White clay also occurs for the production of true chinawares. Much pottery is made without the aid of a wheel. Firing takes place in holes in the ground or in regularly constructed kilns.

Glazed wares, some of which have earned international fame, are manufactured by dressing unfired wares with lead slag, or galena, from the silver mines of the Shan State. It seems likely, in fact, that the Shans were responsible for introducing most pottery techniques into Burma.

The ceramics of different regions of the country are esteemed for special purposes; the black pottery of Tavoy for self-cooling water containers; the salt-glazed jars of Upper Burma for bathrooms; the wares of Papun for their high quality; smaller vessels from Upper Burma for pickle storage.

The most characteristic employment of glass mosaic is in the decoration of wooden buildings and on pagodas, images, and containers for religious use. Notable examples of these applications can be seen on the Shwedagon pagoda. The technique is not Burmese in origin but seems to have been borrowed from Thailand in the eighteenth century. The best artisans are said to be Shans.

For centuries Burmese craftsmen have worked in gold, silver, and copper alloys. In using them they have attained a high degree of skill, although the work, like that of the woodcarvers, is more distinguished by boldness and feedom than by meticulous finish. Burmese silverware, some dating back to the thirteenth century, is of deservedly high repute, although much modern work is but an imitation of traditional wares.

Jewelry making is another art in which much internationally admired work has been achieved. The production of jewelry and setting of jewels in gold is still a major occupation, and such items are an essential part of every Burmese woman's wardrobe. Rubies, spinels, sapphires, emeralds and diamonds are all richly and hansomely set. Diamonds and emeralds are not found in Burma, but diamonds are especially sought after by Burmese women whose ambition it is to own a full set of diamond jewelry. Jade of the highest quality is found in Burma but is not used there as a precious stone. The main demand for jade comes from Japan and China.

In bronze and brass the achievements of Burmese foundries are considerable. Most products are dedicated to religious ends. Of particular note is bell casting, the greatest one being the Mingun bell, some twelve feet high, ten feet in outside diameter, and weighing about eighty tons. Other great bells exist, but none of comparable size. These products are actually gongs rather than bells because they have no clapper and must be struck from the outside. Small gongs and cymballs form a large part of the

Burmese orchestra, and these too are often of exquisite craftsmanship.

Literature

Traditional Burmese literature ended with the monarchy in 1885. This ancient literature was written in the form of manuscript books in Buddhist monasteries or in the courts of kings and princes. Its sources were court life in Burma and religious themes. The treatment tended to rely upon the supernatural, the imaginative, and the miraculous.

During the latter half of the nineteenth century writers came under European influence. Printing became a factor in publishing, and the court, a source of both themes and patronage, disappeared.

The twentieth century ushered in a new kind of prose literature. Modern novels began to appear, soon followed by novelettes. The dominant stream in Burmese literature, however, continued to be religious writing. The leading figure of this period was a monk named Ledi Sayadaw. He wrote over fifty works, primarily religious treatises. His writing style, like that of his contemporaries, was classic.

The founding of the university at Rangoon in 1920 gave an impetus to Burmese literature. Dramas were translated, original work was encouraged, and rhymed poetry in short forms thrived. One of the difficulties writers encountered was linguistic because English was the language used in government. A sign that this obstacle was being overcome was the admission of U Sein Tin, who had been graduated with honors in Burmese, into the Civil Service. He became prominent in fiction and essays distinguished by their realism and simple style.

Various government agencies and private learned societies became interested in the preservation and publication of inscriptions and the Burmese classics. This led to a revival of interest in earlier Burmese literature and to the use of the older and simpler but classic style in contemporary writing. The most prominent figure at the beginning of this reformation was U Pe Maung Tin, professor of Burmese and later head of the university at Rangoon.

Contemporary with U Sein Tin were U Wun and U Thein Han, both of whom were educated in part in England. They initiated a style that reduced florid ornamental usages and eliminated involved subordinate sentences, which had characterized the earlier classic writing. The publication of collections of stories and poems by writers connected with the university brought this new style to public attention. The period became one of increasing translation and adaptation of English folk tales, fiction, and history.

In the early 1930s a group of writers was intent on introducing contemporary ideas from the West. Prominent in it were U Nu and Thein Pe Myint. It organized the Nagani (Red Dragon) Book Club modeled on the Left Book Club in England. During the four years of its existence the club issued a number of translations and original works dealing with revolutionary and leftist topics.

The criticisms produced by members of the club were directed at almost every institution, a well-known example of which was *Tet Pongyi* (The Progressive Monk) by Thein Pe Myint, published in 1935. This book was an attack on modern monks who relaxed their traditional discipline and was an attempt to reform the monastic order. As a writer and a thinker, Thein Pe Myint was highly regarded for his clear, forceful style and his rich sense of humor.

World War II and the Japanese occupation checked the growth of literary activity until after 1946; then, despite internal strife, a flood of cheap booklets and pamphlets was issued. They contained chiefly stories of love and adventure and some wartime narratives reflecting the recent experience of the Burmese people and introducing many new words and phrases along with foreign ideas. There was also a plethora of leftist political literature. Among the more purely literary and serious writers of recent times are the historian U Yaw; Shawe U-daung, author of the *Golden Peacock;* U Aye Maung, professor of Burmese at Rangoon; and Maung Htin Aung, who specialized in folklore.

Left-wing writers are distinguished by language with Communist overtones. Three novels—*Mo Auk Myebin* (The Earth Under the Sky) by Min Aung (1948), *Min Hmudan* (The Civil Servant), by Tet To (1950), and *Tathtega Myat Ko Ko* (The Noble Brother from the Army) by Thadu (1952)—have been awarded prizes for their literary merit. The most respected authors are men who already occupy stations of prestige in the society as teachers or government officials.

Learned Societies and Museums

The cultural revival in Burma was abetted and supported by the work of a number of private and official learned societies and by government action to establish and maintain national museums to collect and display historical records and achievements. Three of these were specialized departments of the Ministry of Culture; the other four were private institutions.

The archaeological department in the ministry was given the responsibility for maintaining ancient monuments, for conducting epigraphical research, and for exploring and excavating historical sites. It also maintains small museums at some of these sites. The ministry's Department of Ancient Literature and Culture compiles bibliographies of Burmese books; collects, classifies, and preserves published and unpublished literary works of Burmese writers; edits classical works for publication; and does research in the cultures of indigenous peoples. The Department of Music and Drama in the ministry standardizes, notates, and publishes classical songs and records ancient styles of music and singing.

One of the oldest and most active of the private learned organizations is the Sarpay Beikman Management Board. This group, formerly called the Burma Translation Society, produces, translates, publishes, and distributes books in Burmese and indigenous languages and encourages research in Burmese literature and fine arts. It was, and remains, in the forefront in providing textbooks for Burmese schools. The board also maintains a public library in Rangoon stocked with over 50,000 volumes, about 30,000 of which are in Burmese.

The remaining three privately operated learned groups are the International Institute of Advanced Buddhist Studies, The Burma Council of World Affairs, and the Burma Research Society. The Buddhist institution is world famous as a center of research and study in Buddhist subjects. In addition, it maintains a public library and a museum in Rangoon. The library is on the grounds of the Kaba-aye pagoda and contains 17,000 volumes, 7,000 periodicals, 7,650 palm leaf manuscripts, and 1,022 folding parchment and brass plate manuscripts. The various manuscripts are priceless and constitute one of the world's most fruitful reservoirs for serious scholars interested in Buddhism. The Burma Council of World Affairs promotes the study of Burma and international questions to develop informed opinion of world affairs and Burma's past, present, and future role in the community of nations. The Burma Research Society promotes both cultural and scientific studies and research relating to Burma. It publishes the *Journal of Burma Research Society* twice a year.

The government has established and maintains five museums devoted to developing public interest in Burmese culture. The Bogyoke Aung San Museum in Rangoon has 571 exhibits on the life and works of General Aung San, who was an underground leader against the Japanese during World War II and later became a patriot in the fight for independence. The National Museum of Art and Archeology, also in Rangoon, is the nations's largest and most celebrated. It displays 1,652 exhibits of antiquities, has 354 paintings by Burmese artists, and features a small replica of the Mandalay Palace. State libraries and museums are located at Kyaukpyu, Moulmein, and Mandalay. The museum at Kyaukpyu has 104 exhibits of silver coins, costumes, and other artifacts; the museums at Moulmein and Mandalay have 300 and 350 exhibits, respectively, all dealing with general cultural subjects.

PUBLIC INFORMATION

Communication Patterns

The government, through the Ministry of Information, controls the output of all media of communications, either by owning and operating them outright or by imposing censorship on nongovernment forms. Most newspapers are published in Rangoon; all radio broadcasting is centered at the capital and there is no television; motion picture theaters are found primarily in urban areas; book production is low; and the transportation system does not provide easy access to all parts of the country. Language differences further impede ease in communications.

Face-to-face communications and the opinion of local leaders, therefore, are of critical importance, even in urban areas. Rangoon, for example, is divided into wards each with a headman appointed by the police. Within these wards an intimacy and homogeneity similar to village life has developed. The average person turns to his ward headman as an opinion leader just as the villager looks to his local leader for guidance.

Newspapers

There was an estimated total of more than twenty-five daily newspapers in Burma as of 1970. Ten of these were classed as major publications and had a total circulation of 212,500 (see table 2). Seven of the major dailies were owned outright or were operated by the Information Department of Ministry of Information and Culture; the other three were privately owned and published. All but one of the government and one of the private major newspapers were published in Rangoon.

Before 1962 the press was relatively free although the government imposed restrictions when necessary. In 1954 the regime attempted to pass a bill making criticism of government leaders a criminal offense, but the Burma Journalists Association and the minority opposition parties prevented its passage. Thus, between 1948 and 1962 the press, despite times of official hostility and its own weaknesses, fulfilled the role of an opposition party and of a lobby pressure group.

The situation changed radically when the Ne Win government came to power. Tight censorship was imposed on all newspapers,

Table 2. Leading Daily Newspapers in Burma, 1970

Publication	Publisher	Language	Circulation
Kye Hmon	Government	Burmese	51,000
Working Peoples Daily[1]	do	English	22,000
Loke Tha Pyithu Nay Zin	do	Burmese	31,000
Yma Ah-lai	do	do	20,000
Hanthawaddy[2]	do	do	19,500
Guardian	do	English	16,500
Botataung	do	Burmese	4,500
Yango	Private	do	21,000
Burma Khit	do	do	19,000
Ludu[2]	do	do	8,000

[1] English-language counterpart of *Loke Tha Pyithu Nay Zin.*

[2] Published in Mandalay. All others published in Rangoon.

Source: Adapted from *Editor and Publisher International Yearbook, 1970,* New York, 1970.

including its own, by the regime; Chinese-, Indian-, and Pakistani-language dailies were eliminated by a requirement that printing must be done only in Burmese or English. Foreign press services were denied permission to distribute their daily reports directly to any publisher in the country, and a new government agency, the News Agency of Burma (NAB), was created to replace them. Two new daily newspapers were founded by the Ministry of Information to act as official government organs.

In 1971 news from foreign press services—primarily from the Telegraph Agency of the Soviet Union (Telegrafnoe Agentsvo Sovietskovo Soyuza—TASS), Soviet Union; United Press International and Associated Press, United States; Reuters, Great Britain; Agence France-Presse, France; and New China News Agency, Communist China—continued to be received, but all were received in the offices of the NAB. There they were edited before release to domestic publishers, and when one was printed the source always had to be indicated. Reports from these sources concerning the same event often appear side by side in the press, which gives the Burmese a unique opportunity to read news stories from agencies representing different ideologies.

The two daily newspapers created by the Ne Win regime were the Burmese-language *Loke Tha Pyithu Nay Zin* and its English-language counterpart, *Working Peoples Daily.* Each had its own staff and offices although both were official government organs.

Before 1969 the government expanded its newspaper interests by nationalizing five other, formerly independent, dailies. They were the *Kye Hmon, Yma Ah-lai, Hanthawaddy, Guardian,* and *Botataung* publications. At the time of nationalization, *Hanthawaddy* was transferred to Mandalay. Thus, in 1970 the official government organs had a combined circulation of 164,500, or about 77 percent of the national total. The government uses its daily newspapers to present ideas and attitudes on both domestic and foreign policy in order to test the response of those most concerned. This is particularly noticeable in the different attitudes taken toward Communist China, in the criticism of public officials, and in articles dealing with the profit motive.

Among the government newspapers the *Working Peoples Daily,* both in its Burmese and English editions, serves to stimulate government officials through criticisms in articles and editorials and to gain public support of government programs. International news is usually reported objectively, but an anti-Western bias may often be detected.

Kye Hmon has the largest circulation in Burma and is the most widely read daily. It concentrates on national news, particularly stories concerning agriculture and the economy. *Yma Ah-lai* is cautious and optimistic in tone. It tries to avoid any position that might be controversial.

Hanthawaddy covers national and international news and prints student and literary supplements. Its main concerns include the problems of developing nations, world food production, international relations, and the arms race. The *Guardian* has a distinguished history and fills its columns with international news. It has a daily feature column dealing with events in communist countries. There is practically no news of Burmese affairs, but that which does appear is favorably slanted. *Botataung* is both anti-Chinese Communist and anti-West. Articles dealing with capitalism, the increasing crime rates in the United States, and other subjects unfavorable to the United States image are frequent and present the advantages to be derived from socialism in nation building and in eliminating injustices. The primary international concern appears to be that of guarding the rights and interests of developing nations.

The three private daily newspapers, *Yango, Burma Khit, Ludu,* have widely different orientations but are limited by the tight government controls in expressing views on many subjects. *Yango* concentrates on international news and frequently editorializes on the conflict in Vietnam, Indian affairs, and other questions of special importance to Southeast Asia. Little is ascertainable about *Burma Khit* except that its coverage is general, well balanced, and largely of local interest. *Ludu* has a strong anti-United States editorial policy. It criticizes United States intervention in Vietnam and notes the danger of the hostilities affecting other Asian nations. It praises Burmese traditions but calls for improvements in education, medicine, and agriculture.

There is very little variation in the size, format, and makeup of the leading daily newspapers. All are of standard size and consist of approximately eight pages. One or two editorials usually appear near the front, and sports news is featured near the back. The daily radio programs and movie features are noted, but there is almost no advertising.

Radio

Radio listening is very popular and accessible to virtually everyone. The number of radio receivers was stated by United Nations sources to be 388,000 in 1968. Most were equipped to receive shortwave broadcasts. Radios receive maximum usage because privately owned sets habitually are turned up high enabling people in the streets to listen. Teashops where Burmese go for conversation and gossip all have radios for their patrons, and the army is provided with sets that are placed in central meeting places or villages in the most remote regions.

There is only one broadcasting service, the government-owned and -operated Burma Broadcasting Service (BBS). The entire system is located at Rangoon and operates over twelve transmitters. Two of the transmitters are mediumwave, using 50-kilowatt and 5-kilowatt power on wavelengths of 955 and 1135 kilohertz (kilocycles) respectively. Nine of the transmitters are shortwave; all are of 50-kilowatt power and operate in the 4, 5, 6, 7, and 9 megahertz (megacycles) bands as required. One transmitter is a low-powered (250 watts) FM (frequency modulation) installation for local Rangoon coverage only.

Only programs in the domestic service are broadcast, and there is no international service. Approximately two-thirds of the BBS programs are in Burmese; about one-third are in English; and a small portion of the newscasts are in the Shan, Karen, Kayah, Kachin, and Chin languages. Program content is devoted to folklore and popular music, education, news, and government information. News is presented in a noncontroversial manner, emphasizing national affairs and the progress of government programs. Educational broadcasts are usually pitched at the secondary school level, but many include vocational training for persons of all ages. Occasionally, programs are devoted to English-language lessons. Government information programs concern rural development, civics, art and science, and health and hygiene.

Films

The Burmese attend many motion pictures. As of 1970 there were 450 theaters in the country, having about 365,000 seats. Attendance figures indicate that the average Burmese sees a film feature about eight times a year. A film council has been created to give governmental direction and assistance to the film industry.

The Motion Picture Agency Board, the Film Censor Board, and the Film Academy Award Board are government agencies concerned with films, and there has been some criticism of their effectiveness. The minister of information and culture has publicly expressed his displeasure that none of the Burmese film productions had expressed a nation-building theme or contributed to the national orientation of the people. Through its newspapers the regime has also criticized the industry for copying United States films that concentrate on themes of physical love.

The Motion Picture Agency Board has exclusive authority to bring foreign films into the country and imports about 200 each year, primarily from the United States and India. Most imports are love stories, comedies, and action films that contain much violence.

Publishing

In 1970 there were ten publishing houses, which together published about 2,000 titles. These included about 86 translations, most of them from English and classical Greek and Latin works, although some were from Russian, German, and French (see table 3).

Only Ava House, a state firm, is permitted to import books, periodicals, and other printed matter. The import policy is permissive, and publications from many countries are available. About 2,000 copies of each issue of the United States news magazine *Time*, for example, are sold weekly, and a dozen copies of the *New York Times* are imported for distribution to top-ranking government officials.

Government Information

The Revolutionary Council is the policymaking body and the final authority in both the party and the government. The party publishes propaganda, including books on such things as the speeches of Ne Win, a collection of articles on party affairs, and biographies of resistance fighters who became national heroes. It also publishes the *Party Affairs Bulletin* and the *International News Bulletin*.

Table 3. *Major Publishers in Burma, 1970*

Publisher	Field of interest
Hanthawaddy Press	General books and periodicals
Knowledge Publishing House	Travel, fiction, religion, politics, and directories
Kyipwaye Press*	Arts, travel, religion, fiction, and children's books
Myawaddy Press	Military books, journals, and magazines
Sarpay Beikman Management Board	Literature, fine arts, and general
Shumawa Press	All kinds of nonfiction
Shwepidan Publishing House	Philosophy, politics, law, and religion
Smart and Mookerdum	Arts, children's books, fiction, and nonfiction
Than Mylt Wadi Publishing House	Scientific and technical books
Thu Dhama Wadi Press	Religious books

* Located in Mandalay; all others, in Rangoon.

Source: Adapted from *The Far East and Australasia, 1970: A Survey and Directory of Asia and the Pacific,* London, 1970.

Forward, published twice a month by the Ministry of Information, is the official organ of the Revolutionary Council. Its circulation of almost 100,000 made it in 1971 the most widely distributed periodical in the country. Themes of national unity and culture are emphasized, but articles on current affairs, traditional culture, and sports appear regularly.

Government seminars and national holidays also provide opportunities for the Revolutionary Council to present its message to the people. The most important formal contacts between the government and local leaders are the annual, weeklong Peasants Seminar and the Workers Seminar. These are held during the week preceding Workers Day (May 1) and Peasants Day (May 2). During the week, officials meet with worker and peasant delegates and review and outline their programs. Freedom of speech, criticism, and questions are allowed, but the communication is primarily from the officials to the delegates. At the end of the week the special days are celebrated by speeches, parades, and rallies followed by a closing banquet for the delegates.

National holidays are the occasions for mass rallies, demonstrations, exhibitions, and speechmaking. Independence Day (January 4) and Union Day (February 12) are most prominent. Union Day commemorates the 1947 conference at which national and ethnic minority leaders reached agreement on the formation of the Union of Burma.

Foreign Information

In 1970 thirty-seven members of the world community of nations, including ten communist countries, had embassies of their own or were represented by the embassy of a friendly power in Burma. Most of those with embassies had some form of information program. Certain countries with consular representation in Burma also conducted such programs. These included East Germany, North Korea, the Republic of Korea, North Vietnam, and the Republic of Vietnam. All operate under the same government restrictions that severely limit the amount of information that may be distributed and prohibit the use of controversial, polemical, or ideological material. The Ministry of Information reviews all information to be printed and, after printing, is responsible for its distribution. Films and exhibits, which may be shown only on diplomatic premises, must be approved by the ministry before exhibition.

Government restrictions have meant that foreign missions follow similar patterns in presenting their views. The program of the United States Information Service is typical. One thousand copies of a daily news bulletin and 5,000 copies of a monthly bulletin are sent to the ministry for distribution, and documentary and educational films are given to the central government library to be used as it wishes. The United States has succeeded in obtaining invitations for sports figures to hold clinics and in 1970 and 1971 the United States also sponsored education exhibits, a visit by the Apollo XIV crew, and the Count Basie and Duke Ellington orchestras. The Soviet Union and Eastern European communist countries have in recent years presented athletes as well as various cultural missions, including press, information, health, and education groups.

Radio, because of its popularity, is used extensively by foreign countries. The British Broadcasting Corporation daily beams programs into Burma. Radio Peking broadcasts a steady stream of propaganda in Burmese. More popular than either of these is All-India Radio, which concentrates on music and entertainment. The Voice of America broadcasts one hour a day in Burmese and also transmits an extensive program in English for Asian listeners. Its programs, devoted to sports, science, agriculture, news, and music, are estimated to have a daily audience of about 2,000 listeners.

CHAPTER 7

RELIGION

Theravada Buddhism, one of the two major forms of Buddhism, is the dominant and official state religion of Burma. Estimates on the number of its adherents vary, ranging from a low of 75 percent to a high of 85 percent of the total population. Minority religious groups of significance include the Indians, who are Hindus; the Pakistanis, who are Muslims; the Chinese, who are a mixture of Buddhists, Taoists, Confucians, and ancestor worshipers; Chins, Kachins, Karens, and Europeans, who are Christians; and the indigenous ethnic peoples, who are basically animists. None of these minority religious groups accounts for more than a small percentage of the total population.

The dominance of the Buddhist religion is indicated by the fact that almost every village supports at least one *kyaung* (monastery or monastery school). Buddhist pagodas dot the landscape in both Upper and Lower Burma, and yellow-robed *pongyi* (Buddhist monks) are characteristic figures of daily life. Over 99 percent of the ethnic Burmans (see Glossary) are Buddhists, as are an equal percentage of the Shan, the Mon, the Palaung, and the Pa-o Karen branch of the Karen ethnic groups. All of the other indigenous ethnic groups have some Buddhist adherents as well (see ch. 4, Social Systems and Values).

Christian missionaries have long been active, primarily in the delta and in the frontier areas. In 1970 an estimated 3 percent of the population was Christian, the majority belonging to the Karen (except the Pa-o Karen branch) ethnic group. Accurate information of the division of Christians according to denomination in 1970 was not available, but the Roman Catholic, the Anglican, the Methodist, the Seventh-Day Adventist, and the American Baptist churches predominated in the initial missionary effort. Activities of the missionaries were centered mainly on education, medical care, and social welfare.

Although the great majority of the Burmese are formally committed to Buddhism as the established religion and identify themselves as Buddhists, actual religious behavior consists of much more than purely Buddhist beliefs and practices. Before the introduction of Buddhism from India, the Burmese had indigenous beliefs centered on the propitiation of *nats* (spirits). This older religious complex persists as the dominant belief system among many of the remote hill tribes.

Among the Burmans, the Shans, the Karens, and some other groups, Buddhism was adopted in addition to the existing religious system, but it did not wholly displace it. In some sophisticated urban circles Buddhist doctrine has supplanted *nat* worship and other folk practices. In rural areas, however, elements of Buddhism and spirit worship have combined to form an integrated religious system that is peculiarly Burmese.

BURMESE BUDDHISM

Like the other great world religions, Buddhism was altered in form and content as it spread from one country to another. Its expansion began soon after the death of Gautama Buddha, who lived and taught in northern India in the sixth century B.C. The faith spread first throughout India and Ceylon and then was carried by monastic missionaries to the countries of Southeast and Central Asia and to China, Korea, and Japan. During the early centuries of Buddhism a schismatic movement concerning the Buddha's philosophical and spiritual teachings arose among Indian adherents. As a result Buddhism has been split for over 2,000 years into two major schools—the Mahayana, or Greater Vehicle, and the Hinayana, or Lesser Vehicle. Although in India many adherents of the Mahayana school objected to some of its beliefs and practices, this school nevertheless became the popular religion of Tibet, Nepal, Mongolia, China, Korea, Japan, and Vietnam.

The Hinayana form had become firmly established in Burma by the eleventh century. The preferred term its adherents use for their religion is Theravada, or the Way of the Elders. It embraces the system of beliefs recorded in the ancient Pali (see Glossary) literature and is believed by its followers and by many scholars to represent most faithfully the original ideas and intent of the Buddha. The Theravada form is the principal formal religion of Burma, Ceylon, Thailand, Laos, and Cambodia.

As an outgrowth of the Indian philosophies that preceded it, Theravada Buddhism uses ancient Hindu-Indian concepts as basic philosophical assumptions. Buddhism represents a departure from these older doctrines, but their primary assumptions remain vital to the mechanics of Buddhist theory. The Buddhist and the Hindu alike see the universe and all forms of life as parts of a process of eternal flux, which is cyclical and recurrent. For the individual, this means that his present life is merely a phase in an endless progression of events that neither ceases with death nor continues indefinitely in some heavenly afterlife. Life and death are merely alternate aspects of existence, marked by the transition points of birth and deanimation. The individual thus is essentially a role player, who is continually reborn in new guises, not all of which are necessarily human. It is possible, for example, that a man's next existence may be in the form of a god or of a nonhuman animal. This endless cycle of rebirth in which all creatures are involved in known as *samsara*, the wheel of rebirth or "perpetual wandering."

As samsaric existence proceeds, what the individual becomes is not determined by a creator god nor by a purely capricious fate. His future life, rather, is directly dependent upon his conduct in this and previous lives through the workings of *karma* (a religious doctrine that involves the workings of an impersonal law of causation—see Glossary). The daily acts of the individual have inevitable consequences that determine his future existence. Each act, mental or physical, affects the role that the individual will play in his next life.

Theoretically, through moral behavior and good deeds, a sincere Buddhist can anticipate a constantly improving status in social and material terms as well as in spiritual rewards. These are not the ultimate objectives of Buddhism, however, because the individual remains tied to the wheel of *karma* in an endless round of existences. The essence of Buddha's message, instead, is to effect a complete escape from the tyranny of rebirth. This escape manifests itself as an entrance into *nirvana*, a state of enlightenment and true wisdom, which is the ultimate goal of conscientious Buddhists. *Nirvana* involves the negation of all that the individual experiences during the cycle of rebirth and is described as the extinction of all greed, delusion, and hate. The Buddhist strives continually to perfect himself through the many stages of his existence, conquering worldly desires by concentration and meditation in an effort to achieve *nirvana*.

THE MONASTIC ORDER

The Pongyi

The *pongyi*, or Buddhist monk, is a living symbol of the Burmese religion. The essence of the monastic life is to make the most of the fortunate incarnation as a human being and thereby hasten progress toward *nirvana*. The monk's strict adherence to a life of self-denial and meditation, his renunciation of the world, and his observance of the rigid monastic vows are evidence of his greater nearness to the ultimate goal of all sincere Buddhists. It is his status in this regard that entitles him to the respect and support of the layman. The term *pongyi* literally means "great glory," indicating the great reverence in which the monk is held by those still involved in worldly pursuits. There is also an order of Buddhist nuns, but they are less numerous and are not accorded the honor that the monks receive.

Theravada Buddhism does not acknowledge the existence of a Supreme Being, nor is the Buddha a higher power who may be called upon to intervene in human affairs. In this context the *pongyi* is in no sense a religious intermediary but is concerned primarily with his own salvation. He is not obligated to perform any duties with respect to laymen. In practice, however, most monks expound the scriptures, give advice on village matters, and take part in religious ceremonies when requested to do so. Their function as village teachers is still carried on in many areas. Their functional value resides simply in their existence. Through gifts of food and support to the *pongyi* a layman increases his own merit and furthers his own search for *nirvana*.

The *pongyi* is subject to a total of 227 rules of conduct, which among other things prohibit taking food after midday, using any personal adornment, and accepting or using money. Should he violate any of the precepts, particularly major ones, such as the vow of chastity, he may be expelled from the monkhood. A *pongyi* is prohibited from owning anything other than the few things considered necessary for the monastic life, such as a begging bowl and the yellow robe.

It is impossible to give an exact figure for the number of monks in Burma at any one time because of the relatively easy entry and departure from the monastery. Many individuals enter the monkhood for only a short time and never intend to commit themselves for life. Those who take the monastic vows and make such a commitment are probably in the minority. One estimate placed the total number of monks at 800,000. This figure, however, apparently referred to all males, including the novices and students, who had spent some time in the monastery. Another estimate, considered fairly accurate in 1970, excluded novices and those who might stay temporarily in the monasteries and gave a more probable figure of 100,000.

The many men who become fully ordained *pongyis* and strictly observe the rules of the monastic order testify to the strong religious feeling that is the basis for much Burmese behavior. Although most are motivated by sincere belief, there are many monks who enter the monastery to escape some difficulty in the outside world. The gradual decline in monastic discipline, first noticed in the early years of the twentieth century, has persisted into the 1970s and continues to be a problem of great concern, particularly to the older and particularly learned monks and to serious Buddhist laymen. The monkhood has been criticized for the ignorance and illiteracy of some of its members, but others are noted scholars who have devoted their lives to a study of the Buddhist scriptures.

Monasteries

Outside nearly every Buddhist village in Burma is a monastery *(kyaung),* a fenced compound on sacred ground that contains the living quarters of the monks. Some monastery compounds contain several dwelling houses, and larger monasteries may have, in addition, separate buildings that are used as kitchens, bathhouses, sleeping quarters, and libraries. Pagodas are not usually part of a monastery compound.

The daily routine of the monastery is designed to encourage meditation and freedom from the cares of the world. Prescribed duties, other than those concerned with meditation, are few. Monks are expected to afford the people the opportunity to gain merit by contributing food as they circulate through the village in the early morning hours. This collection duty is usually performed by the younger monks and novices. No food is eaten after the noon meal, and the day is spent primarily in studying the scriptures, in teaching younger monks and novices, or in meditation. The education of the village children was formerly a major activity, but by 1970 this had become a responsibility of the secular schools. Despite the emphasis on meditation, the monastery is not isolated from everyday village life but, in fact, is the social hub of the village. It is often the center for the spirited and colorful Buddhist village festivals and has a great educational and formative influence on the lives of the villagers.

The Sangha

The *sangha,* or Buddhist monkhood, is a loosely structured institution. The primary requirements for membership are that one be a male and at least twenty years of age. A monk may leave the *sangha* at any time.

There is little in the way of formal organizational structure within the Burmese *sangha,* though such a structure did exist under the Burmese kings. At the top of an administrative hierarchy was the *thathanabaing,* a meritorious monk who was appointed by the king to serve as the head ecclesiastical authority. The country was divided into a number of districts, each under the leadership of a senior monk, who served mainly as an intermediary between the monasteries and the *thathanabaing.* At the bottom of the hierarchy were the monasteries, controlled by a senior monk or abbot.

The monastic hierarchy all but disappeared under the British, who showed no interest in promoting the *sangha*. As a result there has been little coordination within the *sangha*, and discipline has become a matter for each monastery to deal with individually. This factor of decreasing control has been one of the major reasons for what has been considered by the more devout Buddhists to be a decline in morality and discipline within many monasteries.

There are a number of traditional sectarian differences among Burmese Buddhists. Some of these sects are based on differences of opinion as to the prevailing nonatheist doctrine of Buddhism, though such differences have always been slight and the sects have not attracted many people. Although sectarian differences based on points of monastic conduct also exist, they are of minor importance, and many laymen are unaware of them. Of far greater importance than these sectarian differences are the developing associations within the *sangha*, which cut across all sectarian lines and seek to organize large bodies of monks for action programs.

The Sangha and the Government

The *sangha* is seen by the Burmese as something detached from the rest of society, although ultimately dependent upon it. The sincere monk is bound by rules of monastic discipline to avoid secular involvements and devote himself to religion. Yet the great local influence wielded by the monks, partially through their roles as educators and advisers on personal and moral problems, has made them traditionally powerful agents of social control.

The Burmese monarchies recognized the potential of the *sangha* and maintained parallel civil and ecclesiastical agencies to censor and discipline the monkhood. The latent political power inherent in the *sangha's* role became apparent during the latter part of the colonial period when a number of urban monks became actively involved in the nationalist movement. Some of them became martyrs to the nationalist cause, although participation in politics generally met with disapproval as a departure from the rule of monastic discipline. Despite this disapproval, political activity and demonstrations by members of the *sangha* have occurred from time to time since independence, even though the national cause is no longer an issue.

After gaining independence, the Burmese government was anxious to restore the *sangha* to the position it had occupied during the days of the Burmese kings. Active programs of legislation were initiated, and efforts were made to increase the *sangha's* opportunities and incentives for formal study. These efforts stressed the unity of religion and government and, as a result, Buddhism was declared the state religion by a 1961 constitutional amendment.

The relationship between the government and the *sangha* changed abruptly after the coup of 1962. The new chairman of the Revolutionary Council reserved most of the religious legislation of the previous government and adopted a policy tantamount to a separation of church and state. Because there is disagreement as to where the religious and secular lines of authority should be drawn, relations between the *sangha* and the government often have been strained since the coup.

BUDDHIST CEREMONY AND RELIGIOUS SYMBOLISM

Pagodas

Theravada Buddhism, as practiced in Burma, contains relatively little religious symbolism and has no churches in the Western sense nor any formal religious services. The most important religious symbols, however, are associated with Buddhist beliefs and are obvious and omnipresent. The thousands of pagodas, raising their gilded spires, express dramatically the position of the formal religion. The number and size of these pagodas are among the most striking features of the culture, as are the ubiquitous yellow-robed monks. Images and paintings of the Buddha appear everywhere—on pagoda platforms and monasteries, in homes and classrooms, at bus entrances, and on wall calendars.

There are many kinds of pagodas, and at least one dominates the scene in every village. The basic practical function of all of them, ad distinguished from their symbolic character, is that of a reliquary. The most important pagodas are shrines containing sacred relics— remains and images of either the Buddha or of his noteworthy followers. Many pagodas are said to contain a hair of the Buddha, and the world famous Shwedagon pagoda in Rangoon was built to contain eight hairs of the Buddha. One in particular, the Botataung pagoda, in Rangoon, was destroyed during World War II. In the postwar reconstruction of the building, the fabled hair and other relics were actually found in an elaborate container that had been enclosed in the base of the old shrine.

Domestic Shrines

Most Burmese houses have some kind of Buddhist shrine, either a small picture or image of the Buddha. There are, however, no prescribed rituals that are observed in connection with it. Some families place daily offerings of fresh water, food, and flowers before the shrine, and members of the family may genuflect before it while Buddhist scriptures are being recited. In theory, nonetheless, devotional prayer has no place in Buddhism because Buddha is not a high deity to whom one can appeal. The Buddhist has no cause to pray at such a shrine in his home or at a pagoda but only pays homage to the Buddha. In some villages and in many urban areas small groups have been formed to meet in the evening and meditate or receive instruction in Buddhist doctrine and philosophy.

Buddhist Holidays

The Burmese are primarily an agricultural people keenly aware of the changing seasons. All of Burma's religious holidays are calendrical events, indicating the importance of these seasonal changes. The most important one is Thingyan, the Water Festival. It occurs in April but is not precisely datable because the Burmese lunar calendar varies in its yearly cycle. Thingyan has no basis in Buddhist scripture, and its original significance was probably that of an agricultural ritual that acquired Buddhist meaning and symbolism. The ceremonial exchanges of water that mark the holiday are part of a tradition borrowed from India. Thingyan is believed to signal the descent of Thagya Min, king of the *nats,* from his mountain home. For traditional Burmese it marks the coming of the new year and anticipates the end of the hot season and the coming of the monsoon rains. Water symbolizes purity and generally represents a gift that brings good results. During Thingyan ceremonial gifts of water are made to the monasteries and to the monks. There are formal exchanges of water and a ritual washing of sacred objects, such as pagodas and images of the Buddha.

In the villages Thingyan is the only holiday observed by everyone. All work comes to a halt for about three days, and classes are dismissed from school. As the holiday wears on, the air of solemnity and restraint declines, expecially in urban centers, and the water exchanges become jovial mutual dousings by peer groups and individuals. In rural areas such riotous behavior is restricted mostly to the youngsters.

Another important holiday is Buddha Day, which occurs in mid-May and commemorates the birth, enlightenment, and death of the Buddha. It is marked on the lunar calendar by the full moon of Kason and is ritually celebrated by sprinkling the roots of the sacred Bo trees, under which Buddha achieved enlightenment.

Another important holiday is Dhammasetkya, which occurs at the full moon of Waso in mid-July. It commemorates the Buddha's first sermon and his renunciation of worldly life for that of a mendicant ascetic. It initiates a period of restricted social activity, comparable to the Christian Lent, when neither marriages and other personal celebrations nor any public festival may be held. The day itself is the occasion for offerings of flowers at pagodas and sacred places as well as the donation of robes to the monks and the strict observance of Buddhist precepts.

Second in importance to Thingyan is the mid-October Festival of Lights known as Thadingyut. Its arrival signifies the end of the Dhammasetkya period as well as the end of the rainy season. It is an occasion for great joy among the Burmese, who express their high spirits by lighting thousands of lamps and candles on trees, houses, monasteries, and pagoda platforms. Explanation given for the ritual is that it is the anniversary of the descent of the Buddha from the heavens. Gifts are made to the monks, and families take this time to visit pagodas and other holy places.

Tazaungdaing, which follows the Festival of Lights by a lunar month, is more widely celebrated in Lower Burma than in Upper Burma. It is the primary occasion for holding ceremonies in which the community presents robes, bowls, and other monastic necessities to the monks. The traditional custom of holding all-night weaving competitions is a featured part of Tazaungdaing in many communities. Honor is awarded to the unmarried girl who first completes the five yards of cloth necessary for a monk's robe.

The final calendrical event of national significance is the Harvest Festival, occurring in late February. Like most other holidays, it falls on a Buddhist duty day (*ubonei*) and has assumed Buddhist connotations. It is, however, more directly concerned with *nat* propitiation because the intervention of these powerful spirits is needed for a successful harvest.

In addition to the nationally celebrated holidays, there are many local pagoda festivals, which occur annually during the hot season, from March through May. These colorful festivals center on the symbolic Buddhist pagodas and have the atmosphere of a carnival or county fair rather than that of a purely religious observance. Public entertainment in the form of fireworks, circuses, and plays ordinarily accompanies the celebration.

Routine and Periodic Observances and Rituals

The donation of food to the Buddhist monks is a daily event in the life of the average Burmese Buddhist. It is the householder's best opportunity to improve his *karma* regularly through performing a good deed. The monk is bestowing a favor through his visit to a home because it gives the householder a chance to earn merit. The daily ritual represents a reciprocal responsibility for both the donor and the recipient. At least one monk or a novice passes each house in the village or town, receiving contributions of rice or a few vegetables in his alms bowl. There is no acknowledgement on the part of the monk nor any suggestion of a favor being granted because of the ritual nature of the event. Monks are occasionally given breakfast at the donor's home in elaboration of this ritual. This earns even greater merit for the donor.

Another periodically observed religious event is the duty day, which occurs almost weekly. These duty days occur at the full and dark moons of each month and on the eighth day after each, punctuating secular life in much the same way as the Christian Sabbath. Devout Buddhists refrain from working on duty days and visit the monastery instead to hear the scripture recited by a monk. Older people may observe such ascetic discipline as fasting after midday. There are some indications that only a small segment of the rural population regularly visits the monastery on these days. It appears that the merit acquired through such attendance is not great enough to compensate for the interruption of normal activity.

There are several Buddhist rituals that occur at important points in the life cycle of the individual. The first ceremony takes place when the child is about a week old and consists of a ritual cleaning, during which the baby's head is shaved. There is no formal ritual attached to naming a child, although the occasion may involve elaborate feasting and entertainment. The name is largely determined by reference to astrological interpretations. Whereas Buddhist doctrine acknowledges no relationship with this type of determinism, monks are often the respected interpreters of signs and omens. Technically, such acts represent a repudiation of monastic discipline and are frowned upon by the *sangha*.

The most important life cycle ritual is the *shinbyu*, the initiation of every boy as a novice in the Buddhist monastic order. The *shinbyu* ceremony includes a large amount of religious symbolism. An individual is not eligible to become a *pongyi* before the age of twenty, but the high cultural value attached to monastic life imposes this ceremony on adolescent boys. The social necessity of the initiation reinforces the spiritual value of the act and adds to the status of the *shinbyu*.

The *shinbyu* has a considerable effect on the social role and behavior of the boy experiencing initiation. When the youth discards his ceremonial costume and accepts the monk's yellow robe, his life style is abruptly transformed from that of carefree childhood to that of austere monastic discipline. It is a remarkable transition in terms of the behavioral demands upon the youth and the change in social attitude expressed toward him. This monastic life is usually temporary, but thereafter the youth is expected to be more mature and responsible. Personal choice determines how long the boy stays in the monastery. Few persist in the monastic role, although they may return to it in later years.

The *shinbyu,* as well as the comparable *natwin* (ear-piercing) ceremony for girls, may also be the occasion for an almsgiving celebration in which gifts are presented to the local monastery. The cost of these gifts and other festivities sometimes constitutes such a great expense that the sponsor's family is forced to sell valued possessions or go into debt. The elaborate and expensive ceremonial is nowhere called for in Buddhism, and some Buddhist monks have commented with distaste upon these extravagant gestures. Participants, however, justify their action in terms of the religious merit acquired by the donor.

Neither a funeral nor the service of a monk is strictly necessary at the burial of the dead. Usually, however, there is a relatively simple funeral service in which a monk plays the cheif religious role. Unlike some Southeast Asian people, the Burmese do not cremate their dead, except in the case of famous monks and some wealthy or especially pious people. The monks lead the funeral procession to the grave and recite scriptural passages that are calculated to remind the mourners that life is preparation for death and the gateway to a fuller existence. This Buddhist interpretation introduces a rational element into an emotionally charged situation. The element of social crisis and uncertainty is reflected in the recognition of supernatural forces unrelated to Buddhist doctrine. A ceremony may be performed to make certain that the soul, believed to be a butterfly, has flown from the body. Money is placed with the deceased, for there is a mythical river that must be crossed and the ferryman must be paid.

THE ROLE OF BUDDHISM IN BURMESE SOCIETY

Role in Daily Life

Educated Burmese often maintain that Buddhism is not a religion but a way of life and, in attempting to dissociate it from supernaturalism, they cite the fact that it is a pervasive element in Burmese culture, influencing every aspect of social and individual life. Buddhism provides a moral code and serves as a framework against which most Burmese behavior is measured and interpreted. There is no clear line between the secular and the religious considerations of daily life, and Buddhism gives meaning and significance to activities that are only slightly related to religion. It influences the reactions to any given situation and becomes a point of reference for the typical Burmese interpretation of events.

The high status value attached to being a good Buddhist encourages general conformity to Buddhist behavior norms that define moral and upright behavior. The average person tries to observe the five basic precepts that enjoin Buddhist morality. These are to abstain from taking life, from stealing, from committing adultery, from telling a lie, and from partaking of intoxicants. These and numerous other precepts are socially valued because they permit the observer to acquire merit that will ensure an improved future existence.

In reality, all of these rules, even the most basic ones, are commonly interpreted in terms of a given situation. No one will pretend that these ideals of conduct are rigidly observed by all individuals. In defining social relationships and social situations, however, the Burmese do pay deference to them. For example, the fisherman is often stigmatized and relegated to a low social status because his occupation violates the first precept against taking life. Even though he may not actually kill the fish, his action in removing them to dry land causes them to die naturally, and he is aware of violating a fundamental Buddhist principle. Most fishermen, therefore, are non-Buddhists; if they are Buddhists, their intention is the determining factor in judging moral rectitude.

Strict Buddhists will have no part of any occupation that is directly or indirectly involved in taking life. Others may rationalize their vocation is a number of ways, or they may attempt to compensate for their bad *karma* by the performance of meritorious deeds. Even those who outwardly are substantial citizens worthy of respect and deference will be held in low esteem if they have intentionally and repeatedly violated the precepts.

Role in Intergroup Relations

As the dominant faith, Buddhism enjoys a unique position in society as an important symbol of Burmese culture. The number of Burmese who are professedly non-Buddhist is extremely small, although there are some large ethnic minorities that differ from the national norm. Even among these people, however, Buddhism has been transmitted with fairly good success in an effort to unify national society. As part of the assimilation of these groups into the national culture, the process is a continuing one. Proselytizing among the non-Buddhist minorities constituted much of the religious revival that began after independence. A school was established at Yegu for educating and training special missionary monks who carried Buddhism into the Chin, Kachin, and Kayah hill areas where they had been forbidden to propagate their faith before independence.

The significance of this missionary effort is twofold. Primarily it illustrates the value of Buddhism as an important cultural theme and as a source of pride upon which nationalist feelings can be based. The Burmese Buddhist views himself as the agent of civilization bringing enlightenment and culture to the non-Buddhist minorities. Any feeling of superiority that the Burmese express may well be voiced in terms of the presence or absence of Buddhism among another people.

Buddhist missionary activity also illustrates the nonexclusive character of Burmese Buddhism. Non-Burmese are not only eligible to become Buddhists; they may do so without abandoning their traditional beliefs and customs. Symbolically, therefore, something is gained and little, if anything, is lost.

The religious affiliations of the foreign minorities have deterred assimilation in some cases, as with the Indians and Pakistanis, though they are of minimal importance in other cases, as with the Chinese. Buddhism originated in India but died out there long ago as a significant movement. Most Indians in Burma are Hindus, and most Pakistanis are Muslims. Religious differences have accentuated the hostile attitudes that the Burmese and the Indian immigrants have felt toward ony another. Although Buddhism is tolerant of competing faiths, the individual Burmese is easily aroused by remarks or actions he feels are insulting to his religion. Many incidents of violence between Buddhists and Muslims or Hindus have occurred for such reasons.

Except for a small number of Chinese Muslims, the Chinese minority group is of little significance as a deviant religious element. Buddhism is a part of Chinese religious tradition, although it no longer has maximum influence in that culture. The religious customs of the Chinese in Burma do not usually parallel those of the Burmese, though both are often Buddhist. The Chinese, in fact, may be ignorant of much of the content of Burmese religion. Ascendant Chinese families, however, often adopt Burmese religious forms, particularly if these forms have important prestige value, which they find useful. It is not unusual to find prominent Chinese merchants erecting Burmese-style pagodas or sponsoring elaborate shinbyus for their sons, especially if their wives are Burmese. The true content of Burmese religion may become more important to second-generation Chinese, who often are the children of intermarriage and may identify with Burmese culture. Generally, the Chinese community in Burma, as in other communities throughout Southeast Asia, is not noted for any strong religious orientation.

SPIRIT WORSHIP

A number of indigenous animistic beliefs and practices combine with Buddhism to form a unified system that is the sum of Burmese religious behavior. Buddhist doctrine offers a way to ultimate salvation in the distant future but offers little comfort or aid in the more immediate dangers and emergencies of daily life. In Burma, and in other Buddhist countries of Southeast Asia, security in daily affairs is obtained through the propitiation of spirits, astrology, fortunetelling, the use of charms and amulets, magical tattooing, and alchemy. In 1970 the people, especially those in rural villages, still consulted their astrologer, made offerings to spirits and, at the same time, observed Buddhist beliefs and practices as related to their spiritual existence in the next life.

The most important category of spirits consists of the *nats*, and their propitiation is called *nat* worship. The *nats* are a heterogeneous group incorporating a central core of thirty-seven main or royal *nats*; the *nats* of the fields, trees, wind, and rain; the house guardian *nats*; and the harvest *nats*. The *nats* are chiefly evil powers and, if ignored, can bring trouble to mankind. At best, they sometimes offer protection from other more dangerous *nats*.

Religious practices relating to the *nats* include propitiation through offerings of money, flowers, or food at special shrines. In many villages there are women who act as spirit mediums and use their close contact with the spirit world to foretell the future, to attempt to cure illness, and to gain the favor of the *nats* for other reasons.

To a considerable extent, belief in *nats* is interwoven into the context of Buddhism. *Nats* appear as characters in legends of the Buddha, which are commonly taught to children. Scenes depicting *nats* appear on many pagoda platforms, and at times of crisis a Buddhist monk may be called so that his presence will counteract the influence of the spirits. The *sangha* officially condemns *nat* worship, astrology, and magical beliefs as being contrary to Buddhism. This feeling is shared by many educated urban Burmese, but belief in the spirits and the desire to know the future are still too strongly implanted to be suppressed.

SECTION II. POLITICAL

CHAPTER 8

POLITICAL SYSTEM AND VALUES

The political system, developed under military rule after March 1962 and still in effect in 1971, concentrated government authority in the Revolutionary Council. In his capacity as chairman of the council, General Ne Win, leader of the group that seized power in 1962, headed the government and was vested with supreme executive, legislative, and judicial authority. Simultaneously, he was leader of the nation's only authorized political organization, the Burma Socialist Program Party (BSPP) (see ch. 9, Political Dynamics).

The Revolutionary Council's concepts and aims for reconstructing society, as reflected in party documents and statements of its leaders, are referred to by the leadership as the Burmese Way to Socialism. On matters relating to government leadership, ideology was pragmatic, claiming that concepts and practices would be borrowed and utilized without concern for their source. As it developed, the ideological framework became authoritarian socialism, conforming broadly to the East European communist models in its provision for highly centralized government controls and utilization of mass organizations under parallel party control to gain broad support.

General Ne Win stated that the military-directed government and the party, as established in 1962, were transitional institutions in the development of a socialist democratic state. He indicated that the party would be transformed into a "people's party." The socialist democratic state in its fully matured form was not defined, but in 1971 indications were that the existing system of controls would continue as the framework and doctrine for future developments.

When it assumed control, the Revolutionary Council proclaimed that parliamentary democracy had failed. It proceeded to abolish all elective governmental bodies and establish organs whose membership was appointed and closely controlled by the highly centralized authority of the military elite. A hierarchical organization was established under the control of the Central Security and Administrative Committee as the primary means to govern the nation. Committees known at each level as the Security and Administrative

143

Committee extended down to the villages. Many of the governmental institutions and practices of a routine nature were continued from the parliamentary period and reoriented to be consistent with the Burmese Way to Socialism. The party had the function of providing leadership and organizing public support for government policies and programs (see ch. 9, Political Dynamics). In effect, it was an instrument of governmental policy with powers paralleling that of formal government agencies.

The traditional indifference of the largely rural population and of Buddhist layman toward participation in government tended to restrict support for government operations and programs no matter what the system of rule. This phenomenon was a deterrent to the efforts of the Ne Win regime to establish a viable government, as it had been in the period of parliamentary government before 1962.

Political values of the majority of the population traditionally have been strongly oriented toward traditional Buddhist thought. Avowing its aim to remold society, the Revolutionary Government of the Union of Burma made a strong effort to develop a new set of values in which traditional thought would be combined and made congruous with contemporary socialist democratic values devised by the council. The major sources for the social democratic values were Marxism-Leninism and the statements and writings of Aung San, leading founder of independent Burma.

Lack of cooperation and intermittent insurgency, continuing into 1971, by minority ethnic groups who resented control by a Burman-dominated central government had a strongly adverse effect on the Revolutionary Government's efforts to unify the nation. They also had been a source of serious difficulty under parliamentary government before 1962.

BACKGROUND

The experience under British colonial rule had fundamental influences on the development of Burma's governmental institutions that were particularly apparent during the parliamentary period from 1948 to 1962. Although parliamentary government was abolished by the Revolutionary Council, British influences, many of them modified by the system of centralized control, were much in evidence in governmental institutions and practices in 1971.

The British introduced a legal code which, in practice, was combined with Burmese traditions. After 1962 the Ne Win regime politicized important segments of the legal system, but many of the British influences continued.

The British also provided the example for parliamentary government and a modern civil service. Although these and other innovations were not entirely in consonance with Burmese culture and were directed by persons of non-Burmese origin, they furnished a basis on which to build a more modern state. In addition, the British completed the conversion of local government from a system based on personal loyalties to one oriented on government service within a fixed territorial administration (see ch. 3, Historical Setting).

Although British policy called for preeminence of British interests, Burmese nationalism and demands for self-government gained attention in the early twentieth century. The British policy of according privileges and preferences to non-Burman minority ethnic groups in order to maintain control over the Burmans encouraged ethnocentrism, which after independence was a major deterrent to national unity.

After World War II Aung San, one of the Thirty Comrades who fled to Japan under charges of subversive activities in the early days before the Japanese invasion of the country, was instrumental in obtaining British consent to separate nationhood and the calling of the Constituent Assembly in 1947 not long before his assassination.

The system for designating political administrative divisions and subdivisions of territories developed under British rule was adopted in 1948 and has remained essentially the same since 1962. Burma proper is divided into the seven divisions of Mandalay, Irrawaddy, Pegu, Magwe, Tenasserim, Arakan, and Sagaing. The remaining area includes the states of Shan, Kawthule (formerly Karen), Kayah (formerly Karenni), and Kachin and the Chin Special Division (see fig. 3). As defined in the 1947 Constitution, the word *state* meant the executive or legislative authority of the union and such other jurisdictions as the Constitution and Parliament recognized. The Shan, Kachin, and Karenni states were established by the 1948 Constitution, and provisions were made for the creation of a Karen state. Various changes and modifications in state designations and boundaries were effected after 1948. The twelve major entities were divided into districts, numbering forty-eight in 1970. Districts, in turn, were divided into townships. The lowest political administrative unit in the countryside was the village; in towns and cities, it was the ward. Although it was not a part of the formal hierarchical structure, the village tract, consisting of from five to ten villages, was utilized for administration of various government programs.

Under the Revolutionary Government the relationship between political administrative organizations and six military regions known as commands was particularly close. Military officers of the commands exercised control over all the positions in the political administrative organizations and occupied positions from which they could exercise overall authority, down to and including the district level.

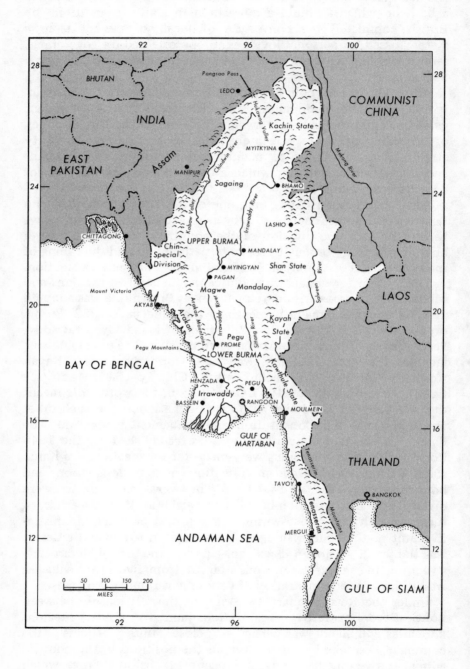

Figure 3. Political Administrative Divisions of Burma, 1971

146

The Constitution embodied the principle of popular sovereignty and made provision for four main organs of government; the presidency, the Parliament, a union government, and a union judiciary. Executive power rested primarily with the prime minister, and he and his cabinet constituted the union government, which was collectively responsible to the Chamber of Deputies. Legislative power was vested exclusively in two chambers of Parliament: the Chamber of Deputies, whose membership was based on population of constituent jurisdictions; and the Chamber of Nationalities, a name indicative of the non-Burman ethnic character of some of its constituencies. A fixed schedule allocated a total of 125 seats in the Chamber of Nationalities to the constituent states, Chin Special Division, and the remaining territories of the Union of Burma. Most representatives were elected to this chamber; exceptions included the inherited seats in the Shan State and Kayah State (see ch. 3, Historical Setting).

The relationships between the territorial divisions of the union as described in the Constitution constituted a cross between a federal and a unitary system rather than a purely federal structure as the name Union of Burma might imply. The divisions of Burma proper were governed directly from Rangoon, but the other territories were given some degree of autonomy. In the territories there was a division of responsibilities under which certain powers were reserved for the central government. The Constitution granted the right to secede after ten years to the jurisdictions outside Burma proper, except that Kachin State was specifically denied this privilege. An amendment in 1951 also denied this right to the newly created Karen State, later known as Kawthule State.

Fundamental individual rights relating to equality before the law, freedom of conscience, and freedom of religion were included in Chapter Two of the Constitution. Some of the rights listed were subject to considerations of public order, morality, and health, but they had legal force. The special position of Buddhism as the faith of the majority of Burmese citizens was recognized in this chapter. In 1961 an amendment made Buddhism the state religion. Certain privileges that were intended for guidance purposes but lacked legal recognition were enumerated in Chapter Four. These concerned the privilege to work, maintenance in old age and sickness, education, and leisure.

The Constitution did not mention the word *socialism,* but the socialist and welfare state orientation was reflected in those sections that set forth the relationship of the state to private property. The rights of private property and private initiative in economic matters were guaranteed, but the doctrine was enunciated that these rights were not to be used in a manner that would be detrimental to the general public. The Constitution also declared that private property could be limited, expropriated, nationalized, or acquired by the central government when required by the public interest. It was specified that the Burmese state would be the ultimate owner of all land, but there was no provision in the Constitution for compensation or reimbursement for assumed land.

NATURE OF THE POLITICAL SYSTEM

Centralized Military Control

In 1962, when General Ne Win seized key governmental installations and imprisoned Prime Minister U Nu, a number of his supporters, and many other political leaders, it was not immediately clear as to what kind of political system would be established. The change was made almost without bloodshed, and only communist leaders called the action a coup at that time. Deposed politicians and minority ethnic elements tended to look upon military rule as an interim measure and an interruption of parliamentary government. Within a month, however, the new government, called the Revolutionary Government of the Union of Burma and headed by the Revolutionary Council of seventeen military officers, initiated a system of highly centralized control and rule by decree.

Upon taking over the government, the council announced that existing laws and institutions would remain in effect until changed or superseded by new laws. On March 3, 1962, the national Parliament was dissolved, and soon all elective positions were filled by appointed officials. Officially, the Constitution of 1947 was not repealed or suspended. In practice, only those provisions that had not been superseded by action of the Revolutionary Council were applicable, and the council tended to avoid making references to them.

The regime made no provisions for elections or for expression of opinions except through party-controlled organizations and on some minor issues in the press. The power of the military was supreme, and military officers or persons approved by the regime controlled government operations and security at all levels of government. The nucleus of Ne Win followers attempted to set the example and was the guiding force of the BSPP, which was put forward as a transitional organization in the building of a "people's party." All opposition parties were abolished in 1964, and after that time all social and professional organizations came under the party.

Observers noted that the attitude of the military elite reflected an atmosphere of confidence, readiness to grasp at quick solutions, and fluctuations between inaction and aggressive action. At the same time the concentration of the decisionmaking process frequently caused leaders in the lower echelons of government to postpone action or resort to committee solutions on matters that required decision. Long delays ensued over minor questions while instructions were awaited from the central authorities.

Government Ideology

The concepts and ideas expressed in the documents and public statements of the Revolutionary Council and reflected in the institutions and practices developed after 1962 combine the influences of traditional Burmese values, Marxist-Leninist precepts, and Aung San's formulations for independent Burma. In 1971 the military regime's philosophy of government was identical to the party ideology (see ch. 9, Political Dynamics). The Revolutionary Council's political guidelines were to be found in: a party document of April 1962 entitled *The Burmese Way to Socialism*; a statement of party philosophy of January 1963 called the *System of Correlation of Man and His Environment*; a booklet published in September 1964 called *The Specific Characteristics of the Burmese Socialist Program Party;* and the speeches of General Ne Win and other party leaders at the Fourth Party Seminar in 1969.

The declared aims of the military rulers reflected in these sources were to remold society, transform existing institutions to meet the special needs of Burma as interpreted by the leadership and replace parliamentary democracy with socialist democracy. The structure and operations of government were left to the Revolutionary Council, the only governmental organization mentioned in the party documents. The socialist democracy envisaged by the leaders would have centralized control of society, and the leadership would combine the will of the individual and the group. The people would follow the socialist leaders.

Party leaders did not make clear what the exact nature and structure of government would be after the transition to socialist democracy. The statements of General Ne Win indicated that the general framework of the existing system of controls would continue as the foundation for future developments. Speaking about the draft party constitution in 1969, he observed "We have yet to openly seek and obtain the people's mandate. We had to assume the responsibility and the leadership because the Revolutionary Council was not born of deliberate design and preparation but was brought into being by dire necessity . . . To put the affairs of state on an enduring constitutional basis a constitution must be found and time is now ripe for that task."

Noting that the Revolutionary Council resembled a military council and had as its backbone the armed forces, he suggested, without fixing a time, the transition to a political system headed by a party. Since the military are also the elite in the party his proposal, if adopted, would not change the basic power structure in the foreseeable future.

The Revolutionary Council's major effort to elaborate its philosophy, *The System of Correlation of Man and His Environment,* used phrases from Marxist-Leninism, traditional Buddhist thought, abstract metaphysics, and everyday thinking. Attempting to provide a philosophy that met both material and spiritual needs, it gave considerable emphasis to humanistic factors in the historical process. Individual freedoms were hardly mentioned, but the state's responsibilities in the reconstruction of society were emphasized (see ch. 9, Political Dynamics).

The economic goals set forth in the basic documents were to raise the standard of living by expanding production, to assure everyone of a means of livelihood, and to create a society where justice would prevail. Individuals would contribute according to their ability and receive on the basis of the quality and quantity of their production. An effort would be made to narrow the gap between the more affluent and the poor. Differences in economic status would continue, however, because men do not have equal mental and physical capacities. The means by which these goals would be achieved called for the planned development of all the means of production and entailed the nationalization of all facets of the economy.

Aung San, an authentic national hero because of his exploits in the independence movement, came to be revered by the Ne Win regime as one of the founding fathers of Burmese socialist democracy. His "Blueprint for Free Burma," written in Japan before World War II, contained many of the general concepts that found expression and practice after 1962. Aung San declared, "What we want is a strong state administration . . . There shall be only one nation, one state, one party, one leader . . . Everyone must submit to the state which is supreme over the individual." At one political gathering he stated that sovereignty must be fully and firmly vested in the people, but at the same time he indicated that a centralized authority, not necessarily an elective government, would ensure basic rights and provide for the needs of the people.

The ideology, when viewed in its entirety, envisioned the Revolutionary Government as being on the side of independence, socialism, national unity, socialist democracy, and the people in struggles where the opposing forces included imperialism, capitalism, separatism, and leftist-rightist extremism.

150

STRUCTURE AND FUNCTIONING OF GOVERNMENT

The Administrative Framework

The framework of the government in 1971 contained many of the ministries and much of the routine administrative machinery established during the parliamentary period. The most significant innovations after 1962 were the concentration of power in the Revolutionary Council and the creation of a control apparatus consisting of what the government called "security and administrative committees." There was no document that fixed the structure of government, and the Revolutionary Council created, changed, or abolished whatever organizations it saw fit.

The Revolutionary Council

The Revolutionary Council, representing the power of the military elite, stood at the apex of the governmental structure. In early 1971 there were eleven members in addition to the chairman, all selected by General Ne Win. Tenure of office and the number of members depended on the desires of the chairman. Seven of the original seventeen members had resigned or been removed by 1965. The council accorded virtually unlimited powers to its chairman, and a feeling of trust and mutual dependence appeared to prevail between the members and General Ne Win. The extent to which differing views were expressed in council meetings was generally not made known; indications were that after 1966, when economic problems caused the regime to reevaluate its position, General Ne Win tended to delay when there was not consensus among members.

Students of government, in analyzing the bureaucracy after independence, noted that Colonel Hla Han, a graduate physician, and Colonel Maung Lwin, a trained army physician, were among the few council members who had had advanced training. The council members' capacity to perform as government administrators and planners was put into question in the late 1960s when many state-directed economic programs lagged (see ch. 11, Character and Structure of the Economy). Indications in the early 1970s were, however, that council members and other high-level administrators were performing more efficiently, having gained from their experience of the past several years.

The major organizations subordinate to the Revolutionary Council at the national level were the Council of Ministers and the Burma Socialist Program Party. The concentration of control over these organizations and their principal subdivisions, which included the ministries, the Central Security and Administrative Committee, and the party central committees, was accomplished by appointing council members to head them (see fig. 4).

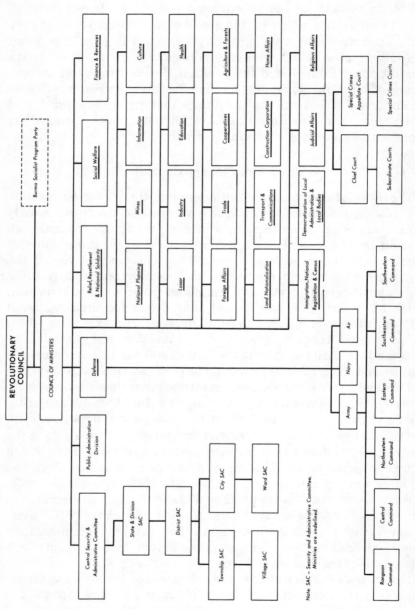

Figure 4. Organization of the Revolutionary Government of the Union of Burma, December 1970

For example, in early 1971 the chairman of the Revolutionary Council was also chief of staff of the Burma Defense Services, head of the party and its central committees, chairman of the Council of Ministers, and minister of defense. A second council member was vice chief of staff of the Burma Defense Services, minister of national planning, minister of finance and revenues, and general secretary of the party. A third held the portfolios of five ministries: home affairs; judicial affairs; religious affairs; immigration, national registration and census; and democratization of local administration and local bodies. He was also chairman of the Central Security and Administrative Committee. Another member was head of four ministries: information; culture; social welfare; and relief, resettlement and national solidarity.

One council member commanded a military region called the Central Command but did not serve as head of a ministry. Many council members also served as chairmen or members of one or more committees and boards concerned with policy, coordination, and execution of programs in addition to their ministerial and party assignments.

The Council of Ministers

Since the membership of the Council of Ministers was nearly identical to that of the Revolutionary Council, it was difficult to differentiate its functions from those of the council. As chairman of the Council of Ministers, General Ne Win organized subordinate elements and made appointments at his discretion. Ministry assignments were made on the basis of personal preference, and ministers sometimes headed several ministries simultaneously without any obvious relationship between their respective functions.

Under the Council of Ministers, the Public Administration Division concerned itself with personnel policies, administrative procedures, and the development of organizational concepts. The Secretariat in each of the twenty-four ministries played an important role in directing administrative affairs. Under parliamentary rule before 1962 and in the early years of the Revolutionary Government, the secretary, the most influential individual in the ministry, was a senior civil servant in nearly every ministry. By 1970 more than half of the civilian secretaries had been replaced by military officers and, in at least one 'ministry, the secretary's position has been abolished and replaced by that of deputy minister.

The ministries carry out the normal functions associated with their designations. Some, however, include corporations that function as business enterprises. For example, the People's Bank of the Union of Burma is a part of the Ministry of Finance and Revenues, and the Myanma Oil Corporation is under the Ministry of Mines.

The Security and Administrative Committees

The Central Security and Administrative Committee had primary responsibility for administering laws, programs, and directives, coordinating government operations, and maintaining public discipline. All other agencies under the Council of Ministers were required to work in concert with it. Security and administrative committees at all lower levels were controlled by the central committee and carried out similar functions.

The groundwork for a new system of controls was laid during the 1958—60 caretaker period with a revision of the previous system of governing councils as the leadership sought to promote cooperation between the military and the public. In 1962 the military leaders replaced the governing councils with security and administrative committees at all levels. Before 1958 the governing councils were directed by politicians and civil servants and frequently included elected representatives of the area that the council governed. The new committees were staffed entirely by appointed officials and, down to district level, were headed by military officers. At lower levels they were under the control of the local military commanders but were frequently chaired by local leaders.

The commanding officers of the six military regional commands were the most powerful representatives of the government in their areas of responsibility. Each held one or more Security and Administrative Committee chairmanships in the major political subdivisions within his command. Other military officers, with the rank of colonel or lieutenant colonel, were chairmen of the governing committees at division or equivalent level, and usually district chairmen held the rank of major. In addition, in 1969 four of the regional commanders were appointed to deputy minister positions in the central government.

At all levels the most important elements of the security and administrative committees, in addition to the military, were the police and the government administration representative. The representative held the title of commissioner at division and constituent state level, district officer (deputy commissioner) in the districts, township officer in townships, and headman at the village level. The commissioners and their equivalents worked under the general supervision of the Ministry of Home Affairs and carried out the tasks concerned with routine administration. At district and higher levels they were civil servants appointed by the central government.

Acknowledged and acceptable local leaders were usually selected as township officers and village headmen (see ch. 4, Social Systems and Values).

The Judiciary

When the Revolutionary Council proclaimed on March 7, 1962, that existing laws would continue in effect until repealed or amended, it provided also that established courts would continue to function. Major changes were initiated within a month, and by 1971 the courts and laws had been revamped to make them accord with the Burmese Way to Socialism. Over 115 laws, including new and amending acts, were promulgated from 1962 to 1968.

The Chief Court, the court of final appeal for all cases except special crimes, was created on April 1, 1962, and the Supreme Court and the High Court were abolished. Also, at this time, certain rights providing recourse to constitutional remedies, such as habeas corpus, mandamus, and prohibition, were suspended. A new category of courts was created in 1962 to deal with special crimes. These were the special crimes courts, established in the larger towns and cities, and the Special Crimes Appellate Court.

In early 1971 the Ministry of Judicial Affairs included the courts, the attorney general's office, the inspector general of prisons, and the Translation and Law Revision Department. Colonel Kyaw Soe, the minister of judicial affairs, directed the hierarchy of security and administrative committees and the National People's Police, thereby controlling both law enforcement and judicial functions. In addition, he was chairman of the Revolutionary Government's Judicial Affairs Committee.

The court system included the regular civil courts and ordinary criminal courts that functioned under the Chief Court. In 1971 the chief justice was Maung Maung, a British-trained jurist. The courts retained many of the law codes and practices from the parliamentary period while attempting to incorporate the concepts of the new order. The special crimes courts were not under the control of the Chief Court. They worked closely with the security and administrative committees, and appeals were heard by the Special Crimes Appellate Court, whose membership usually included at least one Revolutionary Council member. The other element of the court system, at the local level called "people's courts" by the government, was in early 1971 not fully established.

The regular civil courts included the Rangoon District Magistrate's Court and its subordinate courts throughout the country and the district judges' courts and their lower courts. Sometimes it was necessary for a judge's court to try cases in more than one district because not every district had its own court. Criminal cases of a nonpolitical nature were tried in the district magistrate's courts and their subordinates and the sessions courts (see ch. 14, National Defense and Internal Security).

The special crimes courts were created to deal with acts of insurrection, crimes against public safety, and acts that endangered culture and the national economy. In 1963 they were authorized to try any criminal case under any existing laws and to impose whatever legal punishment they saw fit, including the death penalty. Working in close cooperation with the governing committees, the special crimes courts became a primary instrument for maintaining political control.

The Central Security and Administrative Committee can initiate a Special Crimes Court trial for any case it considers necessary. Divisional-level and district committees exercise similar power, but they must first obtain approval from the central government. Investigating teams—consisting of a committee member, a local citizen, and a police representative—exercise broad authority to interrogate suspects and search areas for possession of unauthorized goods. They can seize illegal goods and reprimand offenders. Appeals relating to investigating team actions go to the Security and Administrative Committee for the area or the special crimes courts.

The people's courts at the local level were instituted to involve the peasants and workers in the effort to reduce minor economic offenses against the state. Their work mostly concerned black-market activities and violations that degraded production efforts.

The operations of these courts expanded as what the government called "people's peasants' councils" and "people's workers' councils" came into existence at enterprises and in communities. In early 1971 the people's councils were not yet established in some places, and the people's courts were likewise not operating in all areas.

The Civil Service

The Civil Service tended to lose its distinctive character after 1962 as state employment rapidly increased following the nationalization of many enterprises. The military often took over administrative positions previously held by civil servants, and they and party officials rather than the Public Service Commission exercised primary control over the selection of senior-level personnel.

By 1962 the prestige of the Civil Service had already decreased from the privileged position it held under British rule. The exodus of British civil servants at independence and of others of foreign descent soon thereafter resulted in the loss of many highly qualified personnel, for whom replacements were not available. Another adverse factor was the reduction of pay scales in 1948 and, despite inflation in prices in the 1950s and 1960s, no action was taken to adjust wages. The creation of corporations and boards in the early 1950s provided job opportunities and tended to reduce the attractiveness of the Civil Service. By the mid-1950s there was little competition for professional-level government positions. The swelling tide of college graduates soon thereafter increased the number of applicants, but the quality was below pre-World War II standards.

Politicians during the parliamentary period frequently looked upon senior civil servants as competitors for power, and they were hesitant to delegate them authority, a move that might lead to a Civil Service elite. Political leaders made use of the Civil Service, but there was no large influx of politicians into permanent government service. Competition and distrust among politicians, the military, and civil servants during the 1955—58 period were major factors in bringing about duplication and excess paperwork, which bogged down government administrative machinery. When the caretaker government was given control in 1958, the Civil Service became an active partner with the military in the effort to invigorate administration. After 1962 the military took a less friendly attitude toward senior civil servants and removed a number of senior officers from positions of influence.

The Public Service Enquiry Commission, headed by the chief justice, made extensive recommendations for improving public administration after making visits to Western European and Commonwealth nations in 1961. One recommendation called for a constitutional guarentee of tenure for civil servants. Few of the recommendations were acted upon. The significant changes in civil service and public administration under the Revolutionary Government were brought about largely by circumstances rather than design. The military leaders showed no inclination to give a constitutional guarantee of tenure in civil service.

Although it was critical of the large bureaucracy of the parliamentary government, the Revolutionary Council expanded the permanent government service even more. In late 1963 they gave permanent status to persons in temporary employment; this was about one-third of the estimated total of 300,000 workers. Distinctions between professional level and less skilled employees were abolished, and benefits were made more nearly equal for all employees. The nationalization of enterprises contributed to a considerable increase in state employment after 1963. The total number of state employees in fiscal 1967/68 was estimated at 783,230, of which 288,700 were in administration. Data were not available to indicate the number of civil service status.

A number of measures were taken to develop a cadre of public servants who would support the Burmese Way to Socialism. The Public Service Commission was revised, and appointments came under the control of the military rulers. Political influence was recognized by requiring that appointees be cleared by the party. The Public Administration Division under the Council of Ministers, in addition to devising improved organizational schemes and administrative practices, also established training programs for government workers. In 1965 the Central Services Training School was begun at Phaunggyi. It provided indoctrination in the Burmese Way to Socialism and instruction in military subjects, administration, and fields related to the students' future assignments. By mid-1970 over 8,500 cadre government workers, many of them from the township level, had completed courses at this school.

In late 1970 a committee, composed of senior representatives from the Public Administration Division, the Ministry of Home Affairs, the Central Security and Administrative Committee, the Ministry of Immigration, National Registration and Census, and the Central People's Workers' Council, was charged with the task of drawing up procedures to bring about uniformity in promotions in the various departments and provide for advancement based on merit with no allowance for undeserving favorites. This step reflected a growing concern with these issues.

Government in the Constituent Units

The Revolutionary Government continued to govern the divisions of Burma proper directly from Rangoon, but it took away the partial autonomy that the other constituent jurisdictions exercised before 1962. In January 1964 the government decreed that there would be one set of laws for all elements of the union. Officials appointed by the Revolutionary Government replaced those selected by the people, and controls were increased over organs of government. In the first years of military rule there was an effort to extend Burman cultural domination over the entire country, but by the late 1960s this policy had been modified, and ethnic minority groups were accorded the right to maintain their own customs and folkways as long as they did not foster political disunity.

Because of continuing widespread insurgency and lawlessness, there were constant efforts to extend control over areas where insurgents or lawless elements operated. In 1970 regular army forces, sometimes supplemented by the People's Militia, mounted operations periodically. Also, teams directed by a member of the local Security and Administrative Committee and consisting of military, party, and civic action personnel visited areas of marginal security to extend and strengthen government control. Their work, called five-column operations, included the fields of security, economy, health, education, and administration.

The security and administrative committees are the primary governing bodies in the constituent states and the Chin Special Division at all levels. These jurisdictions, unlike those of Burma proper, also have a council for state affairs, for example, the Council for Shan State Affairs. The number of members on a council varied slightly, but the average in early 1971 was five. The Security and Administrative Committee chairman for the area was usually a council member, and usually one or more ethnic minority representatives were included. Periodic meetings were held between the Revolutionary Council and each of the constituent councils. Continuity in relationships was maintained through the Revolutionary Council's State Liaison Committee.

The state ministries that had operated under the state councils before 1962 were abolished, and the appointed councils were permitted to develop their own administrative organizations. The security and administrative committee and the national ministries, however, took over many of the functions previously performed by state and local government.

POLITICAL VALUES AND ATTITUDES

In 1971, and during the whole period after independence, a gap existed between the political values and attitudes held by the political elite and the general population. The political leadership was change oriented and a force for developing a modernized society of Burmese design, but the bulk of society, largely rural and Buddhist, remained tradition oriented.

Since the ordinary peasant lives in a limited world, his ambitions and ideals are related primarily to his personal life and fundamental identification with family rather than with political affairs. Traditionally, fear of central authority has caused him to look upon government as something to be protected against and avoided. Political leaders are frequently the subject of private conversation, but there is a strong tendency on the part of villagers to leave politics to those who govern. Participation in the political process was encouraged under parliamentary government by elections, debates, and expression of public opinion in the news media and by demonstrations. The Revolutionary Government after 1962 eliminated most of these devices for participation in government and substituted mainly party-controlled channels, such as peasants' and workers' seminars. Some free expression of opinion was continued in the press within well-defined limits.

If acceptance of the political system by the public is used to measure political development after 1948, indications are that little improvement was made. The pervasiveness of the forces to preserve a closed community that protects the cultural heritage tends to permit the ingress of governmental sovereignty only during duress or with strong promises, such as greater security and substantial material benefit. In most areas of questionable security, villagers avoid commitment to either the state or insurgents.

Commonly held concepts of power also contributed to widespread apathy toward involvement in politics. They emphasized the individual and took into account his influence in the community but not in the context of organized government. Certain basic teachings of Buddhism, including freedom of thought, self-reliance, and moderation in desires, were fundamental in shaping values relevant to individualism and power (see ch. 4, Social Systems and Values).

Persons who demonstrate such leadership qualitites as industry, alertness, mercy, patience, judgment, and perspective are influential in shaping attitudes among villagers with respect to politics as well as other matters. Many of them were community leaders under the parliamentary government, and those who are acceptable to the Revolutionary Government are sometimes selected for village and township-level leadership positions under the overall control of the local military commander.

During the postwar movement for independence the authority of national leaders was widely accepted by the predominant Burman group as well as the many disparate ethnic groups. After independence the integrating forces of nationalism began to crumble with the outbreak of widespread insurgency in 1948; respect for national authority became a problem that plagued every government thereafter. The ill-defined goals of the Anti-Fascist People's Freedom League (AFPFL), which dominated the government and the highly factional character of national politics during the 1948-61 period, contributed to the government's failure to elicit broad public participation in government and enhance its authority.

Periodic insurgency resulting from the efforts of the Burman-dominated central government to extend Burman culture into areas inhabited mainly by ethnic minorities also eroded governmental authority (see ch. 9, Political Dynamics). After 1962 the Revolutionary Government relied heavily on the military to assert its authority, and simultaneously it attempted to increase public participation in government programs by organizing the peasants and workers under party control.

Since religion traditionally held a prominent position in Burmese national life, the attitudes of rulers toward relations between church and state were critical in maintaining public support. Before the mid-1960s monks traditionally played an active role in politics, and the *sangha* (see Glossary), despite its lack of unity, had a strong influence on government.

The strongly pro-Buddhist government of U Nu, although widely accepted by the majority of the population, caused strong resentment among Muslims, animists, and even secular-minded Buddhist elements of U Nu's own political party. The imposition of punishments for a slaughter of cows, as a violation of religious principles, in 1950 had wide impact because it was a symbol of dominance of the majority Buddhist community. Other actions followed that brought a close relationship between church and state and deepened antagonisms among non-Buddhists. When this drift culminated in 1961 in the amendment to the Constitution establishing Buddhism as the state religion, the linking of church and state was opposed by secular-minded members of the Anti-Fascist People's Freedom League, the military leadership, the non-Buddhist minority ethnic groups (see ch. 3, Historical Setting).

The Ne Win regime not only made it clear that Buddhism would not be accorded a position of deference but also proclaimed the right of everyone freely to profess and practice religion. *The System of Correlation of Man and His Environment* gave considerable attention to traditional Burmese thought and attempted to show the compatibility of Buddhism and Marxism-Leninism in its Burmese form. Government actions in the 1962-64 period brought strong reactions from *sangha* associations, however. The Revolutionary Council criticized spirit worship and involved itself in church affairs, but it was the large-scale nationalization and the reduction in resources of wealthy laymen who supported Buddhist institutions that brought the strongest reaction from the monks. Many clergymen privately denounced the Revolutionary Government as being communist, to which the party replied with a denial and an elaboration of its aims (see Ch. 9, Political Dynamics).

The protests of the monks had a moderating effect on the council's efforts to diminish the power of the *sangha,* but the initiation of the requirement in 1964 that all social and professional organizations had to be under party control brought an end to the monk's associations and soon diminished the involvement of the *sangha* in politics. The policies and actions of the council in the 1963-65 period, inimical to the prestige and power of the *sangha,* resulted in the loss of support of a traditionally influential and respected element of society.

After 1965 the Revolutionary Council increasingly attempted to maximize its legitimacy by emphasizing the importance of religion in improving the quality of spiritual life of the individual, the commonality of socialist and Buddhist fundamental principles, and the wrongness of abusing or exploiting religion for individual or political gain. It continued to support the doctrine that a distinct line of demarcation must be maintained between secular and religious activities. In order to broaden its base of support, the Revolutionary Government in the early 1970s gave increased emphasis to the need for religion, advocated the unity of religious and socialist ideology, and pointed out that failure to give adequate attention to religion can bankrupt national ideals.

Individuals who have chosen to be active in politics have shown a strong tendency to break associations when frustrated in their attempts to achieve positions of dominance. Fracturing of loyalties led to a multiplicity of parties based on personal followings and frequently to insurgent activity during the parliamentary period. Although the political environment changed after 1962, these same attitudes continued to prevail.

Socialism was introduced in the 1930s through the study of Marxism. Burmese leaders of Marxist persuasion synthesized socialist values with those of Buddhism in order to make them more appealing to the people. In the struggle for independence many people shared the antipathies of their leaders toward British colonial policy and its associated capitalist laissez-faire system. It therefore was relatively easy to promote socialism as an alternative in the struggle for independence.

Political leaders after independence were generally consistent in emphasizing neutralism and socialism. U Nu tended to give socialism a strong Buddhist flavor. In 1958, however, he rejected Marxism, which came from the leadership, and declared his support for true socialism, which came from the people. The Revolutionary Government under General Ne Win shifted to Marxist-Leninist concept of a vanguard party as the leader in the development of a socialist society. The extent to which the masses shared the views of the leadership in socialism cannot be readily determined.

National pride was reflected in widespread reverence for, and commemoration of, Aung San. Accounts of his deeds and works increasingly resembled those of a folk hero, and the memorial erected in his honor was looked to as a place for paying tribute to the state.

The state seal bears scrollwork at the base with the legend "The Union of the Republic of Burma." In the center portion there is a map of Burma and the motto, "The pursuit of unity is happiness and prosperity." Three heraldic cheetahs of classic Burmese design guard the map. Three is the auspicious number, and cheetahs and Burma enjoy astrological kinship.

Other symbols and sources of pride are revealed in the flag and anthem. The national flag is designed to symbolize national unity. It is red with a blue canton in which there is a large white five-pointed star, with five smaller stars between the points representing the states. The national anthem reflecting pride in the struggle for independence is "Kaba Makye" (Our Free Homeland).

CHAPTER 9

POLITICAL DYNAMICS

In early 1971 political energies were focused on the achievement of three major national objectives: restructuring the political system in accordance with General Ne Win's Marxist-colored state ideology called the Burmese Way to Socialism; laying the foundation for a new state constitution dedicated to the establishment of a "socialist democratic state"; and strengthening national solidarity by suppressing civil insurgency that had plagued successive governments since independence.

The political instrument responsible for achieving these objectives was the Burma Socialist Program Party (BSPP), also known as the Myanma Socialist Lanzin Party or simply as the Lanzin party. Headed by General Ne Win, concurrently chairman of the Revolutionary Council and the Council of Ministers, the party has functioned as the ruling political organization since it was founded in July 1962, four months after the constitutional government of Prime Minister U Nu was overturned in a military coup.

The only legal political party in the country, the Burma Socialist Program Party in early 1971 was making necessary preparations so that it could broaden its base of popular support and pave the way for the inauguration of what General Ne Win called "direct participatory democracy." These preparations were to culminate in the party's first national congress.

The dominant power group continued to be the military. Senior army officers held all positions in the Revolutionary Council, the supreme power organ of the state, and in the cabinet; they also served in key positions of the party (see ch. 8, Political System and Values). Members of the defense services remained the dominant group within the party. Since 1962 the military has maintained the position that it was the only political force capable of leading the people, steering the country through crises, and pulling the nation back from the brink of total disintegration. Efforts were underway in 1970 and 1971 to change the image of the army to that of the "people's army" and to convince the public that the army derived its strength from the peasants and workers and thus was the only leadership group that could effectively promote the welfare of the working class.

Meanwhile, the military leadership continued to affirm the often-professed position that political power would be restored to "its original and rightful owner, the people" as soon as the party evolved into a viable people's party and saboteurs and obstructionists in the country were successfully eliminated.

As envisaged by the leadership, the peasants and workers were considered the most revolutionary and progressive forces in the emerging political structure. The party's efforts were aimed at evoking voluntary support from these two groups. Other groups, such as students, youth, and intellectuals, had not been prominently mentioned in party publications by late 1970. Political rallies as reported by Burmese public sources were concerned mostly with laudatory affirmation of the party ideology, program, and leadership. Marxist assumptions and terminology were dominant in the party's effort to communicate with the people and in its policy statements. There were few overt signs of mass protests except for infrequent outbursts of student anger at campus regulations; some of these demonstrations turned into antigovernment slogan shouting and street violence. In the mid-1960s many of the young, militant Buddhist monks were protesting against what they called the government's communistic and antireligious policies, but they were reported as being relatively calm in 1971.

Political activities were carefully monitored by the authorities, and there were no legitimate channels of political expression other than the party and its auxiliary organizations. Public criticism of, or opposition to, the one-party political system was officially discouraged.

As a result, former Prime Minister U Nu's bid to regain power from General Ne Win and to restore parliamentary democracy had to be formulated outside the country—in Thailand, but without official approval of the Thai government. U Nu, reported variously in 1971 as being in self-imposed exile in Thailand and as being somewhere inside Burma, declared his intention in 1969 to overthrow the Ne Win leadership by peaceful or violent means. In this effort he was reported to have been supported by armed insurgents belonging to some ethnic minority organizations who joined him in an alliance known as the National United Front, which was formed in May 1970.

In 1971 the continuation of insurgency in many parts of the country, especially in border regions adjoining China, Laos, and Thailand, remained a critical problem for the regime. In addition to a number of communist rebels divided into rival factions, dissidents from at least three of the most numerous minorities—the Shans, Karens, and Kachins—were in armed rebellion, harassing the government security forces, preying on uncooperative villagers, disrupting transport and communication facilities. In 1970 the total number of armed insurgents was estimated to be as many as 17,000 men, not counting some 5,000 communist combatants and remnants of the Nationalist Chinese troops believed to be operating in the Burmese-Thai-Laotian border regions (see ch. 10, Foreign Relations).

POLITICAL POWER AND MILITARY RULE

Sources of power and the manner in which this power was exercised after 1948 shifted between civilian and military. Between 1948 and 1958 and again between 1960 and 1962, civilian politicians held the reins of government. Between 1958 and 1960 and since 1962, the military has been the dominant group. Until the military takeover in March 1962, senior civil servants also played a prominent role, but not as important as that of principal politicians or military officers.

Until September 1958, when Prime Minister U Nu invited General Ne Win to form a caretaker regime, politics was dominated by popularly elected leaders associated with the Anti-Fascist People's Freedom League (AFPFL) (see ch. 3, Historical Setting). Unlike the senior civil servants who had gained access to power and prestige mostly through educational achievements, these leaders owned their postindependence prominence to their wartime participation in student-nationalist activities.

Most politicians played a leading role in the ostensibly independent Burmese government installed by the Japanese during World War II, then conspired to rid the country of the Japanese, and negotiated successfully for independence from the British. They were closely identified with the people, having led and taken part in the wartime popular movement. They formed the backbone of the ruling AFPFL, drawing their mandate through periodically held general elections. They sought to manage the affairs of state through legislative means or, failing this, through factional manipulation.

The AFPFL leaders gradually eroded the power of senior civil servants who, along with their British counterparts, had in effect constituted the government before independence. They found it necessary, however, to rely on these members of the bureaucracy in carrying out political decisions and government programs. Thus the civil servants continued to enjoy considerable power and latitude because of their general competence and familiarity with the framework of government that was of British origin in theory and practice (see ch. 8, Political System and Values).

Working relationships between the career politicians and senior civil servants were not, however, always harmonious because of their differences in temperament and background. Many AFPFL leaders reportedly shared the view that the civil servants should broaden their perspectives by recognizing the expanded and changed role of government from its prewar preoccupation with preserving law and order, dispensing justice, and collecting taxes to that stressing social and economic development. They often brought political pressures to bear on the operation of the civil service, and in the process they often failed to place full trust in the ranking civil servants, who in their view continued to represent the values and practices associated with the British. On the other hand, the civil servants, who were conscious of their former status and educational superiority, expressed resentment at being supplanted in power and social position by those whom they regarded as less than their equals. They found they had no alternative, however, than to accept the preeminence of career politicians in the government.

Nevertheless, it was the combination of the civil service and the AFPFL that maintained a semblance of political continuity and stability. After the mid-1950s, however, leaders of the AFPFL were unable to initiate concerted, effective action because of personal and ideological tensions among themselves, as manifested in a split in the AFPFL in early 1958. At issue was the question of whether the popularly endorsed political leadership and parliamentary democracy were capable of providing a basis for stability and progress.

The AFPFL politicians themselves were aware of their own power limitations when confronted with crisis situations. When Prime Minister U Nu asked General Ne Win to take over the reins of government, the general responded by replacing AFPFL leaders with military officers and senior civil servants in key positions of the administration.

The background of the military officers was similar to that of the civilian leaders. The officers as a whole had a lesser degree of formal education than the civil servants and had been active participants in the wartime nationalist, revolutionary movement. Both the civilian and military leaders were imbued with Marxist ideology similar to the social democratic movement in Great Britain. As a group, the military was more disciplined and efficient than its civilian counterpart.

The civilian-military differences may be traced to the experiences of the two groups. Given the nature of parliamentary politics that emphasized degrees of responsiveness to public opinion, the political leaders sometimes avoided taking action in order not to alienate any segment of the electorate. They valued the virtue of compromise and used patronage and favors to solidify their competing positions.

True to its tradition of nonpartisanship, the military at first was reluctant to assert itself politically at the expense of civilian leaders.

During its first eighteen months of caretaker government from 1958 to 1960, the military curtailed partisan politics and ruled by decree, but there was no attempt to ignore constitutional restraints on the manner in which state power was to be exercised. Under military rule the economy reached the greatest production level in the history of independent Burma. Rebel activities, which had seriously threatened internal security in 1958, were sharply reduced. By 1960 the situation had been sufficiently stabilized to permit the holding of elections and to restore constitutional rule, again under U Nu.

Upon his assumption of power in 1962, General Ne Win blamed the party politicians for political paralysis, economic stagnation, mounting indications of separatist pressures in frontier states, religious tensions, and worsening internal security situations (see ch. 3, Historical Setting). The group that carried out the coup formed the all-military, seventeen-member Revolutionary Council. The council arrested most party politicians and suspected secessionists, forced many senior civil servants to retire from government serivce (the number of civil servants retired by the military reaching as many as 2,000 between 1962 and 1970), and appointed military officers as ministers and department heads. As chairman of the Revolutionary Council, General Ne Win assumed full executive, legislative, and judicial powers.

The military distaste for the pre-1962 parliamentary partisan politics was expressed in its April 1962 announcement asserting the need for creation of a new society in which the welfare of the working class would be especially promoted. In July 1962 the Burma Socialist Program Party (BSPP) was founded as the political arm of the military leadership. In a continuing attempt to popularize the party as the sole legal political organization of the nation and remove the institutional base for any political opposition, the government in March 1964 abolished all other parties.

By 1966 there had been growing indications that the government's socialist aims were not widely supported in the country. In a consequent effort to ease internal tensions and elicit the broadest possible support from every segment of the public, the government began releasing many of the political prisoners who were detained at the time of, or after, the 1962 coup. By late 1968 all but 880 of the more than 8,500 detainees had been freed. U Nu was one of those released in 1966.

In December 1968, in still another attempt to bridge gaps between the military and former party politicians, General Ne Win appointed thirty-three civilian leaders as members of the Internal Unity Advisory Board. The general asked the board to offer suggestions on means of establishing internal unity as well as on political, social, and economic problems and to report its recommendations no later than the end of May 1969.

The board was not unanimous in its proposals, which were submitted in June 1969. In a separate report, U Nu called for a speedy return to parliamentary democracy by transferring power to a popularly elected government. The remaining thirty-two leaders presented two alternate proposals in their sixty-four-page report. The first one, endorsed by twenty-one leaders, called for the adoption of "democratic socialism" as the goal of the state, to be achieved through the pre-1962 multiparty parliamentary political system; three of these leaders differed with the rest by opting for a unitary rather than a federal form of government. The second proposal, supported by eleven leaders, favored the establishment of a "socialist democracy" through the working-class-oriented, one-party political system.

Apart from their differences in the form of political system, the thirty-three members generally shared the view, though differing in emphasis, that: a broader national leadership composed of military officers, career politicians, and representatives of national ethnic groups and various functional groups be formed; peace be negotiated with insurgent groups; political prisoners be unconditionally released and multiparty activities be revived; and a constitution be drafted by a national front for approval by a constituent assembly or through a popular referendum. On nonpolitical matters, the report called for the introduction of a mixed economy; a sweeping review of all nationalized enterprises so that only essential sectors be retained for purposes of state operations; and acceptance of more foreign aid for the development of the nation's heavy and basic industries.

General Ne Win reacted by stating that the formation of a broad representative national government was still premature, but he also stated that his government had no intention of retaining power indefinitely. In November 1969 he rejected U Nu's proposal, declaring that he would have no part of the system that served "the interests of the exploiting moneyed people." He also vetoed the idea of a multiparty system, asserting that the disunity of the people would be in direct proportion to the number of political parties. On the other hand, he took note of the fact that the eleven leaders, who had submitted the second proposal, had "the interests of the peasant and worker classes as the core and kernel of their proposals." He took the occasion to reaffirm his previous position that "we must go the way of true socialism."

Meanwhile, in August 1969 in London, U Nu announced the formation of a movement for the restoration of parliamentary democracy in Burma. The announced purpose of the movement was to depose General Ne Win by peaceful means or by force of arms if necessary. The movement was to be led by his new Parliamentary Democracy Party, established in Bangkok. In May 1970 U Nu made it public that a national united front was formed as an alliance of political and insurgent groups opposing the Ne Win rule. Two months later, the front claimed the support of 20,000 troops from various minority groups. The Ne Win government asserted on the other hand that total strength of the front's army would amount to no more than 2,000 men, which some experienced observers believed to be a more accurate count.

In early 1971, as in years before, the ranks of the military remained fairly solidly behind the Ne Win government. There were few overt signs of serious internal strife within the councils of power. Conflicts within the ruling hierarchy were usually resolved by the removal of the disputants.

Two notable cases of power struggles within the military concerned Brigadier Aung Gyi and Brigadier Tin Pe. Brigadier Aung Gyi and General Ne Win were comrades in arms during World War II and played a leading role in the 1962 coup, as did Brigadier Tin Pe. During the first nine or ten months of military rule, Aung Gyi became the most influential member of the Revolutionary Council next to General Ne Win and established a reputation as a pragmatic and popular leader. The dispute leading to his resignation in early 1963 centered on his advocating a middle way to socialism that would permit some private sector activity and participation of political parties. He was opposed by a more dogmatic, militant group under Brigadier Tin Pe. Aung Gyi's removal served to accelerate the pace of the Burmese Way to Socialism.

In November 1970 Brigadier Tin Pe resigned from the Revolutionary Council and the Council of Ministers under obscure circumstances. Apart from his failing health, not much was known about the reason for his departure. After the retirement of Tin Pe, Brigadier San Yu emerged apparently as the most trusted confidant of General Ne Win.

THE BURMA SOCIALIST PROGRAM PARTY

The Burma Socialist Program Party (BSPP) in 1971 continued to serve as the Revolutionary Council's political arm for educating the people in the ideology of the Burmese Way to Socialism, for providing an organized channel for popular participation and involvement in the socialist efforts of the regime, and for building the image of the Ne Win government as the true friend and protector of the working people.

The party was founded in July 1962 in order to provide an organized popular base for implementing the Burmese Way to Socialism, which was officially described as the only practical program capable of rehabilitating and developing the nation. Although there were at the time several other political parties that had been active before the coup, the party was actually the only functioning entity at that time because most former party politicians were taken into custody beginning in March 1962. There were three major political organizations before they were banned in March 1964 under the Law to Protect National Solidarity. These were: the Pyidangsu (Union League) Party, the party of U Nu, which was in power at the time of the coup; the Anti-Fascist People's Freedom League (AFPFL) the chief opposition to U Nu; and the National United Front (NUF) a coalition of minor parties, of which the principal affiliate was the Burma Workers and Peasants Party (BWPP) (see ch. 3, Historical Setting).

Ideology

The ideological basis of the party was set forth in April 1962 in a policy statement called the Burmese Way to Socialism. This statement enunciated the goal of establishing a "socialist democratic state" in which the means of production would be owned by the state. This goal was to be achieved by a middle-of-the-road transitional program, avoiding the so-called evils of deviation toward right or left. According to the statement, in the country's march toward socialism all able-bodied men would work according to their ability and would be compensated according to "the quantity and quality of labor expended." It was also noted in the statement that "fraudulent practices, profit motive, easy living, parasitism, shirking and selfishness" would have no place in a new socialist Burma.

The main political support for the Burmese Way to Socialism was to come from the peasants and workers, or "the vanguard and custodians of a socialist democratic state" as the statement described the two working groups. After rejecting the utility of parliamentary democracy for Burma, the Burmese Way to Socialism expressed the need for establishing a new kind of political and administrative structure that would be more attuned to the requirement of a new socialist society. Thus it stated:

> In our road to socialism the existing bureaucratic administration is a big stumbling block. To achieve our aims with this effete machinery is impossible. Steps will be taken to remove this bureaucratic machinery and lay firm foundations for a socialist democratic one.

In an attempt to offer a more systematic explanation of the party's socialist position the Revolutionary Council in January 1963 published a document called *The System of Correlation of Man and His Environment*. This document used many Marxist terms and abstract metaphysical concepts of apparently Buddhist origin.

As the party moved progressively toward the left after Brigadier Aung Gyi's departure in February 1963, an increasing number of party statements began emphasizing the importance of ideology as a prime motivating force of revolution.

In 1963 and 1964, however, indications were lacking that the party's political thinking was widely appreciated except among the coterie of party enthusiasts. The party ideology was too esoteric and remote for all but a small portion of the entire population to comprehend, and it was coming under growing criticism by a number of young militant Buddhist monks who publicly accused the government of being communistic and anti-Buddhist.

In September 1964 the party issued a lengthy statement, denying any link with communism and insisting on sharp and vital differences betwen itself and communist parties. It declared that these communist parties did not permit their members to have any religious faith or worship and would hold the doctrines of Marx, Engels, Lenin, Stalin, and other leaders of world communism to be "absolute, complete and infallible truth." By contrast, the Lanzin party emphasized that it gave full freedom of conscience and religion to those who believe and worship and to nonbelievers and free thinkers alike.

The party pointed out another difference by stating that it would hold no economic, political, or social doctrine to be infallible or absolute. It did not single out any single foreign ideology as the mainspring of its programs and policies, although acknowledging a debt of gratitude to Marxist-Leninist thinking. It took pains to emphasize, however, that:

> The BSPP. . .studies the texts and treatises of the Marxist-Leninists and of the non-Marxist-Leninists alike. In no area, political, economic or others, is the study restricted. What is good and useful for the human society in the Union of Burma will be extracted in its essence, adapted and applied.

Then it went on to explain the manner in which this process of adaptation and application took place in the country.

> The official ideology of the BSPP is constituted in the Burmese Way to Socialism and the philosophy of the Burmese Way to Socialism . . .The System of Correlation of Man and His Environment, or, in other words, the Correlation of Mind and Matter, which the Revolutionary Council has deeply considered and clearly proclaimed, forms the guide to action of the BSPP. To put it in yet another way, the BSPP is guided by a philosophy of humanism based on the system of dielectical objective realism.

In early 1971 the party continued to reaffirm the correctness of the Burmese Way to Socialism as a guiding light in building a new Burma. At the same time, however, it left open the possibility that the party ideology would have to be modified as the organization gained more practical experience in the course of nation building.

Structure

The party was organized as a transitional cadre organization, which, according to its 1962 charter, meant a party that performed such basic functions as recruiting nucleus personnel called cadres and training and testing them by assigning duties. The intention of the Revolutionary Council was that quality, rather than quantity, would be stressed during the initial phase of party construction.

Part of the party's preparation for its first national congress was an effort to complete a draft party constitution that would supersede that adopted in July 1962. According to fragmentary information available in early 1971, the party's intention was to shift the principle of organization from centralism to democratic centralism, a term described by the party as "a harmonious combination of the democratic process and centralism." Democratic centralism was also referred to in party publications as a "democratic central control system."

Democratic centralism was explained by the party as a necessary basis for ensuring intraparty democratic practices. Specifically, these practices meant that party committees from the basic to the central levels would be elected, thus making committee members accountable to their respective constituencies. In addition, democratic centralism required that committee members must act within the framework of the party constitution and abide by decisions of the Party Congress. Similarly, party committees and members at vaious levels must follow the decisions and directives of higher committees, the minority following the decisions of the majority and the majority respecting the opinion of the minority.

The party constitution of 1962 vested the supreme authority of the organization in the Revolutionary Council, which had the ultimate power of control and supervision over both the party and the government (see ch. 8, Political System and Values). The council appointed three bodies—the Central Organizing Committee, the Party Discipline Committee, and the Socialist Economy Planning Committee, all headed by General Ne Win (see fig. 5).

In 1971 the party had, in addition to its national headquarters in Rangoon, fifteen territorial subdivisions, each under the control of a divisional supervisory committee appointed by the Revolutionary Council. The party subdivisions reported to both the Central Organizing Committee and the country's six regional military commands, whose commanders were also chairmen of the divisional supervisory committees within their respective jurisdictions.

In early 1971 the lowest unit of the party hierarchy was a cell, consisting of from three to fifteen members. Three to nine cells made up a party group. At the next higher level, a party section (also called branch or fraction) existed, composed of at least three

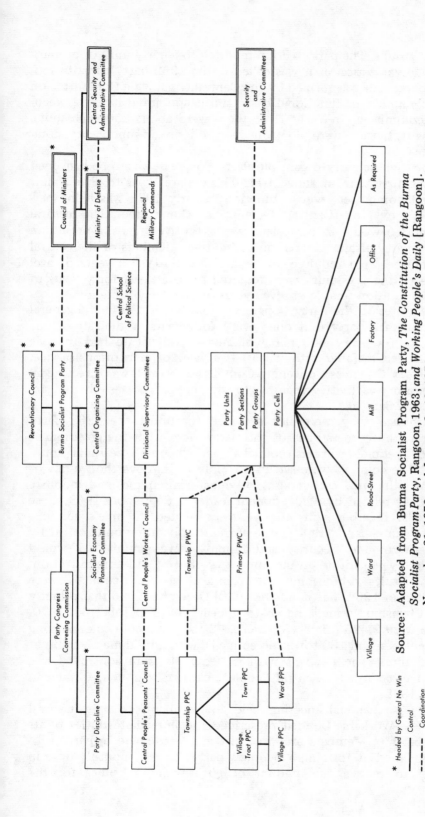

Source: Adapted from Burma Socialist Program Party, *The Constitution of the Burma Socialist Program Party*, Rangoon, 1963; and *Working People's Daily* [Rangoon]. November 21, 1970, and January 8—12, 1971.

Figure 5. Organization of the Burma Socialist Program Party, February 1971

* Headed by General Ne Win

——— Control
----- Coordination
——— Government agencies

173

party groups. The party section reported to a party unit, or primary party organization as it was called in the 1962 party constitution. The party unit was formed by the Central Organizing Committee on a geographical or functional basis, and it appointed its own executive committee. In early 1971 there were about 350 such units, whose activities were controlled by divisional supervisory committees.

The highest party organ, the Party Congress, was to be convened for the first time in June 1971. This congress was to elect a new central committee, whose function in early 1971 was being performed by the Central Organizing Committee. The central committee would in turn elect two executive organs, a presidium and a party affairs supervision committee. Members of the central committee were required to be at least thirty-five years of age; those of the presidium were required to be at least forty years of age, in addition to at least seven years of membership standing.

Delegates to the Party Congress would be elected at the general meeting of a party unit once every four years at the rate of one delegate for every 500 party members. A delegate had to be a full-fledged member with at least five years of meritorious service. The Party Congress Convening Commission, which was directing all preparatory activities relating to the congress, was chaired by Brigadier San Yu.

Although they were not provided for under the 1962 party charter, the cornerstones of the party were what the government called "people's workers' councils" and "people's peasants' councils." The councils were set up not only to improve the welfare of the working masses but also to educate, discipline, and mobilize them. As related by a government leader in September 1968, these councils, together with the yet-to-be-created "people's administrative councils" to replace the currently operating units called by the government "security and administrative committees," would eventually constitute an instrument of control and administration.

The rules establishing the people's workers' councils were adopted in 1964, but it was not until December 1966 that primary and township councils began to appear. As of October 30, 1970, there were 2,425 primary councils, 72 township council organizing committees, and 180 township councils, with a total membership of 1.5 million. The people's workers' councils were controlled and coordianted by the Central People's Workers' Council, formed in April 1968.

In a semiannual meeting held in October 1970, the Central People's Workers' Council prescribed the immediate duties of its membership. Members are: to assist and participate in party activities aimed at forming a people's party; to pay monthly dues in order to reduce the amount of government subsidies for the people's workers' councils; to work harder in an attempt to produce more goods and to reduce the government's budget deficit; to assist the Ministry of Cooperatives in its efforts to organize cooperatives in the country; and to organize mass meetings aimed at expressing popular appreciation for the sacrifices of the army and national ethnic groups in the frontier areas.

At the October meeting, many delegates expressed the view that the hierarchy of people's workers' councils was overcentralized and that more power should be delegated to lower bodies if the whole scheme were to succeed. A Burmese source publicly described the Central People's Workers' Council as "the post office," implying that this body was concerned more with correspondence and administrative routines than with substantive issues relating to workers' welfare.

The people's peasants' councils first appeared in March 1967. Placed under the Central People's Peasants' Council (set up in February 1969), the councils had the special purpose of awakening the rural population to the so-called evils of capitalism, feudalism, and landlordism. By November 1970 the councils had been operating in 9,294 of the country's 14,250 villages, with a claimed membership of more than 5.76 million, and in 227 townships (two-thirds of the total number of townships), with a membership in the township councils of 34,300.

Members of the people's peasants' councils were assigned the functions of producing more agricultural commodities, assisting the party in its efforts to establish a socialist economy, aiding in national defense as militia, and promoting the class alliance between the workers and peasants.

Membership

A party member must be at least eighteen years of age and must have accepted the Burmese Way to Socialism as his guiding ideology. Membership is divided into full-fledged members, candidates, and sympathizers. Applications for membership must be approved by the Revolutionary Council. Once accepted as a candidate member, the applicant is placed on two years' probation and is then eligible for promotion to regular member status. A regular member, according to a party publication, must have demonstrated "loyalty to the country, loyalty to the Party, good character, satisfactory discharge of duties assigned by the Party, firm conviction in the Lanzin (Socialist program), acceptance and practice of ideology, practice of collective leadership and work, practice of democracy in the Party, self-criticism and winning the love and regards of the working people." Surveillance over the conduct of individual members is the responsibility of political intelligence units, which were introduced shortly after the Chinese riots in Rangoon in June 1967. A principal task of these units was to detect pro-Chinese agents who might have infiltrated the party ranks.

A candidate member may withdraw from the party, but a regular member, according to the 1962 party statute, has no right to resign from the party. A full-fledged member can vote at party meetings, elect party officers, and hold elective office.

As of February 20, 1971, there were 72,509 regular members, of whom the army accounted for 41,052. The number of regular members represented an increase of about 53,000 over the number only seven weeks earlier. At the end of July 1970 there had been only 859 regulars. This sharp increase was a result of the screening and promotion procedures that were instituted after the party announced its decision in November 1969 to broaden the base of popular support and hasten the pace of becoming a people's party.

The party had started with a total of 20 regulars in 1962, this number increasing to 24 as of January 1970; of the 24, 13 regulars were members of the Revolutionary Council. In March 1963 it began accepting membership applications, and by the end of 1965 it had 99,638 candidate members and 167,447 sympathizers. By October 1966 the number of candiate members more than doubled, and that of sympathizers rose to 812,611. The increase in the number of sympathizers resulted from the party's decision in September 1966 to regard as sympathizers all those who had applied for membership.

At the end of June 1969, the latest date for which figures were available, the occupational breakdown of 257,200 candidate members was: 91,801 army personnel; 86,155 workers in state sectors (including civil servants) and 30,873 workers in nonstate sectors; 22,670 peasants; 3,446 policemen; and 22,255 others.

Indications in 1971, as in earlier years, were that about four-fifths of the entire party membership were from urban areas. Members of the armed forces, civil servants, and police continued to account for nearly two-thirds of the total membership. Party leaders continued to express their disappointment with the lack of progress in party building among the rural population. They blamed "saboteurs, opportunists, and hangers-on" who were said to be everywhere, "even in the ranks of the armed forces and the government departments."

The training of party cadres is the responsibility of both the Central School of Political Science at Mingaladon, established in July 1963, and the Central Services Training School at Phaunggyi, opened in 1965. Under the direction of Colonel Maung Lwin, a member of the Revolutionary Council and a cabinet minister in 1971, the Central School of Political Science sponsored intensive

176

training—courses lasting from three to nine months—in leadership skills, basic military science, principles of socialist economy, public relations, and party ideology and philosophy. It also conducted two-month reorientation courses for advanced party cadres as warranted. By mid-1970 a total of 9,719 cadres, including 1,017 women, had completed training. By June 1969 about 13,400 soldiers and civil servants had participated in the school's periodic lecture programs.

Placed under the Ministry of Home Affairs, the Central Services Training School offered special programs to civil servants in various subjects relating to party ideology, economics, public relations, code of conduct, military science, and farming. During training, the civil servants were urged to participate actively in party activities, thus abandoning their tradition of nonpartisanship in political affairs (see ch. 8, Political System and Values).

Members of the armed forces were trained separately through their own ideological indoctrination programs, instituted in August 1966. In January 1971, in a further effort to politicize the military, armed forces education committees (also called in-service educational committees) were created within all military units. Special emphasis was placed on the idea that the armed forces constituted the only leading force capable of building socialism, safeguarding independence and sovereignty, enhancing national economic development, and promoting national solidarity. Other common themes were that the army and politics could not separated; that the army should be transformed into a people's army; and that the army was composed almost exclusively of "sons and daughters of peasants, workers, and patriots."

Leadership

In 1971 Chairman Ne Win was assisted by Brigadier San Yu, general secretary of the Central Organizing Committee, and Colonel Than Sein, joint general secretary. Among other leading figures of the party were Brigadier Thaung Dan, Brigadier Sein Win, Colonel Kyaw Soe, Colonel Thaung Kyi, Colonel Maung Shwe, Colonel Maung Lwin, Colonel Hla Han, and Colonel Tin U. All of these men were members of the Revolutionary Council, and all but Colonel Tin U (commander of the Central Command) held one or more cabinet portfolios. Colonel Thaung Kyi and Colonel Maung Shwe were chairmen of the Central People's Peasants' Council and the Central People's Worker's Council, respectively.

General Ne Win expressed concern as early as 1966 over the possible emergence of one-man rule and of an antidemocratic personality cult. Subsequently he repeated a warning against this possibility, advising that the best way to combat this was for the party to exercise collective leadership. In September 1968 he pointed out that concentration of power in a single faction or group would have dangerous consequences. In November 1969, on the occasion of the party's fourth seminar meeting, the general proposed that the draft party constitution then being debated should contain provisions by which leadership could be prevented from perpetuating itself.

In his speech to the party seminar, General Ne Win also expressed the view that the base of political power should be broadened. Thus he stated that "democratic appearances are absent and it may look as if the members of the Revolutionary Council are responsible only to themselves. We have yet to openly seek and obtain the people's mandate." He then emphasized the need of managing the affairs of state "on an enduring constitutional basis."

OTHER POLITICAL FORCES

In September 1968 General Ne Win declared that "politicians, army personnel, civil servants, the intelligentsia, peasants and workers—all must participate in the practice of politics." Later he described this form of popular involvement as direct participatory democracy, a term that was appearing with increasing frequency in party literature in 1971. In the party-controlled scheme of politics, however, students, youths, intellectuals, and Buddhist monks were not assigned any significant role, at least up to 1971.

Since 1962 political activities nevertheless have remained the concern mainly of a limited number of persons in the armed forces, civil service, and police. The peasants and workers who were being exalted as the vanguard of revolutionary forces have been overshadowed by the political activists of bureaucratic origin. Party leaders have continued to express the view that the ideological consciousness of the working people should be further aroused and heightened before they could be assigned the leading role in the current phase of socialist revolution.

Indications persisted that, even among the most politicized segment of the population, the nature of political involvement was not above suspicion. In December 1970 the party stated that some 43,000 out of its 257,500 candidate members were not actively engaged in party activities and urged those people to contact their nearest party unit so that they would not lose their rights.

In February 1969 some of the delegates in attendance at the first seminar of the Central People's Peasants' Council took the occasion to complain that some local council members did not obey rules, had only a scanty understanding of party ideology, and resorted to black marketeering. Lack of coordination among local councils and failure of council members to understand their duties and responsibilities were another common source of dissatisfaction. A similar situation also existed among the workers' movement. Thus in January 1971 an influential, government-controlled English-language daily in Rangoon editorially commented that, despite the Central People's Workers' Council directive urging all local council members to minimize waste and increase production, this appeal remained on paper "since the beginning of the revolutionary socialist workers' movement."

In the late 1960s the government began its limited efforts to bring students, youth, and intellectuals into the mainstream of national politics. The party position toward students and youth has generally been ambivalent since 1962. Although it repeatedly has stated that the future of the nation belonged to the youth, it has done little to organize young people for any partisan purposes. Indications were that students and youths would not be asked to play any significant role, at least until the party felt that there were sufficient cadres to penetrate and organize the ranks of the youth and students. In December 1970 Brigadier San Yu admitted that "the Party has made only a start in organizing the youths."

Traditionally, student activists were mostly leftist oriented and constituted only a small number but were able to influence the majority of the student population on issues ranging from purely campus matters to politics. Since 1962 there have been sporadic incidents of student violence. The first was in July 1962, when a small student protest against regulations limiting campus activities erupted into a mass demonstration at Rangoon. The disturbance was brought under control but not before 15 students were killed and scores wounded as a result of firing by the army. In December 1969 in Rangoon more than 1,000 university students, who were unable to obtain tickets for an athletic event, clashed with police, shouting antigovernment slogans. The government ordered universities closed for nearly a month in mid-December 1969, in order to "relieve parents" from worrying over the disturbance.

The government blamed both leftist and rightist saboteurs for the student riots and condemned their alleged tactics of using their "sons, daughters, and young relatives to carry out anit-people activities." At the same time, it urged parents and elders supporting the socialist revolution to give correct guidance to their offspring, noting that the government was educating students to become builders and defenders of the Burmese socialist system.

In early 1971 it was difficult to determine the political orientations of the study population. The government-controlled newspapers seldom carried any item relating to the attitudes and reactions of the student population toward various official exhortations, such as that the university should be transformed into the training center of the working people's children or that it could no longer function as "the spawning pool of bureaucrats and bourgeoisie."

It was readily apparent, however, that a major source of tension and anxiety among students and educated youth was the continuing problem of unemployment for them. Since the mid-1960s the two arts and sciences universities have been producing about 5,000 graduates annually, and at most only about half of them have been able to secure some sort of employment. In early 1971 the number of unemployed college graduates was estimated to be as great as 20,000.

In 1967 the government helped in the formation of a writers' and journalists' association. This measure was part of its continuing efforts to remold the intellectual group, a frequent target of government attack as an ally of the so-called capitalist class. In early 1970, for example, the government's doctrine was that, although a majority of the intellectuals came to identify themselves with the interests of the working class, some intellectuals were showing contemptuous attitudes toward manual workers. Scholars, journalists, and technicians were being told that they should become socialist, renouncing and discarding old ideas and attitudes not in keeping with party ideology.

The *sangha* (Buddhist monkhood) constitutes a potential source of political activity because Buddhism has traditionally influenced the sociopolitical values and attitudes of some 85 percent of the total population (see ch. 4, Social Systems and Values; ch. 8, Political System and Values). There is a monastery in virtually every village, and in the towns *kyaungtaiks* (clusters of monasteries) house up to 1,500 monks. As nationalists and defenders of the faith, the monks have become a familiar feature of the political scene in recent decades, although their involvement in temporal matters is not sanctioned under the code of monastic discipline (see ch. 7, Religion).

The politics of the monks was confined mainly to an urban setting, especially Rangoon and Mandalay. Before 1962 their numerous associations acted as pressure groups, supporting politicians and parties during elections, and sometimes as a useful tool of the government in opposing communism. Street demonstrations, the adoption of resolutions, sit-ins, and threats of direct action or political reprisals were the common techniques they used in seeking to enhance the status of Buddhism as the state religion. Buddhist agitations reached critical proportions in 1960 and 1961, culminating in a constitutional amendment in August 1961 during the reign of Prime Minister U Nu. The amended constitution stated: "Buddhism being the religion professed by the great majority of the citizens of the Union shall be the State religion." A few weeks later the State Religion Promotion Act was passed, enabling the government to render the assistance for the propagation of Buddhism.

Almost immediately this measure aroused a storm of protest from the country's religious minorities—Muslims, Hindus, Christians, and animists. In an attempt to calm the minorities, the U Nu government in November 1961 passed another constitutional amendment providing for safeguard measures relating to minority religions, but this antagonized many Buddhist monks.

After the military assumption of power in 1962, the Revolutionary Council stated that it would follow the policy of minimum participation by the government in religious affairs and that it would not favor any one religion at the expense of others. This policy was in line with General Ne Win's position, publicized as early as 1945, that the army should show no official sympathy with any particular religion because of the country's multireligious character. The relationship between the *sangha* and the military soon showed signs of tension as the government instituted measures designed to prevent religion from being mixed with politics.

In May 1962 the Buddha Sasana Council, which had been formed in 1951 by the U Nu government to promote the revival of Buddhism, was ordered dissolved. At the same time the Ne Win leadership withdrew the state grant designated for Muslim organizations, thus discontinuing its predecessor's policy of contributing state funds for the promotion of all religions in the country.

Buddhist discontent with the government's socialist policies deepened rapidly, if only covertly. Many monks opposed General Ne Win's nationalization measures, which they believed violated the Buddhist injunction against stealing. They protested loudly against the new government order issued in April 1964 that directed all religious organizations to register with the authorities so that "the use of [a] religious name or religious reason for carrying on other activities" could be prevented. Despite General Ne Win's personal appeal to the monks to refrain from political activities, a wave of antigovernment Buddhist demonstrations erupted in Upper Burma, especially in and around Mandalay; the protesting monks asserted that "the Sangha masses are doubtful as to whether the Revolutionary Council shows as much respect to Buddhism as it does to socialism."

In March 1965 about 2,000 monks of all sects gathered near Rangoon to discuss a government proposal asking the *sangha* to purge itself of the so-called political pseudo-monks and to creat a new, all-sect congregation called the Buddha Sasana Sangha Organization. Deliberations were stormy, however, with many participatnts protesting against a measure requiring all *sangha* members to carry identification cards issued by the organization.

The government asserted that about 80 percent of those present supported its proposal, but a sizable number of monks walked out in protest.

In April there were massive demonstrations in Mandalay against the Buddha Sasana Sangha Organization and the government, resulting in the arrest of 92 leading monks on the grounds of "acting as stooges of capitalistic economic insurgents." More than 70 former party politicians were also taken into custody because of suspected complicity in the disorders. In addition as many as 1,000 Buddhist laymen were arrested on charges of conspiring to lure the monks into politics. In May 1965 General Ne Win went to great lengths to explain that his government was not anti-Buddhist or affiliated with communists.

After 1965 the Buddhist monks did not organize campaigns of protest or direct confrontation with the police. The Buddha Sasana Sangha Organization continued to exist but with only minimal impact on the *sangha* as a whole. An uneasy, undeclared truce continued between the government and the *sangha*. After the late 1960s indications were that the authorities were intensifying their efforts to enlist the support of monks in their counterinsurgency operations, especially in frontier regions. Also tangible was the party's publicity campaign purporting to prove that the Burmese Way to Socialism and Buddhism were inextricably bound to each other, both in theory and in practice.

On the other hand, it was becoming increasingly evident that the place of Buddhism in Burma under Ne Win was not to be what it had been in previous centuries. Echoing official positions, a Burmese source in 1971 asserted that, if Buddhism was to contribute its share to the socialist construction, the people should recognize the fact that "the outdated medieval conception of religion" was now "totally alien to the present age of secularity." Another source went as far as to comment that, with the development of science and technology, it was no longer necessary "to posit a supernatural creation as a theory to explain the existence of everything in the universe."

INSURGENCY AND NATIONAL UNITY

Since independence the inextricable problems of national unity and insurgency have troubled successive governments, civilian and military alike. The problems have been complicated by a combination of at least three major reasons: the persistence of separatist demands among the country's ethnic minorities, which are officially described as national races; the communist attempts to subvert governments in Rangoon and impose their own brands of sociopolitical systems; and the evidence of Communist Chinese support to not only the communist rebels but also some insurgent minorities.

Long before the country's independence a multitude of ethnic groups in the frontier regions had varying degrees of internal freedom that they enjoyed in exchange for their support of British authority. Thus, on the eve of independence, the country's founding fathers went to great lengths to assure that the minorities were accorded sufficient protections and rights under a federal scheme of government. Some ethnic groups, such as the Shans and Kayahs, were given the right to secede from the union after ten years from the date on which the Constitution came into effect. Furthermore, in an attempt to ensure the representation of these groups at the highest echelon of decisionmaking processes, the 125-seat Chamber of Nationalities was created for the ethnic minority groups (see ch. 3, Historical Setting; ch. 8, Political System and Values). Nevertheless, the minorities as a whole continued to agitate for the fullest possible autonomy within the union, prompted mainly by their growing concern that the majority Burmans would eventually encroach on their inherited ways of life (see ch. 4, Social Systems and Values).

Within six months of independence the Karens, the largest of the discontented minority groups, were in armed rebellion, thus joining a band of Communists who had already launched armed struggles. The civil insurrections were soon joined by other minority groups, each independent of the other. Resulting chaos was a major contributing factor in U Nu's decision in 1958 to step down from the premiership and ask General Ne Win to restore law and order in the country.

In March 1962 the Revolutionary Council defended its takeover on the grounds that, among other reasons, the military had to act to prevent the onset of national disintegration. In fact, in many of the frontier regions the government's authority had been increasingly challenged by armed insurgents, and what was initially a moderate autonomy movement had been giving way rapidly to a secessionist movement. The Ne Win leadership declared that a small country like Burma would "sink like Laos and Cambodia" if frontier states were permitted to secede from the union.

The government quickly cracked down on dissident leaders among the minorities, rounding up some thirty Shan leaders on the ground that they had advocated a policy prejudicial to national interests. It abolished the existing elective state councils in frontier areas and replaced them with appointive state supreme councils and generally tightened control of administrative and internal security measures by establishing a military-led hierarchy of security and administrative committees (see ch. 8, Political System and Values).

In April 1963 the government initiated a major step in seeking to end the insurgency by offering amnesty to all rebels; two months later it went further by proposing unconditional peace parleys to all insurgent groups. Peace talks were held with all communist factions, the Shan State Independence Army, the Kachin Independence Army, Mahn Ba Zan's Karen National Defense Organization, the Mon National Defense Organization, and the National Democratic United Front, a coalition of many radical leftist organizations.

In November 1963 the government had to acknowledge publicly that peace negotiations had failed. Hostilities continued as before. A notable exception was the peace parley with the Karen National Defense Organization. In March 1964 the government and the Karen group signed a peace agreement by which minor concessions were granted to the minority group. The state of peace was precarious, however, and the Karen group resumed hostilities in 1967.

After the peace negotiations failed, the government intensified its suppression campaigns, combining with them the initiation of modest developmental activities in the areas of education, health, agriculture, welfare, industry, and communications. According to a government source, the amount of resource allocations for the states in fiscal year 1969/70 was nearly K64 million (4.76 kyat equal US$1) as compared to K15.3 million in 1961/62.

Among other measures designed to make government authority felt in frontier areas were: forming party organizations including people's peasants' councils and people's workers' councils; supporting Buddhist missions as a counterweight to communist propaganda efforts; sponsoring mass rallies in support of government policies and party ideology; and holding "appreciation" meetings for members of the armed forces manning defense posts in frontier areas.

Another major government measure was the decision in 1964 to apply a uniform set of laws to every state of the union in which the administration of justice was based on customary laws of minorities involved. The purpose of this measure was to standardize not only judicial but also administrative procedures throughout the country in an effort to raise efficiency and promote the common awareness of national identity.

An important feature of the government's policies on national unity was the Academy for Development of National Groups, established originally in 1964 at Sagaing but moved to Ywathitgyi in 1968. The purpose of the academy was to train high-school-age students as cadres for service in their respective areas of ethnic origin. Officially described as an "essential sector in the anti-imperialist struggle for Burmese unity as a State," this school offered a four-year program of studies. As of October 1970 the academy had 425 students, who represented forty-seven ethnic groups of the union. In 1970 a Burmese source commented with a note of pride that Burma was one of the four countries in the world to have such a training center, along with the Soviet Union, Communist China, and North Vietnam. Persons of superior caliber from various minorities were also sent to the Central School of Political Science for advanced political and administrative training.

The government's policy on the indigenous cultures of various national ethnic groups was generally circumspect. In 1971 it continued to recognize that the national groups could freely preserve and develop their language and culture as long as they did not adversely affect the unity of the nation. The government was quite firm, however, in its rejection of autonomist or secessionist demands of all sorts.

By 1971 the government had been able to assert that, because of the leadership of the Revolutionary Council and the party, it had done away with capitalism and exploitation in all states and that the Burmese Way to Socialism had opened the eyes of the minorities politically, economically, and socially. It was evident, however, that not all frontier peoples shared the official contention. Armed insurgency by both Communists and minority groups continued with little sign of cessation in the near future.

Indications in 1971 were that the government was firmly in control of much of Upper, Central, and Lower Burma, or Burma proper as they are collectively defined. The authority of the central government was contested in border areas of Kachin, Shan, and Kawthule states and, to a lesser degree, in parts of Sagaing, Arakan, Irrawaddy, and Chin divisions as well as in certain areas of the Kayah State. There were continuing reports of sporadic guerrilla activities even in areas that were considered to be secure.

As available in fragmentary form in 1970 and 1971, estimates of the number of insurgents were varied and conflicting. Most observers agreed that published figures were generally conjectural and had no firm basis. Nevertheless, the frequently cited figures for insurgents among ethnic minorities ranged in 1970 from 13,000 to 17,000. Listed by group, the Karens accounted for 7,000 to 7,500 rebels; the Shans, 3,500 to 5,000; and the Kachins, 3,000 to 4,500. There were reports of rebels among the Mons, Arakanese, and Chins, but their combined strength was considered by the authorities to be insignificant.

Communist insurgents, composed of both Burmans and members of minority groups, were estimated to number about 5,000 in 1970. Of this total, the Communist Chinese-supported Burma Communist Party (White Flag) accounted for 4,000 to 4,500; the rival Communist Party of Burma (Red Flag) had about 500 insurgents. Since 1967 the White Flag Communists have lost considerable strength in their traditional operating areas of central Burma, largely as a result of internal disunity and of more effective operations by the Burmese security forces.

After mid-1967 the communist rebels became a source of grave concern to the government because of mounting evidence that they were supported by Communist China. Their activities were extensive, especially in upper Shan State, where they set up the Northeast Command. They received material assistance from Communist China, and some of them, apparently recruited from both sides of the frontier, also received training in Communist China. From 1968 through 1970 there were frequent reports of clashes between Burmese security forces and the communist rebels in the frontier areas. Thus in March 1968 General Ne Win remarked publicly that his army had much difficulty in fighting these communist insurgents because of the proximity of disturbed areas to the border. He stated, "We have to be very careful lest our bullets go into the other country."

CHAPTER 10

FOREIGN RELATIONS

In 1971 the dominant feature of Burmese foreign relations was, as it has been consistently since independence in 1948, the country's strict adherence to its avowed policy of nonalignment. Burma's leaders have defended this policy as best suited to their domestic and external objectives of national security, internal cohesion, and economic development. Thus the country was not allied with any single nation or bloc of nations in order to refra.n from involving itself in international affairs that might compromise its nonaligned position.

As of 1970 Burma had diplomatic representation in forty nations, of which twenty-two were being served by resident missions. These missions were scattered throughout the world, except in countries in Africa and Latin America. Relations with all countries were generally correct or cordial and were free of tensions. A notable exception was its ties with Communist China, which were strained after mid-1967 but were showing signs of some improvement in 1971. The government of Burma took the position that it would continue to strive for the restoration of formerly friendly relations with Communist China and expressed hope that the communist neighbor would reciprocate in earnest. Although the Burmese have traditionally feared the Chinese a treaty of friendship and mutual nonaggression was signed between the two countries in 1960, the only such treaty to be signed by Burma up to 1971.

Mutually beneficial economic relations existed with many countries. To some of these Burma exported rice to pay for commercial imports as well as economic and technical assistance. The country was seeking and receiving economic aid from any source that it believed would not infringe on its sovereignty and independence. Disillusioned with foreign aid that Burma felt was being exploited by the donor as an instrument of persuasion, the government in Rangoon continued in 1971 to decline any assistance unless it could pay for it or unless there was the firm assurance that political strings were not attached.

The Burmese leadership's desire since 1962 to eliminate as much foreign influence as practicable from the country has led to a reduction of cultural and economic contacts with the outside world. All business enterprises of any importance, many of them foreign owned, have been nationalized, and foreign nationals not electing to apply for Burmese citizenship have been repatriated. Foreign aid programs have been reduced, and foreign credits have often gone unused. Until restrictions were relaxed in July 1969 and again in 1970, foreign tourists were not encouraged to enter the country, nor were foreign correspondents. In 1971 foreign and domestic news was still being channeled exclusively through the government-controlled News Agency of Burma (NAB). Foreign correspondents were still not encouraged in 1971 to visit the country, but they were not completely banned.

Since independence the foreign policy of the government has not been openly questioned by the people nor has parliamentary debate led to any significant policy change. With each new government the continued pursuit of a policy of nonalignment has been both assumed and accepted. The majority of the people appeared unconcerned with foreign affairs, and those ethnic minorities that are organized have concentrated on their own domestic objectives.

BASIS AND CHARACTER OF FOREIGN RELATIONS

Independence and entry into the community of nations came at a time when the cold war between the communist and noncommunist nations was most intense, but Burmese leaders showed little interest in the ideological conflict. Instead, in defining their foreign policy priorities, they focused on three major interrelated objectives, the choice of which was dictated by problems relating to the immediacy of national survival.

These objectives were to preserve the nation's territorial integrity by following a policy of caution and accommodation in relation to Communist China; to seek internal unity by suppressing civil insurgencies and forging a common ground for loyalty to Rangoon; and to diversify and modernize the economy, thus reducing the country's overwhelming dependence on rice exports for foreign exchange. These objectives determined the country's neutral and nonaligned foreign policy.

U Nu, who was deposed as prime minister in 1962 and who was a principal architect of this policy, has defined nonalignment as an impartial examination of every external issue on its merits; friendly relations with all nations possible; and acceptance of aid in the creation of a welfare state, provided the aid is freely given and does not detract from Burma's sovereignty. In practice, this policy has meant nonparticipation in any power bloc. Since 1962 General Ne Win has added another dimension to this policy by seeking to eliminate foreign influence, communist and noncommunist alike.

The achievement of foreign policy objectives hinged most of all on peaceful and neighborly relations with Communist China. Burma shares a 1,358-mile border with its Chinese neighbor, whose historic claims to several tracts on the Burmese side of the frontier had been a major source of anxiety to the government of Burma until the issue was settled in a 1960 agreement. After independence Burma's anxiety was heightened by the fact that communist rebels as well as some ethnic minorities in the frontier regions launched armed insurgency with instigation and support from across the border (see ch. 9, Political Dynamics).

Feeling that it alone was not capable of coping with the growing power of Communist China, Burma sought the support of the United Nations. That the Communist Chinese threat to its existence was uppermost in Burmese minds was attested to by Prime Minister U Nu, who stated after his country joined the United Nations:

> We were not prompted by considerations of . . . aid, education missions . . . and such other benefits likely to accrue from our membership. These things, however desirable, are immaterial. What was foremost in our minds was the expectation of United Nations assistance if our country should be subjected to aggression by a stronger power.

It was also fear of Communist China that influenced Burma's attitude toward the Peking regime in late 1949. Thus, a noted Burmese scholar asserted that "the fear of aggression was at the back of the Union Government's mind when it decided to be the first to recognize the new Communist regime in China" in December 1949.

The Burmese feelings of insecurity were further aroused in 1950 when Communist China seized Tibet and intervened in the Korean conflict. As a result, the country defended the United Nations police action in Korea, but the same consideration that impelled the Burmese faith in the world organization also caused Burma to refrain from condemning Communist China as the aggressor. When Burma realized that the United Nations was being transformed into an instrument of the cold war, it quickly became disenchanted with the world organization. Burma began the search for a new formula of peace.

By 1954 a Sino-Soviet strategy of more active cooperation with nonaligned Asian nations had emerged, and Communist China and India had subscribed to the "Five Principles of Coexistence." First enunciated by Prime Minister Jawaharlal Nehru of India, these principles called for mutual respect for each other's territorial integrity and sovereignty; mutual nonaggression; mutual noninterference in each other's internal affairs; equality and mutual benefits; and peaceful coexistence. Burma has subscribed to these principles, which became the basis for the 1960 treaty of friendship and mutual nonaggression with Communist China. The treaty made it mandatory that Burma refrain from joining any alliance directed against the communist regime. For its part, Communist China pledged not to interfere in Burma's internal affairs.

Burma's opting for a nonalignment policy was influenced by an equally compelling reason—desire to trade with all nations and to seek aid from all possible sources. Since independence Burma has relied on rice exports for much of its foreign exchange earnings, about 60 to 70 percent of its total annual export earnings (see ch. 13, Trade and Transportation). As a result Burmese leaders sought friendly relations with countries of all ideological orientations. At the same time, these leaders accepted foreign aid in an attempt to diversify the economy, reduce dependence on rice, and promote economic development.

Burmese leaders have refused to join the Southeast Asia Treaty Organization (SEATO) on the assertion that this regional defense organization was pro-Western and against Communist China. Although Burma is a member of the Colombo Plan (see Glossary) and the Economic Commission for Asia and the Far East, it has refused to join any other regional body, again on the ground that participation in any grouping of nations would hinder international or regional cooperation. It even turned down the invitation to participate in the United Nations Conference on Trade and Development held in Algiers in October 1967. It also declined to take part in any conference where it might be forced to take sides in the Sino-Soviet dispute.

The nation's refusal to associate with any bloc of countries was illustrated again at the Consultative Conference of Nonaligned Nations, held in Belgrade in July 1969. At the conference, the Burmese delegation declared that many nonaligned nations would face difficulties if they tried to form a separate bloc and that such a bloc was bound to clash with the big powers sooner or later. The delegation thus stated that it could not agree to the formation of a "nonaligned or third world bloc."

POLICY FORMULATION AND IMPLEMENTATION

The making of foreign policy has always been handled by the prime minister or, in the case of the government in power in 1971, the chairman of the Revolutionary Council. The Ministry of Foreign Affairs has the formal responsibility, but important matters, such as the border agreement with Communist China or aid pacts with foreign countries, have been personally handled at the highest level of government. Great care has been taken in selecting officials to conduct foreign affairs. These officials are chosen on the basis of merit and loyalty. In 1971 the minister of foreign affairs, as in the case of all cabinet members, was a military officer.

In a continuing effort to improve ministerial performance, the government in January 1971 reorganized the Ministry of Foreign

Affairs into five departments: political; United Nations and economic; international organizations; protocol and consular; and administration. The Political Department includes three geographical divisions: Asia and the Pacific; Africa and the Middle East; and Europe and the Americas.

The alternatives and means available to policymakers have been limited. Internal conditions, the proximity of Communist China, and the treaty of friendship and mutual nonaggression signed with Communist China in 1960 have helped to inhibit an activist foreign policy. A sizable portion of government resources is channeled toward combating civil insurgencies. Moreover, the country is forced to refrain from involving itself in any situation that might conceivably be viewed by Communist China as threatening its national security. Burma apparently has not been regarded by any of its neighbors as posing a military, economic, or psychological threat.

Lacking the capabilities and resources to pursue an activist foreign policy and avowedly seeking to be left alone, Burma has depended on the written and spoken word as a substitute for power in dealing with other nations. Adherence to agreed principles of international law and pursuit of a nonprovocative policy of nonalignment are relied on in place of military and economic power in pursuing a course designed to keep the country out of ideological and national conflicts that might threaten its existence.

In 1970 Burma had diplomatic representation with forty countries—sixteen in Asia; eleven in Western Europe; nine in the communist world; two in the Middle East; and two in North America.

RELATIONS WITH COMMUNIST CHINA

Relations with Communist China were cordial during much of the postindependence period but became strained in June 1967 because of disturbances involving local Chinese in Rangoon. Although signs of some improvement in these relations began to appear in 1969, there were also continuing indications of apprehension regarding Communist China's intentions. Formal relations between the two countries began in December 1949 when Burma became the first noncommunist nation to recognize the new regime in Peking. Thereafter, Burma sought the good will of Communist China by its policy of accommodation and neighborliness.

An issue that initially caused considerable anxiety on the part of both sides was the presence on Burmese soil of thousands of troops remaining loyal to the Republic of China (Nationalist China) that Communist China considered a threat to its southwestern flank.

Known in Burma as the Kuomintang (see Glossary) irregulars, these troops poured across the border into neighboring Burma in late 1949 to escape the victorious communist forces in Yunnan. By the end of 1950 they had reached a strength of about 10,000 men and had established bases of operations in northeastern Burma from which to conduct raids into Yunnan. Much to the embarassment of the government of Burma, they had also occupied a sizable portion of the area between the Salween River and the Burmese border adjoining Communist China, Laos, and Thailand.

The irregulars posed a serious problem to Burma's efforts to maintain internal and external peace. On the one hand, they began joining with local rebel groups, thus intensifying Burma's civil insurrection problem. On the other, they increased their strength to about 12,000 men by 1952, organized the so-called Yunnan Province Anti-Communist National Salvation Army, and conducted further raids in to Yunnan. As a consequence, Burma became apprehensive that these activities would provide a pretext for a Communist Chinese invasion. The Burmese concern was heightened by occasional reports of Communist Chinese incursions into the Shan State beginning in 1952.

In mid-1952 the Burmese security forces consequently began intensifying their operations against the irregulars but with limited results. Communist China offered help in ejecting the Nationalist troops, but Burma refused for fear of massive Chinese intervention.

In March 1953 Burma turned to the United Nations for assistance in resolving the issue of the irregulars by filing a complaint of aggression against Nationalist China. In April a General Assembly resolution was passed, deploring the presence of foreign forces in Burma and urging all interested parties to assist in the peaceful evacuation of these forces to Taiwan, but the Burmese were unsuccessful in having Nationalist China named as an aggressor.

On a United States initiative, a four-nation joint military commission (including Burma, Nationalist China, Thailand, and the United States) was formed in May under United Nations auspices, and met at Bangkok to discuss evacuation measures. By mid-1954 a total of 6,000 persons including dependents, had been repatriated to Taiwan. On a visit to Peking in December 1954 Prime Minister U Nu assured the communist regime that his government would not allow its territory to be used for any purposes prejudicial to the interests of Communist China. Continuing efforts to remove the irregulars led to a second evacuation of about 4,200 men and dependents in early 1961. In April 1961 the prime ministers of Burma and Communist China jointly stated in Peking that the two countries would "when necessary, act in coordination and cooperation to solve" the issue of the "remnant Kuomintang troops in Burma."

Relations with Communist China were affected also by a border problem dating back to 1886, when China and Great Britain first agreed that the common frontier be jointly delimited and demarcated at a later date (see ch. 3, Historical Setting). The issue remained dormant until 1956, when a Rangoon newspaper reported the presence of Communist Chinese troops in several disputed areas of northeastern Burma; although the report was denied at first, the government of Burma later confirmed it.

Four years of intermittent negotiations resulted in a Sino-Burmese border agreement initiated in January 1960. The agreement ceded small tracts of disputed territory to Communist China in return for permanent Burmese rights to a much larger tract obtained from China by the British in 1897 under what was termed a lease. It also provided for a joint committee to survey and demarcate the boundary. After the completion of demarcation in September 1960, the border pact was formally signed in Peking in October 1960.

The 1960 treaty of friendship and mutual nonaggression between the two countries was to be valid for ten years unless abrogated sooner by either side. The treaty was to remain in force "without any specified time limit" if it survived the initial ten years, but it is still subject to termination on a one-year advance notification. By 1971 neither country had publicly indicated any intention to terminate the treaty.

The two countries entered a new era with the signing in January 1961 of an agreement on economic and technical cooperation. This pact provided for Chinese goods and services to be sent to Burma on an interest-free credit basis "without any conditions and privileges attached" and the sale of Burmese rice to Communist China. The loan, equivalent to US$84 million, was repayable in ten years from 1971 in installments, using either Burmese goods or the currency of a third country to be designated by Communist China. The agreement provided that the loan would be utilized over a six-year period beginning in October 1961 but that the utilization period could be extended by mutual consultation. As of September 1967 Burma had utilized roughly 40 percent of the credits, and none has been used since then. Further data had not been made public by 1971.

Communist China's ability to exert pressure on overseas Chinese in Burma through political and economic means was curbed in 1962 when General Ne Win seized power and took steps to remove foreign influence in the country. All foreign cultural and propaganda activities were banned, including those of the New China News Agency, whose headquarters were raided. Promulgation of the Enterprise Nationalization Law in 1963 brought under government control the two banks in Rangoon owned by Communist China, and Chinese schools, which earlier had been forced to follow a

Burmese curriculum, were taken over by the state (see ch. 6, Education, Cultural Activities, and Public Information).

Nevertheless, the two neighbors were able to maintain friendly relationships in this period, with frequent exchanges of visits between leaders of the two governments. Communist China sought to use Burma as a model to demonstrate to other countries that it could pusue a proper and peaceful relationship with its neighbors. Burma, for its part, welcomed this lack of interference from a regime that posed a potential threat to its existence.

Relations with Communist China deteriorated sharply after the 1967 disturbances that involved clashes between local Chinese residents and Burmese, creating ill feelings in both countries. The so-called June 22, 1967, incident broke out when Chinese students in Rangoon, obviously inspired by the "great proletarian cultural revolution" then underway in mainland China, defied Burmese authorities, protesting against their order forbidding the wearing of Mao Tse-tung badges. In reaction, several days of anti-communist Chinese disturbances broke out in Rangoon and elsewhere. Communist China countered by accusing the Ne Win leadership of being a "fascist military dictatorship" and of following a policy of calculated anti-Chinese persecutions. In August the Chinese Communist Party publicly declared for the first time its support of the "people's revolutionary armed struggle" led by the Burma Communist Party (White Flag), the principal pro-Chinese insurgent group long dedicated to the overthrow of what it termed the "reactionary and revisionist" Burmese government (see ch. 9, Political Dynamics).

As a result, both countries reduced their respective ambassadorial representation to the level of charge d'affairs. By November 1967 Communist China had withdrawn 412 engineers and technicians working on various aid projects underway in Burma, thus for all practical purposes suspending its economic and technical assistance program to Burma.

Burmese reaction was generally circumspect. The Ne Win leadership sought to restore the pre-1967 relationship by treating the June 1967 incident as a purely local phenomenon rather than one instigated by Communist China. Thus, General Ne Win declared in a major policy speech delivered in Nobember 1969:

> We should like to restore the cordial and friendly relations which formerly prevailed between our two countries. We shall strive towards that end, but it takes two to make a friendship, and it is up to the other side also to try. We regard what has passed as past, the unhappy incident of 1967, and we only wish to heal its wounds and erase the scars it might have left on our minds.

In November 1970 Burma had reinstated its ambassadorial representation to Peking; in March 1971 China sent an ambassador to Rangoon. Meanwhile the tone of the attacks on Ne Win emanating from Peking softened considerably after late 1969, and during the latter part of 1970 and the early months of 1971 there was no Chinese propaganda support for the Communists in Burma. There were continuing indications, nevertheless, that Burma was uneasy about reports of Communist China aiding not only the White Flag communist rebels but also the Kachin and Karen insurrectionists (see ch. 9, Political Dynamics).

RELATIONS WITH INDIA AND PAKISTAN

Relations with India have been marked by ambivalence. In the early years of independence the mutual respect felt between prime ministers U Nu and Nehru stood in contrast to the feeling of animosity most Burmese had towards the Indians who, during the period of British colonial rule, held most of the positions of political and economic importance.

Burmese-Indian cooperation in the 1950s was not limited to the personal friendship of the two prime ministers. India supported Burma's bid for admission to the United Nations, wrote off 70 percent of Burma's pre-1947 debt, purchased Burma's rice surpluses, and approved the diversion to Burma of British arms shipments during the most critical period of insurrection from 1948 to 1950. In 1951 the two signed a treaty of friendship.

Relations during the 1960s remained formally friendly, although the death of Nehru and the accession to power in Burma of General Ne Win's nationalistic group of leaders led to domestic policies in Burma that exacerbated the usual antipathy of the Burmese toward people from India. Promulgation of the Enterprise Nationalization Law in October 1963, though not directed against any particular foreign group, hit the Indian community the hardest.

Indians have dominated the twentieth-century economic life of the country. They were successful in business and agriculture. Of the business enterprises nationalized by Burma, some 60 percent were estimated to be in Indian hands. Together with the Chinese, they were granted over 80 percent of the export licenses issued by the government and were often accused of charging usurious rates on loans to Burmese. The Enterprise Nationalization Law put them out of business, and by mid-1968 nearly 158,000 Indians had left the country, leaving fewer than 200,000 Indians still to be repatriated.

The Indians leaving the country were given nothing for their property, forbidden to take even personal articles, and limited to carrying out small sums of currency. The issue of compensation for the Indian assets left behind was among the major items discussed by Indian Prime Minister Indira Gandhi and General Ne Win in

Rangoon in March 1969. The two leaders also discussed measures under which Burmese citizenship could be granted to about 60,000 Indians choosing to remain in the country.

The two countries have cooperated in their common efforts to tighten border security. In early 1966 Burma assured India of its assistance in preventing Naga and Mizo secessionist rebels on the Indian border from using Burmese territory as a staging point for anti-Indian guerrilla activities. In a related area of mutual concern, both countries in March 1967 reached an agreement concerning the demarcation of more than 900 miles of common border. By May 1970, about 400 miles of the border had been demarcated. On the economic level, in 1969 India agreed to supply Burma with rail and track equipment valued at the equivalent of US$9 million on an eight-year, deferred-payment basis.

In 1952 Pakistan and Burma signed a treaty of friendship that formalized relations that have been amicable. The forty-five-mile portion of their common border, corresponding to the ever shifting channel of the Naf River, provided a minor point of contention that was resolved in a 1966 protocol setting a fixed boundary; the demarcation of the disputed boundary was completed in May 1968.

Relations with Pakistan were not adversely affected by Burma's nationalization measures, although some 4,500 Pakistanis were forced to give up their assets in Burma. By mid-1967, nearly 15,000 Pakistanis had been repatriated. In the late 1960s bilateral efforts continued to improve communications and increase trade between the two countries.

RELATIONS WITH OTHER ASIAN COUNTRIES

In 1971 Burma and Thailand were making every effort to maintain proper and friendly relations despite a history of friction. Thai-Burmese wars in the eighteenth and nineteenth centuries still produce a strong emotional reaction among some of the people of both countries.

In 1953 Thailand refused to admit Burmese observers at the staging points used for the evacuation of the Nationalist Chinese irregulars. Burma, dissatisfied with the results of the evacuation, resumed action against the irregulars and in the process accidentally bombed a Thai village. The Thai premier accused Burma of "general unfriendliness." Burma apologized and offered K20,000 (4.76 kyat equal US$1) compensation. Thailand returned the money to Prime Minister U Nu, who, in turn, gave the check to his ambassador to Thailand to be used for the purpose of performing works of merit in Thailand. This exchange was followed by a Burmese-Thai communique waiving all World War II claims held by Burma against Thailand. In 1956 a treaty of friendship was signed.

Burmese efforts to avoid incurring the enmity of a country that shares a 1,000-mile border were dictated mainly by the persistance of insurrections among its ethnic minorities, the Shans in particular, who straddle the Thailand border and speak a dialect of the Tai language. Although the Thai government disclaimed any connection with the Shan insurgency, the Shan rebels are reported to be commanding some sympathy among their ethnic counterparts in Thailand. The same thing was true, perhaps to a greater degree, among the Karens. Nevertheless, lack of effective control by both governments in these frontier areas had not eliminated the activity by early 1971 (see ch. 9, Political Dynamics).

Since 1969 Burma and Thailand have been watching closely the movements of U Nu, who in October 1970, after a year of self-imposed exile in Thailand, was reported in Bangkok newspapers to have slipped back into Burma in an attempt to regain power from General Ne Win. In October 1969, while announcing the granting of political asylum to U Nu, the government of Thailand had assured the Burmese counterpart that U Nu would not be permitted to engage in any activity against Ne Win during his stay in the country. Burma reacted coolly. In 1970 there were conflicting public reports as to whether U Nu was in Burma, Thailand, or somewhere else. In January 1971 Thai Prime Minister Thanom Kittikachorn officially announced that initial police investigation produced evidence of U Nu's presence in Burma. In an effort to establish his country's impartiality, the Thai prime minister also stated that his government would review the activities of U Law Yone, who at that time was serving as U Nu's deputy in Bangkok.

Relations with other Asian countries have been limited, except with Japan. Malaysia, Singapore, and especially Ceylon are markets for Burmese rice. Burma has not developed close ties with the Philippines. In November 1970, however, at the invitation of the president of the Philippines, General and Madame Ne Win paid a goodwill visit to Manila. Burmese relations with Cambodia and Laos were still limited in early 1971, although Burma had played a role in the Geneva Conference on Laos in 1961-62, and the country had ambassadors in both Laos and Cambodia.

Ties between Burma and Indonesia, which is a principal buyer of Burmese rice, have been fairly close. During Indonesia's struggle for independence, Burma denied the use of its airfields and airspace to Dutch planes. The governments of the two countries cooperated closely at the Bandung Conference of Afro-Asian Countries in 1955. Sukarno's policy of confrontation against Malaysia in the 1962-65 period and the withdrawal of Indonesia from the United Nations were reproved by Burma but did not affect surface relations with Rangoon. Despite the reorientation of Djakarta's politics after Sukarno's departure, the two countries continued to maintain cordial ties in 1971.

Burma has withheld diplomatic recognition from governments of North and South Vietnam and similarly from North and South Korea, although all four maintain consuls general in Rangoon. Burmese policy has been to avoid involvement in the controversies between elements of divided states.

Relations with Japan have special importance in view of Burma's need for external assistance. Under the treaty of peace signed with Burma in November 1954, Japan agreed to provide over a ten-year period the equivalent of US$200 million in war reparations and the equivalent US$50 million in economic assistance. In April 1959, however, Burma demanded additional reparations from Japan on the ground that other countries that had not suffered as much severe wartime damage had obtained a disproportionate share of reparations payments. Intermittent negotiations led to the conclusion in March 1963 of an economic and technical cooperation agreement under which Japan pledged to furnish, in addition to the US$200 million, the equivalent of US$140 million in capital goods and services over a twelve-year period. Under this agreement Burma renounced any right to demand further claims.

In February 1969 Japan made commitments to extend the equivalent of US$30 million in commercial loans over a three-year period. These loans were to be used to finance Japanese-aided projects relating to automobile assembly plants and factories manufacturing irrigation pumps and electrical appliances. In April 1970 General Ne Win visited Japan to participate in Burma Day celebrations held at Expo '70, Osaka, Japan.

RELATIONS WITH THE UNITED STATES

In 1971 Burmese-United States relations were friendly and free of tension. They were based on mutual recognition of the two countries' foreign policy positions. The United States continued to support Burma's policy of adhering to strict neutrality and non-alignment. Although disagreeing with United States policies toward Vietnam, Burma refrained from publicly criticizing the United States regarding this issue.

The United States historically has supported Burmese aspirations for national independence. After 1948 and especially after the Communist Chinese seizure of Tibet in early 1950 and Peking's intervention in the Korean conflict later in the year, the United States sought to assist Burma's efforts to promote economic development, strengthen internal security, and resist any external aggression. Economic assistance, exchanges under the Fulbright program, and United States Information Service programs were warmly received at first in Burma. The United States economic aid program was discontinued in 1953, however, at the request of the Burmese government, which asserted that it considered it to be immoral to receive aid from a nation that was indirectly assisting the Chinese irregulars operating on its territory, thus complicating Rangoon's relations with Communist China.

Economic cooperation was resumed in 1956 under a Public Law 480 agreement providing for sale to Burma of surplus agricultural commodities for local currency. Between 1956 and 1966 more agreements were signed for the provision of technical services, loans to help finance economic development projects, and a dollar loan to help the Burmese government purchase transportation, communications, and other equipment for its police. In June 1958 a military sales agreement was also signed; deliveries under this accord were completed in 1971. From the local currency paid by Burma for the agricultural goods, the United States has also extended grants and loans for development purposes.

Since 1962 the Ne Win government's policy of excluding foreign influence has affected the United States along with Great Britain, India, and Communist China. The teaching of English was dropped in the primary schools. The Fulbright, Asia, and Ford Foundation programs were discontinued, and the United States Information Service Library was closed. Overall relations with the United States, nevertheless, continued to be friendly.

In September 1966 General and Madame Ne Win paid a state visit to Washington, and the prime minister exchanged views with President Lyndon B. Johnson. In a joint communique, the two leaders reaffirmed their belief that mutual respect, noninterference, and equality among all nations were "the basic principles underlying the creation of a stable, peaceful international order." They also agreed that "every nation should have the right to choose its own political, economic, and social systems and its own way of life free from any outside interference or pressure." Many observers commented that this visit helped to enhance the already cordial ties existing between the two countries.

RELATIONS WITH THE SOVIET UNION

Burma exchanged ambassadors with the Soviet Union in 1951, but it was not until 1954 that the first broader contacts, in the form of the exchange of cultural missions, were made. The first Burmese-Soviet trade agreement, signed in 1955, set the pattern for subsequent accords. Soviet assistance is paid for, to avoid creating unwanted obligations or to invite any outside interference. From 1955 through 1970 technical, cultural, and defense missions were exchanged periodically.

The experience of the Soviet Union in building a modern industrial state has impressed observers in Burma, where the leadership has generally referred to itself as Marxist but not communist. Despite the ideological affinity of the leadership of the two countries, the Soviet Union was at first cautious in its approach toward the military regime of Ne Win. In 1962 it was slow in affording diplomatic recognition to the new government. A leading Soviet expert on Burma at the time asserted that, although Ne Win's policies were supported by all progressive organizations, his government did not recognize the special role of the working class and the decisive significance of Marxism-Leninism as a theoretical weapon in the Burmese effort to introduce scientific socialism.

Bilateral contacts between Burma and the Soviet Union increased as Burma's relations with Communist China deteriorated after mid-1967. In late 1967 Burma accepted small amounts of arms assistance from the Soviet Union, which also sought to increase its economic assistance. In the latter half of 1967, when relations with Communist China reached a low ebb, the Soviet Union expressed its support for Burma's position against Peking. In 1969 Moscow commented favorably on the "non-capitalist road" that Burma was said to be taking in its effort to establish a socialist society.

On the eve of the twenty-third anniversary of Burma's national independence in January 1971, Soviet press and journals commented favorably on the Ne Win government's policies and programs relating to workers' and peasants' councils, which they asserted were serving as "bases for carrying out socio-economic reforms" (see ch. 9, Political Dynamics). These sources also took note of the fact that the armed separatist struggle instigated by "the feudal-landowner circles in some national districts" as well as "the fratricidal armed struggle" waged by the Red Flag and Peking-supported White Flag communist rebels were not in the interest of Burma. For its part, however, the government of Burma, in an attempt to maintain neutrality, refrained from taking an open position on issues affecting the Sino-Soviet dispute.

RELATIONS WITH COMMONWEALTH COUNTRIES

Burma's attitude toward Great Britain has been marked by a combination of respect for British ideals and residual anticolonial sentiments. Burmese unwillingness to join the British Commonwealth was caused for the most part by the lingering fear expressed by some leaders that British influence would return through a new form of nominally co-equal but British-dominated association.

Nonetheless, Burma's leaders have acknowledged a debt to Great Britain, both in obtaining independence peacefully and in suppressing the activities of communist insurgents as the country was emerging into statehood. Under the Nu-Attlee Agreement of October 1947, which provided the basis for Burma's independence in the following January, the British agreed to the cancellation of debts owed it and, under a supplementary defense agreement, also pledged to provide arms and training to the Burmese army for a four-year period. The British arms proved vital to preserving the integrity of the new Burmese state.

Great Britain, like other countries, has seen its cultural programs and activities eliminated under the Ne Win government. British libraries and schools have been closed, and its commercial enterprises have been nationalized. Stringent visa policies have also affected the activities of British correspondents, who had more contacts in Burma than any other foreign jounalists. In October 1966 Burma left the sterling area, thus severing the last of formal ties it had inherited from British rule.

Nevertheless, in 1971 the bonds of friendship between individual Burmese and Britons remained substantial. During August and September 1967 General Ne Win visited London for a medical checkup. His subsequent trips to London were in May and June 1968, twice in 1969—in April and May and, in July and August—and in May and June 1970. His most recent visit to London for reasons of health was in January 1971.

FOREIGN ASSISTANCE

In 1970 Burma was receiving economic and technical assistance on a reimbursable basis from countries of widely differing ideological orientations, as well as some non-reimbursable reparations assistance. The country was insisting that no political strings be attached to any aid. The most preferred form of aid for Burma was credit extended on a government-to-government basis and repayable over a specified period. Burma was generally against any private investment or joint venture with foreign governments. Actual amounts of aid received from individual countries are difficult to ascertain since these frequently are much less than the amount initially pledged by a particular country. This results from the fact that for various reasons Burma has been slow in utilizing available loans.

Japanese

Japanese reparations to Burma for damages suffered during the Japanese invasion and eighteen months of occupation during World War II have been the largest single source of external assistance to the country. Between 1955 and 1970 Japan agreed to provide

Burma the equivalent of about US$450 million in loans and capital goods and services, much of which has been supplied according to schedule.

The most important project completed with Japanese help has been a large hydroelectric plant and dam at Baluchaung (see ch. 12, Agriculture and Industry). Goods awarded to Burma have included railway equipment, automobiles and buses, and agricultural implements. Under the 1963 agreement on economic and technical cooperation, Burma built plants for the manufacture of agricultural implements and household electrical appliances and assembly plants for trucks, buses, and compact sedans. In 1969 Burma was importing from Japan heavy machinery, motor vehicles, military communications equipment, and construction materials with funds supplied by Japan under the 1963 agreement. In late 1970 a fertilizer plant, built with the US$8-million credit Japan had agreed to provide in 1966, began operating at Sale. Between 1968 and 1969 Japan trained seventeen Burmese engineers and technicians for the fertilizer plant under construction. Japanese assistance has also been directed to oil exploration off the Arakan coast under an agreement signed in December 1968. In late 1970 negotiations took place between the two countries concerning the terms of exploitation of offshore oil on the Arakan coast and elsewhere.

United States

The history of the United States aid to Burma has been affected not only by the inexperience of both countries in administering aid programs in the early 1950s but also by their different attitudes toward communist regimes, particularly the Chinese. In 1971 the only United States aid to Burma consisted of completion of commitments made in earlier years. The last aid agreement between the two countries was negotiated in 1966.

Economic assistance, first begun in 1950, was welcomed by many Burmese. It was aimed at rehabilitating the economy, which had been damaged during World War II and by postindependence civil insurgency. By mid-1953 a total of US$20 million in grants were given for use in the improvement of transportation, financing of commodity imports to relieve shortages, and promotion of agricultural development and health facilities.

By 1953, however, differences had emerged between the two countries regarding the most desirable form of development assistance. The Burmese had become suspicious that the United States was not so much concerned with their own development effort as with a short-range program designed to prevent their country from being taken over by Communists. Furthermore, the Burmese were suspicious of the possible relationship of the United States to the activities of Nationalist Chinese irregulars in Burma. The result of these differences was Burma's request for termination of aid from the United States.

In the following years Burma turned more toward communist countries for assistance, especially in disposing of its large stocks of rice, markets for which had been affected by United States food aid programs in other food-deficit Asian countries. In February 1956, however, Burma again signed an agreement with the United States providing for the sale of US$21.7 million worth of surplus United States agricultural commodities in Burma, to be repaid over a period of forty years; 80 percent of the repaid funds—payable in kyats or dollars—were to be used in Burma for development projects, the remainder being used to defray official United States expenses within the country.

In March 1957 the United States advanced a credit of US$25 million to help finance economic development projects, to be repaid in the same manner as the Public Law 480 commodity sales agreement. Much of this credit was devoted to improving the country's inland water transportation system and land and water resources development projects; as of 1969 most of these projects had been completed.

Under a dollar loan agreement signed in May 1958, Burma was able to purchase US$8.8 million worth of transportation, communications, and other equipment for its police force. In June 1958 a military sales agreement was signed between the two countries; under this accord, the United States agreed to sell, for local currency, equipment and materiel that Burma needed in suppressing insurgencies of both internal and external origin.

Additional agreements signed in 1958 and 1962 provided for a total of nearly US$28 million worth of agricultural commodities to be sold for local currency. In 1962 the United States also extended a loan of US$34 million to finance the purchase of equipment with which Burma was to reclaim ricelands in Pegu and Irrawaddy divisions.

In 1959 the United States agreed to grant US$28 million as a dollar contribution to finance the construction of a highway from Rangoon to Mandalay and an additional US$2 million toward the construction of buildings at Rangoon University. The university project was partially completed by 1966, but in a disagreement over the design and route of the highway the Ne Win government in 1964 asked the United States to terminate the road project.

The last of the aid agreements to be signed was in 1966, when the United States pledged to transfer to Burma the equivalent of about US$17 million worth of local currency for economic development purposes.

Communist

Economic assistance received by Burma from communist countries is for the most part in the form of barter trade agreements. These countries take surplus rice from Burma and, through multilateral clearing accounts, settle in goods and services.

The first aid pact with a communist country was concluded with the Soviet Union in 1957. In return for a number of what the Soviet Union called "gift" projects, such as the construction of an institute of technology, a hotel, a hospital, a theater, a sports stadium, a swimming pool, a conference hall, and a permanent exhibition hall, the Burmese were to meet all local costs and deliver specified amounts of rice to the Soviet Union over a period of twenty years. This agreement differed little from the straight barter agreements and dissatisfied with the scheme, the Burmese government cancelled the agreement in 1959, with only the first three projects having been completed.

In 1958 the Soviet Union made a loan equivalent to between US$4 million and US$7 million to meet the cost of building irrigation dams, which were completed in 1967. In 1965 it also extended a credit equivalent of US$1 million for the purchase of tractors and agricultural equipment and a loan of US$3.9 million, part of which was to be used for the purchase of equipment needed for surveying irrigation projects. In December 1969 the Soviet Union also signed a US$1.7 million loan agreement for the rehabilitation of the Mawchi tungsten and tin mines. In October 1970 it was announced that the Soviets would extend technical assistance in the medical field in the form of four experts and US$22,000 worth of medical equipment. In 1971 there were also three hydraulic engineers with the Department of Irrigation and eight professors at the Institute of Technology (Rangoon).

Communist Chinese aid was given under the 1961 agreement for economic and technical cooperation, which provided a credit equivalent to US$84 million, to be utilized by the end of September 1967. The projects agreed upon between the two countries included the enlargement of Burma's steel mill and the construction of two hydroelectric power plants; tire, textile, plywood, paper, and diesel engine factories; two sugar mills; two bridges; and an orchard farm.

By mid-1967 one sugar mill, one bridge, and the orchard farm had been completed, and work had been in progress on the textile and paper mills and the two hydroelectric plants. Except for the second bridge, completed by the Burmese in July 1968, and the plywood factory, finished also by them in October 1969, the status of remaining incomplete projects was uncertain because, for all practical purposes, aid from Communist China had been suspended since the disturbance in June 1967.

Burma has also received varying amounts of assistance from Eastern European countries. In 1962 Romania provided technical assistance in exploring and drilling for oil. In 1964 Yugoslavia extended a credit equivalent to US$8 million for unspecified agricultural and industrial projects; in 1966 an additional credit equivalent to US$8 million was given for the purchase fo unspecified factory equipment. In 1964 East Germany advanced a credit equivalent to US$14 million for health, educational, and sports projects; furthermore, in 1966 it provided another credit equivalent to US$14 million to be used by the end of 1970 for the purchase of industrial plants and equipment from East Germany. Poland agreed in 1966 to furnish the equivalent of US$10 million for the purchase of Polish machinery and equipment for the construction of industrial plants; as of May 1970, however, none of this US$10 million had been utilized.

Other Assistance

In 1962 West Germany provided the equivalent of US$8.8 million in official loans and guaranteed a private credit of US$2.5 million. In addition, it agreed in 1967 to finance the construction of a fertilizer plant at Kyunchaung, with a credit of K19 million. The construction was completed by the end of 1970. When General Ne Win visited Bonn in October 1968, West Germany raised its loan of US$8.8 million to US$12.5 million and the private credit from K12 million to K28.5 million. The official loan was unrestricted, to be used how and where the Burmese government desired. Part of the private credit was to be devoted to the purchase of new ships for the Burmese merchant marine. These ships were to be constructed in Hamburg. Other projects underway with West German help were tile and canning factories, a spinning and weaving mill, and a plant to manufacture diesel engines, electric motors, and power tillers. A glass-bottle factory and two brick factories were completed in 1969.

In September 1970 West Germany and Burma signed two aid agreements calling for a long-term loan of the equivalent of US$6 million for both onshore and offshore oil exploration and exploitation and a grant of about US$2 million to be used for the services of experts and the delivery of equipment. Under the September agreements, a West German firm began in late 1970 a seismic survey of the potentially oil rich Gulf of Martaban. Another agreement for technical cooperation in the exploration of mineral resources was signed with West Germany on February 15, 1970.

Aid from Great Britain has been channeled through the Colombo Plan. Assistance has been mainly educational, technical, and medical. Great Britain has supplied educational and scientific equipment to Rangoon University as well as to various technological and agricultural institutes.

Australia, also operating through the Colombo Plan, has provided both capital and technical assistance. In the late 1960s it was providing fertilizers, irrigation pumps, railway cars, and technical training. By the late 1960s it had given approximately K55 million in assistance.

Burma has also received aid from both regional and international organizations. By mid-1966 it had received a total of the equivalent of US$8.15 million in grants from the Colombo Plan countries. For purposes of technical training, it sent between 1952 and mid-1967 a total of 1,498 trainees and students to thirteen countries of the Colombo Plan: 483 to Australia; 473 to Great Britain; 172 to Canada; 91 to New Zealand; 88 to Japan; 79 to India; 33 to Pakistan; 31 to Singapore; 19 to Ceylon; 15 to Malaysia; 10 to Indonesia; 2 to the Philippines; and 2 to Thailand. During the same period specialists and consultants visited Burma; among the most important contributing countries were Great Britain, Japan, Australia, New Zealand, India, and the United States.

Canada has been another donor of assistance, also through the Colombo Plan. In late 1970 Burma was interested in obtaining Canadian assistance in mining and in the timber industry.

INTERNATIONAL AND REGIONAL ORGANIZATIONS

Burma joined the United Nations in April 1948 and has since participated actively in the world organization. In 1953 Burma turned to the United Nations General Assembly for assistance in evacuating Nationalist Chinese irregulars to Taiwan. In 1956 it offered to send troops to participate in the United Nations peacekeeping action in the Gaza Strip. In 1960 it dispatched a small group to the Congo in support of United Nations forces there.

Burma became a member of the Colombo Plan in 1952 and has actively participated in its student and technical exchange programs; it served as host for the 1967 ministerial meeting of the Colombo Plan held at Rangoon in December. Nevertheless, as of early 1971 it has refrained from joining any of the numerous regional organizations organized by its neighboring countries. For example, despite a standing invitation for membership, Burma had yet to associate with the Association of Southeast Asian Nations (ASEAN), set up in 1967 by Thailand, Malaysia, the Philippines, Indonesia, and Singapore. Another organization that Burma refused to join was the Asian Development Bank, which was inaugurated in 1966 under United Nations auspices. Some observers have commented that Burma's disinclination to participate in these bodies stemmed from its apprehension that Communist China might misinterpret its motives.

In 1971 Burma was represented on the following specialized agencies of the United Nations: the International Atomic Energy Agency; the International Labor Organization; the Food and Agriculture Organization; the United Nations Educational, Scientific and Cultural Organization; the World Health Organization; the International Bank for Reconstruction and Development; the International Finance Corporation; the International Development Association; the International Monetary Fund; the International Civil Aviation Organization; the Universal Postal Union; the International Telecommunications Union; the World Meteorological Organization; the Intergovernmental Maritime Consultative Organization; and the Interim Commission for the International Trade Organization. Burma was also a contracting party to the General Agreement on Tariffs and Trade.

SECTION III. ECONOMIC

CHAPTER 11

CHARACTER AND STRUCTURE OF THE ECONOMY

The country's fundamentally agrarian economy has developed around its rich agricultural and forested lands and its abundant fishery resources. In 1970 agriculture, forestry, and fishing together accounted for about 35 percent of the country's gross national product (GNP). Other than the processing of agricultural products, industry was still in an embryonic state and generated 11 percent of the GNP. Producing units, whether in farming, fishing, forestry, or industry, were for the most part small. The preponderant agricultural sector comprised an export component of basically one staple cash crop—rice—and one forestry product—teak—superimposed upon an extensive subsistence base, including handicraft industry. Trade and finance, including rice marketing, accounted for 34 percent of the GNP. The 20-percent balance of national output originated in other sectors, including 9 percent from government services and 7 percent from transportation and communications.

The majority of the people in 1971 were primarily agricultural workers, with low incomes and a 40-percent illiteracy rate. The bulk of the country's manpower was unskilled and, because of primitive production techniques, lack of modern tools and equipment, and inadequate training, productivity was quite low. In addition to these factors, because of the steady growth of population, the GNP per person in 1971 was calculated as among the lowest in Southeast Asia and probably below the pre-World War II level in real terms.

In 1971 the country was predominantly rural, with only about 12 percent of the labor force, estimated at 10.5 million persons in 1968, living in urban areas. In 1968 agriculture employed over 65 percent of the labor force; manufacturing, about 7 percent; mining, under 1 percent; construction, about 1 percent; transport and communications, almost 3 percent; and other sectors, about 22 percent.

The Revolutionary Government of the Union of Burma had demonstrated its intent to pursue a course of total socialization. In the nine-year period from March 1962 to March 1971 the government has nationalized banking, insurance, foreign trade, domestic wholesale trade, most retail trade, shipping agencies, motion picture houses, and many printing and publishing firms. Also nationalized were the petroleum industry, most of the mining industry, most of the nation's sawmills, and most manufacturing enterprises employing twenty-five or more persons except those rice, flour, and oil mills that were seminationalized—that is, privately owned but operating under the control of government supervisory committees (see ch. 12, Agriculture and Industry; ch. 13, Trade and Transportation).

In the resulting situation of an overburdened administrative machinery and in the absence of sufficient price and other incentives, economic activity had tended to slacken, despite the country's large agricultural, timber, and mineral potential. The nation had taken only limited recourse to long-term borrowing abroad and had avoided arrangements with foreign capital to exploit its resources. The government had published in March 1971 the draft First Four-Year Plan for submission in June 1971 to the first national congress of the Burma Socialist Program Party (BSPP). The draft plan would cover the four-year period beginning October 1, 1971.

There had been a problem in the 1960s and early 1970s of growing unemployment and underemployment, particularly among the educated. Strikes were not permitted; labor disputes were submitted to local conciliation committees consisting of labor officers. During the late 1960s a network of workers' councils had been formed to complement the local conciliation committees in the implementation of wage policy.

Joint consultative committees, comprising representatives of both workers and employers in factories, work places, and industrial establishments, had been formed to enable the workers to participate, according to a uniform procedure, in the management and operation of the industrial enterprises of the country, as provided in the 1964 Law of Fundamental Rights and Responsibilities of Workers (see ch. 12, Agriculture and Industry).

Rice represented half the value of all agricultural output. Minor crops included sugar, peanuts, beans, peas, corn, sesame, tobacco, fruit, tea, wheat, and rubber. Although overall agricultural acreage was about 12 percent above pre-World War II levels, that devoted to rice was in 1971 still below the 1939 magnitude. Production of rice, however, had increased because of improved farm practices, but exports had declined sharply. In 1963 the country still led the world in rice exports, with 1.7 million tons, nearly 30 percent of the world rice trade. From 1963 to 1968 rice exports had declined because a rising share of government rice procurement has been used to meet domestic needs. In 1969 the country exported 541,000 tons, less than 10 percent of world trade. Rice, together with oilcakes, metal concentrates, and teak—a government monopoly, with production in 1970 substantially below the pre-World War II level—accounted for over 85 percent of total exports in 1970.

The country's trade and payments position had deteriorated in the late 1960s and early 1970s, mainly because of the decline in rice exports. As a result, essential imports of consumer goods and capital goods for development have had to be curtailed. The distribution of the country's export trade was dominated by the rice-consuming countries of Asia; the most important sources of imports were the countries of Western Europe, Japan, and Great Britian.

Evidence of inflation included a persistent disparity between official and unofficial exchange rates. Practical self-sufficiency in basic food requirements at the village level, however, generally immunized the rural population from the hazards of the monetized part of the economy. The inflation had been caused in part by an increased money supply and in part by inadequate government distribution of goods.

During 1970 the country had been experiencing a substantial expansion of bank credit related to a considerable accumulation of government rice stocks and to limited rice export sales. Lower government revenues associated with reduced rice incomes had contributed to a growing fiscal deficit. A serious decline in the country's international reserves, which fell by 30 percent in 1970 to the lowest level in fifteen years, had limited monetary expansion but might lead in the period beyond 1971 to a further reduction in imports and thereby aggravate existing pressures on prices.

In 1970 exports had fallen to their lowest level since independence was attained in 1948. Exports had reached their post-World War II peak in 1963 and in the intervening seven years had fallen almost annually for a total drop of 60 percent over the period. One reason for the drop in export earnings had been the depressed state of the world rice market in the early 1970s. The country's rice export prices had declined by 31 percent in two years, with about half the fall occurring in 1970.

A continuing serious handicap facing the economy was the festering insurgency, although its effect was difficult to measure in statistical terms. The insurgency had hampered the extraction of teak, mineral ores, and precious stones. Combating the insurgency also represented a drain on the economy in terms of resources allocated to the defense services, which in 1971 were 35 percent of regular government expenditures (see ch. 14, National Defense and Internal Security).

Another serious strain on the economy was the virtual extinction of the country's managerial and professional class that occurred after the Revolutionary Government assumed power. Between 1962 and 1971 at least 220,000 persons had emigrated, and perhaps 2,000 senior civil service officials had been forcibly retired or removed from office. Their replacements, often military officers, had generally been either inexperienced or unqualified. Some evidence had appeared by 1971, however, that the new managers were learning their work and that some good appointments had been made by the government. Progress has been slow, however, perhaps because no comprehensive system has existed for advancement by merit. Uncertainty about tenure has prevailed at all executive levels, and the primary criterion for senior appointments as of 1971 still appeared to be political reliability (see ch. 8, Political System and Values; ch. 9, Political Dynamics).

The government was aware that no substantial material incentives to individual enterprises or managers were provided under the existing system. The government took the position that employees should not be motivated by considerations of material gain but should instead be impelled by moral precepts and by having a theoretical voice regarding the economy through what the government called "people's workers' councils" and "people's peasants' councils" (see ch. 12, Agriculture and Industry). Other incentives approved by the government included nonmaterial awards, such as the titles "Model Worker" and "Hero of Socialist Labor."

Executives in the state enterprises were not well paid. One aspect of the nationalizations had been the subsequent huge reductions in salaries of the executives of the nationalized firms, usually by more than 50 percent. Bonuses for good performance did not exist at any levels of the state enterprises, and overtime pay was rarely permitted. The workers could not easily be discharged, but executives could be removed. Civil service officials and employees had received no increase in salaries and allowances from 1962 to 1971 (see ch. 8, Political System and Values).

The government's main criterion for judging the operations of the state enterprises was their ability to meet production targets. Considerations of quality, service to customers, or maximization of profits were secondary elements in the government's view. This attitude was reflected in the poor monetary performance of the state enterprises. As of 1971 the state enterprises had registered an overall deficit in all but one of the preceding eight years.

Although the country's economy had been described as one of state monopolies, these monopolies had only limited autonomy. They were not free to determine prices for their products, to fix salary scales, or to decide what persons should fill senior positions. Their entire income was required to be transmitted to the government Treasury, whereas their spending was dependent on government budget allocations, adjusted quarterly.

The government also realized that organizational rigidities often impeded progress toward efficiency. State factories were ordered to obtain their raw materials from a particular trade corporation, with the supplies being brought by the State Transport Board, and to sell their products to another trade corporation, with the goods again being moved by the State Transport Board (see ch. 13, Trade and Transportation). If any link in this fixed chain of distribution broke, the whole system became semiparalyzed, according to the numerous complaints, printed in the controlled government press, of congestion of goods, shortages, or spoilage of goods by inordinately long storage.

The economy was also distorted by having three kinds of pricing systems. These were a limited free market in certain foodstuffs and locally made household items, a low price level for rationed goods that were either imported or produced in state factories, and a pervasive black market in rationed or smuggled goods. By 1971 smuggling and the black market were flourishing and played an important role in the supply and allocation of scarce commodities.

ECONOMIC STRUCTURE

In a policy declaration of May 1962, setting forth the principles of the Burmese Way to Socialism, the Revolutionary Government stated that the vital means of production and distribution should be nationalized in order to carry out its socialist plan. Accordingly, the banking system, foreign trade, domestic wholesale trade, and most of the retail trade were nationalized during the ensuing years. All important industries were either nationalized or placed under supervisory committees, and a policy of not approving new private investments was adopted. In 1963 the Land Tenancy Act was promulgated, entrusting the village land committees with the right of allotting land to tenants. Two years later the government abolished the payment of all tenancy rents.

In December 1968 the Revolutionary Government nationalized: all motion picture theaters and film exhibition business; many sawmills and their milling business; and 168 industrial establishments, including 60 in the textile industry, 28 in foodstuffs, 23 in chemicals, 16 in metals, 9 in engineering, 2 in porcelain and pottery works, and 30 in various other industries, such as rubber, leather, and umbrellas.

Between December 1968 and June 1969 an additional large number of industrial and other enterprises—including motion picture theaters, sawmills, shipping agencies, publishing houses, and printing works—most of which were already controlled by supervisory committees, were nationalized. As of the first quarter of 1971 no compensation procedures for the owners of these enterprises had yet been decided. It was the Revolutionary Government's general policy, however, to retain former owners as salaried managers after nationalization.

All private banks—fourteen foreign and ten domestic—had been nationalized in February 1963. The two foreign banks owned by Communist China had voluntarily surrendered all claims to compensation. Following an appeal of the original findings of a compensation commission, according to which five of the twelve other foreign banks were entitled to compensation totaling K1.4 million (4.76 kyat equal US$1), the decisions were revised in early 1969 on the basis of a formula more favorable to the banks. As of the first quarter 1971 final decisions were still pending for four banks that had appealed the revised decisions to the chairman of the Revolutionary Council. The various reports of the compensation commissions on other nationalized foreign firms, including foreign companies that had participated in joint ventures with the government, were also still under consideration as of the first quarter of 1971.

There were 1,254 public factories in operation in 1969, and 54 factories were under construction. At the same time there were 16,149 private factories, of which only 27 were government controlled. About two-thirds of the private factories had less than ten workers, however, and few employed more than fifty.

In 1971 the Revolutionary Government's economic policy aimed at specified types of ownership and operation within the country's economic system. These were: state ownership of key industries pertaining to production and consumption, excluding agriculture; state supervision of industries that in accordance with policy were supposed to be state owned but had not yet come under full state ownership; cooperative ownership of agricultural and commercial enterprises that could not yet be nationalized; and private ownership of enterprises that were not owned by the state or by the cooperatives.

In accordance with these guidelines, the Revolutionary Government had announced in May 1970 a comprehensive plan for cooperatives, which was to be implemented under the responsibility of the Cooperative Council. The council was headed by the minister of cooperatives and included several other ministers and representatives of the Burma Socialist Program Party, the Central People's Workers' Council, the Central People's Peasants' Council, and other organizations (see ch. 9, Political Dynamics; ch. 12, Agriculture and Industry).

Under the Union of Burma Cooperative Societies Law of 1970, promulgated by the chairman of the Revolutionary Council on May 28, 1970, cooperative societies were to be organized in three types. These were consumer cooperatives, production cooperatives, and savings and credit cooperatives. There were to be eight categories of production cooperatives: farming, gardening, fishing, stockbreeding, forest, mineral, manufacturing, and handicrafts. Other types of cooperatives were to be introduced when necessary.

The existing agricultural multipurpose cooperatives would be reorganized as consumer cooperatives, and consumer cooperatives would also be formed in urban areas. Heads of families permanently residing in an area were eligible for membership with equal shares. The consumer cooperatives would provide a supply of food also to nonmembers, although preference would be given to members. Farming, or agricultural production, cooperatives would be formed on the basis of village tracts, usually consisting of from five to ten villages. Members would also in this case contribute equal shares.

Manufacturing production cooperatives would be formed on the basis of industries and territories; for example, a weaving cooperative would have as its members weavers from a group of five or six villages. Members were to enjoy benefits according to their work and shares, which would not be of equal value. Savings and credit cooperatives would be formed on the basis of work establishments. Permanent members of the work establishments were eligible for membership and would be required to contribute equal shares. These cooperatives would also accept savings, which would be paid interest. The funds derived from shares and savings would be used as loans to needy members. All cooperatives would have to carry out their ventures with their own savings or with capital borrowed from the People's Bank of the Union of Burma, if necessary; no private investment would be accepted.

The cooperatives would be organized as a system of primary, township, and central cooperative societies, where all the registered primary cooperatives within a township were eligible for membership in the township cooperative, and all registered township cooperatives functioning in the townships were eligible for membership in the central cooperative. The position in 1970 with respect to the then-existing cooperatives was: agricultural production cooperatives, 12,563 societies with 3,805, 375 members; manufacturing production cooperatives, 27 societies with 16,850 members; services cooperatives, 271 societies with 78,263 members; savings and credit cooperatives, 328 societies, with 70,875 members; and general cooperatives, 67 societies with 13,211 members.

In 1971 the targets of the Revolutionary Government's cooperative plan included the formation of 24,304 primary cooperative societies with a total membership of more than 10 million persons. Within this grouping the plan aimed for 10,000 consumer cooperatives with 5 million members, 304 savings and credit cooperatives with 80,000 members, 13,000 agricultural production cooperatives with 5 million members, and 1,000 manufacturing production cooperatives with 15,000 members.

Township cooperatives were scheduled to number 311, with 24,304 members. There would be one central cooperative, with 311 members. The township cooperatives would have the responsibility of operating a wholesale shop, a commodity center, and a cooperative brokerage and would control and coordinate the activities of the primary cooperatives among themselves and with those of other townships. The central cooperative would not itself deal in trade but would be responsible for supervising, coordinating, and organizing the business ventures of the primary and township cooperatives. All the cooperatives would be controlled by the Cooperative Directorate, operating under the broad supervision of the Cooperative Council.

The government anticipated that the 1970 membership in cooperatives of 4 million persons would ultimately be expanded to 21 million persons, or the entire adult and adolescent population, with the bulk of membership to be fifty-family cooperatives at the village level. According to the Revolutionary Government's comprehensive cooperative plan, the government would play primarily an educational role, whereas decisions about distribution and production would devolve to village and township leaders.

Through the first quarter of 1971 a few pilot consumer cooperatives had been established. The remarks on cooperatives in the major speech delivered by the chairman of the Revolutionary Council in November 1969 and subsequent authoritative pronouncements had made it clear that the state would supply the staff of the cooperatives; they would be members of the Burma Socialist Program Party or retired army personnel. Governmental policy announcements and the provisions of the Cooperative Societies Law also specified that the state would have the determinative say in the system by various controls and through the right to appoint one-third of the members of each cooperative committee. The public was to supply the capital and would be allowed to elect the other two-thirds of the committee members.

When the chairman of the Revolutionary Council announced the plan to introduce a system of state-controlled cooperatives, he explained it largely in terms of helping to solve the chronic problem of distribution, which was blamed for the general scarcity of consumer goods, and to mobilize more loan capital for consumers. He stated that the new cooperatives would replace much of what remained of private enterprise and certain state trading activities. The deputy minister of cooperatives, speaking at a later date, preferred to use the justification that the new cooperative system "is designed to completely abolish capitalism in all its manifestations."

The reported reaction of the public to the new cooperative program had been generally apathetic or skeptical through the first quarter of 1971. Residents asked privately how the consumer cooperatives could be expected to solve the shortage of consumer products. At best, they saw the cooperatives dispensing rationed items more honestly than the unpopular people's retail shops (see ch. 13, Trade and Transportation).

216

ECONOMIC DEVELOPMENT POLICY AND PLANNING

As of the first quarter of 1971 the country had no formally adopted development plan. During 1969 and 1970 and the first quarter of 1971 the practice was to work within the annual budgetary procedures and, given the broad framework of development priorities, to adjust implementation to the availability of resources.

The draft First Four-Year Plan, to cover the fiscal period 1971/72 to 1974/75, was part of the "Guide to Economic Planning for the Union of Burma" to be submitted to the first national congress of the Burma Socialist Program Party, scheduled for June 1971. The guide stated that plans for each year of the First Four-Year Plan period would be made within the plan framework, and annual budgets would be prepared on the basis of these yearly plans.

In 1971 the broad rationale of the government's economic development policy continued to be to increase primary output to achieve surpluses for export that would make possible a larger inflow of imports, notably materials, spare parts, and equipment, and in this manner to attain a higher rate of capital utilization and investment. The government was convinced that greater imports of intermediate goods, spare parts, and equipment were essential to facilitate the full utilization of existing productive capacity as well as the expansion of capacity. Agriculture had received principal emphasis because the country's endowment of resources made such emphasis appropriate. Investment resources devoted to industry had in the late 1960s and early 1970s exceeded those allocated to agriculture because of the greater capital intensity of industry and the need for a broadened industrial base to provide the foundation for agricultural development—for example, supplying implements. The regime also has as an objective the creation of industries capable of saving foreign exchange.

In agriculture the government's efforts in 1971 continued to be directed toward both more intensive and more extensive cultivation, the latter mainly by enlarging the size of holdings by cultivation of fallow and waste land. In its efforts to raise agricultural productivity, the governmental authorities had focused on extension services, for example, providing incentives in the form of fertilizers, seeds, credit, and other facilities in specific areas where certain crops had been selected for cultivation on the basis of soil analysis and climate. To deal with the problem of small uneconomical holdings, joint working had been encouraged in order to facilitate the use of mechanized methods. Voluntary groupings of landless agricultural laborers had been given preferred treatment in the distribution of cultivable wastelands and reclaimed alluvial islands.

217

In addition, land had been redistributed with a view to the abolition of tenancy and the settlement of landless laborers. Virtually all the country's farms were worked privately, with agriculture representing the largest single segment of private-sector activities. In the agricultural sector, emphasis had also been placed on irrigation projects and programs, including the use of more machinery, pesticides, and chemical fertilizers. Two fertilizer plants under construction in the early 1970s, with a combined capacity of 120,000 tons, were expected to be completed sometime in the early 1970s. They would, however, satisfy only a part of projected needs because the government expected consumption of fertilizer to increase sharply in the late 1970s.

The mobilization of resources for investment through the generation of increased exportable surpluses had continued to encounter difficulties in the late 1960s and early 1970s. The world market outlook for rice had worsened in that period because of the increased availability of rice in a number of Asian countries, such as India, Indonesia, Japan, Pakistan, and the Phillipines. The government had recognized by 1969 that the country would have to adjust to a weak world market for rice in the medium-term future—that is, in the next five to ten years. Diversification of exports, for several years a broad goal of the Revolutionary Government's economic policy, had therefore become more urgent by 1970.

To achieve diversification of exports, there was scope in early 1971 for increasing the production and export of some commodities, such as pulses, oilcakes, and cotton. World demand for timber continued strong in 1971, but security problems in the timber areas limited the possible growth in production and exports. There was in 1971 considerable potential in crude oil and other mineral resources. The government had concluded, however, that to expand the scale of exploitation of these resources, more exploration, additional technical knowledge, and investment on a substantial scale in equipment as well as in transportation and storage facilities would be necessary. The government estimated that, because the amount of capital necessary to produce an additional unit of output tended to be high in the case of such investments and because the gestation period tended to be long, a marked increase in output was unlikely until the late 1970s.

In the first quarter of 1971 the governmental authorities continued to aim at a growth in output of paddy, or unmilled rice, that allowed for increased domestic consumption and exports. The country's output of paddy had fluctuated in the 1960s around an unchanging average level. As domestic consumption in that decade had apparently grown faster than population, the annual exportable surpluses had declined by 1971 to a level considerably below the amount of rice available for export ten years earlier.

As of the first quarter of 1971 the government considered that, in relation to the area of the country and its ample natural resources, the country could be said to be underpopulated. The government believed, therefore, that there was no need in the early 1970s for a population policy. Family planning assistance by the medical profession was not permitted, nor was foreign exchange granted for family planning materials, except for limited serious medical cases.

GOVERNMENT FINANCE

The State Budget

The consolidated budget of the government sector, comprising the national government, the states, the boards and corporations of the state enterprises, and the local governing bodies, is known as the state budget. Although the consolidated budget covers all public boards and corporations, the loan transactions of these financial entities remain outside the budget.

The budget figures appear in three versions: the original estimates, issued in the period immediately preceding each new fiscal year (October 1 to September 30); the revised estimates, made in the middle of the fiscal year; and the accounts, or actuals, calculated after the close of the fiscal year. The original estimates generally present a more favorable picture of income and expenditures than do the two subsequent presentations. For example, in 1969 the original estimates showed an overall deficit of K114 million; the revised estimates, a deficit of K261 million; and the accounts, a deficit of K301 million.

The consolidated budget might be considered as comprising four categories of income and expenditures: regular government, state boards and corporations, various special financial accounts, and foreign loans and grants. Regular government means current expenditures for ordinary government activities under the ministries. The state enterprise sector (the state boards and corporations) accounted for about 75 percent of total income and expenditures. State enterprises are not allowed to retain their income but are required to transfer it to the Consolidated Cash Fund, from which funds are returned to the enterprises according to budget allocations revised quarterly.

As of the first quarter of 1971 the amount of data available on the budget was limited. Many of the details were not made public. No analysis of the budget was published, and there was no public discussion of budget policies and priorities. The budgets were announced by decree, and the controlled press urged the people to fulfill the government's program.

The budget in effect in the first quarter of 1971—that is, the budget covering the period from October 1, 1970, through September 30, 1971—proposed record high totals of income and expenditures and an overall deficit of K196 million. This deficit represented about 2 percent of planned expenditures and was equivalent to about 8 percent of the money supply as of September 30, 1970. The full potential inflationary effects of a budget deficit of this magnitude on the expansion of the economy appeared to informed observers to be reduced by an excess of imports over exports, largely financed by a further reduction of foreign exchange reserves. This pattern of events had prevailed in the latter half of the 1960s.

From 1964 to 1969 actual income and expenditures had proved in each of the five years to be lower than originally planned. This trend demonstrated both the slackening performance of the economy, as shown in the income side of the budget, and the willingness of the fiscal authorities to reduce planned expenditures sharply in order to avoid excessive deficit financing. In 1969, the latest year for which actual accounts were available, income finished 12 percent less than originally projected in the budget estimates, and planned expenditures were reduced 10 percent below their original level. The revised estimates for 1970 showed income 10 percent and expenditures 7 percent lower than planned.

The state enterprise sector of the budget was in 1971, as in previous years, expected to provide an overall surplus, although the projected amount of K22 million was relatively low. The state enterprise sector, however, had registered deficits in every year but one of the 1962-70 period. In 1970 the state enterprise sector showed a deficit of K173 million, compared to the surplus of K33 million projected in the original budget estimates.

Expenditure

The significant aspects of the expenditures portion of the budget were primarily the indications of the government's economic development priorities, the importance of defense spending, and the apparent lack of interest by the Revolutionary Government in the minority-dominated areas of the country (see ch. 4, Social Systems and Values). Public investment comprised the capital expenditures of the state enterprises and regular government. In absolute and percentage terms, public investment had been increasing, whereas private investment appeared to be negligible. In 1966 the amount of public investment was K576 million, or 7.4 percent of the year's budget. By 1970 public investment had risen to K881 million, or 10.2 percent of the budget. For 1971 the goal was more than K1 billion, or 10.7 percent of the budget.

The government's economic development priorities were shown by the emphasis on industrialization in the division of public investment. The priorities for 1971 were: manufacturing, 39 percent; infrastructure (electric power, transport, roads, and buildings), 22 percent; government, 19 percent; primary production and related sectors (agriculture, irrigation, forestry, mining, and fisheries), 18 percent; and others, 2 percent.

Defense outlays of K601 million for 1971 constituted the single largest expenditure of regular government, consuming about 35 percent of regular government expenditure. In absolute terms the amount was about 6 percent higher than in 1970.

Budgeted and actual government expenditures also indicated the extent of the government's interest in the minority-dominated hill areas—Shan, Kachin, Kawthule, and Kayah states and Chin Special Division (see ch. 4, Social Systems and Values). These five areas cover 48 percent of the country's total land area and hold around 17 percent of the population; most of the country's chronic insurgency is located in these areas. For several years the Revolutionary Government had repeatedly claimed that it was doing more for these areas, especially in health and education, than its predecessor governments had done. The budget figures tended, however, to present a contrasting appearance. In both absolute and percentage terms, the Revolutionary Government appeared to be doing less for these hill areas than previous governments had done.

In 1962, the year in which the Revolutionary Government assumed power, regular government expenditure—current plus capital accounts—in the five areas was K77 million. Through 1971 the expenditure had not subsequently reached that amount. During the seven years—1962 through 1969—for which the budget accounts were available, annual expenditures in these areas averaged K62 million. For 1970 the revised budget estimates show a rise to K75 million, but for 1971 the original estimates indicate a decline to K73 million.

The percentage of regular government expenditures devoted to these hill areas was also a significant indicator of the Revolutionary Government's performance. In the last pre-Revolutionary Government budget, that covering 1962, the share of regular government spending in the five areas was 6.8 percent. Under the Revolutionary Government, the figures had been lower. From 1963 to 1970 the percentage of regular government expenditures in these areas had averaged 4.2 percent; for 1971 the budget estimates allocated 3.8 percent of regular government expenditures to these areas.

Income

Under the budget system of the Revolutionary Government all income, whether from taxes, ordinary receipts of state enterprises, or other sources, is given to the Consolidated Cash Fund, from which allocations are made to the state agencies and enterprises, subject to quarterly adjustments. The state enterprises had, therefore, little control over the income they earned. Data on the state enterprises suggested that the surpluses of profitable enterprises—for example, banking and insurance—were used to help meet the deficits of less profitable enterprises.

The main sources of government income in 1971 were, in order of magnitude: income of state enterprises, taxes, repayment of loans and advances, and foreign loans and grants. The actual income of the state enterprises had generally fallen below their expenditures. The state enterprises, therefore, rather than being a net contributor to budgetary income, had been instead a drain on income.

One apparent cause of the continuing losses of most of the state enterprises had been the pricing policy imposed by the Revolutionary Government. With the exception of a few commodities, the pricing policy of the public boards and corporations, such as the Industrial Development Corporation and its affiliated industrial enterprises, was based on the principle that goods produced are sold at cost to the trade corporations, which add certain prescribed margins to arrive at the retail prices. The Central Trade Organization fixed prices and rates of margin so that the lowest rates should apply to essential goods; medium rates, to conventional goods; and high rates, to luxury goods. The production costs of the state enterprises are defined as including depreciation, and also interest in the case of funds borrowed from abroad, but not if the funds are provided by the government. In the late 1960s the production costs of the state enterprises had been increasing by from 2 to 5 percent annually.

The state boards and corporations draw for their requirements on the Consolidated Cash Fund. These drawings are not considered as borrowings, and therefore neither repayments nor interest are required. The performance of the state boards and corporations, however, is reviewed periodically by the Taxation and Finance Committee, which may require the elimination of any deficits that do not arise as a result of specific government policies. This committee is headed by the minister of finance and revenues, and representatives of certain other government departments and the People's Bank of the Union of Burma serve on it.

In the consolidated budget, income from taxes was paired with regular government expenditures. In the late 1960s and early 1970s tax income had generally failed to match regular government expenditures. For 1971 income from taxes was expected to be 5 percent less than in 1970. The two most important types of taxes were income taxes and customs receipts. Income taxes were levied on individuals and on government-run enterprises, boards, and corporations, as well as on those few businesses remaining in private hands in 1971.

Because of very high rates of income tax, imposed shortly after the Revolutionary Government assumed power, income from tax sources had been higher under the Revolutionary Government than in the pre-1962 period. For 1971 the receipts from the income tax were estimated at K635 million. This sum, however, was 37 percent less than the peak year of 1965, when the government levied many arbitrary assessments against private individuals and businesses, leading in many cases to bankruptcy. Customs receipts in the early 1970s had also fallen below earlier levels; the estimated 1971 receipts of K220 million were about 40 percent less than the intake ten years earlier, when the country's foreign trade was more vigorous (see ch. 13, Trade and Transportation).

The third principal source of income was repayments of loans and advances. This source had also tended under the Revolutionary Government to become a net negative item. New loans—almost exclusively to farmers—and advances had together exceeded repayments. The problem did not arise with loans because repayments in the late 1960s and early 1970s had exceeded new loans, but with advances that were, in effect, interest-free loans to state enterprises and ministries.

If the income from state enterprises, taxes, and repayments is inadequate to cover aggregate state expenditures, the two principal means of meeting the difference are foreign aid and deficit financing. For 1971 foreign loans and grants were expected to provide K323 million, or 3 percent of the consolidated budget receipts. If realized, this sum would represent a 50-percent increase over the 1970 level. Receipts from foreign aid had been slowly rising in the 1968-70 period, but in every year under the Revolutionary Government the original budget estimates had tended to show more foreign aid receipts than had actually been received.

In the first quarter of 1971 data were not available as to how the overall budget deficits, after inclusion of foreign aid, had been financed under the Revolutionary Government. The government's public announcements merely stated that the deficits had been financed "by the banking system" without further explanation.

The Public Debt

Because public debt transactions are included within the budget itself, the conventional budget deficit represents only part of the overall deficit. The public debt is represented by government borrowings from the People's Bank of the Union of Burma. The internal public debt consisted of Treasury bills, bonds, and government-guaranteed debentures. Treasury bills are three-month obligations, bearing 1 percent interest annually, whereas Treasury bonds are medium-term obligations; the three-year bonds bear interest at 2½ percent, and the five-year bonds bear interest at 3 percent. Subsequent to the assumption of power by the Revolutionary Government in March 1962, the internal public debt had risen from K1.4 billion to K2.6 billion at the end of September 1970. In the same period the external public debt had increased from the equivalent of K300 million to the equivalent of K694 million. The major creditors were the United States, Communist China, and the International Bank for Reconstruction and Development (IBRD, commonly known as the World Bank). Debt service payments on conventional loans—that is, excluding suppliers' credits—totaled 8 percent of export earnings in 1967, 10 percent in 1968, and 12 percent in 1969.

GOVERNMENT BANKING

People's Bank of the Union of Burma

As of the first quarter of 1971 all of the country's banks had been merged into one entity—the People's Bank of the Union of Burma. This arrangement had been formally described as the mono-bank system. Beginning with the nationalization of the private commercial banks in February 1963, the Revolutionary Government had undertaken a program for the eventual amalgamation of all the country's banks into a single, government-owned bank. The Revolutionary Government's program was considered by international financial observers to have been inspired by the system in Communist China, where the People's Bank of China had been established in December 1948.

On July 1, 1966, the Revolutionary Government formally announced its intention to combine all the country's banks into a single bank. On April 27, 1967, the chairman of the Revolutionary Council promulgated the Union of Burma People's Bank Law of 1967 as a first step in establishing a monobank system. Certain parts of the law went into force on August 9, 1968, pursuant to a governmental notification; the primary action was to establish and appoint the bank's board of directors.

On November 1, 1969, the following financial institutions were amalgamated with the People's Bank of the Union of Burma: the Union Bank of Burma, the Industrial Development Bank Limited, the Union of Burma Insurance Board, the Savings and Securities Department, the People's Loans Company Limited, and three of the nationalized commercial banks. In addition, the basic laws for the Union Bank of Burma and the Insurance Board were repealed.

The second and final merger occurred on February 1, 1970, when the State Commercial Bank, the State Agricultural Bank, and the remaining nationalized commercial banks were amalgamated with the People's Bank. On the same date, the basic laws of the State Commercial Bank and the State Agricultural Bank were repealed.

As constituted in the first quarter of 1971, the People's Bank performed a wide variety of functions, serving as a central bank, commercial bank, industrial bank, savings bank, agricultural bank, consumer-finance company, and general-insurance company. The preamble of the People's Bank Law stated the government's rationale for the decision to create a single financial institution: "It is desirable to have the various existing undertakings on banking, money lending, currency and credit, savings bank, foreign exchange, insurance, and so forth, grouped together into one and placed under a single institution to assist in the development of socialist economy in the Union of Burma." By establishing a single bank, the government hoped to improve the mobilization of resources and to have a more centralized and better coordinated control of the existing financial institutions. The bank's basic objectives, as defined in the People's Bank Law, were to stabilize the kyat at home and abroad, to encourage economic progress, and to increase the income of the country's citizens, particularly peasants and workers.

The responsibilities of the financial institutions incorporated into the People's Bank had been taken over by its different divisions, each headed by an executive director. The bank was under the general supervision of a board of directors, which consisted of the chairman and deputy chairman of the board, the executive directors of the bank, and certain other members, all of whom were appointed by the government. In 1971 the secretaries of the ministries of finance and revenues, national planning, agriculture and forests, industry, and trade were members of the board of directors.

In an organizational listing issued in September 1970 the bank had a central office, which carried out central banking functions. In addition, the bank had ten divisions: administrative, internal audit and inspection, foreign exchange, agricultural finance, insurance, savings and securities, research and training, industrial finance, small loan, and banking. After the final amalgamation in February 1970, the People's Bank reportedly had a total staff of over 7,000 employees.

The basic capital of the People's Bank was K200 million, all of which had been contributed by the government. In addition, the bank had a reserve fund of at least K50 million, also contributed by the government. At the end of each financial year one-fourth of any surplus funds arising from the bank's operations are to be allocated to the reserve fund until the fund is equal to the bank's original capital. Thereafter, any surplus is to be paid to the government. The remaining three-fourths of any annual surplus is to be paid to the government.

The bank offered three types of savings instruments: ordinary savings accounts yielding 2 percent annually, five-year cash certificates yielding 2.5 percent, and twelve-year savings certificates yielding 4.5 percent. If the bank should need additional loanable funds, these could be provided from the government's general revenue.

The bank planned to conduct a wide variety of lending and other activities. These would include providing agricultural credits through the village banks and cooperatives and also directly to agriculturists. To the extent that it was necessary, the bank planned to establish branch banks down to the township level, agency banks in large villages, and village banks in every village. Some of these outlets can then be used for providing credits directly to the agriculturists.

The bank also planned to extend industrial loans and short-term petty loans against movable property. The bank also served as fiscal agent and broker for the government and handled the accounts of the state boards and corporations. All government treasuries and subtreasuries have been absorbed by the bank. The bank also conducted all insurance operations for the country.

The interest rates charged by the bank ranged from 4 to 6 percent. All credits to state corporations or advances to the government carried a rate of 4 percent, whereas the rates on overdrafts ranged from 4.5 to 6 percent. For personal loans and housing mortgages, the rate was 6 percent. Most loans were short term, meaning up to three years, and were extended to state enterprises; the bank also extended some medium-term loans of from three to five years and some long-term loans of from five to fifteen years.

The amount of credit outstanding to the private sector had been declining steadily, being K94 million at the end of 1969, compared with K99 million at the end of 1968 and K103 million at the end of 1967. As of the first quarter of 1971 the bank was still formally left with its traditional functions to give credit to the private sector as well as to the government. Credits to the private sector in the late 1960s had been mainly consumer loans made against such collateral as jewelry and real estate, and the volume had not been large. New loans extended to the private business sector were limited in extent, and not many old loans were renewed. Private businessmen generally either had to provide their working capital themselves or borrow it from private moneylenders, who were allowed to charge up to 18 percent annually. The bank credit requirements of the private sector had declined, however, because the trade corporations supplied raw materials on credit to all private industrial enterprises managed by supervisory committees and accepted their finished products in payment. Agricultural credit was not included in banking statistics.

The bank was subject to only two major financial restraints in its operations. One of these was the requirement in Article 21 of the People's Bank Law that the bank shall maintain gold and foreign exchange assets at a level equivalent to at least 25 percent of the amount of currency in circulation. The government is empowered under Article 22 of the law to suspend the requirement for a specified period. On July 1, 1970, the official holdings of gold and foreign exchange were equal to slightly over 25 percent of the amount of currency in circulation.

The second restraint related to advances extended to the government by the People's Bank. Under Article 55 of the People's Bank Law, such advances cannot legally exceed 15 percent of the estimated revenues of the government for the financial year in which the advances are made, and they must be repaid within six months of the date of the advance. This restraint was largely without meaning, however, because the government could still obtain funds from the bank by selling it securities, there being no specific limit on this type of transaction. In addition, this rule could be suspended under powers granted the government by Article 71 of the People's Bank Law; this article authorized the government "to make such provisions as it may deem desirable or necessary for removing any difficulty that may arise in enforcing the provisions of this law."

Currency, Credit, and Money Supply

In the 1960s and early 1970s, although the official rate of exchange had remained fairly stable at K4.76 to the United States dollar, a free market in currency had indicated that the kyat's real value had declined. Gold and other currencies were reportedly being exchanged in 1970 against the kyat at a rate three to four times higher than the official rate; this ratio had prevailed for almost a decade.

The internal money supply consisted of currency in circulation and demand deposits. It followed a seasonal fluctuation based on the cycle of the rice harvest. Currency and credit begin to expand in December at the beginning of the harvest season, rise to a peak in April, and begin to fall in June. The major factor in this seasonal fluctuation is the level of credit offered to farmers and rice millers.

In 1971 the major source of government loans to cultivators was the Agricultural Finance Division of the People's Bank. This division had assumed on February 1, 1970, the functions of the superseded State Agricultural Bank, which had operated as an independent agency from 1953 through January 1970. The State

Agricultural Bank had provided government funds to farmers through village banks and cooperative societies. It had been completely owned and controlled by the government, and during the 1966-69 period official agricultural loans in the country were extended by the State Agricultural Bank. In the late 1960s this bank operated through a network of about 40 district branches and approximately 11,000 village banks. Because of poor loan repayments, the State Agricultural Bank was short of financial resources in the 1960s and was heavily dependent on the government for new loanable funds. In the 1960s there had been frequent reorganizations of the government's system of agricultural credits.

The agricultural credit policy of the government aimed at providing farmers with official loans at low interest rates in lieu of private credit at much higher interest rates. Agricultural credit extended by government agencies was predominantly short term because major land improvements were undertaken directly by the government. The repayments of agricultural loans, however, had been seriously incomplete. In 1966 the government had decided that loans would be extended to individual farmers only through cooperatives or other farmers' groups, which would be collectively responsible for repayments. For this purpose, a village tract, consisting of about five to ten hamlets, was treated as a unit. To qualify for a new loan, such a cooperative or group would have to repay a minimum of its previous borrowings.

The principle of joint responsibility was made more effective in 1967 by allowing groups of cultivators in single hamlets with good repayment performance to form units that would qualify for fresh loans. Among such groups, only those that had no outstanding loans to repay were being advanced new loans. Beginning with the 1970 monsoon season, the joint responsibility was, in general, reduced to cover only a village instead of a whole tract, and defaulters would be expelled from the village banks.

Effective October 15, 1964, a system of advance purchases of paddy had been introduced under which each farmer was entitled to sell in advance up to five baskets per acre. Advance payments had been made by the State Agricultural Bank, acting as agent of the Union of Burma Agricultural Marketing Board, through what the government called "security and administrative committees," which delivered the cash to the farmers. The security and administrative committees also supervised the delivery of crops that had been sold in advance.

In October 1965 the government had announced certain modifications in the advance purchase system. Advance payments were made directly by Trade Corporation No. 1, which replaced the Union of Burma Agricultural Marketing Board in December 1965. The farmer could sell paddy in advance up to five baskets per acre cultivated, subject to an overall ceiling of 100 baskets (or 4,600 pounds) per farmer. Repayments could be made either in cash or in kind, whereas previously repayments were only in kind. To improve the collection of repayments, advances were made to village cooperatives or other farmers' groups rather than to individual farmers. These groups jointly guaranteed the repayment of the advance received. Farmers who failed to repay their loans were not allowed to sell under the advance purchase plan. This system of advance purchases had remained in effect through the first quarter of 1971.

In 1971 there was very little information available on private moneylending activities, but most reports indicated that the general public, particularly the farmers, were heavily dependent on private moneylenders as a source of credit. Rough estimates suggested that farmers utilized private moneylenders to meet about three-fourths of their credit needs. During the pre-World War II period the predominant moneylenders in the country had been the Indian Chettyars. Although by 1971 the Chettyars had largely disappeared, they had generally been replaced by Burmese moneylenders. During the post-World War II period Chinese moneylenders, particularly the gold merchants and goldsmiths, had also been active, but in the late 1960s and early 1970s their role had been diminishing.

The interest rates charged by private moneylenders varied substantially, and only very broad estimates of actual rates could be made. Various reports indicated that, in general, the lowest rates for the best customers on secured credits ranged from about 2 to 4 percent per month. Unsecured loans tended to range between 5 to 10 percent per month, and some rates were higher.

The total money supply had increased from K2.2 billion at the end of 1966 to K2.3 billion at the end of 1969; the increase was slightly over 4 percent in 1967 and less than 2 percent in both 1968 and 1969. As of March 31, 1970, the total was K2.6 billion. Most of the money supply consisted of currency in circulation, which amounted to K1.6 billion at the end of 1966 and which had increased to K1.8 billion by the end of 1969; the total on September 30, 1970, was K2 billion

BALANCE OF PAYMENTS

As measured by monetary movements, the balance of payments showed an overall deficit of US$53 million in 1969, compared with a deficit of US$41.2 million in 1968, a deficit of US$18.9 million in 1967, and a surplus of US$7.1 million in 1966. As in 1968, a large deficit in 1969 on goods, services, and miscellaneous capital accounts was partly offset by official grants and loans. The trade deficit in 1969 was smaller than in 1968, but there was a substantial increase in debt repayments, and receipts in 1969 from grants and loans were substantially lower than in 1968. The overall balance of payments deficit, which had been financed in 1968 mainly by short-term credits from banks abroad, was financed in 1969 to a greater extent by drawing down official reserves.

According to the balance of payments data, exports in 1969 reversed the declining trend of the late 1960s by showing an increase of 15 percent to US$125.1 million, whereas imports declined to US$142.1 million, so that the trade deficit was reduced in 1969 by US$51.2 million to US$17 million. Net payments on services accounts were US$32.7 million in 1969, compared with US$24.8 million in 1968. Recorded private capital movements subsequent to 1964 had been negligible. Official debt repayments increased from US$8.8 million in 1968 to US$29.7 million in 1969, principally because of repayment of suppliers' credits of US$17.7 million received in 1968. The decline of US$15.2 million in 1969 in receipts from suppliers' credits almost accounted for the fall in total loans and grants receipts from US$45.8 million in 1968 to US$29.2 million in 1969.

During 1969 US$44 million of the balance of payments deficit for that year was financed by utilizing the country's foreign exchange reserves, whereas bank liabilities increased by US$9 million. In July 1969 the country's total gold and foreign exchange holdings consisted of slightly over one-half in gold, with the balance in foreign exchange divided among West German marks, United States dollars, British pounds sterling, Swiss francs, and other currencies; the total value was denominated in United States dollars and amounted to US$161 million on July 31, 1969. Total gold and foreign exchange holdings, which had declined from US$190 million at the end of 1967 to US$181 million at the end of 1968, fell further to US$140 million at the end of 1969.

The total gold and foreign exchange holdings at the end of 1969 were equivalent to 99 percent of imports in 1969. The People's Bank Law stipulated that the value of the People's Bank holdings of international reserves must be equal to not less than 25 percent of the currency in circulation. At the end of 1969 about US$100 million of the official reserves were required minimum reserves, leaving official free reserves of about US$40 million. Short-term bank credits abroad at the end of 1969 amounted to US$45 million, compared with about US$36 million a year earlier and US$3 million at the end of 1967.

Despite the country's initial allocation of special drawing rights under the International Monetary Fund (IMF) and the US$12 million purchases from the fund in January 1970 under a one-year standby arrangement, the country's international reserves declined further to US$99 million at the end of May 1970. One-quarter of the country's gold reserves, valued at US$84 million, was disposed of in August 1970, and another quarter was disposed of in 1971.

CHAPTER 12

AGRICULTURE AND INDUSTRY

Agriculture continued in early 1971, as it had for centuries, to be the predominant sector of the economy. Despite almost two decades of effort to diversify agriculture, the country relied heavily on rice, the most important crop for both domestic consumption and export. Per capita agricultural production and rice surpluses for export generally declined in the 1966-70 period in comparison with the preceding decade, however. Lack of incentive for the cultivators was a basic factor. By early 1971 a satisfactory system had not been devised to induce farmers to produce for the government-monopolized market (see ch. 11, Character and Structure of the Economy).

Industry is keyed to agriculture, with about 70 percent of manufacturing relating to food products, mostly rice. The policy since about 1957 has been to emphasize industries that support agriculture and enhance the value of farm exports and at the same time to develop as rapidly as possible the production of import-substitute commodities.

Despite priority for more than a decade to the industrial sector in the allocation of public investment and abundant, widely dispersed raw materials, industry in early 1971 was in a low state of development, and production activities were generally in a stagnant condition.

The country is rich in natural resources. Good soil combined with favorable climate provide an excellent base for agriculture. Millions of additional acres of fallow but cultivable land are available, and expansion of irrigation could add substantially to crop acreages. There are large reserves of teak and hardwood and more than adequate expanses of coastal waters and inland streams and ponds for development of the fishing industry. Indications in early 1971 were that mineral deposits, although not thoroughly and completely evaluated, were large. Many mineral reserves are located in remote areas where lack of security restricts exploitation and lack of transportation facilities presents problems (see ch. 2, Physical Environment and Population).

Nationalization of most large private industries after 1963 and expansion of government control over agriculture and industry had not resulted in greater productivity by early 1971. State monopoly of marketing and price fixing of major crops tended to keep prices depressed on the legitimate market; it also brought forth a black market, which flourished after 1966. The establishment of what the government termed "people's workers' councils" and "people's peasants' councils," begun in the late 1960s, was continuing in early 1971. These efforts had as their primary objectives the strengthening of government controls over the peasants and workers and the improvement of productivity.

In early 1971, and periodically through the entire time since independence, the activities of armed robbers and bandits (dacoits) and insurgents restricted the exercise of government controls over agricultural and industrial activities, particularly in remote areas. Resulting disruptions in production and transportation caused significant losses to the economy. Shortages of capital and of experienced management and technically skilled personnel were continuing basic problems that tended to impede agricultural and industrial development (see ch. 8, Political System and Values; ch. 14, National Defense and Internal Security; ch. 11, Character and Structure of the Economy).

The manpower base is quantitatively more than adequate to provide workers, but there are widespread shortages of experienced managerial and technically skilled personnel. The lack of a disciplined labor force and the disinclination of workers to submit to the regimentation required in factories were continuing impediments to industrial development. Labor unions went into eclipse when the political parties that supported them were banned by the revolutionary government after the 1962 coup (see ch. 2, Physical Environment and Population; ch. 4, Social Systems and Values).

THE RESOURCE BASE

In 1969 about 24 percent of the land area was cultivable, and roughly 13 percent was under cultivation. The per capita acreage of agricultural land was 1.5 acres. In fiscal year 1967/68 as revealed in the latest available government statistics, the land area, in millions of acres, consisted of: cultivable raw land, 21.6; land under cultivation, 19; unused land, 6.3; forest reserve, 22.2; and other land, 98.1. Almost 4 million acres of arable land were considered unstable for cultivation, principally because of excessive flooding of the Irrawaddy and Sittang rivers and the Arakan and Tenasserim coasts during the season of heavy rains, in July and August. Losses from weather vary from year to year; during the 1959-69 decade the low was 1.07 million acres—lost in 1964/65—and the high was 2.65 million acres—lost in 1966/67. Replanting of rice one or more times is frequently required because of floods.

In fiscal 1968/69 about 2 million acres were irrigated by the use of canals, streams, and pumps. Irrigation is carried out principally in central Burma, where annual rainfall is twenty-four to forty inches but is badly distributed, falling almost entirely during a five-month period. About 80 percent of the irrigated acreage, including multi-crop areas, was in rice. The area under irrigation expanded gradually during the 1960s, from 1.26 million acres in 1960/61 to 2 million acres in 1968/69. The total had been 1.56 million acres in 1940/41, but heavy damage was inflicted during World War II and during the widespread insurgency from 1948 to 1951. During the 1960s the government tended to place greater emphasis on expansion of irrigation in the dry zone rather than on reclamation of fallow land abandoned earlier in the delta. Concern for improvement in the distribution of food was a probable contributing factor in this decision.

In 1970 there were numerous long-term projects with planned acreage to be irrigated. The largest of these (and their acreage) included: Mu Valley, 700,000; Sedawgyi Reservoir, 148,643; Kinywa Reservoir, 129,013; Nyaung-kyat Reservoir, 119,287; and Hanthawaddy Flood Control in the Sittang Valley, 115,000.

Banditry and hostile insurgency acts in the late 1960s and 1970 imposed serious limitations on the expansion of the area under cultivation. They also tended to reduce the intensity of cultivation in areas where security was questionable.

The lower valleys of the Irrawaddy and Sittang rivers and their deltas are the centers of a major agricultural region covering the districts of Rangoon, Pegu, Tharrawaddy, Hanthawaddy, Insein, Bassein, Henzada, Myaungmya, Ma-ubin, and Pyapon. This basin contains deep fertile alluvial soils and has an annual rainfall of from 80 to 130 inches. It is agriculturally the most productive area and provides the bulk of the country's rice. Conditions for rice cultivation are near optimum because of reliable precipitation and adequate sun during the growing season.

The 100-mile wide valley extending northward over 200 miles from Thayetmyo forms another agricultural region that is characterized by a long dry season. It is often referred to as the dry zone even though annual precipitation is from twenty-four to forty inches. The area around Mandalay, lying generally between Kyaukse on the south and the Ye-U Canal on the north, has been irrigated extensively for centuries and normally produces a rice surplus. The remainder of the dry zone in the Central Valley is generally a rice deficit area but self-sufficient in most other food crops.

The shallow undulating valleys and ridges of the Pegu and Arakan mountains and the Shan Plateau have some common characteristics and are cultivated. Soils are generally shallow, subject to erosion, and exhausted quickly unless conservation measures are practiced. Annual rainfall is from twenty-four to forty inches.

Until the 1960s the country's subsurface resources were largely unexplored, and only 30 percent of the area had been geologically surveyed and mapped by 1966. Assistance was provided from several outside agencies. In the 1960s United Nations experts surveyed the potential of the Bawdwin mine complex, which had been operated by the British and even earlier by the Chinese; the Krupp interests of West Germany made a survey of the country for coal and iron deposits, and Romanian experts assisted with oil explorations. In 1970 a West German firm began sizable offshore oil explorations, with seismic surveys beginning in the Gulf of Martaban. Offshore activities had been initiated in the previous year along the Arakan coast with a seismic survey by a Japanese firm under contract.

The best known deposits of nonferrous metals are in the area worked by the Bawdwin mine complex near Namtu in the northern Shan State (see ch. 2, Physical Environment and Population). Ore reserves in this area as of 1968 were estimated at 6 million tons, with 11.2 percent lead, 5.6 percent zinc, and 0.3 percent copper. Silver content was estimated at 7.8 ounces per ton. The percentages of metallic content of extracted ores dropped from an estimated 34 to 13 between 1958 and 1968. Other reported deposits include: lead near Maymyo, near Yezintaung, in the Bawsaing area, in Kyaukse District, and in the Loisin and Luphan areas of the Shan State; zinc near Lonchiek and Maymyo; and copper in the Mongwa and Bhamo districts near Heho and at the Sakataung mines.

The high-grade tin and tungsten reserves at the Mawchi mines have been depleted. The low-grade remaining reserves were reportedly to be evaluated and exploited with assistance from the Soviet Union. The Karen range east of Pyinmana was reported to hold reserves of tin and tungsten.

The Burmese government and the Soviet Union signed an agreement in December 1969 providing for a US$1.7 million rehabilitation loan for the Mawchi mines. Although Soviet technicians reportedly have conducted surveys, rehabilitation apparently had not yet begun in early 1971. Security has reportedly been a problem in the area.

The lignite deposits at Kalewa had been estimated at 128 million tons by the Krupp survey, and more recently a surface vein was reported in Thayet District. The Shan State iron ore reserves were estimated to be in excess of 100 million tons in the area of Taunggyi. There were other reported deposits in Shan State and elsewhere. Known deposits of iron, as well as coal, were low grade and would require large investments in transportation if developed. Limestone deposits in Meiktila District were estimated at 40 million tons.

The major older oilfields of Chauk and Yenangyaung continued to be active, using secondary methods of extraction. Some of the newer fields have not produced as expected. The fields at Mann and Prome were among the most productive newly found sources in 1970. Total oil reserves were estimated at 140 million barrels in 1969.

AGRICULTURE

Land Tenure and Farm Credit

The nationalization of land and measures to assist tenant farmers after World War II had brought by the mid-1960s a significant change in the distribution of land ownership and tenancy. The legal position of the cultivator landlord in 1970 was not entirely clear; he could divide, transfer, or sell land to persons in the village where cultivators of the area lived, but the government claimed formal title to all land. Persons classified as tenants were assured a high degree of tenure on the land they cultivated as a result of measures enacted in 1963 and 1965, which freed them from rents and property seizures for bad debts. The net effect was to make tenants virtual owners of the land they worked.

In fiscal 1967/68 about 86 percent of farmowners and tenants held 10 acres or less and about 55 percent of all cultivable land; about 14 percent held from 10 to 50 acres and about 43.5 percent of all cultivable land; and about 1 percent held more than 50 acres and approximately 1.5 percent of all cultivable land. The average cultivator landlord held 4.4 acres, whereas the average tenant farmer worked about 5.5 acres. The net effect of the fragmentation of large holdings after independence was to increase subsistence-type farming. Many farmers were without adequate implements and draft animals, and frequently those with larger plots could not afford hired help for the replanting of rice and other investments necessary to produce for the market.

The system of landownership and tenancy that developed in Lower Burma under British rule caused deep resentment against landlords, especially those of alien origin, and strongly influenced agrarian reform after independence (see ch. 3, Historical Setting). In early 1971 the traditional strong feeling against so-called capitalist landlords continued to be important in agricultural policy and propaganda. Landownership was no problem in the outlying areas and, consequently, the Constitution of 1947 made the land nationalization acts applicable to the divisions of Burma but not to the states.

Feelings against the Chettyars—a moneylending caste of Indian origin who became landlords through defaulted peasant debts during the period of British rule—were particularly strong. After the opening of the Suez Canal in 1869 and demands for Burmese products increased, farmers from the older rice-producing areas of central Burma migrated to the undeveloped delta area to the south, where they received free grants of from ten to fifteen acres. They lacked funds, however, to finance their crop and became dependent upon the Chettyars. Interest rates were generally very high, and charges from indigenous lenders were usually higher than those of the Chettyars. Nevertheless, as increasing numbers of cultivators became insolvent and forfeited their holdings, resentment mounted against landlords, especially the Chettyars, who had come to hold about 25 percent of the agricultural land of Lower Burma by the mid-1930s. By the 1938-39 period 59 percent of the farmers in that region were tenants.

The appropriation of land from landlords began during World War II, when many Chettyars and others of foreign origin departed. Nationalization of land was initiated before independence, but it was not until the 1953-58 period that it was effected on a large scale. State holdings were further expanded, to a total of 8.7 million acres, under an April 1965 decree that abolished all land rents and expropriated tenanted land. A hierarchy of land committees was established in the early 1950s to facilitate the transfer of appropriated land to cultivators. The Land Tenancy Act of 1963 gave these committees the right to allot tenancies, thereby weakening the position of landlords. Another act the same year, the Law to Protect the Rights of Peasants, aimed to assist the indebted peasants by prohibiting seizure of land and farm equipment for default on loans. Although agriculture had come increasingly under state control by 1970, collective farms had been organized only on a minor scale and were confined to a few reclamation settlement schemes.

One of the government's aims after independence was to furnish the small farmer with at least minimal needs for short-term credit and to reduce the peasants' reliance on private lenders whose rates were exceedingly high. During the 1945-52 period rates from private sources were even higher than before World War II—frequently 48 to 60 percent as compared to 7 percent for government loans—and five-sixths of farm credit came from nongovernment lenders. In 1953 the State Agricultural Bank was created, and loans to farmers were made through the district and village banks. During the decade ending in 1962, K681 million (4.76 kyat equal US$1) were lent, of which 74 percent was recovered.

When the Revolutionary Government of the Union of Burma came to power, it increased allocations for loans. Repayments soon declined, and a system of collective security was introduced in 1965 whereby the village tract, usually consisting of from five to ten villages, became the primary unit to which loans were extended. During the 1966-70 period the government banking system was given greater responsibility for the credit program, and annual loans were roughly half that of fiscal 1964/65, when K324.3 million were disbursed. Revisions in this period included designation of the village rather than the tract as the primary unit for lending.

By 1970 the problem of loan default had become sufficiently acute that it was a subject for discussion in the officially controlled press. One account said that as much as K263 million arrears had accumulated.

The farmers' needs for credit were largely short-term requirements. Cultivators had received the nationalized land without obligation, and pre-World War II debts were written off. The scale of state agricultural credit during the 1950s and 1960s placed it in the category of welfare for the neediest peasants, mostly rice farmers, but it was inadequate to boost production above subsistence requirements. In the late 1960s loans were allotted at the rate of K25 per acre, an amount considered adequate for land preparation and sowing of seed but not sufficient in most cases to permit much in the way of additional expenditures, such as transplanting of rice and the use of fertilizers.

Agricultural Practices

Crop patterns are divided into three categories, taking into account rainfall, soil, and topography. The first, known as *le* cultivation, is predominant in the lower valleys of the Irrawaddy and Sittang rivers, in the delta area, in Akyab District, and on the coasts of Arakan and Tenasserim divisions. In these areas the fields are periodically inundated by rainfall and the overflow of rivers. Rice is grown on about 90 percent of the cultivated area, and the farmers frequently have fruit and vegetable plots for their own use. No important second crops are grown after the rice harvest.

Another type of cultivation, known as *kaing,* is practiced in the central part of the country, north of the area of *le* cultivation, along the lesser rivers and streams that sometimes overflow. The land is well watered but not subject to erosion and is frequently double cropped. Conditions are suitable for various crops other than rice. Beans and peas are grown frequently as a second crop during the cooler dry season.

A third type, *ye* or shifting cultivation, is practiced in the dry areas of most of the rest of the country. When the amount of rainfall in the uplands of central Burma permits, double cropping is often practiced.

The power for propelling farm implements is provided mainly by draft animals. Cattle are most commonly used and are best suited for the drier parts of the country. On the average a pair of oxen can work 10.8 acres. Water buffalo are preferred for use in the inundated rice fields of Lower Burma. Small horses and some mules are used for transport in the hilly regions of the Shan State. Draft requirements of small farmers frequently were not met because the distribution of animals was uneven. There were 3,469 tractors in agricultural use in fiscal 1968/69, and on the average each plowed only 189 acres. Utilization was low, and the government tractor stations were the most unprofitable sector of the state enterprises: village cooperatives were given in 1968/69 an opportunity to produce tractors on the installment plan. In 1970 lack of spare parts was reportedly a problem.

The use of chemical fertilizers, almost negligible before World War II, increased during the 1950s and 1960s but was still on a very small scale in 1970 and limited generally to rice. Utilization reached a high of 162,000 tons in fiscal 1967/68; the annual average for 1962 to 1967 was about 24,000 tons and about 75,000 tons for 1969 and 1970. Crops can be grown on much of the land without commercial fertilizers, but yields of rice and most other principal crops do not compare favorably with those of many other countries. In 1968 rice yields per acre in Burma ranked thirteenth among major rice-producing nations.

The use of insecticides generally increased in the decade preceding 1968 but then decreased, reportedly, because of concern for the environment. In fiscal 1968/69 a little over 500,000 pounds of insecticides in powdered form and 36,000 gallons in a liquid state were utilized.

High-yield varieties of rice were introduced in the middle 1960s. One variety was reported to have given yields about three and one-half times above normal. In fiscal 1969/70 an estimated 8 percent of rice acreage was planted in the new strains. Conversion to the varieties has moved slowly because they require better soil and more complex growing procedures than ordinary rice. Also, some new strains of rice do not appeal to the palate of all Asians.

Agricultural Production

Data for the 1966-70 period indicated a state of stagnation in agricultural production and a decline in real terms of the farm sector's contribution to economic growth. Estimates by the Food and Agriculture Organization (FAO) for this period placed actual annual growth in terms of agricultural gross national product (GNP) at 2.3 percent, as compared with a planned rate of 6 percent. After 1940 the trend was one of rapid population growth without comparable increases in agricultural production and thus a drop in per capita productivity. During the 1960s the index of per capita agricultural production was highest in 1962 and lowest in 1966. Burma lost its position as the leading exporter of rice in the middle-1960s, and yearly exports for the 1967-69 period were only about one-third of the annual average for the 1957-66 period.

Efforts after independence toward greater diversification of crops were only modestly successful. Increases in the production of wheat, peanuts, and sugar were achieved, but rice, the mainstay of the diet, lost little of its relative importance. In the early 1970s unpromising prospects for world rice prices were causing the government to continue to encourage diversification.

The proportion of total cultivated area in rice remained fairly steady at about 65 percent after independence and in the late 1960s was about 12.5 million acres. Crop acreage and production for other crops tended to fluctuate (see table 4).

Edible oil crops are important because Burmese cooking requires large amounts of oil. Sesame oil is most popular, but production is inadequate to meet domestic demand. Yields per acre average only thirty pounds. An effort has been made to increase peanut oil production. The result has not been entirely satisfactory because fields planted to peanuts eroded badly during the dry season. In some years production of edible oils has not met domestic requirements.

Beans and peas are widely grown, particularly in the northern dry zone. In quantity these legumes were second only to rice as a crop export in the late 1960s.

Sugar and jute are important to the economy, and strong emphasis is placed in gaining self-sufficiency in refined surgar and sacks fabricated from jute. Conditions are favorable for growing sugarcane, but requirements for refined sugar, estimated at 70,000 tons in fiscal 1967/68, had not been met by 1971. The acreage planted to jute increased by about 63,000 acres from 1961 to 1969, reaching 120,000 acres in 1969/70, but sack production was not adequate to meet domestic needs.

Generally, there were adequate supplies of at least some kinds of food available. Tomatoes, mustard, radishes, onions, and peppers are produced by nearly every family for home consumption. A great variety of fruits are grown in almost all parts of the country. The important fruits are mangoes, bananas, pineapples, and citrus. Coconuts are plentiful, and the yield in 1968/69 was estimated at about 45 million tons.

Animals are of importance primarily for draft and transport and, to a lesser extent, for fertilizer. The Buddhist beliefs of the majority of the population tend to discourage the use of animals for food. In fiscal 1968/69 the approximate numbers of animals reported in official statistics were: cows, 7.2 million; buffalo, 1.5 million; goats, 0.9 million; pigs, 1.7 million; and chickens, 10.2 million. Selective breeding has been virtually impossible because of the lack of

Table 4. *Crop Acreage and Agricultural Production in Burma, Selected Years, 1962-69*[1]
(in thousands)

	1962/63		1966/67		1967/68		1968/69	
	Acres	Tons[2]	Acres	Tons[2]	Acres	Tons[2]	Acres	Tons[2]
Rice	11,953	7,544[3]	12,326	6,532	12,193	7,647	12,402	7,896
Wheat	162	32	372	66	235	50	150	25
Peanuts	1,536	425	1,132	273	1,259	365	1,500	392
Sesame	1,576	84	1,910	56	2,050	106	2,037	82
Cotton	551	54	487	56	526	73	389	54
Jute	53	11	69	13	87	22	99	21
Beans and peas	1,710	317	1,768	241	1,616	248	1,751	294
Sugarcane	117	1,272	155	1,557	146	1,423	162	1,287
Tobacco	124	58	140	60	157	67	145	56
Rubber	184	14	216	11	219	12	220	12
Corn	350	62	223	53	232	64	216	61
Peppers	134	23	116	18	128	20	139	26
Onions	53	95	45	77	46	73	43	60
Potatoes	55	62	24	21	19	28	22	41

[1] Fiscal year is October 1 through September 30.

[2] In metric tons.

[3] Unmilled rice.

Source: Adapted from *Far Eastern Economic Review Yearbook, 1970,* Hong Kong, 1970, p. 86; and *Far Eastern Economic Review Yearbook, 1967,* Hong Kong, 1967, p. 130.

fencing except on a small scale at government stations that were established to improve animal husbandry.

Lumber and Fishing Industries

Forests cover almost half of the total land area and contain many varieties of commercially valuable timber, of which teak is by far the most important. Although the country has been for many years the world's leading exporter of teak, it has had difficulty in managing and developing its forest resources since independence. The forest areas, being more difficult for the government to secure than the cultivated areas, were frequently subject to disruption by insurgency forces. The loss, by government action, of persons of foreign derivation experienced in forestry, large losses of elephants trained for forestry tasks during World War II, and shortages of machines contributed to the low level of teak production in the postwar period.

By 1971 teak production had not been restored to the immediate prewar level of about 450,000 tons annually. Production in fiscal 1968/69 was 320,000 tons. Processing of teak was especially vulnerable to the disruptions of insurgency. Trees are girdled and then allowed to stand for three years before felling. This practice makes it possible to float the logs, which in a green condition will not float. Felled trees may be en route to the sawmill for an additional three years. Insurgency interfered with forestry management and normal girdling of teak and, in the late 1960s, there also were reports of substantial losses of logs that were being floated to market.

Hardwood production, on the other hand, increased over prewar levels after independence. Total hardwood output in fiscal 1968/69 was 981,000 tons. In the middle 1960s the value of timber exports, largely teak, rose to second place after rice.

Timber resources were nationalized in 1963, and the State Timber Board was given a monopoly over logging, milling, and exporting of lumber. In early 1971 foreign trade involving forestry products was under Trade Corporation No. 16, and administrative controls over forests were exercised by the minister of agriculture and forests.

Fish constitutes a major source of protein in the Burmese diet, and efforts were being made to meet domestic needs. Coastal fishing expanded during the late 1960s but in early 1971 was still in the early stages of development. The government encouraged the stocking of ponds and other inland fish-growing areas. The number of fisheries increased from 3,465 in fiscal 1961/62 to 3,710 in 1968/69. About 90 percent of these were under government lease in the 1960s. The output of freshwater fish in 1968/69 was 114,000 tons, and the state-owned deep sea-fishing industry produced about 294,000 tons. Fish imports dropped after 1965 and were relatively small during the late 1960s.

Government's Role in Agriculture

The government's contribution to agriculture after World War II was primarily in the nationalization and redistribution of land and in providing credit to the poorest cultivators. Although there had been repeated assurances to the peasants that agriculture merited priority in national economic development, viable programs to increase production had not appeared by early 1971. The attitude of the Revolutionary Council, in many respects like that of the parliamentary government, was that smallholder production should improve without extensive help from the state once the peasant was relieved from capitalist exploitation, given land tenure, protected from loss of his property because of indebtedness, extended limited credit, and assured of modest but guaranteed prices for his produce.

The Revolutionary Government increased the percentage of capital expenditures on agriculture slightly during the 1962-66 period, but from 1966 to 1970 the proportion was about the same as in the 1950s. By the beginning of 1971 the net effect of measures to aid agriculture had been to raise the margin for consumption by the farmer and to reduce that for savings and investment.

Although he was confronted with increasing pressures and propaganda from the government in early 1971, the peasant continued to make most of his own decisions concerning planting, cultivation, and marketing. In some areas, however, farmers were required to grow crops specified by government officials. Until the late 1960s, when a hierarchy of people's peasants' councils began to appear, the government had not undertaken seriously the organization and control of peasant farmers. Cooperatives had been encouraged in the 1950s, and by the middle 1960s there were over 12,000 such organizations of all types, including those in agriculture. In practice, they were relatively unimportant during the parliamentary period, and until 1970 the Revolutionary Council tended to overlook them.

In May of 1970, after the country had experienced serious distribution problems, General Ne Win announced plans to establish viable cooperatives for producer, consumer, and savings and credit activities. Indications were that the cooperatives were to be an adjunct to what the government called "security and administrative committees," and their objectives included the improvement of distribution of consumer goods and increased efficiency in the system of government purchase of crops.

Leaders of the revolutionary regime formulated plans for a hierarchy of peasant councils in the early 1960s, but the system did not take root until about 1967. The purpose of these councils is primarily to educate the peasant so that he will give full support to all government programs. Their functions include the management of rural affairs and the supervision of distribution of agricultural implements, land, and consumer goods to the peasants. These councils, according to government leaders, are also to have a voice in matters relating to agricultural economics.

In 1969 all organizations concerned with agriculture were under one head, Colonel Thaung Kyi, the minister of agriculture and forests and also secretary of the Peasant Affairs Division of the Burma Socialist Program Party's Central Organizing Committee. Colonel Thaung Kyi became chairman of the Central People's Peasants' Council formed in early 1969. At the first meeting of this council, from February to March 1969, General Ne Win stated that the most important task in agriculture was to educate the peasantry. Rural assistants, appointed by the government and in 1969 numbering 3,688, had the task of helping to educate the farmers, including assistance in technical matters. Peasants' seminars were held on a broad scale, from the national to the local level. The Central School of Political Science turned out hundreds of trainees each year to act as cadre for the establishment of the peasants' councils.

Government purchases of principal agricultural products had a major influence on the agricultural economy. After October 1963 the state was the sole legal purchaser of rice. The government monopolies also included wheat, corn, cotton, rubber, mustard, and castor seeds. In 1965 the government Trade Corporation No. 1 took over domestic purchases of agricultural products from the Union of Burma Agricultural Marketing Board, the organization that succeeded the State Agricultural Marketing Board originally established by the British in 1946. Also, export and import of agricultural and other products came under the government Trade Corporation No. 22 in 1965.

Until 1966 the abundance of rice enabled the government to maintain a one-price system, but the poor rice crop in that year, coupled with distribution problems, led to the growth of a black market. Relaxations were made temporarily to permit private traders to purchase some food items. In 1970 the government purchasing system applied to all major crops, but indications were that there was a considerable black market, particularly in rice. The monopoly system tended to keep agricultural prices depressed and to encourage subsistence farming, limiting the amount of products available to the government (see ch. 13, Trade and Transportation).

INDUSTRY

Industrial Development

Industry is dominated by the processing of rice and timber, the country's most readily available raw materials. Manufacturing enterprises have long been centered on the Rangoon area. Except for food and lumber, manufactured items are not adequate to meet domestic needs. The manufacturing sector of the economy is small in comparison with agriculture. It contributes about 10 percent of the gross national product and employs less than 10 percent of the work force.

From 1952 to 1957 the government placed strong emphasis on the diversification of industry as a step toward eventual economic independence. Experience during this period showed that ventures into an excessive number of fields were not advisable. Shortages of capital and other factors required that plans be modified. After 1957 the policy was to emphasize industries that supported the primary production sector—which includes agriculture and forestry—and, to the extent resources would permit, to produce import substitutes, thereby attaining the best possible position in foreign exchange. The efforts to diversify by early 1971 had resulted in the construction of plants to produce sugar and other foodstuffs, fabrics, items from clay, fertilizer, and other goods. Some progress has been made toward self-sufficiency, but the costs have been in many instances inordinately high. Frequently, new manufacturing enterprises were established and given unrealistic safeguards from foreign competition without regard for economy of operation.

Government Role in Industry

Although the move toward nationalization of enterprises and state socialism was begun soon after independence, the nationalization of private industries did not begin on a large scale until 1963. The revolutionary government's program of that year, the Burmese Way to Socialism, called for the virtual elimination of both private industry and foreign investments in Burma. By early 1971 most industrial establishments with twenty-five or more employees and a number of those with more than ten were fully nationalized, the state controlled the bulk of privately owned industries through government supervisory committees. In fiscal 1968/69 there were 1,248 state-owned factories and workshops and 16,149 privately owned industrial enterprises in operation (see ch. 11, Character and Structure of the Economy).

From 1948 to 1957 the government gave strong emphasis to the establishment of state enterprises in the heavier industries under joint agreements with foreign firms. New enterprises were given tariff protection, and the government was liberal on the licensing of imports of industrial raw materials. The joint venture was seen as a means to further the government's socialist aim of public ownership. By 1957 serious financial difficulties had developed, and a complete halt was called to new industrial investment by the state.

Although in order to attract badly needed capital increased incentives were provided to private domestic and foreign investors, the state in 1960 nevertheless formed the Burma Economic Development Corporation (BEDC) to control certain enterprises and took action to give full control of joint enterprises with foreign investors to Burmese interests. The previous year the decision had been made to discontinue the practice of ten-year guarantees against nationalization and to make this a subject for negotiation between the government and foreign investors.

The turn toward socialization of industry during the 1963-71 period generally lacked planning and organization. After the Revolutionary Council's announcement of its intention to eventually assume control of all industry in early 1963, the enterprises operated by the Defense Services Institute, founded in 1951, and the BEDC were placed under the centralized control of the Industrial Development Corporation (IDC), which had been established in 1952. For industry the closest resemblance to a government-planned development program by early 1971 was a timetable for the 1970-77 period to construct factories at the rate of about five per year. The practice was to work within annual budgetary procedures.

In 1970 the Ministry of Industry, the Industrial Raw Materials Committee, the IDC, the Mineral Resource Development Corporation, various numbered trade corporations of the Trade Council, and other organizations were concerned with industrial operations and development. Indications were that major decisions were made by the Revolutionary Council but that administrative controls were not closely coordinated. The supply of competent managerial personnel was not adequate to provide essential long-term planning and operational supervision of industrial development.

The acquisition of capital for investment in industrial development and expansion has presented continuing difficulties for the government. In early 1971 further progress was highly dependent upon government financing. The nationalization of many privately owned enterprises, mostly without compensation, after 1963 strongly inhibited private investment. By 1970 virtually all industries belonging to persons of non-Burmese extraction had been nationalized, and an important entrepreneurial element of industry was consequently disestablished. New foreign private investment was not permitted, and foreign companies were allowed to operate only if invited and only under contract with the government.

The prevailing attitude was self-reliance and caution concerning foreign assistance. Only United Nations or foreign government aid was accepted for development of industry or other purposes. The restrictive policies of the Revolutionary Council brought reductions in the inflow of long-term foreign capital; for the 1963-68 period the inflow averaged about US$8 million a year, as compared with US$14 million a year in the six years before 1963.

Industrial Production

Although the value of manufactures increased from K3.59 billion in fiscal 1961/62 to K5.18 billion in 1968/69, the increase was not steady and did not keep pace with requirements. Total production in 1963/64 and 1965/66 was below that of the previous year, and output of specific industries fluctuated from year to year. In the late 1960s and in 1970 production problems mounted, bringing industry to a state of stagnation.

The rapid moves toward a socialist economy after 1962 resulted in some disruption of production. Shortages of capital and of managerial and technically skilled personnel and an inadequate transportation system were basic problems that became even more critical as widespread banditry and disruptions by insurgents mounted. Inadequate supplies of spare parts for industrial machines, lack of raw materials, and labor problems resulting from an undisciplined work force also detracted from production efforts. In 1966/67 industrial output did not exceed two-thirds of installed capacity. Qualified observers reported that factory managers were sometimes directed to maintain their work force even when they lacked raw materials or when machinery was inoperable in order to reduce unemployment problems.

The predominance of the food-processing industries is revealed in data for fiscal 1968/69. In that year, when the value of manufactured goods was estimated at K5.18 billion, the contributions, in percent, for industries were: food and beverage, 60; textiles, 14; housing and household goods, 7; metal industries, 6; personal goods and raw materials, 3; transport equipment, 2; and other, 8. Manufactured items, except for foodstuffs, were generally limited to the most essential commodities required by the population (see table 5).

The processing of rice into finished form, including the production of rice bran oil, was by far the largest sector of the food industry. Production from peanuts, sesame seed, and cottonseed of

*Table 5. Production of Various Commodities in Burma, Selected Years, 1961-69**

Commodities	Units	1961/62	1964/65	1967/68	1968/69
Sugar	thousand tons	55	64	65	57
Salt	do	124	146	139	176
Yarn	do	3	5	7	7
Gunny sacks	hundred thousands	126	266	219	174
Umbrellas	thousand dozens	102	138	113	110
Fountain pens	thousands	n.a.	225	309	500
Soap	thousand tons	44	30	28	36
Matches	thousand boxes of 1,200	306	293	297	300
Candles	thousand tons	8	7	6	7
Brick	hundred thousands	91	831	993	1,000
Cement	thousand tons	33	136	158	200
Iron nails	do	n.a.	2	5	4
Gasoline	hundred thousand gallons	476	439	467	480
Kerosine	do	450	464	593	627
Aluminum utensils	do	41	37	16	22
Stoves	thousands	39	40	48	36
Radios	do	n.a.	19	24	31
Motor cars	numbers	n.a.	1,157	1,535	1,676
Water pumps	do	300	2,000	1,535	1,815

n.a.—not available.

*Fiscal year is from October 1 through September 30.

Source: Adapted from Union of Burma, *Report to the People by the Union of Burma Revolutionary Council on the Revolutionary Government's Budget Estimates for 1969-70,* Rangoon, 1970, p. 60.

cooking oils, which are widely used throughout the country, is an important industry. Per capita production of oil was about 9 pounds per year. A major effort was made in the late 1960s to make the country self-sufficient in sugar production. The requirement for over 70,000 tons was not met by 1971 despite the opening of new mills at Namti and Bilin in 1966 and efforts to expand production at the Zewaddy and Pyinmana plants. Output for 1969-70 was estimated to be below the 57,000 tons produced the previous year.

The country was highly dependent on imports of fiber because most domestic cotton was too coarse to make into cloth unless combined with long fiber types. There were no domestic substitutes available. Despite government efforts to promote production of cotton, acreage dropped from 567,000 in fiscal 1965/66 to about 362,000 in 1969/70 and output from 46,000 long tons down to an estimated 34,000 long tons in the same period.

The production of cement was revitalized in the early 1960s with restoration of a plant at Thayetmyo. Before the war this plant had supplied more than 90 percent of requirements. Production rose steadily in the late 1960s, reaching 200,000 tons in fiscal 1968/69, and then decreased slightly, by an estimated 10,000 tons, in fiscal 1969/70. Domestic supply was not adequate, and imports, lower after the middle 1960s, were required.

Production of iron and steel, consisting of ingots, castings, and semimanufactures, was 46,000 tons in fiscal 1968/69. The only plant of importance was the Ywama mill in Rangoon, built in 1957 with West German assistance. Electrically operated and capable of producing 20,000 tons annually, this mill has operated at less than capacity, and some of its original capabilities have been abandoned because usable scrap metal has been in short supply and less than estimated when the plant was planned.

Installed electric capacity in fiscal 1968/69 was 196,050 kilowatts. For 84,450 kilowatts of this total, the using elements were connected with hydroelectric generators; for 111,600 kilowatts, with thermal generators. The total power generated was 441.96 million kilowatt-hours. Almost half, or 154.3 million, of the total kilowatt-hours utilized were for industrial purposes. Over 300 towns and more than 400 villages were supplied with electricity.

The industry was nationalized in 1953, and all aspects of electric power were under the government's Electricity Supply Board. The largest hydroelectric facility was the station on the Baluchaung River, which in 1970 supplied 80 percent of Rangoon's power needs. The concentration of industries and people in the Rangoon area made it the largest consumer of electric power.

The output of the mining industry was relatively insignificant (see table 6). Only about 0.5 percent of the labor force was

Table 6. *Production of Certain Minerals in Burma, Selected Years, 1961-69*[1]
(in metric tons)

Mineral	1961/62	1964/65	1968/69
Refined lead	16,615	15,693	9,500
Antimonial lead	376	561	300
Zinc	14,225	14,131	9,000
Nickel speiss	520	266	115
Copper matte	354	310	160
Tin	900	910	499
Tungsten	1,440	70	155
Coal	n.a.	8,200	13,000
Jade	51	34	1
Silver[2]	1,436,955	1,204,130	810,000

n.a.—not available.

[1] Fiscal year is October 1 through September 30.

[2] In ounces.

Source: Adapted from Union of Burma, *Report to the People by the Union of Burma Revolutionary Council on the Revolutionary Government's Budget Estimates for 1969-70*, Rangoon, 1970, p. 55.

employed in it. The low metal content of major deposits and the necessity to transport ores long distances were basic factors that tended to discourage new exploitation. Lack of security at mining sites and along transportation routes and shortages of trained personnel were additional strong adverse influences.

Most of the mining industry has been nationalized. Plans called for taking over the remaining private mines when their licenses expired. Nationalizations in 1969 included precious stone and jade extraction enterprises.

The largest mining complex and, in the late 1960s the only one operating regularly, was the People's Bawdwin Industry. The Mawchi tin and tungsten mines, once the second largest complex and a leading world producer, were largely destroyed during the World War II period.

Oil extraction was developed to a relatively high degree during the period of British rule, reaching a level in the 1930s of from 6 million to 6.5 million barrels a year. The Burmah Oil Company was the dominant producer and after independence became a joint state-private enterprise. When the industry was nationalized in 1963, it became the People's Oil Industry. In 1970 it was renamed the Myanma Oil Corporation. Heavy damages were inflicted on the industry during World War II, and widespread insurgency from 1948 to 1950 brought further losses. In 1955 production of crude petroleum was only 20 percent of the prewar level. In fiscal

1962/63 production reached approximately 4.5 million barrels and then fell below that level for the next three years. Output increased steadily during the 1966—70 period, reaching 6.4 million barrels in 1969/70. Imports took a downward turn from 1966 to 1969, and it appeared that crude oil requirements, estimated at 7 million barrels, would be met in the early 1970s. Domestic requirements increased, however, and in 1969/70 the amount of imports rose. Nevertheless, a determined effort was being made in early 1971 to attain self-sufficiency in crude petroleum.

In fiscal 1969/70 the country's two refineries, in Syriam and Chauk, produced 239,700 gallons of refined products. These plants worked at less than full capacity because of crude oil shortages; in 1969/70 their production was about 87 percent of capacity. Imports of finished oil products were a continuing necessity.

Labor

Available data indicate that there are adequate numbers of people to meet manpower requirements, but widespread shortages of technically skilled workers and persons with managerial talent existed during the 1960s and continued to exist in early 1971. The latest complete census was in 1931, and statistics on total population and the labor force are generally estimates after that date, based on surveys or studies conducted at various times (see ch. 2, Physical Environment and Population).

In fiscal 1967/68, when total population was estimated at 26.4 million, the labor force was estimated at almost 10.5 million (see table 7). At that time the total population included 14.3 million persons in the working-age group (fifteen to fifty-nine years of age), of whom about 49 percent were males. About two-thirds of the labor force were employed in agriculture; a little over 8 percent, in trade; and about 7 percent, in manufacturing. None of the other sectors of the economy employed more than 3 percent. More than 92 percent of the work force was in private employment in 1967/68; however, this percentage was decreased somewhat by extensive nationalization of enterprises in late 1968 and in 1969.

Unemployment was highest in the greater Rangoon area and in Mandalay in the late 1960s. Accurate data were not available for overall unemployment. Work applications, an indicator of unemployment, were at a level of about 700,000 in 1968 and 1969. The jobless rate for the urban work force was estimated at 6 percent in 1969, and underemployment was considered to be at about the same level.

The large number of young university graduates without jobs in fiscal 1968/69 caused the government to establish a committee to

Table 7. Estimated Labor Force in Burma, 1967/68 *
(by number of persons)

Sectors	State-owned enterprises	Private enterprises	Total
Agriculture	30,000	5,280,000	5,310,000
Livestock and fishery	3,000	148,000	151,000
Forestry	53,000	27,000	80,000
Mining	17,000	37,000	54,000
Manufacturing	62,400	705,600	768,000
Power	10,000	n.a.	10,000
Construction	68,400	41,600	110,000
Communication	73,830	239,170	313,000
Social service	94,200	80,000	174,200
Administration	288,700	n.a.	288,700
Trade	82,700	770,000	852,700
Part-time workers in paddy fields	n.a.	1,500,000	1,500,000
Other	n.a.	847,400	847,400
Total	783,230	9,675,770	10,459,000

n.a.—not available.

*Fiscal year is October 1 through September 30.

Source: Adapted from Union of Burma, *Report to the People by the Union of Burma Revolutionary Council on the Revolutionary Government's Budget Estimates for 1969-70*, Rangoon, 1970, p. 6.

cope with the problem. At the same time that the country lacked experienced, technically trained personnel, there was an oversupply of university graduates in some technical fields, such as mechanical and electrical engineering. The regime's sensitivity to the attitudes of students tended to give ideological factors an important place in the appointment of graduates. Labor recruitment is highly centralized under government control. The public employment exchanges, numbering sixteen in 1969, were the major agencies for hiring.

The Revolutionary Council generally displayed a paternalistic attitude toward labor in disputes between workers and employers and in situations where government policies were not being contested. It showed firmness at times against recalcitrant workers, but on the whole it had not been able to remold the people's cultural attitudes that traditionally have prevented the development of a high state of discipline in the labor force. Low productivity and absenteeism were continuing major problems. These were aggravated by lack of material incentives. Government measures by early 1971 had brought few and limited benefits for the worker. Primary emphasis was placed on improving production as a means to improve the welfare of the labor force as a whole (see ch. 5, Living Conditions).

Although the Revolutionary Council had issued decrees amending certain laws concerning labor, in early 1971 it still utilized many regulations passed during the parliamentary period. The 1964 Law of Fundamental Rights and Responsibilities of Workers drew on existing codes, but it served mainly as a manifesto for the new regime to express the hopes and expectations of the working people. The Trade Disputes Amending Law of 1963 established the Central Labor Committee, replacing the former Court of Industrial Arbitration; this act took final authority over labor disputes away from the courts and placed it in the hands of the Revolutionary Council.

At the top, the Central Organizing Committee of the ruling Burma Socialist Program Party exercises control over labor matters through the Directorate of Labor. The minister of labor administers governmental programs, and the hierarchy of workers' councils are the primary means for the Burma Socialist Program Party to reach the mass of workers. In early 1971 Colonel Maung Shwe, minister of labor, was also Chairman of the Central People's Workers' Council.

The system of workers' councils, which resembled the pattern of those in the Soviet Union, was planned in the early 1960s but was not implemented until 1967. The need to develop reliable organizers was probably a delaying factor. By 1970 there were 2,398 councils at the primary level, and the system was being expanded as rapidly as resources would permit. The party central leadership maintained control and exerted its influence by appointing one-third of the membership of all councils and by appointing at all levels a labor affairs officer who conducted administrative training courses. The major purpose of the councils is to serve as a transmission belt between the Revolutionary Council and the mass of workers and to facilitate government control. They are not looked upon as bargaining agents to further the workers' interests.

Labor unions came to an end with the passage of the Law to Protect National Solidarity in 1964, which forbade labor, or any other element of society, to affiliate with any political party except the Burma Socialist Program Party. During the parliamentary period unions were utilized to gain support for political factions but they lacked any real power to further labor interests.

Before the 1962 coup Burma was active in the International Labor Organization (ILO) and had subscribed to twenty-one of its conventions. The Ne Win government has mainly played the role of an observer in ILO meetings, but it has made use of the organization's services. It has continued to abide by ILO decisions based on conventions to which Burma had subscribed.

Wages did not rise enough to keep pace with the rising cost of living during the late 1960s and 1970 and were relatively low. More than one member of the average urban family had to work to meet even a minimum living standard. In 1969 the average unskilled worker received K122 per month. Expenses of the average household—consisting of two adults and three children—for maintaining a minimum standard was estimated at K178.6 per month. Government pay scales fixed in 1948 were not raised despite inflation.

The government's policy in newly nationalized enterprises was generally to raise wages for unskilled workers to the minimum paid government employees and to lower the pay of skilled and professional personnel to that of government employees of the same category. Wages were usually paid at a monthly, daily, or hourly rate in government establishments, on a piecework basis in cottage industries, and in kind for hired labor in agriculture. The Revolutionary Council, when it came to power, expanded application of minimum wages and established the minimum monthly rate at K82 and the daily minimum rate at K3.15.

The primary means to induce greater incentive and productivity are the model-worker program and appeals to the worker to increase output for the benefit of society as a whole. Outstanding workers were selected and given acclaim with the hope that others would emulate their performance. In fiscal 1968/69, 638 model workers were designated. Indications were that special vacation privileges accorded to model workers did not provide as much appeal as expected. The wage system made no provision for extra pay for overtime work or bonuses for above-normal output.

The normal working day is usually eight hours for adults, and the work week is forty-four hours in most factories. Employees in shops and commercial establishments generally work forty-eight hours a week. The workday for laborers in agriculture is frequently longer than for other workers and during the busiest seasons may be up to twelve hours per day. Leave is supposed to be granted for the country's national holidays. Total paid leave for nonagricultural workers varies from about three to five weeks per year. Workers with more than six months' service are entitled to thirty days' paid medical leave annually.

Technology

The country relies very heavily on foreign and international agencies for technological assistance. Research efforts are almost entirely concerned with application of already-developed technology. The Union of Burma Applied Research Institute directs experimental work in industrial fields. Its program in 1969 included the construction of a pilot papermill and installation of imported machinery to make paper from yarn and wastepaper. The government took a liberal attitude toward, and participated in, international industrial and trade fairs as a means to further technological development.

CHAPTER 13

TRADE AND TRANSPORTATION

Subsequent to its assumption of power in 1962 the government progressively nationalized domestic wholesale trade, most retail trade, shipping agencies, foreign trade, and almost all other sectors of the economy. Transport facilities, except for some private operations in inland waterway transport and trucking, also became a government monopoly. By 1971 distribution of most goods was under the ownership, control, or supervision of the government in pursuit of its objective of socialization of the economy (see ch. 11, Character and Structure of the Economy).

Internal marketing of all imported goods and all goods produced in government-owned or supervised industries, except for cooking oil, was the exclusive right of the government. The government also monopolized the purchase and distribution of rice, cotton, tobacco, wheat, sugarcane, and jute (see ch. 12, Agriculture and Industry). The government shared the catching and marketing of fish and the marketing of cooking oil with the private sector. Trade in other agricultural commodities, meat, poultry, secondhand goods, and products of small private industries and handicraft operations not using imported materials was conducted in the private sector.

In the case of external trade, foreign purchasing policies were adjusted to specific needs as determined by the government to support its economic objectives. An annual import program was therefore prepared as part of the foreign exchange budget. On the basis of estimated foreign exchange receipts, allocations were made for estimated import requirements for capital and maintenance goods, raw materials, and spares. With respect to consumer goods, allocations were being made in 1971 only for certain essential scarce goods.

The country continued its traditional reliance upon rice and teak as its main sources of export earnings; exports of rice were near half of total exports in 1970 and sales of teak provided some 23 percent. The country's principal imports were machinery and transport equipment, metal and metal products, and textiles. The country's principal trading partners were Japan, the countries of Western Europe, India, and Great Britain.

By 1971 nationalization of trade had not brought many of the benefits sought by the program. There were widespread supply shortages in the official retail stores, and an extensive black market, with considerable smuggling, had developed. Other deficiencies in distribution had become a cause of concern to the government. A shortage of qualified personnel, poor coordination among state enterprises, inadequate information on production and consumption patterns, and overtaxed storage and transportation facilities were cited by the government as major causes of the difficulties in commodity distribution.

Railways, airlines, inland waterways, ocean shipping, and communications facilities are state controlled and managed by government boards directly responsible to the appropriate ministry. The country's facilities for ground transportation were largely destroyed during World War II, and subsequent road and track construction was concentrated on repair and replacement. For trade and transporation, the country continues to be primarily dependent upon its waterways. The Irrawaddy-Chindwin river system provides 1,500 miles of navigable water transport throughout the year and handles most of the coastal shipping headed for major ports in India, East Pakistan, and Malaysia. Rangoon is the natural focus of ocean transportation, with supplementary ports handling minor trade. The national airline, Union of Burma Airways, provides both internal and external service, the latter in competition with other international airlines.

The transportation network has become overstrained. The state-owned railway has been carrying three times the number of pre-World War II rail passengers with two-thirds as many passenger coaches. As many as 27 percent of the locomotives have been out of order at any one time. In 1969 there were 10 percent fewer freight cars than in 1939. The annual report of the Inland Waterways Transport Board stated in 1969 that only thirty-three of the sixty routes once maintained by the nationalized Irrawaddy Flotilla Company were in operation. Because of the obsolete condition of the fleet of the Inland Waterways Transport Board, there were 63 percent more breakdowns during 1968 than in 1963.

Telephone facilities outside Rangoon are quite limited. In 1971 radiotelephone service connected the country with most of the countries of Asia, the United States, the Soviet Union and Switzerland. Internal communication was also largely by wireless. A direct telegraphic link connected Rangoon and Osaka, Japan, but service to all other countries had to be routed through India and Ceylon.

NATIONALIZED DISTRIBUTION

In 1971 the official distribution system was administered by the Trade Council, which was established in October 1965 to replace the earlier People's Stores Corporation. The Trade Council was responsible for formulating trade policy; both domestic and foreign trade operations were under its supervision. The council consisted of twelve members, including the minister of trade, who was the chairman, and several other ministers. The day-to-day business of the council was managed by the Executive Committee of three members, headed by the minister of trade. The Trade Council and the Executive Committee together were known as the Central Trade Organization.

The Trade Council established twenty-two trade corporations in December 1965. The corporations were managed by trade corporation committees, which were directly responsible to the Trade Council. Most of the corporations were engaged in the domestic distribution of specified categories of commodities, both imported and domestically produced. The Myanma Export-Import Corporation, also known as Trade Corporation No. 22, was the only exporting agency and also handled all imports for use by the private sector. Government departments and agencies imported goods for their own accounts. Certain agencies, such as the People's Oil Industry and the State Timber Board, engaged in internal distribution of their production.

The Trade Council determined how trading was to be conducted in each locality, whether through a people's retail shop, village cooperative shop, private registered retail shop, department store, or people's market. At the local level, the Trade Council is represented by the five-man Township Trade Committee. The function of these committees is to purchase, store, transport, and deliver commodities for the local distribution system.

In January 1966 two notifications were issued that added certain items to the list of commodities that could be traded only by government agencies, thereby restricting private trading to meat, fruits, perishable vegetables, confectionery, handicrafts, and most products of cottage industries. The notifications also provided for stricter enforcement of existing regulations prohibiting trading by the private sector. As a result, a large number of private retail shops closed, and the burden on the overstrained state trading system was further increased.

Many problems arose after the nationalization of the distribution system. Overhead costs, partly because of overstaffing and large unsold inventories, proved to be excessive. The government believed that these problems were primarily the result of three factors: inadequate statistics on consumer demand, inventories, and production; a severe shortage of qualified personnel to operate the system; and insufficient storage and transportation facilities.

The government has been aware of the deficiencies in the distribution system and has taken certain actions to improve it. Beginning in June 1966, consumer committees had been organized in the towns to help plan the procurement, stockpiling, and sale of goods by the local people's retail shops, which dealt primarily in basic foodstuffs and textiles. The committees were also responsible for the operation of a system of household purchase booklets. These had been introduced on a nationwide basis in 1964 in order to produce an equitable distribution of scarce commodities in the different townships and to prevent hoarding and trading in the black market. The consumer committees allocated such commodities to the local households on the basis of their estimated requirements.

The effectiveness of the consumer committees, however, was not as great as the government had expected, partly because of lack of cooperation on the part of other elements of the distribution system and partly because of the failure of some committees to perform their duties satisfactorily. An important measure taken to improve the distribution system had been the partial decontrol of domestic trade implemented during 1966.

In September 1966 the government authorized the private sector to engage in domestic trade in thirty-four food items previously distributed only through public channels, including potatoes, peas, onions, garlic, coconuts, tea, domestic tobacco, prawns, and fish. Private dealers were authorized in the following month to trade in forty-two minor forestry products that had been distributed through cooperatives since October 1963. In November 1966 domestic trade in groundnuts, groundnut oil and oilcake, sesame, and sesame oil and oilcake was opened to private traders.

In 1967 supply shortages in the official retail outlets became serious, and most goods, including rice, were sold on a quota basis when available. This situation caused certain modifications in the policy of decontrol. The measures taken in 1966 had partly relaxed the prohibition on private dealing in controlled foodstuffs by exempting the purchase, storage, movement, and milling of controlled foodstuffs for household consumption. Effective February 15, 1968, the free movement of controlled foodstuffs was limited to within the same township, and movements between townships were again prohibited.

To introduce greater efficiency in the operations of the state retail shops, the government in 1970 appointed regional supervisors, who were responsible for controlling and directing supplies to the shops and preventing excessive accumulation of inventories. The distribution had also become more oriented toward essential goods, among which were distinguished type 1 and type 2 goods. Type 1 goods comprised primarily basic foodstuffs, such as rice, that were consumed daily. Type 2 goods were other essential goods that were not required to be distributed daily—for example, textiles. The practice in 1971 was to inform trade agencies at the township level on the type and amount of goods they would receive during the year, so that the township trade committees could make their plans in such a way as to enable them to distribute type 1 goods at regular intervals to meet the normal needs of consumers. Type 2 goods were sent as and when they were available, but each consumer would ultimately get his full quota in a year.

The government hoped that competition between the state retail shops and the consumers' cooperatives, which would be given more scope under the government's cooperative plan announced in May 1970, would lead to a more efficeint system of distribution. Consumers' cooperatives would be allowed to purchase supplies not only from state trading corporations, as was the case for state retail shops, but also from producers' cooperatives and from private traders. Financing of the consumers' cooperatives in excess of the funds available from membership subscriptions would require borrowing from the banks at the prevailing rate of interest (see ch. 11, Character and Structure of the Economy). By the early months of 1971 consumers' cooperatives were being set up in various areas to serve as pilot projects for expansion of the program throughout the country.

FOREIGN TRADE

All exports and imports are made by the government through the Myanma Export-Import Corporation. The corporation negotiates and signs contracts with foreign importers and handles all exports. The State Timber Board, however, deals directly with foreign importers for the sake of administrative convenience (see ch. 12, Agriculture and Industry). Contracts negotiated by the board are then approved by the corporation and carried out in the name of the corporation. The proceeds from exports must be surrendered to the People's Bank of the Union of Burma within six months from the date of shipment (see ch. 11, Character and Structure of the Economy).

There is a list of prohibited exports: iron and steel, brass, copper, and aluminum and scraps thereof; foreign manufactures; and commodities of domestic origin that are to be conserved for domestic use. All exports to the Union of South Africa and to Rhodesia are prohibited. In the case of export sales on an f.o.b. (free-on-board) basis, buyers are free to choose any shipping line as the carrier; exports on a c.i.f. (cost-insurance-freight) basis are usually shipped on vessels of the Burma Five Star Line or vessels designated by it.

The Myanma Export-Import Corporation imports goods for use by the private sector. No private individual or organization may import any goods or act as a commission agent. The Myanma

Export-Import Corporation issues proposals for the import requirements of other trade corporations or government agencies and negotiates and signs contracts with foreign suppliers. Various other government agencies, such as the Industrial Development Corporation, transport organizations, ministries, and other boards and corporations, import goods for their own use, as well as goods under loan and aid agreements, in the name of the Myanma Export-Import Corporation (see ch. 12, Agriculture and Industry).

To pay for their imports, the government departments and agencies and the Myanma Export-Import Corporation obtain foreign exchange allotments on a quarterly basis from the foreign exchange subcommittee, which consists of representatives of the Ministry of Finance and Revenues and the Ministry of National Planning. Letters of credit are opened by the People's Bank of the Union of Burma against these allotments, which serve as exchange permits. Because imports have to be made in the name of the Myanma Export-Import Corporation, applications for letters of credit made by government agencies are countersigned by it. All payments for imports are made through the foreign exchange division of the People's Bank of the Union of Burma.

Import requirements of the private sector, including all consumer goods requirements, are determined by the twelve-member Trade Council, comprising the minister of trade as chairman and other ministers dealing with econimic matters. Current import requirements of other government agencies, including ministries, departments, boards, and corporations, are calculated in the course of the preparation of their annual fiscal budget estimates. All these claims are fitted together into an import program within the foreign exchange budget by the Ministry of Finance and Revenues.

Imports of capital goods financed by project loans and grants are approved automatically once the project has been approved. For all other imports the general order of priorities gives precedence to raw materials, spare parts, and capital goods over consumer goods. Imports of consumer goods are usually limited mostly to scarce essentials; this restriction is imposed to conserve foreign exchange and to protect domestic industry. If foreign exchange receipts fall short of budget estimates, the import program is revised in the light of this order of priorities.

Imports of a few commodities, including opium and similar narcotics, and all imports from South Africa and Rhodesia, are prohibited. All imports are purchased on an f.o.b. basis, and shipments are made on vessels owned or chartered by the Burma Five Star Line, whenever possible, or vessels designated by it. Vessels owned or chartered by the Burma Five Star Line carried an estimated 70 to 80 percent of the country's imports in 1970.

In 1969 the country's foreign trade activity recorded the second lowest level since World War II. Exports were K598 million (4.76 kyat equal US$1) or about 6 percent of the gross national product (GNP), showing the further decline of the role of exports in the economy (see ch. 11, Character and Structure of the Economy). Exports other than rice and teak were primarily metals and ores, pulses, rubber, and oilcakes. The 1969 import figure of K677 million was a minor increase over the post-World War II low of K673 million in 1967 and represented around 7 percent of the GNP.

In early 1971 the country had bilateral trade agreements in force with eight countries: that is, with North Korea, Bulgaria, Hungary, East Germany, South Korea, Romania, Poland, and India (see ch. 10, Foreign Relations). The agreement with Romania was concluded in February 1969; that with Poland, in January 1970; and that with India in May 1970. These agreements were all general trade agreements; no commodities were listed nor was there any provision for quotas or clearing accounts. Payments must be made in transferable pounds sterling or other mutually agreed upon convertible currency. The agreements were automatically renewable from year to year unless cancelled by either party. The bilateral trade and payments agreement with Communist China that was concluded on January 9, 1961, expired on June 30, 1966, and was not renewed; the outstanding balance of the equivalent of about US$420 was settled in pounds sterling. In early 1971 the country did not have any bilateral payments agreements.

Composition of Trade

Exports

During the 1960s the volume and total value of exports of rice and rice products had fallen steadily after the high point in fiscal 1961/62 (October 1, 1961, to September 30, 1962), when they reached 1.8 million tons at a value of K852 million. The totals dropped to 1.5 million tons and K761 million for 1963/64, 1.3 million tons and K645 million for 1964/65, 1.1 million tons and K563 million for 1965/66, 649,000 tons and K375 million for 1966/67, 347,000 tons and K238 million for 1967/68, and 364,000 tons and K235 million for 1968/69.

The 1960s were characterized by a sharp increase in the quantity of rice used domestically. The decline in output of paddy (unmilled rice) in 1965/66 and 1966/67 resulted in a substantial fall in government procurement from a husked-rice equivalent of 2.5 million tons in 1964/65 to 1.3 million tons in 1966/67 (see ch. 12, Agriculture and Industry). Despite the approximate 7 percent recovery in output of paddy in 1967/68, government procurement showed only a 5 percent increase. The quantity retained by cultivators increased from 2.5 million tons in 1965/66 and 1966/67 to 3.1 million tons in 1967/68, reportedly as a result of dissatisfaction with government procurement prices.

In 1968/69, however, government procurement increased to 1.8 million tons. With government domestic sales accounting for slightly over 1 million tons, the exportable surplus for the fiscal year was about 800,000 tons. As a result of severe difficulties in marketing the exportable surplus on the weakened world rice market, however, exports failed to keep pace with the increased availabilities. The consequence was a substantial increase of about 400,000 tons in government stocks during that fiscal year. The price of rice per ton at which the government was able to conclude sales contracts with foreign buyers, commonly termed the unit price, also fell by 16 percent in 1968/69 and another 14 percent in 1969/70.

During the 1960s exports of teak were the country's second most important earner of foreign exchange. The volume of exports had ranged between 154,000 tons in 1963/64 to the 100,000 tons recorded in 1966/67 and 1967/68. The highest total amount in export earnings of teak during the 1960s occurred in 1968/69, when receipts reached K159 million. This figure represented a volume of 130,000 tons, however, and a decline of 21 percent in the unit value of teak exports in 1968/69 compared with the previous year. The lower average export price was primarily caused by an increased share in exports of planks, which receive lower prices than logs.

The country had little difficulty in finding export markets for teak. Its export was limited by internal difficulties in extracting, milling, and transporting. Illegal felling and theft of logs in transit to the mills of Rangoon and Moulmein had continued to take place; much of this material ultimately arrived at the sawmills of the private sector.

Miscellaneous exports included tin. Exports of this commodity during the 1960s were at their highest value in 1964/65, when export receipts were K52 million. The complex of tin mines at Mawchi in Kayah State had not been able to resume regular operations after World War II, because the area has seldom been controlled by the national government (see ch. 14, National Defense and Internal Security). In 1968/69 exports of tin reached a volume of 19,000 thousand tons and a value of K29 million.

Exports of agricultural products other than rice and teak included pulses, oilcakes, and rubber. In 1968/69 exports of pulses were 46,000 tons at a value of K32 million, and exports of oilcakes were 88,000 tons at a value of K25 million. Exports of rubber increased in 1968/69 to 13,000 tons at a value of K27 million, from

6,000 tons and earnings of K9 million in the previous year. During the 1960s exports of cotton gradually diminished and by 1968/69 had ceased completely.

Imports

During the 1960s the relative importance of imports of machinery and transport equipment increased; by 1968/69 this category of imports was clearly the most important. Imports of machinery and transport equipment had also increased in absolute value from K188 million in 1961/62 to the 1968/69 total of K301 million, or around 40 percent of the total value of all imports. The value of imports of machinery and transport equipment in 1968/69 was more than three times greater than the value of the second most important category, metal and metal products, for which K93 million was spent. Imports of textiles, which in the first half of the 1960s had reached relatively high totals, had in 1968/69 been reduced to the comparatively low level of K86 million. Other categories of imports, which were high enough in total values to warrant separate grouping in the trade statistics, included raw materials, paper and paper products, foodstuffs and tobacco, pharmaceutical products, and rubber manufactures. Miscellaneous imports amounted to K119 million in 1968/69.

Direction of Trade

In early 1971 the latest data available from Burmese governmental authorities on the principal markets for the country's exports and principal sources for its imports, expressed on a calendar-year basis, covered trade in calendar 1968. The country's major foreign trading partners in 1968 in terms of value of total exports and imports were Japan, the countries of Western Europe, India, and Great Britain. One major change in the pattern of the country's foreign trade during the 1960s was the diminution of Communist China as an export market and the sharp drop in imports from that source. Sales to Communist China fell from K81 million in 1964 to K10 million in 1968. Imports from Communist China, which had reached K152 million in 1964, dropped to K8 million in 1968.

Another substantial alteration in the country's pattern of foreign trade during the 1960s was the drastic decline in the country's sales of its major export, rice, to its traditional export markets for that product. During the 1964—68 period export sales of rice fell as follows: Indonesia, K157 million to K40 million; Ceylon, K129 million to K42 million; Pakistan, K67 million to K4 million; Malaysia, K67 million to K1 million; and the Philippines, K43 million to zero.

Japan

The largest value of total trade with one country in 1968 was recorded with Japan, which supplied over 20 percent of imports and bought nearly 10 percent of exports. Japanese purchases continued to be concentrated on beans, rice, timber, and metallic ores. Machinery transport equipment, textile yarns and fabrics, and iron and steel were the major imports from Japan. During the 1960s the country continually ran a large trade deficit with Japan; in 1968 this deficit was K48 million. Imports from Japan in the 1960s averaged about K224 million yearly.

Western Europe

The countries of the European Economic Community (EEC) and the European Free Trade Association (EFTA) plus Ireland and Spain comprise the trading group designated as Western Europe in statistics on the country's foreign trade. Total trade with Western Europe reached K276 million in 1968. In that year, the country ran a trade deficit with Western Europe, with imports of K167 million and exports of K109 million. Trade with Western Europe had declined from the mid-1960s, when total trade reached K357 million. The country's exports to this trading area in the second half of the 1960s had ranged around K119 million annually. The level of imports had fallen from the 1964 total of K243 million to the 1968 total of K167 million.

India

In 1968 India purchased about 15 percent of the country's exports and supplied 20 percent of its imports. For many years before the mid-1960s India had been the country's most important trading partner. Increased production of rice within India and large United States food-aid programs to India, however, had significantly reduced the amounts of the country's rice purchased by India. In 1968, nevertheless, the country's major export market for rice continued to be India, with sales of K78 million for that year, and the timing, amount, and price per ton of India's annual purchases of rice remained in the late 1960s an important factor in the country's annual balance of payments. India was also a major purchaser of the country's exports of tin.

Great Britain

Trade with Great Britain in the second half of the 1960s reached a stable level both in absolute amounts and in relative importance In 1968 exports to Great Britain were slightly over 7 percent of total exports of goods, with teak and animal foodstuffs the major

266

items. Imports from Great Britain in 1968 were somewhat greater than 10 percent of total imports; machinery and transport equipment were the principal items. The general proportion of trade with Great Britain in relation to total exports and imports has prevailed since 1964.

NONGOVERNMENTAL DISTRIBUTION

In 1971 there were very few private registered retail shops in operation, and those that were open for business had few goods available for sale. There was a lack of facilities for storage of highly perishable items such as fish paste and vegetables. Imported goods were available only on the black market. Foreign press observers visiting Rangoon described as worn and threadbare the clothing of much of the population and said that soldiers' uniforms were patched and mended. One block-long building in Rangoon, intended for use as a department store and in operation briefly, had been closed and boarded because there were so few goods to sell.

Hoarding of money by some relatively wealthy persons and the shortage of goods under the government's rationing system led to private dealings among government storekeepers and consumers. The system of sale of goods on the basis of quota slips created many opportunities for the diversion of goods into the black market. The ubiquitous nature of the black market caused it to be given the satirical title of Trade Corporation No. 23 (a reference to the government's Trade Corporation No. 22).

The black market demand for rice and other necessities stimulated acquisitiveness among the cultivators. The price of rice on the black market in 1971 was about five times greater than the price at government outlets. This difference had destroyed the cultivators' traditional habit of saving part of their production to feed their own families because they could sell rice at a high price on the black market and subsequently buy it at a lower price from the government outlets. The result was persistent and heavy demands on the already scarce supply in the government stores.

Officials systematically searched luggage for smuggled goods. Articles in the government press described the methods used in the transfer of the smuggled goods from Moulmein, the major point for entry of contraband items, to Rangoon. In 1970 over K5 million worth of assorted black-market commodities were seized in the district of Moulmein. *Working Peoples Daily* in reporting this named those persons who systematically moved the smuggled goods from Moulmein to Rangoon the "darkness shelterers," or *hmaunghkos*. Traveling on the Moulmein-Rangoon Express, the newspaper's correspondent was struck by the luggage being brought for checking by some of the passengers, mostly women. Almost all of them had small trunks, many battered and apparently well used. All of the trunks were of steel and of striking uniformity in size. The account described the trunks as "all smallish, of manageable proportions, easily slipped under a seat to be hidden or conveniently carried if in a hurry."

As the trunks were weighed at the baggage checkpoint, three government officials—a civilian policeman, a military policeman, and a tax collector—examined the contents. Imported goods that could not be satisfactorily justified to the government officials were confiscated. Before the train's departure, the same officials searched the passenger coaches. They inspected plastic bags and international airline cabin bags, both of which are of foreign origin and are assumed to have been smuggled into the country. The officials confiscated imported goods found in such containers only when they considered the quantities more than sufficient for personal use. The passengers, therefore, divided their illicit goods into small bags that they distributed among accomplices in various sections of the train.

The search party moved through each passenger coach, selecting at random the bags to be searched. After the train's departure, the passengers assembled their goods from the various parts of the train where they had been dispersed. The goods were repacked into compact small bundles. As soon as the train entered the Rangoon metropolitan area and reduced speed, some of the passengers jumped off the train with their bundles. Others pushed the bundles off the train to waiting accomplices along the track.

The same correspondent of the *Working Peoples Daily* described the search and confiscation of smuggled goods hidden under the clothing of female passengers on the Rangoon-Moulmein Express. He reported that foreign-manufactured textiles, clothing, umbrellas, and cosmetics were described to him as being commonly transported in this fashion.

TRANSPORTATION AND COMMUNICATION

Water Transport

Inland water transport is extremely important to the country's economic life because of the division of the country into a series of river valleys separated by mountain ranges (see ch. 2, Physical Environment and Population). There are approximately 5,000 miles of navigable rivers in the country.

The main inland water system utilizes the Irrawaddy River, navigable by shallow-draught vessels for 800 miles above its delta to Bhamo throughout the year and, in the low-water season, when the force of the stream through the narrow defiles slackens, to Myitkyina. The Irrawaddy is navigable from Rangoon by way of the Twante Canal, linking the easternmost mouth of the river to the Rangoon River. The Chindwin River, the Irrawaddy River's most important tributary, is navigable for vessels drawing 2½ feet of water from its mouth at the confluence with the Irrawaddy at Myingyan to Homalin or, occasionally, to Tamanthi (as far north as Myitkyina).

The Irrawaddy River system drains about 65 percent of the country, including the area of greatest population and resources. The Salween River, the longest of the country's rivers, is navigable only for a comparatively short distance, less than 100 miles, beyond which boats cannot ascend because of dangerous rapids. The great rivers—the Irrawaddy, the Chindwin, and the Salween—provide the major natural arteries, but they run only from north to south and therefore have limited usefulness as total links for all parts of the country.

In early 1971 the government was dredging the Irrawaddy and Chindwin rivers to make them navigable throughout the year. The two rivers had been rapidly silting, causing the waterways to become narrower. Although the government was unable to remove all the silt, dredging operations were underway at sites where the silt had become a navigational hazard. The government was also collecting data regarding changes in the courses of the rivers and the silting of the waterways.

The Kaladan River and its tributaries are important as means of transportation along the Arakan Coastal Strip in the northwest, especially for transporting rice to the port of Akyab. The Arakan Coastal Strip is separated from the rest of the country by the Western Mountain Belt and has no railroads and almost no roads. Many other rivers and tidal creeks throughout the country are navigable for short distances and are used by private traffic, mainly small scows and homemade boats plying between villages.

The government's Inland Waterways Transport Board operates all principal routes. It carries the bulk of waterborne commerce, especially important commodities, such as rice, oil, and cement. The total freight tonnage carried by the Inland Waterways Transport Board in 1969 was 1.8 million tons; the total number of passengers carried was 10.9 million. In that year the board was operating only thirty-three of the sixty routes once maintained by the Irrawaddy Flotilla Company, which had been nationalized in 1948. Breakdowns in the fleet of the Inland Waterways Transport Board were increasing in the late 1960s because of the equipment's obsolescence.

The number of good natural harbors is limited. Rangoon serves as the principal center for ocean transportation, handling about 85 percent of seaborne trade. Akyab, Bassein, and Moulmein are secondary ports; there are in addition four minor ports. The three main supplementary ports handle trade in the Arakan Coastal Strip, the Central Belt, and the Shan Plateau. Among the supplementary ports, Moulmein is an important port for exports of timber. Most of the rice destined for export is shipped to Rangoon via the Irrawaddy River or through the approximate 1,700 miles of rivers and creeks in the Irrawaddy Delta. This rice transport is handled by small vessels.

In 1970 construction of a shipyard at Simalaik on the Hlaing River at Rangoon was continuing. It would have docking facilities for private coastal vessels and navy and other government-owned ships of up to 1,700 tons and would be able to build ships of up to 1,000 tons. Through 1969, although the shipyard was not completely constructed, two river gunboats had been built there.

In 1971 the country's only shipping line was the state-owned Burma Five Star Line. It operated a fleet of nine oceangoing vessels and four coastal steamers; overseas destinations included India, Pakistan, Ceylon, Japan, Great Britain, and Europe. In fiscal year 1968/69 the line carried 25,000 passengers and transported 741,000 tons of freight. The line also chartered foreign vessels for shipping exports to European and Asian destinations. In a further extension of nationalization, twenty-four shipping agencies in Rangoon, Moulmein, Bassein, and Akyab were nationalized in 1969.

Rail and Road Transport

Burma Railways, the state-owned railway, in 1970 operated 1,850 miles single-track, meter gauge. Some additional mileage, not being used in 1970, had been abandoned for various reasons. The railways are secondary to inland waterways as a means of transportation. The rail system is oriented on a generally north-south axis, with the main trunkline running through the center of the country from Rangoon to Mandalay. This line then continues northward beyond Mandalay to its terminus at Myitkyina; spurs that branch from this trunkline terminate at Lashio and Myingyan. There is also a 161-mile line from Rangoon to Prome, with a branch to Bassein in the Irrawaddy Delta. An important rail line connects Rangoon with Moulmein and continues about 50 miles farther south.

In 1971 work on a second rail track on the 386-mile Rangoon-Mandalay section was continuing; when completed, this section would be the country's first double-track line. Rail traffic in 1971, therefore, had to be operated on a shuttle system on the single-track rail lines, with trains stopping at several stations to wait until the line ahead was clear. Frequent breakdowns of the locomotives in use in 1971 on the Mandalay-Myitkyina section caused disruptions in communications and transportation. In 1969 the railway had 373 locomotives, 9,344 freight cars, and 1,184 passenger coaches. Passengers carried during fiscal 1968/69 numbered nearly 52,000 for a total of about 1.4 million-passenger miles; 3,335 tons of freight were transported for a total of about 540,000 ton-miles.

In 1969 there were around 65,000 motor vehicles registered in the country and about 16,000 miles of highways, of which 4,200 miles were paved. Most of the roads ran in a north-south direction parallel to the mountains and rivers, and many terminated at inland waterway connections. Somewhat over 190,000 passengers traveled by bus in fiscal 1968/69 for nearly 338,000 passenger-miles; slightly over 2,500 tons of freight were hauled for over 71,000 ton-miles. Road transport was very important for medium and short distances in the country; the bullock and the buffalo, however, continued to be the major form of transport in rural areas where water transport was insufficient.

Air Transport

Air transport is entirely operated by the Union of Burma Airways, which acts as agent for all foreign airlines. Transport of goods and passengers throughout the country by air has been particularly important, in view of the inadequacies of rail and road transport and the fluctuating levels of internal security. In fiscal 1968/69 Union of Burma Airways operated seventeen commercial aircraft— seven Dakotas, five Viscounts, and five Fokker Friendships. In 1969 there were forty-one airfields in the country, thirteen of which were equipped with night facilities and radio controls. Mingaladon airport in Rangoon is a fully equipped international airport. Domestically, Union of Burma Airways in 1969 was serving thirty-three localities throughout the country with forty-six flights weekly. A new airfield, built at a cost of K6.4 million, was opened at Akyab in 1969, with a 6,000-foot runway. The Moulmein airfield was renovated in the same year, and the runway was extended to 8,900 feet.

Union of Burma Airways had in 1970 regular international service to Bangkok, Hong Kong, Calcutta, and Chittagong. Seven foreign airlines served the country. An agreement in 1969 between Burma and Thailand gave Union of Burma Airways landing rights to call at Bangkok on the airline's Rangoon-Hong Kong flight. In the same year the airline leased one Boeing 727 aircraft from a United States airline, which also provided the crew. This plane arrived in July 1969 and was put on the Rangoon-Bangkok-Hong Kong run, with plans to extend the flight subsequently to Japan. In 1970 the airline terminated this lease and purchased a 727 aircraft from another American airline. The government calculated that to make the Boeing 727 venture successful the country would need visits from at least 4,500 tourists annually.

Communications

The director general of posts and telegraphs controls the telephone, telegraph, radio, and postal communications systems. In 1970 there were 24,290 telephones in use, of which 17,500 were in Rangoon; only the telephones in Rangoon were fully automatic. There were 1,039 post offices and 277 telegraph offices in operation in 1969. Internal communication is mainly by wireless. In 1969 there were 370,000 licensed radio receivers, half of which were in Rangoon (see ch. 6, Education, Cultural Activities, and Public Information).

Most external communications are routed through Ceylon and India. A wireless telegraph service, however, allows direct communication with Japan, Pakistan, Hong Kong, Thailand, and the Philippines. In 1969 there were also 104 radio telephone stations providing radio telephone links with most Asian countries, the United States, the Soviet Union, Great Britain, Denmark, and Switzerland. In July 1969 radio telephone service between Burma and Nepal via India was opened.

SECTION IV. NATIONAL SECURITY

CHAPTER 14

NATIONAL DEFENSE AND INTERNAL SECURITY

Burmese national defense forces in late 1970 consisted of an army, a navy, and an air force, all subordinate to the Ministry of Defense, which functioned in the dual capacity of a government ministry and a triservice military headquarters. Command and staff organization was patterned on the British system. The army, with a strength of approximately 120,000 officers and men in 1970, was by far the dominant element; the navy and the air force, with total strengths of about 6,000 and 7,000, respectively, had limited capabilities but often were able to provide effective support for the army's operations. Overall strength of the armed forces was estimated at about 140,000.

The country was almost entirely dependent on outside aid for its armament and equipment as well as for some of its military training. Both the United States and Great Britain made significant contributions to the development of the armed forces over the years. Materiel, however, has not been at a high level of sophisticated weaponry, and the unbalanced forces, although they have some heavy weapons and equipment, have operated primarily as light infantry with negligible supporting arms and services. Despite long involvement in guerrilla-type operations, the military establishment has had little experience in conventional warfare.

The armed forces are maintained entirely on a volunteer basis, except for the conscription of a few needed doctors and qualified technicians. The National Service Law of 1959 provided for universal military service, but it has never been implemented. It has, in fact, never been needed, as voluntary enlistments have met force levels easily. The universities at Rangoon and Mandalay each maintain a corps of student trainees but, other than these, there is no organized reserve or training program. As far as can be determined, there is no overall mobilization plan, and the development of such a plan would be difficult because significant expansion of the armed forces would be restricted by shortages of equipment, facilities, and qualified training instructors.

Military service has received widely varying degrees of acceptance, but by and large the military has been considered a desirable and respected career. The serviceman as an individual has been in a favored segment of society, and his environment and conditions of service have met a relatively high local standard. Although their daily routines are arduous and personnel frequently are faced with the hazards of their calling, the soldier, sailor, and airman have status, a degree of security, and many amenities that would be difficult to achieve in civilian life.

Responsibility for law enforcement and the maintenance of public order is vested in the National People's Police, a large, centralized body within the Ministry of Home Affairs. In 1970 its strength was estimated at about 42,000 members. The force has two main elements: the Rangoon City Police, whose operations are restricted to the metropolitan area of the capital; and the Burma Civil Police, which operates on a countrywide basis. The National People's Police works closely with the army, and in the past the transfer of personnel from one to the other and the periodic absorption of entire police units into the military made it difficult at times to distinguish one from the other. The reorganization of police into the unified National People's Police in 1964 was an effort to set up a civilian force separate from the army that would become exclusively concerned with law and order and the prevention and detection of crime.

The preservation of public order and security has been a major problem because continuing political unrest, marked by violence and revolt, has been widespread. Despite religious and family traditions of respect for authority and adherence to social discipline, the atmosphere of violence and rebellion has encouraged crime and brigandage and has contributed to a manifest disrespect for law and order. The roots of these chronic disturbances go deep into the past and are a heritage of the country's confused and turbulent history. Aggressive opposition to the government has been fomented by longstanding ethnic hostilities, tribal animosities, and separatist aspirations of once-autonomous enclaves and has been further aggravated in recent years by communist-inspired disaffection. The result has been that the civilian police and the armed forces have had to devote much of their energies to its suppression.

Statistics on the incidence of crime were fragmentary and incomplete, but limited records available in 1970 indicated that crimes of violence, armed robbery, and larceny, stemming largely from social tensions and instability resulting from political insurgency, were particularly prevalent. Also of concern was the penal and correctional system, which was outdated and lacked adequate facilities for most effective operation. Some progress in the reduction of crime was claimed by publicity sources in 1970, and in the battle against insurgency the government apparently had achieved considerable success. Barring unforeseen developments, the forces should be able to maintain this momentum toward a sure, if gradual, improvement in national peace, order, and safety.

MILITARY HISTORY AND TRADITION

The country's military tradition combines aspects of its ancient monarchical heritage with the British forms and doctrines of its more recent colonial tutelage. For centuries the Burmans of the central Irrawaddy Valley resorted to armed force to establish or maintain control over their immediate neighbors or to defend themselves. They even undertook protracted and more distant campaigns into China, India, and Siam (Thailand). At one time or another all peoples in the area had been subject to the Burman crown so that militant nationalism became deeply rooted in their culture (see ch. 3, Historical Setting).

For 700 years after the country's unification in 1057, the kingdom experienced local warfare, suppressed uprisings, occasional clashes with neighboring powers, and rare periods of tranquillity. The local nature of these operations and the predominance of Burman victories gave the country a false sense of security. Consequently, there was little incentive to spur improvements or modernization of the armed forces, and they remained stagnant, ignoring the progress being made in the world around them.

After the British annexed Burma in 1886, Burmese military tradition was interrupted, and there was a period of relative tranquillity, during which Burmese military forces virtually disintegrated. In time, the British came to look upon the Burmans as an obviously unmartial ethnic group, and they recruited from non-Burman sources.

There was, nevertheless, some participation in military activities during these years. In 1887 an engineer company was recruited among the Burmans and proved itself capable and resourceful. During World War I four battalions of Burmans were organized as the Burma Rifles and saw active duty in Mesopotamia and Palestine. They established an excellent combat record, but their lax discipline, high absentee rate, and belligerence toward other ethnic groups led to a decision to bar Burmans from the regular forces.

When Burma was separated from India in 1937, a radical change took place in the attitude toward military service. National pride spurred a renewed interest in the country's armed forces, and there was a gradual buildup of indigenous Burmese elements, both as officers and in the ranks. By the beginning of World War II there were several Burmese battalions in the army. These forces were among those that, under Japanese sponsorship, revolted against the British in 1941 and 1942 and, later in 1945 as the Burma National Army, joined forces with the British against the Japanese.

After the war the increase in Burman participation continued and was greatly stimulated by independence in 1948. In 1970, after several phases of development and reorganization in which efforts to desegregate ethnic elements and absorb minority groups were made, the services became an intensely nationalistic force that was predominantly Burman in makeup and outlook. The armed forces are trying to maintain continuity with past tradition by emphasizing those unifying factors that can contribute to the country's well-being and solidarity.

THE ARMED FORCES AND THE GOVERNMENT

Legal Basis

The Constitution of 1947 gave Parliament full authority to raise and maintain armed forces and provided the initial basis on which the Burmese military establishment was founded. This authority disappeared in 1962, however, with the military coup led by General Ne Win. The Revolutionary Council took and remained in power, and in 1970 General Ne Win served as both chairman of the Council of Ministers and minister of defense and also was chairman of the Revolutionary Council, giving him broad authority over the military establishment.

Top Command

Command of the armed forces is channeled downward from the chairman of the Revolutionary Council through the Council of Ministers, the Ministry of Defense, and the chief of staff of the Burma Defense Services. In theory, it is the minister of defense who exercises political and military control and who, under normal circumstances, provides civilian supervision over military activities. He is advised by the Defense Council Executive Committee, a high policymaking body of senior officers that serves as a consultative group on matters of military administration and operation.

The chief of staff of the Burma Defense Services is the supreme operational commander of all military forces, and his office in the Ministry of Defense serves as a general headquarters for the establishment as a whole. He is assisted by three vice chiefs of staff—one each for the army, the navy, and the air force—who are commanders of their respective services as well as deputies to the defense chief, and by the combined Defense Services Staff. The staff has three major components: the Chief of Staff Department, known as the "G" Staff; the Adjutant General's Department, or

"A" Staff; and the Quartermaster General's Department, or "Q" Staff. There are also four special office chiefs: the inspector general, the director of procurement, the controller of military accounts, and the judge advocate general. Each vice chief of staff also has a small staff each organized in similar fashion, to handle particular service operations. Staff responsibilities and functions conform closely to standard British military practice.

Missions

The army has the dual mission of defending the nation's territorial integrity and assisting the police in preserving internal order and security. This entails the traditional military responsibility of maintaining a constant state of readiness to defend the nation and to implement its military policies. The navy, in addition to defending the national coastline and patrolling territorial waters, is charged with patrolling inland waterways and providing transport and tactical support to the ground forces. The air force's mission is the air defense of the country and the provision of air support to the army and the navy.

Conditions since independence, including the absence of any external aggression, have permitted scant attention to the task of defending the country from outside attack, as the military forces have found it difficult to maintain minimum national stability and to counter an endless succession of dissident uprisings. The services have been meeting these commitments effectively, and constant warfare has given them a background of combat experience and an army of battle-hardened veterans. Although emphasis is on infantry rather than a balanced force, the military establishment has been well adapted to Burmese needs as evidenced by the success against various insurgencies.

THE ARMED FORCES AND THE ECONOMY

The ratio of defense spending to the total cost of government has been high, and sums devoted to military expenditures have been rising steadily, keeping pace with expanding national budgets. Published figures indicate that K601 million (4.76 kyat equal US$1) were allotted to defense for the 1970/71 fiscal year. This amount was about 35 percent of the K1.7 billion of current expenditures for ordinary government activities under the ministries, or a little over 6 percent of the gross national product (GNP).

Immediately after independence Burma avoided a serious drain on its limited financial resources by accepting generous British aid in the form of weapons, equipment, and grants. Later, however, the government decreed that no military assistance would be sought or accepted except on a reimbursable basis. Since that time it has purchased some arms and equipment from the United Kingdom and in 1958 concluded a military sales agreement with the United States that permitted Burma to buy military equipment for local currency. Defense costs have been an ever-increasing burden on the national economy.

MANPOWER AND TRAINING

Source and Quality of Manpower

About 250,000 young men reach the military age of eighteen years annually, so there is more than enough manpower to meet the country's military requirements. The number of men in uniform is small in relation to the total population, representing less than 2 percent of the able-bodied males in 1970. The withdrawal of this small number from civilian pursuits has had no appreciable effect on the economy nor has it created any manpower shortages in agriculture or industry. The economy in fact profited somewhat from the service experience of the young men because many of them were able to acquire skills that served them in good stead upon their return to civilian life.

There is a law establishing universal compulsory military service but, except for the single category of doctors and, occasionally, for a few critically needed specialists, the status and benefits offered by a military career have made conscription unnecessary. Although only about one-half of the eligible males are usually found fit for military duty, there are still enough men available to make the selection of applicants a difficult and painstaking process. Aside from ethnic considerations, which frequently complicate selection, the greatest problem has been finding men with educational qualifications and mechanical aptitude to train as technical specialists.

Although under the British men from the minority groups were the mainstay of the Burmese forces, since independence national policies have favored the acceptance of Burmans in increasing numbers, and the leadership has become Burmese. Although Burmans constitute an increased proportion of men in service, there are many men of other ethnic affiliation, particularly Karens, Chins, and Kachins. Minority elements have performed creditably and have been among the best and most reliable troops in the national service. The ethnic Burman tends to be individualistic, with an inherent distaste for regimentation and discipline. He, nevertheless, responds well to capable leadership and in combat usually proves to be a courageous and effective soldier.

278

Procurement and Training of Officers

Procurement of officers is based on voluntary application or on recommendation from the ranks. Qualifying requirements are high and limit applicants to young men with good health and better than average education. Candidates must be high school graduates between eighteen and twenty-five years of age and, in addition to physical qualification, must pass a rigid entrance examination. Most candidates come from urban middle class families, and many are college graduates.

Two principal training facilities turn out officers for the three services, with all cadets receiving the same fundamental instruction before branching out into their respective specialties. The Defense Services Academy at Maymyo, the school for all regular officers regardless of the service they desire, has a four-year course. The academy achieved university status in 1964 and grants bachelor degrees to its graduates. About 100 candidates are admitted each year, and approximately 50 are commissioned at the end of the course. The Officer Training School conducts a six-month course to train emergency or reserve officers and an additional limited number of selected graduates from the University Training Corps. The course is similar to that of the United States Reserve Officers Training Corps.

Graduates of the academy or the training school who enter the army are assigned directly to tactical units or to advanced training in one of several army technical schools. Those going into the navy or air force continue specialized training at either the Naval Training School or the air force Flying Training School, where they receive advanced instruction in their service specialties. The naval school qualifies officers for shipboard duties; the air force school qualifies officers to the pilots or trains them for other aircrew functions.

There are several levels of advanced professional training, and most officers attend either a senior troop school or a staff college in the course of their careers. A variety of schools offer intermediate-level and higher level courses for platoon and company commanders, and there are several advanced branch schools and staff-level war colleges for senior officers. The Defense Services Staff College provides the most advanced training for officers of the three services. It has a nine-month course for selected senior officers that includes administration, tactics, combined operations, and government.

Procurement and Training of Enlisted Personnel

Enlisted personnel for all services are procured by voluntary enlistment. The National Service Law of 1959 was enacted to ensure the availability of manpower in case of emergency rather than because of any problem in maintaining the forces at desired strength. Under its provisions all citizens between the ages of eighteen and forty-five years, both male and female, are subject to compulsory military service for two years. The law has never been invoked, however, and there is no clear indication of what forms and patterns conscription would follow.

Recruiting is handled by boards located at major cities and towns and by itinerant teams that periodically visit outlying rural population center. Candidates are selected on the basis of examination and personal interview. Terms of enlistment range from four to six years, with a commitment to remain in inactive reserve status for a specified period upon termination of the enlistment. There is no reserve organization or program, however, so this has not yet entailed any obligation.

Each service has its own stations for receiving recruits and conducting their basic training. The army has a number of recruit training depots, and the navy and the air force have special installations in their school complexes. Basic training takes about ten weeks, after which a man is given his permanent assignment. Later he may be selected for advanced technical training or be sent to a noncommissioned officers' training school. All three services maintain schools for advanced training in branch specialties, including administrative, technical, and tactical instruction.

Graduates of the University Training Corps who do not go on to train for a commission may be appointed noncommissioned officers, and a number enter the services in this way. Most noncommissioned officers, however, come up through the ranks and are selected on the basis of experience and proven capability. Most of them are career men with several years of service and generally constitute the backbone of the military establishment. A shortage of noncommissioned officers usually exists.

ARMED FORCES ORGANIZATION

Army

Below headquarters, the army operates through six major military districts, designated the Central, Eastern, Southeastern, Southwestern, Northwestern, and Rangoon commands. (In the summer of 1970 a new strategic area command was established to deal with insurgency problems in rural areas of the northern Shan State and the southern Kachin State, formerly under the administrative control of the Eastern and Northwestern commands. This strategic area command is directly responsible to the Ministry of Defense.) Each command is in the charge of a general officer who reports directly to the vice chief of staff (army) and is responsible for all activities in his area. A variable number of combat units are assigned to these districts as dictated by operational requirements. There are also fixed garrisons spread throughout the country; the majority are in the strategic central valley between Rangoon and Mandalay.

Army units in 1971 were mainly infantry, some battalions of which were parachute trained, and included elements of armor, artillery, and engineers as well as administrative support troops. They were organized principally into battalions, the infantry battalion of approximately 750 men being the basic tactical combat unit.

The army's arms inventory is largely of the light-infantry type but also includes fairly substantial quantities of heavy-infantry weapons and some artillery and armor. Most materiel is from British or United States sources, and much of it in 1970 was, or was becoming, obsolescent.

Navy

In 1970 the navy was a small force of about fifty-seven vessels, mostly patrol ships and landing craft. It had one minesweeper, one frigate, a number of gunboats of various sizes, and a few motor torpedo boats. All vessels were of foreign origin, and the navy was dependent on outside aid for spare parts and virtually all naval supplies.

Rangoon is the principal naval base and the location of the naval dockyard as well as storage and supply facilities. There are three naval subcommands—the Irrawaddy, the Tenasserim, and the Bassein naval regions. Units afloat are subordinate to their regional commanders, except for those based on Rangoon, which are directly controlled by the vice chief of staff (navy). Some of the larger vessels operate in ocean waters, but most are used for river patrol duty and support of army operations against insurgents.

Air Force

The air force is small but active, providing limited air-ground support to the army and transportation and medical evacuation for operations in otherwise difficult and inaccessible terrain. Its complement of aircraft totaled about seventy airplanes in 1970, including some jet fighter-bombers and trainers, piston-engine transports, trainers, liaison planes, and helicopters. Pilots are trained locally in sufficient quantity to meet the needs of the force.

Tactical air organization consists of operational wings grouped by function as fighter, transport, and administrative elements. They are based at some fifteen airfields dispersed about the country. The major field is Mingaladon Airfield, Burma's international airport near Rangoon. Most fields have limited fuel storage. Despite its shortages, problems, and limitations, the air force is a valuable asset in the irregular type of warfare in which the armed forces are primarily engaged.

CONDITIONS OF SERVICE

The general environment and physical conditions surrounding garrison life conform to British patterns, most installations retaining the atmosphere of a colonial post. While some army units are assigned to fixed posts, the constant state of hostilities in some areas requires many troops to spend most of their time in the field.

For the most part, the serviceman is well cared for by the authorities, and conditions of service are at a high level of dignity and comfort in relation to local standards. Daily routine is exacting and often dangerous, but discipline is not severe. The serviceman has status, recognition, and security. Military posts compare favorably with civilian facilities, and their type of tropical construction meets the needs of the services. Quarters, food, and pay are as good as a man could find outside the service and, in many cases, considerably better.

There are several advantages that add attraction to a military career, such as accrual of leave, medical care, retirement, and survivor benefits. Pay is considered good in relation to that of comparably skilled groups in the civilian sector. Supplementary allowances for quarters, rations, families, special skills, and hazardous duty substantially augment basic rates to attractive levels. Rations are good and provide greater variety and balance than local dietary patterns provide.

Retirement may be for disability, length of service, or age and can be statutory or granted upon request. Retirement pay may reach a maximum of 75 percent of the active duty rate. There is also a scale of survivor benefits that provide pensions to widows of men disabled or killed on active duty or in action. Leave policies are liberal, men of all ranks accruing thirty days a year. All personnel receive free medical attention, and their families are also eligible when facilities are available.

UNIFORMS, INSIGNIA, AND DECORATIONS

The rank and grade structure of the three services designates personnel as officers and "other ranks." Navy and air force ranks conform to British equivalents; those of the army parallel those of the United States Army.

Officers' insignia are displayed on shoulder boards, and noncommissioned officers' chevrons are worn on the upper sleeve. Officers utilize a system of brass bars, stars, and wreathed, crossed swords. The five-pointed stars are surmounted by the national arms within a circle; the bars represent stylized, extended leaves. Noncommissioned officers' chevrons are worn with the points down; the combat arms use black stripes on a red base, and the colors are reversed for specialists and members of supportive services.

The uniforms of all three services are patterned after those of the British. The navy uses the traditional blue or white, and the air force has a blue uniform similar in color to that of the Royal Air Force. There are three types of army uniform: a service uniform and a field uniform for all ranks and a dress uniform for officers. Enlisted men's uniforms are of cotton, and both types are of similar design, consisting of shirt and trousers tucked into short leggings. The service uniform is khaki, and the field uniform is green.

The officers' dress uniform is khaki worsted or gabardine for summer and a darker colored wool for winter. Officers wear the standard visored cap; enlisted men have a wide-brimmed brush hat of felt or cloth, usually with a chinstrap. All ranks, on occasion, wear a beret or a helmet.

There are three classes of national honors: orders, titles, and decorations, all of which are for military personnel. Two national honors, the Order of the Dhamma and the Order of the Union of Burma, are the country's highest awards. They are presented to three and five classes, the two highest grades being the Grand Commander and the Grand Officer. There are five titles that are given for meritorious service, bestowing on the recipient a lifelong title, which he appends to his name. Each title also carries with it a corresponding medal, which is usually a neck decoration.

There are six decorations for military heroism and for long and meritorious service. The two highest, for valor, are the Aung San Thuriya and the Aung San Tazeit, awarded for exceptional acts of gallantry on the battlefield. Following these in precedence are the Thiha Thura Tazeit, the Thiha Bala Tazeit, and the Thura Tazeit. The final decoration, the Sit Hmu Htan Guang Tazeit, is for long, faithful, and honorable service.

There are other forms of recognition for acts or service that do not warrant a higher award. The British-derived system of "mention in dispatches" has been used extensively, and there is a wide variety of service medals, commemorative awards, and campaign stars that are issued periodically.

LOGISTICS

The Quartermaster General's Department at general headquarters in Rangoon handles logistic matters for the three services, except for major purchases, which are made by the director of procurement. Virtually all military hardware originates outside the country as do most other supplies, although there is some local production of small arms, ammunition, and clothing.

Procurement is complicated by a lack of funds, long supply lines, and the timelag in deliveries from abroad. Distribution is poor because of insufficient transport and a sparse road net. Storage and issue are reasonably efficient from about twenty-five depots, bases, and supply points throughout the country. The general staff has given the matter of logistics maximum attention, and the structure for handling supply and maintenance is well organized. Personnel perform creditably and, in spite of the manifold problems, materials are distributed and are able to maintain the force's operations.

Supplies needed for day-to-day operations are decentralized down to battalion level, but many items, particularly perishable rations, are purchased by units in the field. Battalions also distribute clothing and organizational equipment, and many requisition food, shelter, transportation, and labor from local sources.

In general, individual weapons are sufficient and are maintained in satisfactory condition. Reserve materiel and equipment, however, are limited. Spare parts are critically short, and this situation together with the lack of qualified technicians, so hampers maintenance that frequently much equipment is idle.

Navy logistic activities are centered at the main naval dockyard in Rangoon. Facilities can handle most ship repair, but major overhauls have to be performed abroad. Virtually all naval supplies are stored and issued at the naval supply depot in Rangoon. The principal air force supply and maintenance base is Mingaladon Airfield, where storage, repair, and overhaul activities are centered. A few other bases have minimum facilities for minor maintenance and refueling.

INTERNAL ORDER AND SECURITY

The country's social environment with respect to human behavior has been described as permissive. The people pride themselves on the tolerance of their formal religion and are loath to judge their fellow men. Burmese culture tends to recognize human frailty, and a certain degree of human error is tolerated. Laws and statutes often are not applied rigidly, in the belief that inexorable natural laws taught by Buddhism will in themselves punish the malefactor.

This reluctance to judge another is reflected in an unwillingness to criticize an offender, whether the criticism is directed at a single individual or at society as a whole. This propensity can create a misleading picture of harmony and accord while inner conflicts actually ferment and become acute. Feelings can reach a point where they erupt in sudden explosions, whose roots are not readily discernible, as they did in the Saya San rebellion against the British in 1930 and 1931. Although poorly organized and mystically oriented, this revolt was a spontaneous expression of suppressed grievances that spread swiftly and brought thousands of poorly armed villagers into violent conflict with police and military forces. It was easily subdued, but the fanatical tenacity of the rebels both surprised and shocked authorities. This same pattern is reflected in the individual, and sudden and unexpected violence is a common characteristic of Burmese criminal behavior.

The major problem in maintaining public order and safety in 1970 was disaffection among ethnic minorities. Insurgent uprisings among them, inspired and led mainly by the White Flag party (see Glossary) and to a lesser extent by the Red Flag party (see Glossary), were serious and continuing. The principal leader of the Red Flag Communists was captured in 1970, and the group probably could field no more than a few hundred armed men. The government tried to negotiate with the dissidents in 1963 but failed with all groups except the Karen National Defense Organization. Extremists among the Karens, as well as others among the Kachins and Shan who want secession or extreme autonomy, continued to stir up turmoil (see ch. 9, Political Dynamics).

The principal insurgent group is the White Flag communist organization. It suffered serious setbacks in central Burma as a result of government suppression and bitter internal party disunity. Accordingly a new White Flag group, called the Northeast Command, was formed under Naw Seng, a Kachin trained in Communist China. Supported by Communist China, this group has seriously limited government control measures along the Burmese-Chinese border in northeastern Shan State.

Apart from communist inspiration, minority disaffection, individualism, and disrespect for authority have prolonged lawlessness in some areas. The government has met with some successes in the battle for law and order, but there is still a formidable fight ahead before the country achieves true internal order and security.

THE NATIONAL PEOPLE'S POLICE

The National People's Police, organized under the Ministry of Home Affairs, consists of the Burma Civil Police and the Rangoon

City Police. This centralized force was responsible for law and order on a nationwide basis. In 1964 the police were developed as a unified force that is organizationally independent from the military establishment. The army has continued to dominate the police; however, in 1970 an army officer occupied the principal command position of director general, and army officers had most of the other senior posts.

The mission of the police is to maintain law and order, preserve the peace, protect life and property, prevent and detect crime, and apprehend offenders. They have initial responsibility in controlling subversion but in large-scale outbreaks have to be aided by the armed forces.

Police general headquarters in Rangoon determines policy, supervises operations, and directs the activities of subordinate units. The director general, assisted by a vice director general, reports directly to the minister of home affairs. The Police Council, made up of ranking police, army, and cabinet officials, is the senior policy-making body and serves in an advisory capacity to the force.

Organization and Operations

Police headquarters consists of the staff elements and special activities of the force as well as operational control mechanisms for directing outlying components. It has two special departments and two principal staff sections, the Supply and Finance Section and the Administration and Training Section. These sections handle all matters within their jurisdictions for the entire force on a nationwide basis. There is no separate operations element; rather the chain of command runs directly from the office of the director general to subordinate units in the field.

The two special activities are the Criminal Investigation Department (CID) and the Special Intelligence Department (SID). The mission of the CID is inherent in its name; that of the SID is intelligence and counterintelligence activities. The SID reportedly had a strength of some 500 men in 1970; about one-half were stationed in Rangoon, and the rest were at rural outposts. The CID had a strength estimated at approximately 1,300 men in 1970, assigned to the Crime Bureau, the Scientific Bureau, and the Railway Police Bureau.

The Rangoon City Police is, in effect, an autonomous metropolitan force operating exclusively within the capital city and its environs. It is headed by a director and had a strength estimated in 1970 at about 3,700 officers and men. In addition to regular law enforcement, it is responsible for registration of motor vehicles and the surveillance of foreigners and, with the navy, safeguards the security of Rangoon harbor. Other routine duties include the usual police activities associated with urban life, such as sanitation, traffic control, and the suppression of vice.

The Burma Civil Police comprises all forces stationed outside the capital and forms the bulk of the National People's Police. Its uniformed members are the patrolmen on the beat and the rural constables who protect people and property. Its primary mission is the enforcement of law and order, but its members also guard government property and the residences of high officials. Also, it is often called on to assist in operations against insurgents.

The Burma Civil Police is organized into twelve subordinate geographic regions corresponding to the seven administrative divisions of Burma and one for each of the constituent states. Each region is headed by a director or vice director and is subdivided into districts, subdistricts, stations, and outposts. Much of the operational control of police activities is exercised by the army through its direction of what the government called "security and administrative committees," composed of military and civil officials at the various levels.

Despite the official separation and independence of the police forces, until 1967 there was considerable acrimony and strained relations between the two services. Major police grievances were their apparent subordination to the military and the imposition of army regulations on their units, complaints of low supply priorities vis-à-vis the military, and charges of alleged lack of army support to isolated police posts. It is true that at times numerous police stations were attacked and that no support for them was forthcoming from the army. In most cases, however, this was because the army's lack of mobility made it impossible to reach the outposts in time.

The government has shown an awareness of these problems and deficiencies and constantly has sought to remedy them. Major measures included stopping the integration of better trained police units and individuals into the army, issuing new and better equipment to the police as rapidly as possible, and providing for increased police compensation in the national budget. Police morale has improved considerably and has been reflected in more favorable press coverage and an encouraging new atmosphere of service and cooperation.

Conditions of Service

The average city police headquarters is adequate but far from luxurious. Usually housed in a frame building enclosed by a fence or barbed wire, it offers basic facilities for administration, housing, and supply storage. Most rural police posts are strictly utilitarian, generally consisting of a rustic, fort-like compound, closely guarded and surrounded by barbed wire. Used for housing the garrison and sometimes police families, it can be used for a defense strongpoint when necessary. Mostly, however, rural posts are bases of operations for fixed guard posts and constant area-surveillance patrols.

All but the remotest outlying posts are tied into the police communications net, linking them with headquarters in Rangoon. They are adequately supplied with transportation, and there are generally enough trucks, sedans, jeeps, or motorcycles to meet local needs. Rural patrols are conducted mostly by motor vehicle, but the force also has many patrol boats for covering rivers and coastal areas.

Police Equipment and Training

Much of the police equipment and a great deal of the basic police training in modern techniques originated with a United States program initiated in 1950 and continued until 1965. About US$8.8 million was used to supply the police with arms, vehicles, uniforms, and other needed equipment. As part of the program several Burmese police officers were sent to the United States for advanced training, and many specialists were given instruction in supply, radio maintenance, and antiriot duties. Since 1965, when the program was phased out, some technicians have been sent to police schools in other countries, but there is no indication that this practice is a continuing effort.

The most common form of instruction is on-the-job training in the unit of assignment. The Police Officers Academy in Mandalay conducts annual courses for officer candidates and also has a course of advanced instruction for officers at the intermediate level.

Rank, Pay, Uniforms, and Decorations

With the formation of the National People's Police a new grade structure was introduced. The changes were not radical, and new grades continued to conform closely to British precedents. Ranks below the director level range from constable up to superintendent; usually advancement follows a progressive course up through corporal, sergeant, station officer, and inspector.

Pay increases have brought police compensation into line with equivalent army ranks and have done much to allay police disaffection vis-a-vis the military. The pay was at a level considered good by local standards and consistent with the country's economic level.

Police uniforms closely resemble British military wear for the tropics. Army khaki uniforms with distinctive insignia are worn in the field and in hot weather. For garrison or urban duty enlisted men wear blue trousers with a bluish-gray angora shirt. Headgear is either a beret or wide-brimmed Gurkha hat. Noncommissioned officers wear their chevrons on the right sleeve only.

Officers have a blue or khaki service coat and wear a peaked service cap or a beret for field duty. Noncommissioned officers and officers armed with a pistol; patrolmen carry only a baton unless issued other weapons in an emergency. The Metropolitan Division of the Rangoon City Police—that is, the patrolmen, the traffic police, and the motorcycle squads—have a distinctive uniform consisting of a white jacket worn with dark-blue trousers or breeches.

The police have their own decorations distinct from those of the military, although police may receive any of the national orders. There are four medals specifically for police personnel, one of which is reserved for officers. They are given for gallantry, distinguished service, or conspicuous devotion to duty. The two higher awards carry with them a monetary allowance, rated according to the rank of the recipient.

Related Intelligence Activities

Counterintelligence activities have required as much effort as the control of ordinary crime, if not more, so the police and security agencies have had to work closely together. Two of these, the National Intelligence Bureau (NIB) and the Bureau of Special Investigations (BSI), are most prominent. Although both of these have little responsibility in the criminal field, there was an overlap of interests that often required their joint action with the police in the areas of subversion and insurgency.

The NIB is made up of the country's various intelligence and specialized security agencies—the Military Intelligence Service (MIS) of the Ministry of Defense, the CID and the SID of the National People's Police, and the BSI. Headed by a director of the MIS, the NIB is a component of the Central Security and Administrative Committee. Its main function is the top-level coordination of the intelligence activities of the armed forces, the police, and other civil agencies.

The BSI is directly under the office of the chairman of the Revolutionary Council. It was originally organized to investigate corruption among political leaders and government employees, but this aspect of its work seems to have been dropped. The agency is engaged mostly in investigating possible threats to the regime and running down suspected activity of a subversive or an antigovernmental nature.

THE JUDICIAL SYSTEM

The judicial system originally consisted of the Penal Code and the Criminal Procedure Code and the hierarchy of courts established to adjudicate violations of the law. Both of the codes were adapted from their Indian counterparts—the Penal Code from the Indian Penal Code of 1860 and the Criminal Code from the Indian Criminal Procedure Code of 1898. They were ultimately combined into the Burma Code which, with necessary amendments from time to time, is the law of the land.

Criminal Codes

The Burma Code is a compilation of all statutory laws, acts, and regulations covering various other judicial activities, such as police and prisons. It has ten basic volumes and several augmentations concerned with laws applicable to the states and the special division of Chin. The Penal Code appears in Volume VIII, and the Criminal Procedure Code, in volumes IV and VII. Changes and amendments are published annually and are brought out periodically as the situation requires. The Penal Code is comprehensive and modern. It deals with the competence of the law, categories of offenses and criminal responsibility, and the types and limits of punishments. One section is concerned with offenses germane to the armed forces and serves as the basis for military justice. Two general levels of offenses are recognized: felonies, or serious crimes, and misdemeanors, or minor infractions. Criminal responsibility is precisely defined and takes into account possible extenuating and mitigating factors, such as self-defense or impairment of mental faculties.

Ignorance of the law is not considered an excuse, but involuntary intoxication may be a moderating factor. Children under seven years of age are not held criminally liable for their acts; penalties for minors between seven and twelve years of age are considerably less severe than penalties usually imposed.

The code groups various offenses into broad categories, which, in turn, are broken down into specific types of violations. The major categories distinguish between crimes against the state; against public tranquillity; against persons or property; and against public health, safety, and morality. Other broad areas include offenses against public justice, public servants, coins and stamps, marriage, and religion. There are also brief sections covering defamation, intimidation, insult, and annoyance.

Punishments are treated in some detail and, although courts have some degree of latitude, the range of punishments is carefully defined. Punishments include the death penalty; transportation, which is exile to a penal colony; fine; and imprisonment, which may involve hard labor. The code also authorizes whipping, but this form of punishment is seldom practiced.

Felonies are defined as those crimes subject to the death penalty or imprisonment for three years or more. Misdemeanors are usually redressed by a fine, but they may draw short terms of confinement. There is little information on transporation (penal exile) practice, but in the past it involved shipment of condemned prisoners to detention facilities on offshore islands.

Courts and Criminal Procedures

There are three levels of courts in Burma to deal with criminal matters. The single Chief Court in Rangoon is the country's final arbiter in questions of law and fact, and in criminal matters it is the final court of appeal. Below the Chief Court are sessions courts, established in most principal towns and cities. Sessions courts have original jurisdiction in cases involving felonies and serious crimes for which punishments of five years or more are authorized. Below the sessions courts are the magistrate's courts, found in most localities throughout the country, that deal with lesser crimes for which punishments of not more than two years' imprisonment may be imposed (see ch. 8, Political System and Values).

The Criminal Procedure Code prescribes the competence of each type of court, specifies the functions and responsibilities of judicial officials, outlines rules of evidence, and regulates the conduct of preliminary proceedings and trials. Minor offenses are prosecuted by complaint, and major crimes are prosecuted by indictment, but there is no grand jury.

Minor offenders are brought directly before a lower court judge or magistrate, who prepares charges and issues a summons to the accused; major cases are referred to the attorney general's office, which determines jurisdiction and venue. The code provides for the use of writs of habeas corpus and for the arrangement of bail at the discretion of the court.

THE PENAL SYSTEM

The country's prison administration, under the direction of the Ministry of Home Affairs, is regulated by provisions of the Burma Code. The system is loosely organized, however, and most detention facilities receive little central guidance or supervision. The code provides for certain standards and procedures, but in practice they are not strictly observed. In 1971 there was a prison facility of some kind in most towns of any size, but most of them were old buildings in poor repair that were generally unsanitary and overcrowded.

There is almost no official publication of penal statistics and, of the negligible amount of information put out by the government, virtually none reaches the outside world. Infrequent reports of questionable reliability give an indication but do not provide a clear picture of the situation. The best information available indicates that there were about forty detention facilities in the country in 1971. About ten of these were central prisons; twenty were district jails; and ten were subjails or guardhouses.

The central prisons are the largest and best equipped facilities. They accommodate felons from the cities in which they are located and from its environs. The jails were generally used for short-term prisoners convicted of minor offenses. There is also one reformatory for juvenile offenders, called a training school, located in Rangoon. Juvenile delinquency was increasing in urban areas, but it had not yet reached critical proportions in 1971. The country's average prison population as of the mid-1960s was estimated at approximately 6,000 inmates in any given month.

The central prisons in Rangoon and Mandalay are the most extensive installations. Both are large and secure but lack modern facilities, and conditions in them are described as poor. The rest of the prisons range from crude single detention rooms to sizable city jails. Most consist of a frame or log enclosure surrounded by a barbed-wire fence.

The code prescribed the treatment of prisoners and specified that imprisonment should be for rehabilitation as well as for punishment. There was, however, no indication of any corrective program. None of the country's penal institutions are known to have workshops or handicraft facilities, and none have teachers, social workers, vocational training instructors, or medical personnel assigned to their regular staffs. Nevertheless, the treatment of prisoners is generally good, and Burmese jails compare favorably with most others in Southeast Asia.

BIBLIOGRAPHY OF THE JUNE 1968 EDITION

SECTION I. SOCIAL

RECOMMENDED SOURCES

Brant, Charles S., and Mi Mi Khaing. "Burmese Kinship and the Life Cycle: An Outline," *Southwestern Journal of Anthropology*, VII, 1951, 437-154.

Brown, R. Grant. "The Pre-Buddhist Religion of the Burmese," *Folklore*, XXXII, June 1921, 77-100.

Cady, John Frank. "Political Institutions of Old Burma." (Cornell University, Southeast Asia Program, Data Paper No. 12.) Ithaca; 1954 (mimeo.)

_____. *The Problem of Law and Order in Burma under British Administration*. (Office of Strategic Services, Research and Analysis Branch, R & A No. 1980.) Washington: March 15, 1944.

_____. *Thailand, Burma, Laos and Cambodia*. Englewood Cliffs: Prentice-Hall, 1966.

Embree, John Fee, and Thomas, William L. (eds.) *Ethnic Groups of Northern Southeast Asia*. New Haven: Yale University Southeast Asia-Studies, 1950.

Fielding-Hall, Harold. *The Soul of a People*. London: Macmillan, 1902.

Furnivall, John Syndenham. *Progress and Welfare in Southeast Asia: A Comparison of Colonial Policy and Practice*. New York: Institute of Pacific Relations, 1941.

Gorer, Geoffrey. "Burmese Personality." New York: Institute for Intercultural Relations, 1943 (mimeo.).

Hanks, Lucien M., Jr. "The Quest for Individual Autonomy in Burmese Personality," *Psychiatry*, XII, No. 3, 1949, 285-300.

Hanson, Ola. *The Kachins: Their Customs and Traditions*. Rangoon: American Baptist Mission Press, 1913.

Harvey, Godfrey Eric. *History of Burma from the Earliest Times to 10 March 1824, the Beginning of the English Conquest*. London: Longmans, Green, 1925.

Hobbs, Cecil. "The Burmese Family: An Inquiry into Its History, Customs and Traditions." Washington: 1952 (mimeo.).

Htin Aung (trans.) *Burmese Folk Tales*. Calcutta: Oxford University Press, 1948.

International Labor Organization. "Report to the Government of the Union of Burma on Establishment of a Manpower Information Program." Geneva: 1964 (mimeo.).

Leach, Edmund Ronald. *Political Systems of Highland Burma: A Study of Kachin Social Structure.* London: G. Bell, 1954.

Marshall, Harry Ignatius. *The Karen People of Burma: A Study in Anthropology and Ethnology.* (The Ohio State University Bulletin, Vol. 26, No. 13; Contributions in History and Political Science, No. 8.) Columbus: Ohio State University Press, 1922.

Maxwell-Lefray, C. *The Land and People of Burma:* New York: Macmillan, 1963.

Milne, Mary (Lewis) (Mrs. Leslie Milne). *The Shans at Home.* With Two Chapters on Shan History and Literature by Rev. Wilber Willis Cochrane. London: Murry, 1910.

Mi Mi Khaing. *Burmese Family.* Bloomington: Indiana University Press, 1962.

Nash, Manning. *The Golden Road to Modernity: Village Life in Contemporary Burma.* New York: Wiley, 1965.

Orr, Kenneth G. *Field Notes on the Burmese Standard of Living as Seen in the Case of a Fisherman-Refugee Family.* Rangoon: University of Rangoon, 1951 (mimeo.).

Perera, M. Theodore (ed.). *Gems of Buddhist Thought.* Colombo: M.D. Gunasena, 1950.

Ray, Nihar-ranjan. *An Introduction to the Study of Theravada Buddhism in Burma.* Calcutta: Calcutta University Press, 1946.

Scott, Sir James George. *Burma: A Handbook of Practical Information.* (Rev. ed.) London: Alexander Moring, 1921.

Sein, Kenneth (Maung Khe), and Withey, J. A. *The Great Po Sein.* Bloomington: Indiana University Press, 1965.

Stevenson, Henry Noel Cochran. *The Economics of the Central Chin Tribes.* Bombay: Times of India Press, 1943.

U.S. Department of Commerce. *Basic Data on the Economy of Burma.* (Overseas Business Reports: OBR 63-162.) Washington: GPO, 1963.

U.S. Department of Health, Education and Welfare. Office of Education. *Burma Educational Data.* Washington: GPO 1965.

U.S. Department of Labor. Bureau of Labor Statistics. *Labor Law and Practice in the Union of Burma.* (BLS Report No. 264.) Washington: GPO, 1965.

Walter Reed Army Institute of Research. *Burma.* (Health Data Publications, No. 30.) Washington: Walter Reed Army Medical Center, 1966.

OTHER SOURCES USED

Aligretti, Ted, and Marshall, E. G. "Glimpses of Burma," *Asia* (New York), Spring 1965.

Appleton, G. *Buddhism in Burma.* (Burma Pamphlets, No. 3.) Calcutta: Longmans, Green. 1944.

Asian Recorder (New Delhi), IX, November 12-18, 1963; and October 15-21, 1966.

Brant, Charles S. "Tadagale: A Burmese Village in 1950." (Cornell University, Southeast Asia Program, Data Paper No. 13.) Ithaca: 1954 (mimeo.).

Burling, Robbins. *Hill Farms and Padi Fields: Life Among Inland Southeast Asia.* Englewood Cliffs: Prentice-Hall, 1965.

Butwell, Richard. *U Nu of Burma.* Stanford: Stanford University Press, 1963.

Cady, John Frank. *Southeast Asia: Its Historical Development.* New York: McGraw-Hill, 1964.

Christian, John Leroy. *Burma and the Japanese Invader.* Bombay: Thacker, 1945.

Collis, Maurice Stewart. *Last and First in Burma (1941-48).* London: Faber and Faber, 1956.

———. *Trials in Burma.* London: Faber and Faber, 1938.

Cornyn, William Stewart. *Spoken Burmese,* New York: Henry Holt, 1945.

Demographic Yearbook, 1965. New York: United Nations, Department of Economic and Social Affairs, 1966.

Dobby, E. H. G. *Southeast Asia* (8th. ed.). London: University of London Press, 1964.

Far Eastern Economic Review Yearbook, 1966. Hong Kong: 1966.

Far Eastern Economic Review Yearbook, 1967. Hong Kong: 1967.

Ferrars, Max, and Ferrars, Bertha. *Burma.* (2d. ed.) London: Sampson Low, Marston, 1901.

Furnivall, John Syndenham. *Colonial Policy and Practice: A Comparative Study of Burma and Netherlands India.* London: Cambridge University Press, 1948. (Reissued by the Institute of Pacific Relations in 1957.).

Hall, D. G. E. *A History of Southeast Asia.* New York: Macmillan, 1964.

Harvey, Godfrey Eric. *British Rule in Burma, 1824-1942.* London: Faber and Faber, 1946.

Htin Aung. *Burmese Drama: A Study with Translations of Burmese Plays.* London: Oxford University Press, 1967.

———. *Burmese Monk's Tales.* New York: Columbia University Press, 1966.

———. "The Spirit of the Burmese Folk Tale," *Asia* (New York), Spring 1965, 49-71.

International Labor Organization. "Report to the Government of the Union of Burma on Further Development of Social Security." Geneva: 1964 (mimeo.)

———. "Trade Union Situation in Burma." Geneva: 1962 (mimeo.).

Kessel, Joseph. *The Valley of Rubies.* New York: David McKay, 1961.

Khin Zaw, U. "Burmese Music: A Preliminary Inquiry," *Bulletin of the School of Oriental Studies,* X, 1940, 717-754.

LeBar, Frank M.; Hickey, Gerald C.; and Musgrave, John K. *Ethnic Groups of Mainland Southeast Asia.* New Haven: Human Relations Area Files Press, 1964.

Lehman, F.K. *The Structure of Chin Society: A Tribal People of Burma Adapted to a Non-Western Civilization.* (Illinois Studies in Anthropology No. 3.) Urbana: University of Illinois Press, 1963.

LeMay, Reginald. *The Culture of Southeast Asia: The Heritage of India.* London: Allen and Unwin, 1954.

Mead, Margaret (ed.). *Cultural Patterns and Technical Change.* Paris: United Nations Educational, Scientific and Cultural Organization, 1953.

Milne, Mary (Lewis) (Mrs. Leslie Milne). *The Home of an Eastern Clan.* Oxford: Oxford University Press, 1924.

Moore, W. Robert. "Burma, Gentle Neighbor of India and Red China," *National Geographic Magazine,* CXXIII, February 1963.

Nash, Manning. "Burmese Buddhism in Every Day Life," *American Anthropologist,* LXV, April 1963, 285-295.

———. "Social Prerequisites for Economic Growth in Southeast Asia and Latin America," *Economic Development and Culture Change,* April 1964, 225-242.

———. "Southeast Asian Society: Dual or Multiple," *Journal of Asian Studies,* XXIII, May 1964.

Onslow, Cranley (ed.). *Asian Economic Development.* New York: Praeger, 1965.

Pye, Lucian W. *Politics, Personality and Nation Building: Burma's Search for Identity.* New Haven: Yale University Press, 1966.

Rau, Santha Rama. *View to the Southeast.* New York: Harper, 1957.

Sarkisyanz, E. *Buddhist Backgrounds of the Burmese Revolution.* The Hague: Martinus Nijhoff, 1965.

Scott, Sir James George (ed.). *The Burman, His Life and Notions,* by Shway Yoe. London: Macmillan, 1927.

Scott, Sir James George, and Hardiman, John Thomas Percy. *Gazetteer of Upper Burma and the Shan States.* Rangoon: Government Printing and Stationery, 1900-01.

Seagrave, Gordon Stifler. *Burma Surgeon.* New York: Norton, 1944.

_____. *Burma Surgeon Returns.* New York: Norton, 1946.

Silcock, T.H. *Southeast Asia University: A Comparative Account of Some Development Problems.* Durham:Duke University Press,1964.

Silverstein, Josef. "Problems in Burma: Economic, Political and Diplomatic," *Asian Survey,* February 1967.

Smith, Donald Eugene. *Religion and Politics in Burma.* Princeton: Princeton University Press, 1965.

Spencer, Joseph E. *Asian East by South: A Cultural Geography.* New York: Wiley, 1954.

Spiro, Melford E. "Buddhism and Economic Action in Burma," *American Anthropologist,* LXVIII, October 1966, 1163-1173.

Statistical Yearbook, 1965. New York: United Nations, Department of Economic and Social Affairs, 1966.

Stevenson, Henry Noel Cochran. *The Hill Peoples of Burma.* (Burma Pamphlet No. 6, Burma Research Society.) London: Longmans, Green, 1944.

Thompson, Virginia. *Labor Problems in Southeast Asia.* New Haven: Yale University Press, 1947.

Thompson, Virginia, and Adloff, Richard. *Minority Problems in Southeast Asia.* Stanford: Stanford University Press, 1955.

Tinker, Hugh. *The Union of Burma: A Study of the First Years of Independence.* New York: Oxford University Press, 1957.

_____. *The Union of Burma: A Study of the First Years of Independence.* (3d. ed.) (Issued under the auspices of the Royal Institute of International Affairs.) London: Oxford University Press, 1961.

Trager, Frank N. *Burma, from Kingdom to Republic.* New York: Praeger, 1966.

United Nations. *Compendium of Social Statistics, 1963.* New York: 1963.

_____. Economic Commission for Asia and the Far East. *Economic Survey for Asia and the Far East, 1965.* New York: 1966.

U.S. Department of Health, Education and Welfare. *Social Security Programs Throughout the World, 1964.* Washington: GPO, 1964.

U.S. Department of State. *Burma-China Boundary.* (International Boundary Study No. 42.) Washington: 1964.

_____. *Burma-Laos Boundary.* (International Boundary Study No. 33.) Washington: 1964.

_____. *Burma-Thailand Boundary.* (International Boundary Study No. 630). Washington: 1966

Walinsky, Louis. *Economic Development in Burma. 1951-1960.* New York: The Twentieth Century Fund, 1962.

Wichmann, Arthur A. "Burma: Agriculture, Population and Buddhism," *American Journal of Economics and Sociology,* XXIV, January 1965, 71-83.

Williams, Lea E. *The Future of the Overseas Chinese in Southeast Asia.* New York: McGraw Hill, 1966.

(Also used in the preparation of this section was *Keesing's Contemporary Archives* [Bristol], from 1964 through May 1967.)

SECTION II. POLITICAL

RECOMMENDED SOURCES

Butwell, Richard. *U Nu of Burma*. Stanford: Stanford University Press, 1963.

Clubb, O. E., Jr. *Effect of Chinese Nationalist Military Activities in Burma on Chinese Foreign Policy*. N. pl.: Rand Corporation, 1959.

Crocker, Isabelle. *Burma's Foreign Policy and the Korean War*. Santa Monica: Rand Corporation, 1958.

Nash, Manning. *The Golden Road to Modernity: Village Life in Contemporary Burma*. New York: Wiley, 1965.

OTHER SOURCES USED

Barnett, A. Doak. *Communist China and Asia*. New York: Harper, 1960.

Cady, John F. *Thailand, Burma, Laos, and Cambodia*. Englewood Cliffs: Prentice-Hall, 1966.

Dupay, T. N. "Burma and Its Army: A Contrast in Motivations and Characteristics," *Antioch Review*, XX, Winter 1960-61.

Eckstein, Alexander. *Communist China's Economic Growth and Foreign Trade*. New York: McGraw-Hill, 1966.

Hinton, Harold. *China's Relations with Vietnam and Burma: A Brief Survey*. New York: Institute of Pacific Relations, 1958.

Johnson, John (ed.). *The Role of the Military in Underdeveloped Countries*. Princeton: Princeton University Press, 1962.

Kaznacheev, Aleksend. *Inside a Soviet Embassy*. Philadelphia: Lippincott, 1962.

Kuhn, Ferdinand and Delia. *Borderlands*. New York: Knopf, 1963.

Lyon, Peter. *Neutralism*. Blackfiars: Leicester University Press, 1963.

Maung Maung. *Burma in the Family of Nations*. Amsterdam: Djambatan, 1956.

_____. *Burma's Constitution*. (2d. ed., rev. and enlarged.) The Hague: Martinus Nijhoff, 1961.

Publishers International Yearbook. London: A. P. Wales, 1965.

Pye, Lucian W. *Politics, Personality and Nation Building*. (A Yale Paperbound). New Haven: Yale University Press, 1962.

Sarkisyanz, E. *Buddhist Backgrounds of the Burmese Revolution*. The Hague: Martinus Nijhoff, 1965.

Scalapino, Robert A. (ed.). *The Communist Revolution in Asia*. Englewood Cliffs: Prentice-Hall, 1965.

Sigmund, Paul E. (ed.). *The Ideologies of the Developing Nations*. New York: Praeger, 1963.

Silverstein, Josef, and Wohl, J. "University Students and Politics in Burma," *Pacific Affairs*, XXXVII, Spring 1964.

Sinai, I. R. *The Challenge of Modernisation: The West Impact on the Non-Western World.* New York: Norton, 1964.

Smith, Donald Eugene. *Religion and Politics in Burma.* Princeton: Princeton University Press, 1965.

Thomson, John S. "Marxism in Burma." In Frank N. Trager (ed.), *Marxism in Southeast Asia.* Stanford: Stanford University Press, 1959.

Tinker, Hugh. "Politics in Burma." In Saul Rose (ed.), *Politics in Southern Asia.* New York: St. Martins Press, 1963.

————. *The Union of Burma: A Study of the First Years of Independence.* (3d. ed.) (Issued under the auspices of the Royal Institute of International Affairs.) London: Oxford University Press, 1961.

Trager, Frank N. *Burma, from Kingdom to Republic.* New York: Praeger, 1966.

United Nations Educational, Scientific and Cultural Organization. *Radio and Television in the Service of Education and Development in Asia.* No. 29. Paris: 1967.

von der Mehden, Fred. *Religion and Nationalism in Southeast Asia.* Madison: University of Wisconsin Press, 1963.

Walinsky, Louis. *Review of Economic Developments in Burma.* New York: The Twentieth Century Fund, 1962.

World Radio, TV Handbook. (21st ed., J. M. Frost.) Hellerup: World Radio-Television Handbook Company, 1967.

(Also used in the preparation of this section were: *Asian Recorder* [New Delhi] and *Keesing's Contemporary Archives* [Bristol], from 1962 through May 1967.)

SECTION III. ECONOMIC

RECOMMENDED SOURCES

Nash, Manning. *The Golden Road to Modernity: Village Life in Contemporary Burma.* New York: Wiley, 1965.

Tinker, Hugh. *The Union of Burma: A Study of the First Years of Independence.* (3d. ed.) (Issued under the auspices of the Royal Institute of International Affairs.) London. Oxford University Press, 1961.

Trager, Frank N. *Burma From Kingdom to Republic.* Washington: Praeger, 1966.

U.S. Department of Labor. Bureau of Labor Statistics. *Labor Law and Practice in the Union of Burma.* (BLS Report No. 264.) Washington: GPO, 1965.

Walinsky, Louis. *Economic Development in Burma, 1951-1960.* New York: The Twentieth Century Fund, 1962.

OTHER SOURCES USED

Andrus, James Russell. *Burmese Economic Life.* Stanford: Stanford University Press, 1948.

Balance of Payments Yearbook, XVIII, 1961-65. Washington: International Monetary Fund, 1966.

Burma Revolutionary Council. *State Budget of Burma and Report to the People, 1966-67.* Rangoon: 1966.

Burma. Union Land and Agricultural Planning Commission. *Report 1956.* Rangoon: 1957.

Cady, John Frank. *Southeast Asia: Its Historical Development.* New York: McGraw-Hill, 1964.

Hagen, Everett E. *The Economic Development of Burma.* (Planning Pamphlet No. 96.) Washington: National Planning Association, 1956.

International Labor Organization. "Report to the Government of the Union of Burma on Establishment of a Manpower Information Program." Geneva: 1964 (mimeo.).

_____. "Trade Union Situation in Burma." Geneva: 1962 (mimeo.).

International Monetary Fund. *International Financial Statistics,* XX, No. 3, 1967.

Jacoby, Erich H. "Union of Burma." Pages 83-110 in *Agrarian Unrest in Southeast Asia.* New York: Asia Publishing House, 1961.

Knappen, Tippets, Abbett, McCarthy, Engineers. *Comprehensive Report: Economic and Engineering Development of Burma.* (Prepared for the Government of the Union of Burma.) 2 vols. Aylesbury: n. pub., 1953.

Nuttonson, Michael Y. *Climate, Soils and Rice of Burma: Supplementary Information.* Washington: American Institute of Crop Ecology, 1963.

———. *The Physical Environment and Agriculture of Burma.* Washington: American Institute of Crop Ecology, 1963.

Pick's Currency Yearbook 1966. New York; Pick, 1966.

Sarkisyanz, E. *Buddhist Backgrounds of the Burmese Revolution.* The Hague: Martinus Nijhoff, 1965.

Silverstein, Josef. "Problems in Burma: Economic, Political and Diplomatic," *Asian Survey,* VIII, February 1967.

State Commercial Bank. *Annual Report, 1963-64.* Rangoon: 1964.

Trager, Frank N. "Toward a Welfare State in Burma." New York: Institute of Pacific Relations, 1954 (mimeo.).

U Tun Wai. *Burma's Currency and Credit.* London: Longmans, 1962.

Union Bank of Burma. *Bulletin,* X, 1962.

———. *Regulation of Banks.* Rangoon: 1958.

University of Rangoon. Economic Research Center. *Burmese Agriculture, 1924-41.* Rangoon: 1959.

Wichmann, Arthur A. "Burma: Agriculture, Population and Buddhism," *American Journal of Economics and Sociology,* XXIV, January 1965, 71-83.

Yearbook of Labor Statistics, 1966. Geneva: International Labor Organization. 1966.

(Various issues of the following periodicals were also used in the preparation of this section: *Far Eastern Economic Review* (and Yearbooks) [Hong Kong], from 1962 through May 1967; *International Commerce* [Washington], from January 1966 through May 1967; *International Financial News Survey* [Washington], from January 1966 through May 1967, and *Quarterly Economic Review for Continental Southeast Asia* [London], from 1957 through May 1967.)

SECTION IV. NATIONAL SECURITY

Burma. Revolutionary Council. *State Budget of Burma and Report to the People, 1966-67.* Rangoon: 1966.

Butwell, Richard. *U Nu of Burma.* Stanford: Stanford University Press, 1963.

Cady, John F. *Thailand, Burma, Laos and Cambodia.* Englewood Cliffs: Prentice-Hall, 1966.

Dobby, E. H. G. *Southeast Asia.* (8th ed.) London: University of London Press, 1964.

Dupay, T. N. "Burma and Its Army: A Contrast in Variations and Characteristics," *Antioch Review,* XX, Winter 1960-61.

Johnson, John (ed.). *The Role of the Military in Underdeveloped Countries.* Princeton: Princeton University Press, 1962.

Maung Maung. *Burma's Constitution.* (2d. ed., rev. and enlarged.) The Hague: Martinus Nijhoff, 1961.

Maxwell-Lefray, C. *The Land and People of Burma.* New York: Macmillan, 1963.

Mi Mi Khaing. *Burmese Family.* Bloomington: Indiana University Press, 1962.

Nash, Manning. *The Golden Road to Modernity: Village Life in Contemporary Burma.* New York: Wiley, 1965.

Pye, Lucian W. *Burma's Search for Identity.* New Haven: Yale University Press, 1966.

Scalapino, Robert A. (ed.). *The Communist Revolution in Asia.* Englewood Cliffs: Prentice-Hall, 1965.

Tinker, Hugh. *The Union of Burma: A Study of the First Years of Independence.* (3d. ed.). (Issued under the auspices of the Royal Institute of International Affairs.) London: Oxford University Press, 1961.

Trager, Frank N. *Burma, from Kingdom to Republic.* New York: Praeger, 1966.

Wales, H. G. Quaritch. *Ancient South-East Asian Warfare.* London: Bernard Quaritch, 1952.

Weins, Harold J. *China's March Toward the Tropics.* Hamden: Shoe String Press, 1954.

Wyatt, Woodrow. *Southwards from China.* London: Hodder and Stroughton, 1952.

(Various issues of the following periodicals were also used in the preparation of this section: *Asia* [New York], *Asian Recorder* [New Delhi], *Far Eastern Economic Review* [Hong Kong], *Forward* [Rangoon], and *Keesing's Contemporary Archives* [Bristol], from 1964 through May 1967.)

ADDITIONAL BIBLIOGRAPHY FOR REVISED EDITION

SECTION I. SOCIAL

Badgley, John H. "Intellectuals and the National Vision: The Burmese Case," *Asian Survey,* IX, No. 8, August 1969, 598-613.

———. *Politics Among Burmans: A Study of Intermediary Leaders.* (Southeast Asia Series, No. 15.) Athens: Center for International Studies, Ohio University Press, 1970.

Banerji, S. C. "Buddha Awakes," *Far Eastern Economic Review* [Hong Kong], LXIX, No. 35, August 27, 1970, 15-16.

———. "Human Faces," *Far Eastern Economic Review* [Hong Kong], LXVIII, No. 13, March 26, 1970. 18.

Bell, Donald. "Labor Problems Retard Burma's Economic Growth," *Labor Developments Abroad,* XV, No. 9, September 1970, 1-7,

Berezhkov, V. "Land of the Shans," *New Times* [Moscow], No. 29, July 24, 1968, 22-24.

Bixler, Norma. *Burma: A Profile.* (Praeger Country Profile Series.) New York: Praeger, 1971.

"Burma: The Burmese Way to Despair," *Far Eastern Economic Review* [Hong Kong], LXX, No. 41, October 10, 1970, 13.

"Burma," *Labor Developments Abroad,* XV, No. 12, December 1970, 22-25.

Butwell, Richard. *Southeast Asia Today and Tomorrow: Problems of Political Development.* (2d ed., rev.) New York: Praeger, 1969.

———. *U Nu of Burma.* (2d ed.) Stanford: Stanford University Press, 1969.

———. "U Nu's Second Comeback Try," *Asian Survey,* IX, No. 11, November 1969, 868-876.

Cady, John F. *A History of Modern Burma.* Ithaca: Cornell University Press, 1958.

———. "Modernization vs. Traditionalism in Burma." Pages 17-25 in Burma Research Society, *50th Anniversary Publications: Some of the Papers Read at the 50th Anniversary Conference,* I. Rangoon: Burma Research Society, April 1961.

Caterini, Dino J. (ed.) *Burma: The Golden Country.* N. pl.: Horizons, n. d.

"Censored Slogans," *Far Eastern Economic Review* [Hong Kong], LXVIII, No. 19, May 7, 1970, 13.

Cook, C. "The Mizo and Naga Problems," *Eastern World* [London], May-June 1968, 18-19.

Dalton, James Joseph. "Babes in the Wood," *Far Eastern Economic Review* [Hong Kong], LXIX, No. 34, August 20, 1970, 27-32,

———. "The 1,000-Year Struggle," *Far Eastern Economic Review* [Hong Kong], LXVII, No. 1, March 5, 1970, 18-20, 45.

Donnison, F. S. V. *Burma.* (Nations of the Modern World Series.) New York: Praeger, 1970.

Editor and Publisher International Yearbook, 1970. New York: Editor and Publisher, 1970.

Europa Yearbook, 1970, II: Africa, the Americas, Asia, Australasia. London: Europa Publications, 1970.

The Far East and Australasia, 1970: A Survey and Directory of Asia and the Pacific. London: Europa Publications, 1970.

Far Eastern Economic Review Yearbook, 1968. Hong Kong: FEER, 1968.

Far Eastern Economic Review Yearbook, 1969. Hong Kong: FEER, 1969.

Far Eastern Economic Review Yearbook, 1970. Hong Kong: FEER, 1970.

"Few for U Nu," *Far Eastern Economic Review* [Hong Kong], LXX, No. 40, October 3, 1970, 7.

Frost, J. M. (ed.) *World Radio-Television Handbook.* (25th ed.) Hvidore: World Radio-Television Handbook, 1970.

Garrett, W. E. "Southeast Asia: Pagan on the Road to Mandalay," *National Geographic,* CXXXIX, No. 3, March 1971, 343-365.

Golay, Frank H., et al. *Underdevelopment and Economic Nationalism in Southeast Asia.* Ithaca: Cornell University Press, 1969.

Guyot, James F. "The 'Clerk Mentality' in Burmese Education." Pages 122-227 in Robert O. Tilman (ed.), *Man, State and Society in Contemporary Southeast Asia.* New York: Praeger, 1969.

Hagen, Everett E. "Personality and Religion in Burma," *American Anthropologist,* X, No. 2, April 1968, 357-359.

Hall, D.G.E. *A History of South-East Asia.* (3d ed.) (Macmillan Student Edition.) New York: St. Martin's Press, 1968.

Hanna, Willard A. *Progressive, Productive, Patriotic Burma: The Burmese View of the Ne Win Regime.* (American Universities Field Staff Reports, Southeast Asia Series, XVI, No. 1.) New York: AUFS, January 1968.

Harvey, G. E. *Outline of Burmese History.* Bombay: Orient Longmans, 1926.

Hatley, R. "The Overseas Indian in Southeast Asia: Burma, Malaysia and Singapore." Pages 450-466 in Robert O. Tilman (ed.), *Man, State and Society in Contemporary Southeast Asia.* New York: Praeger, 1969.

Hayden, Howard. *Higher Education and Development in South-East Asia,* I. Paris: United Nations Educational, Scientific and Cultural Organization and the International Association of Universities, 1967.

_____. *Higher Education and Development in South-East Asia*, II: Country Profiles. Paris: United Nations Educational, Scientific and Cultural Organization and the International Association of Universities, 1967.

Hillam, Ray C. "Nationalist Chinese Irregulars in Southeast Asia: Liability or Asset." (Paper presented at the Annual Meeting of the Rocky Mountain Social Science Association, May 1970.) Colorado Springs: Colorado College, May 1970 (mimeo.).

Hinton, Harold C. *Communist China in World Politics.* Boston: Houghton Mifflin, 1966.

Hitson, Hazel. "Family Patterns and Paranoidal Personality Structure in Boston and Burma." Unpublished Ph.D. dissertation. Cambridge: Radcliffe College, 1959.

Holmes, Robert A. "Burmese Domestic Policy: The Politics of Burmanization." *Asian Survey,* XII, No. 3, March 1967, 188-197.

Htin Aung. *A History of Burma.* New York: Columbia University Press, 1967.

Khin Maung Kyi. "Patterns of Accommodation to Bureaucratic Authority in a Transitional Culture: A Sociological Analysis of Burmese Bureaucrats with Respect to their Orientations Toward Authority." Unpublished Ph.D. dissertation. Ithaca: Cornell University, 1966.

Koop, John Clement. *The Eurasian Population in Burma.* (Cultural Report Series No. 6.) New Haven: Yale University Press, Southeast Asia Studies, 1960.

Kunstadter, Peter (ed.). *Southeast Asian Tribes, Minorities and Nations,* I. Princeton: Princeton University Press, 1967.

Kyaw Thet. "Burma: The Political Integration of Linguistic and Religious Minority Groups." Pages 156-168 in Philip W. Thayer (ed.), *Nationalism and Progress in Free Asia.* Baltimore: Johns Hopkins Press, 1956.

Limbin Htaik Tin Lat. "The Hill Tribes of Burma," *Hemisphere* [Australia], XI, March 1967, 33-36.

Lissak, Moshe. "The Class Structure of Burma: Continuity and Change," *Journal of Southeast Asian Studies* [Singapore], I, No. 1, March 1970, 60-73.

_____. "Social Change, Mobilization and Exchange of Services Between the Military Establishment and the Civil Society: The Burmese Case," *Economic Development and Cultural Change,* XIII, Pt. 1, 1964, 12-16.

Luce G.H. "Note on the Peoples of Burma in the 12th-13th Century A.D.," *Journal of the Burma Research Society* [Rangoon], XLII, No. 1, June 1959, 52-74.

_____. "Old Kyaukse and the Coming of the Burmans," *Journal of the Burma Research Society* [Rangoon], XLII, No. 1, June 1959, 75-112.

McGee, T.G. *The Southeast Asian City: A Social Geography of the Primate Cities of Southeast Asia.* New York: Praeger, 1967.

Maung Maung. *Burma and General Ne Win.* New York: Asia Publishing House, 1969.

———. *Burma's Constitution.* (2d ed., rev.) The Hague: Martinus Nijhoff, 1961.

Maung Sein Maung. "Socio-Cultural Values and Economic Backwardness: A Case Study of Burma." Unpublished Ph.D. dissertation. New York: New York University, 1964.

Mendleson, E. Michael. "Religion and Authority in Modern Burma," *World Today* [London], XIV, 1960, 110-118.

Mya Maung. "Burmese Way to Socialism Beyond the Welfare State," *Asian Survey,* X, No. 6, June 1970, 533-551.

Myint, H. "The Inward and Outward Looking Countries of Southeast Asia," *Malayan Economic Review* [Singapore], XII, No. 1, April 1967, 1-13.

Nash, Manning. "Burmese Family and Social Life," *Asia,* No. 11, Spring 1968, 42-53.

———. "The Modernization of Burma." Pages 124-137 in Robert I. Crane (ed.), *Southern Asia.* (Southern Regional Education Board Seminars for Journalists, Report No. 5.) Atlanta: Southern Regional Education Board, 1968.

Nash, Manning, et al. *Studies in Theravada Buddhism.* (Cultural Report Series, No. 13.) New Haven: Yale University Press, Southeast Asia Studies, 1966.

Nu, U. *Burma Under the Japanese.* London: Macmillan, 1954.

Pfanner, David E., and Ingersoll, Jasper. "Theravada Buddhism and Village Economic Behavior: A Burmese and Thai Comparison," *Journal of Asian Studies,* XXI, No. 3, May 1962, 341-361.

Roucek, Joseph S. "Burma in Geopolitics," *Revue du sud-est asiatique* [Brussels], I, 1968, 47-82.

Saimong Mangrai, Sao. *The Shan States and the British Annexation.* (Data Paper No. 57, Southeast Asia Program.) Ithaca: Cornell University Press, 1965.

Sarkisyanz, Manuel. "Messianic Folk-Buddhism as Ideology of Peasant Revolts in Nineteenth and Early Twentieth Century Burma," *Review of Religious Research,* X, Fall 1968, 32-38.

Seagrave, Sterling. "The Minorities Unite," *Far Eastern Economic Review* [Hong Kong], LXX, No. 45, November 7, 1970, 37-39.

———."U Nu Underground," *Far Eastern Economic Review* [Hong Kong], LXX, No. 50, December 12, 1970, 18, 21-24.

Sein Tu. "The Psychodynamics of Burmese Personality," *Journal of the Burma Research Society* [Rangoon], XLVII, No. 2, December 1964, 263-285.

Sidhu, Jagjit Singh. "The Historical Background to Burma's Acceptance of Western Culture," *East Asian Cultural Studies* [Tokyo], VI, Nos. 1-4. March 1967, 41-54.

Silverstein, Josef. "Political Dialogue in Burma: A New Turn on the Road to Socialism?" *Asian Survey,* X, No. 2, February 1970, 133-141.

Smith, Donald Eugene. "The Political Monks of Burma and Ceylon," *Asia,* No. 10. Winter 1968, 3-10.

Solomon, Robert L. "Saya San and the Burmese Rebellion," *Modern Asian Studies,* III, Pt. 3, July 1969, 209-229.

Spiro, Milton E. "Factionalism and Politics in Village Burma." Pages 401-421 in Marc J. Swartz (ed.), *Local-Level Politics: Social and Cultural Perspectives.* Chicago: Aldine, 1968.

The Statesmen's Yearbook, 1969-1970. (106th ed.) (Eds., John Paxton and S.H. Steinberg.) New York: St. Martin's Press, 1969.

Statistical Yearbook, 1969. New York: United Nations, 1969.

Steward, Julian H. (ed.) *Contemporary Change in Traditional Societies,* II: Asian Rural Societies. Urbana: University of Illinois Press, 1967.

Than Tun. "History of Burma: A.D. 1300-1400," *Journal of the Burma Research Society* [Rangoon], XLII, No. 2, December 1959, 119-133.

_____ "Religion in Burma A.D. 1000-1300," *Journal of the Burma Research Society* [Rangoon], XLII, No. 2, December 1959, 47-69.

Thaung, Dr. "Burmese Kingship in Theory and Practice during the Reign of Mindon," *Journal of the Burma Research Society* [Rangoon], XLII, No. 2, December 1959, 171-185.

Theodorson, George A. "Book Review: *The Structure of Chin Society* by F.K. Lehman," *Journal of Southeast Asian History* [Singapore], V, No. 1, March 1964, 198-200.

_____. "Minority Peoples of the Union of Burma," *Journal of Southeast Asian History* [Singapore], V, No. 1, March 1964, 1-16.

Thin Kyi, Daw. "The Old City of Pagan." Pages 179-188 in Ba Shin, Jean Boisselier, and A.B. Griswold (eds.), *Essays Offered to G.H. Luce by His Colleagues and Friends in Honour of His Seventy-Fifth Birthday,* II: Papers on Asian Art and Archaeology. Ascona, Switzerland: Artibus Asiae, 1966.

Tin Hla Thaw. "History of Burma: A.D. 1400-1500," *Journal of the Burma Research Society* [Rangoon], XLII, No. 2, December 1959, 135-151.

Trager, Frank N. "Burma, 1968: A New Beginning?" *Asian Survey,* IX, No. 2, February 1969, 104-114.

_____. "Historical Perspectives on Independent Burma," *Asia,* No. 13, Autumn 1968, 71-91.

Trager, Helen G. *We the Burmese: Voices from Burma.* New York: Praeger, 1969.

Union of Burma. *Report to the People by the Union of Burma Revolutionary Council on the Revolutionary Government's Budget Estimates for 1969-70.* Rangoon: 1970.

Union of Burma. *Statistical Pocketbook.* Rangoon: 1967.

Union of Burma. Embassy in Washington. *People.* Washington: n.d. (mimeo.).

Union of Burma. Ministry of Information. *Burma: A Handbook on Burma with Special Reference to Burmese Customs, Culture, History, Economic Resources, Education, Famous Pagodas and Cities.* Published on the occasion of the Chatta Sangavana (Sixth Buddhist Synod.) Rangoon: Ministry of Information, 1954.

United Nations. Economic Commission for Asia and the Far East. *Economic Survey of Asia and the Far East, 1968.* Bangkok: 1969.

U.S. Agency for International Development. Office of Statistics and Reports. Bureau for Program and Policy Coordination. *Selected Economic Data for the Less Developed Countries.* Washington: GPO, 1971.

U.S. Department of State. *Fact Book of the Countries of the World.* New York: Crown, 1970.

U.S. Foreign Broadcasting Information Service. *Broadcasting Stations of the World.* (23d ed.) Washington: GPO, 1969.

Walinsky, Louis J. "The Role of the Military in Development Planning: Burma." Pages 340-350 in Robert O. Tilman (ed.), *Man, State and Society in Contemporary Southeast Asia.* New York: Praeger, 1969.

White, Peter T. "Southeast Asia: Mosaic of Cultures," *National Geographic,* CXXXIX, No. 3, March 1971, 206-329.

Worldmark Encyclopedia of the Nations, IV: Asia and Australasia. (Ed., Louis Barron.) New York: Harper and Row, 1967.

Yegar, Moshe. "Muslims in Burma." Rangoon: October 1962 (Unpublished manuscript, not available for public distribution).

————. "The Panthay (Chinese Muslims) of Burma and Yunnan," *Journal of Southeast Asian History* [Singapore], VII, No. 1, March 1966, 73-85.

(Various issues of the following periodicals were also used in the preparation of this section: *Forward* [Rangoon], January 1970-December 1970; *Guardian Magazine* [Rangoon], January 1970-December 1970; and the *Working People's Daily* [Rangoon], January 1970-March 1971.)

SECTION II. POLITICAL

Ajia Kyokai. *Tonan Ajia Seiji Keizai Soran-jokan* (General Outline of Southeast Asian Politics and Economy, I). Tokyo: Daiyamondo-Sha, 1957.

Badgley, John H. "Burma's China Crisis: The Choices Ahead," *Asian Survey*, VII, No. 11, November 1967, 753-761.

_____. "Burma's Military Government: A Political Analysis," *Asian Survey*, II, No. 6, August 1962, 24-31.

_____. "Burma: The Nexus of Socialism and Two Political Traditions," *Asian Survey*, III, No. 2, February 1963, 89-95.

_____. "Burma's Zealot Wungyis: Maoists or St. Simonists," *Asian Survey*, V, No. 1, January 1965, 55-62.

_____. "The Communist Parties of Burma." Pages 290-308 in Robert A. Scalapino (ed.), *The Communist Revolution in Asia: Tactics, Goals, and Achievements*. Englewood Cliffs: Prentice-Hall, 1965.

_____. "Intellectuals and the National Vision: The Burmese Case," *Asian Survey*, IX, No. 8, August 1969, 598-613.

_____. *Politics Among Burmans: A Study of Intermediary Leaders.* (Southeast Asia Series, No. 15.) Athens: Center for International Studies, Ohio University Press, 1970.

Banerji S.C. "Buddha Awakes," *Far Eastern Economic Review* [Hong Kong], LXIX, No. 35, August 27, 1970, 15-16.

Bixler, Norma. *Burma: A Profile.* (Praeger Country Profiles Series.) New York: Praeger, 1971.

"Burma." Pages 29-38 in Louis Barron (ed.), *Worldmark Encyclopedia of the Nations,* IV: Asia and Australasia. New York: Harper and Row, 1967.

"Burma: The Burmese Way to Despair," *Far Eastern Economic Review* [Hong Kong], LXX, No. 41, October 10, 1970, 13.

"Burma's Future: A Political Alert," *Far Eastern Economic Review* [Hong Kong], XLIII. January 16, 1969, 105-107.

Burma Socialist Program Party. *The Specific Characteristics of the Burma Socialist Program Party.* Rangoon: Union of Burma, 1964.

_____. *The Constitution of the Burma Socialist Program Party.* Rangoon: Union of Burma, 1962.

Butwell, Richard. "Burma: The Obscure Domino," *Current History,* LXIX No. 352, December 1970, 339-344, 364.

_____. "The Four Failures of U Nu's Second Premiership," *Asian Survey*, II, No. 1, March 1962, 3-11.

_____. *Southeast Asia: A Survey.* (Headline Series, No. 192.) New York: Foreign Policy Association, 1968.

_____. *Southeast Asia Today and Tomorrow: Problems of Political Development.* (2d ed., rev.) New York: Praeger, 1969.

Butwell, Richard. *U Nu of Burma.* (2d ed.) Stanford: Stanford University Press, 1969.

———. "U Nu's Second Comeback Try," *Asian Survey,* IX, No. 11, November 1969, 868-876.

Dalton, James Joseph. "The 1,000-Year Struggle," *Far Eastern Economic Review* [Hong Kong], LXVII, No. 1, March 5, 1970, 18-20, 45.

Donnison, F.S.V. *Burma.* (Nations of the Modern World Series.) New York: Praeger, 1970.

Far Eastern Economic Review Yearbook, 1967. Hong Kong: FEER, 1967.

Far Eastern Economic Review Yearbook, 1968. Hong Kong: FEER, 1968.

Far Eastern Economic Review Yearbook, 1969. Hong Kong: FEER, 1969.

Far Eastern Economic Review Yearbook, 1970. Hong Kong: FEER, 1970.

Far Eastern Economic Review Yearbook, 1971. Hong Kong: FEER, 1971.

Guyot, James F. "Bureaucratic Transformation in Burma." Pages 354-443 in Ralph Braibanti (ed.), *Asian Bureaucratic Systems Emergent from the British Imperial Tradition.* Durham: Duke University Press, 1966.

Halpern, Abraham M. (ed.) *Policies Toward China: Views from Six Continents.* New York: McGraw-Hill, 1966.

Hillam, Ray C. "Nationalist Chinese Irregulars in Southeast Asia: Liability or Asset." (Paper presented at the Annual Meeting of the Rocky Mountain Social Science Association, May 1970.) Colorado Springs: Colorado Springs College, May 1970 (mimeo.).

Hilton, Harold C. *Communist China in World Politics.* Boston: Houghton Mifflin, 1966.

Holmes, Robert A. "Burmese Domestic Policy: The Politics of Burmanization," *Asian Survey,* XII, No. 3, March 1967, 188-197.

Johnstone, William C. *Burma's Foreign Policy: A Study in Neutralism.* Cambridge: Harvard University Press, 1963.

Lissak, Moshe. "The Class Structure of Burma: Continuity and Change," *Journal of Southeast Asian Studies* [Singapore], I, No. 1, March 1970, 60-73.

McLennan, Barbara. "Evolution of Concepts of Representation in Burma," *Journal of Southeast Asian History* [Singapore], VIII, No. 2, September 1967, 268-284.

Maung Maung. *Burma and General Ne Win.* New York: Asia Publishing House, 1969.

———. *"Burma's Constitution.* (2d ed., rev.) The Hague: Martinus Nijhoff, 1961.

Mya Maung. "The Burmese Way to Socialism Beyond the Welfare State," *Asian Survey*, X, No. 6, June 1970, 533-551.

———. "The Elephant Catching Cooperative Society of Burma: A Case Study on the Effect of Planned Socio-Economic Change," *Asian Survey*, VI, No. 6, June 1966, 327-337.

———. "Socialism and Economic Development of Burma," *Asian Survey*, IV, No. 12, December 1964, 1182-1190.

Nash, Manning. "Party Building in Upper Burma," *Asian Survey*, III, No. 4, April 1963, 197-202.

Ne Win. "Address delivered by General Ne Win, Chairman of the Burma Socialist Program Party, at the opening of the Fourth Party Seminar." Rangoon: Central Press, 1969.

Pye, Lucian W. "The Army in Burmese Politics." Page 231-252 in John J. Johnson (ed.), *The Role of the Military in Underdeveloped Countries*. Princeton: Princeton University Press, 1962.

———. *Burma: Opening on the Left in the Military Manner*. Cambridge: Massachusetts Institute of Technology, Center for International Studies, 1963.

Seagrave, Sterling. "U Nu Underground," *Far Eastern Economic Review* [Hong Kong], LXX, No. 50, December 12, 1970, 21-24.

Severino, Rodolfo, Jr. "The Pressures on Burma's Foreign Policy: A Case Study," *Philippine Studies* [Manila], XVI, July 1968, 460-486.

Silverstein, Josef. "Burma: Ne Win's Revolution Reconsidered," *Asian Survey*, VI, No. 2, February 1966, 95-102.

———. "Burma." Pages 75-179 in George McTurnan Kahin (ed.), *Governments and Politics of Southeast Asia*. (2d ed.) Ithaca: Cornell University Press, 1964.

———. "First Steps on the Burmese Way to Socialism." *Asian Survey*, IV, No. 2, February 1964, 716-722.

———. "Political Dialogue in Burma: A New Turn on the Road to Socialism," *Asian Survey*, X, No. 2, February 1970, 133-142.

———. "Problems in Burma: Economic, Political and Diplomatic," *Asian Survey*, VII, No. 2, February 1967, 177-125.

Smith, Donald Eugene. "The Political Monks of Burma and Ceylon," *Asia*, No. 10, Winter 1968, 3-10.

———. *Religion and Politics in Burma*. Princeton: Princeton University Press, 1965.

South-East Asia Treaty Organization. "Burma's Counter-Insurgency Effort," *Trends and Highlights* (RO/TH/283), April 1, 1969, 11-13.

———. "The Burmese Scene," *Trends and Highlights* (RO/TH/299), August 1, 1970, 5-9.

———. "Communist Chinese Subversion in Burma-India Border Areas," *Trends and Highlights* (RO/TH—275), August 1, 1968, 3-8.

———."Communist Reverses in Burma," *Trends and Highlights* (RO/TH/303), December 1, 1970, 20-23.

Tinker, Hugh. *The Union of Burma: A Study of the First Year of Independence.* (3d ed.) London: Oxford University Press, 1961.

Tonan Ajia Chosakai. *Tonan Ajia Yoran* (Outline of Southeast Asia). (1968 ed.) Toyko: 1968.

_____. *Tonan Ajia Yoran* (Outline of Southeast Asia). (1969 ed.) Tokyo: 1969.

_____. *Tonan Ajia Yoran* (Outline of Southeast Asia). (1970 ed.) Tokyo: 1970.

Trager, Frank N. *Burma from Kingdom to Republic: A Historical and Political Analysis.* New York: Praeger, 1966.

_____. "Burma, 1968: A New Beginning?" *Asian Survey,* IX, No. 2, February 1969, 104-114.

_____. "Burma, 1967: A Better Ending Than Beginning?" *Asian Survey,* VIII, No. 2, February 1968, 110-119.

Union of Burma. *Report to the People by the Union of Burma Revolutionary Council on the Revolutionary Government's Budget Estimates for 1969-70.* Rangoon: 1970.

Union of Burma. Director of Information. *Burma: Administrative and Social Affairs, 1962-63.* Rangoon: n.d.

Union of Burma. Revolutionary Council. *The Burmese Way to Socialism: Manifesto of Burma Revolutionary Council.* Rangoon: April 30, 1962.

U.S. Agency for International Development. *U.S. Overseas Loans and Grants and Assistance from International Organizations, Obligations and Loan Authorizations, July 1, 1945-June 30, 1960.* (Special report prepared for the House Foreign Affairs Committee.) Washington: GPO, 1970.

U.S. Department of Commerce. Bureau of International Commerce. "Basic Data on the Economy of Burma," *Overseas Business Reports* (OBR 69-71-C.) Washington: December 1969.

U.S. Department of State. *Fact Book of the Countries of the World.* New York: Crown, 1970.

von der Mehden, Fred R. "The Burmese Way to Socialism," *Asian Survey,* III, No. 3, March 1963, 129-135.

Walinsky, Louis J. "The Role of the Military in Development Planning: Burma." Pages 340-350 in Robert O. Tilman (ed.), *Man, State and Society in Contemporary Southeast Asia.* New York: Praeger, 1969.

Wriggins, W. Howard. "The Presence in Southern Asia of Outside Powers," *The Annals of the American Academy of Political and Social Science,* CCCXC, July 1970, 48-62.

Yearbook on International Communist Affairs, 1969. (Ed., Richard F. Starr.) Stanford: Hoover Institute Press, 1970.

(Various Issues of the following periodicals were also used in the preparation of this section: *Asian Recorder* [New Delhi], January 1956-December 1970; *Daily Press Summary*] Rangoon], October 1970-January 1971; *Far Eastern Economic Review* [Hong Kong], January 1967-March 1971; *Guardian* [Rangoon], January 1970-March 1971; *Keesing's Contemporary Archives* [London], January 1956-December 1970; *New York Times,* July 1967-January 1971; *Washington Post,* July 1967-January 1971; *Working People's Daily* [Rangoon], January 1969-June 1970 and February 1971-March 1971.)

SECTION III. ECONOMIC

Badgley, John H. "The Union of Burma: Age Twenty-Two," *Asian Survey*, XI, No. 2, February 1971, 149-158.

"Burma: U Nu Underground," *Far Eastern Economic Review* [Hong Kong], LXX, No. 50, December 12, 1970, 18, 21-24.

Butwell, Richard. "Burma: The Obscure Domino," *Current History*, LXIX, No. 352, December 1970, 339-344, 364.

Donnison, F.S.V. *Burma*. (Nations of the Modern World Series.) New York: Praeger, 1970.

The Economist Intelligence Unit. *Quarterly Economic Review: Continental Southeast Asia, Annual Supplement 1970*. London: 1970.

Emery, Robert F. *The Financial Institutions of Southeast Asia*. New York: Praeger, 1970.

Far Eastern Economic Review Yearbook, 1967. Hong Kong: FEER, 1967.

Far Eastern Economic Review Yearbook, 1968. Hong Kong: FEER, 1968.

Far Eastern Economic Review Yearbook, 1969. Hong Kong: FEER, 1969.

Far Eastern Economic Review Yearbook, 1970. Hong Kong: FEER, 1970.

Far Eastern Economic Review Yearbook, 1971. Hong Kong: FEER, 1971.

Food and Agriculture Organization. *The State of Food and Agriculture, 1970*. (Preliminary Version, 55th Session, held in Rome, November 17-December 1, 1970.) Rome: FAO, 1970.

Fryer, Donald W. *Emerging Southeast Asia: A Study in Growth and Stagnation*. New York: McGraw-Hill, 1970.

Gallatin International Business Service. *Burma*. New York: Copley International Corporation, 1966.

Golay, Frank H., et al. *Underdevelopment and Economic Nationalism in Southeast Asia*. Ithaca: Cornell University Press, 1969.

Keatley, Robert. "Burma's Sticky Way to Socialism," *Wall Street Journal*, CLXXII, September 16, 1968, 16.

Kirby, E. Stuart. *Economic Development in East Asia*. New York: Praeger, 1967.

Landry, Lionel. *The Land and People of Burma*. (Portraits of the Nation Series.) Philadelphia: Lippincott, 1968.

Morgan, Theodore, and Spoelstra, Nyle (eds.). *Economic Interdependence in Southeast Asia*. Madison: University of Wisconsin Press, 1969.

Mya Maung. "The Burmese Way to Socialism Beyond the Welfare State," *Asian Survey*, X, No. 6, June 1970, 533-551.

Myint, H. *Economic Theory and the Underdeveloped Countries.* London: Oxford University Press, 1971.

Nash, Manning. "The Modernization of Burma." Pages 124-137 in Robert I. Crane (ed.), *Southern Asia.* (Southern Regional Education Board Seminars for Journalists, Report No. 5.) Atlanta: Southern Regional Education Board, 1968.

Richter, H.V. "The Union of Burma." Pages 141-180 in R.T. Shand (ed.), *Agricultural Development in Asia.* Berkeley: University of California Press, 1969.

Schmitt, Hans O. "Decolonization and Development in Burma," *Journal of Development Studies* [London], IV, October 1967, 97-108.

The Statesmen's Yearbook, 1970-71. (107th ed.) (Ed., John Paxton.) New York: St. Martin's Press, 1970.

Tun Wau. *Burma's Currency and Credit.* Bombay: Orient Longmans, 1962.

Union of Burma. *Report to the People by the Union of Burma Revolutionary Council on the Revolutionary Government's Budget Estimates for 1969-70.* Rangoon: 1970.

——. *Statistical Pocketbook.* Rangoon: 1967.

U.S. Agency for International Development. *A.I.D. Economic Data Book: East Asia.* Washington: GPO, 1970.

——. *East Asia: Economic Growth Trends.* Washington: GPO, 1971.

U.S. Agency for International Development. Office of Statistics and Reports. Bureau for Program and Policy Coordination. *Selected Economic Data for the Less Developed Countries.* Washington: GPO, 1971.

U.S. Department of Agriculture. Economic Research Service. *The 1970 Agricultural Data Book for the Far East and Oceania.* (ERS Foreign 267.) Washington: GPO. 1970.

U.S. Department of Commerce. Bureau of International Commerce. "Basic Data on the Economy of Burma," *Overseas Business Reports* OBR 69-71-C.) Washington: December 1969.

——. "Foreign Trade Regulations of Burma," *Overseas Business Reports* (OBR 68-92) Washington: October 1968.

U.S. Department of the Interior. Bureau of Mines. *The Mineral Industry of Burma.* Washington: GPO, 1969.

U.S. Department of Labor. Bureau of Labor Statistics. "Burma," *Labor Developments Abroad,* XV, No. 12, December 1970, 22-24.

Walinsky, Louis J. "The Role of the Military in Development Planning: Burma." Pages 340-350 in Robert O. Tilman (ed.), *Man, State and Society in Contemporary Southeast Asia.* New York: Praeger, 1969.

Yearbook of Labor Statistics, 1969. Geneva: International Labor Office, 1969.

(Various issues of the following periodicals were also used in the preparation of this section: *Guardian* [Rangoon], January 1970-December 1970; and *Working People's Daily* [Rangoon], January 1969-December 1970.)

SECTION IV. NATIONAL SECURITY

Cramer, James. *The World's Police.* London: Cassell, 1964.

Donnison, F.S.V. *Burma.* (Nations of the Modern World Series.) New York: Praeger, 1970.

Europa Yearbook, 1970, II: Africa, the Americas, Asia, Australasia. London: Europa Publications, 1970.

The International Yearbook and Statesmen's Who's Who, 1968. (16th ed.) London: Burke's Peerage, 1968.

The Military Balance, 1970-1971. London: Institute for Strategic Studies, 1970.

Sellers, Robert C. *Armed Forces of the World.* Garden City: Robert C. Sellers and Associates, 1968.

The Statesman's Yearbook, 1970-1971. (107th ed.) (Ed., John Paxton.) New York: St. Martin's Press, 1970.

U.S. Department of State. *Fact Book of the Countries of the World.* New York: Crown, 1970.

GLOSSARY

AFPFL—Anti-Fascist People's Freedom League. The political organization, consisting of a coalition of parties and individuals, that led the independence movement and dominated politics until 1958.

BSPP—*See* Burma Socialist Program Party.

Burman(s)—Member(s) of or descriptive of dominant ethnic group in Burma. A narrower term than Burmese, which is used to refer to all the peoples in Burma and to the national language.

Burma proper—Term in use since British colonial period to designate area of Burma excluding Shan Plateau and the frontier hill territories. Corresponds approximately to the area included in the seven divisions of Mandalay, Irrawaddy, Pegu, Magwe, Tenasserim, Arakan, and Sagaing. The other parts of Burma are four states and a special division. Formerly these were accorded a special status with semiautonomous powers, whereas Burma proper was administered directly by the central government. In 1964 all jurisdictions were placed on the same level in this respect.

Burma Socialist Program Party (BSPP)—The party created by the Revolutionary Government that has governed Burma since March 2, 1962.

Colombo Plan—The Colombo Plan for Cooperative Economic Development in South and Southeast Asia. An international cooperative effort to help countries of the area raise their living standards. In 1971 member nations of the plan included Afghanistan, Bhutan, Burma, Cambodia, Ceylon, India, Indonesia, Iran, the Republic of Korea, Laos, Malaysia, the Maldive Islands, Nepal, Pakistan, the Philippines, Singapore, Thailand, the Republic of Vietnam; and the donor nations, Australia, Canada, Japan, New Zealand, the United Kingdom, and the United States.

Hinayana—Literal meaning, Lesser Vehicle. *See* Theravada.

Karenni—Literal meaning, Red Karen. Former name for member of ethnic group that predominates in Kayah State (formerly known as the Karenni states). *See* Kayah.

karma—A religious doctrine that involves the workings of an impersonal law of causation by which the ethical consequences of one's acts determine his lot in future incarnations or rebirths. Buddhist equivalent of fate or destiny.

Kayah(s)—Member(s) of or descriptive of ethnic group that lives in Kayah State; formerly known as Karennis or Red Karens, the

Kayahs are usually regarded as distinct from the Karens, another ethnic group of Burma.

KMT—*See* Kuomintang.

KNDO—Karen National Defense Organization. An armed insurgent group.

Kuomintang (KMT)—Name for ruling party of the Republic of China. Party was founded in 1912 by associates of Sun Yat-sen after revolution that overthrew Manchu dynasty, replacing it with a republican form of government.

kyat (K)—Unit of currency; 4.76 kyat equal US$1.

Lanzin party—Alternate unofficial name for Burma Socialist Program Party *(q.v.)*. Lanzin is Burmese word meaning program or policy.

Lower Burma—Term in use since British colonial period. Refers to the area annexed by British in 1853. The area, which includes the delta of the Irrawaddy and the mouths of the Pegu and Sittang rivers, is in the southern portion of the country.

Mahayana—Literal meaning, Greater Vehicle. One of the two schools of Buddhism; popular in China, Japan, Korea, Nepal, Tibet, and Republic of Vietnam.

Mon—Member of or descriptive of ethnic group that formerly was the dominant group in the delta area of Burma. Language spoken by the Mons, one of the Mon-Khmer group of Austroasiatic languages. Also is term used by the Shans to designate the Burmans *(q.v.)*.

Myanma—Burmese literary word meaning Burma. Sometimes spelled Myama.

NUF—National United Front. Coalition of parties to oppose the AFPFL *(q.v.)* in general elections of 1956 and 1960.

Pali—Language of the sacred scriptures of Theravada Buddhism.

pongyi—Buddhist monk.

PPC—People's Peasants' Council. Name given each organization for agricultural workers sponsored by the BSPP *(q.v.)*. The Central People's Peasants' Council (CPPC) occupies the highest level in the hierarchy of the PPCs.

PVO—Patriotic Volunteer Organization. Veteran organization established in 1945 and headed by Aung San. The original membership consisted of veterans of Aung San's wartime army, but many new members were recruited in the years immediately after World War II to support AFPFL *(q.v.)* agitation for independence. After independence the PVO split, and one faction joined the insurgent forces.

PWC—People's Workers' Council. Name given each organization for nonagricultural workers sponsored by the BSPP *(q.v.)*. The Central People's Workers' Council (CPWC) occupies the highest level in the hierarchy of PWCs.

pwe—A gathering, a show, or a performance. The principal traditional Burmese theatrical performance.

Pyidawtha—Literal meaning, Happy Land. As used by U Nu, has come to mean welfare state.

Red Flag party—Alternate unofficial name for the Communist Party of Burma, which is also known as the Communist Party of Burma (Red Flag). Members are sometimes called Red Flags. One of two Burmese communist parties. Offshoot and rival of the White Flag party *(q.v.)*.

SAC—Security and Administrative Committee. Unit of administration of the law and maintenance of government control introduced by the Revolutionary Government of the Union of Burma. Hierarchy of SACs extends from national to local level.

sangha—Pali *(q.v.)* term meaning assembly or order of Buddhist monks. Includes ordained monks and novices. Members of the *sangha* reside separately from the laity, usually in a *kyaung* (monastery).

Shan—Member of or descriptive of ethnic group that predominates in the Shan State. A subgroup of the Tai *(q.v.)*.

Tai—Member of ethnic group or descriptive of indigenous speakers of the Tai language. Includes the indigenous Tai of Burma, usually called Shans, and also the Tai of Thailand, Laos, North Vietnam, southern China, and Assam. The name for citizens of Thailand ordinarily is spelled "Thai" in roman letters.

Thakin—Literal meaning, master. Term used as a prefix to a man's name. In colonial period, usually reserved for Europeans, equivalent to Indian word *Sahib*. Adopted as a gesture of defiance by members of nationalist group in 1930s. Thakins founded the Do-Bama Asi-ayon party in 1935.

Theravada—One of the two major schools of Buddhism; the principal religion of Burma and several other Southeast Asian countries. Sometimes known as the Hinayana or Lesser Vehicle school in contradistinction to Mahayana *(q.v.)* Buddhism.

Upper Burma—Term in use since British colonial period designating the area annexed by British in 1886; corresponds approximately to northern half of the country. Includes all of the country except Lower Burma*(q.v.)*, Arakan and Tenasserim (both annexed in 1826), the Shan Plateau, and the territory now included in Kayah State.

White Flag party—Alternate unofficial name for the Burma Communist Party, which is also known as the Burma Communist Party (White Flag). Members are sometimes called White Flags. One of two major Burmese communist parties.

Young Men's Buddhist Association (YMBA)—Private organization formed to provide various social services. Became active in Burmese nationalist politics in early twentieth century.

INDEX

Academy for Development of National Groups: 76, 184

adipati: 42

administration *(see also* Revolutionary Council): 143-147, 151-159; state, 52, 159; town, 145, 154; training, 158, 177, 185, 254; village, 37, 80, 81, 83-84, 145, 154

administrative divisions: vii, 145, 146

Agricultural Marketing Board, State (later Union of Burma): 49, 233, 245

agriculture *(see also* cooperatives; fisheries; rice): viii, 3,6,7, 20, 203, 209, 210, 217, 233, 237-245; education, 109; labor, viii, 209, 252, 255; shifting, 7, 16, 21, 83, 84, 239; small holding, 81, 244

aid, foreign: ix, 50, 94, 98, 187, 188, 190, 193, 194, 198, 199, 200, 201-206, 210, 219, 236, 248, 250, 255, 262, 288; military, 195, 200, 201, 273, 277-278, 281

air force *(see also* armed forces): ix, 273, 276, 277, 280, 281-282, 284

air transport: ix, 258, 271-272

Alaungpaya, King: 31-32, 76

Alaungsethu, King (1112-67): 27

All Burma Peasants Organization: 51

All India Radio: 128

Allies: 41, 42

Amarapura: 26, 32, 34

American Medical Center: 94

Ananda Pagoda: 27, 113

Anaukhpetlun, King (1605-28): 30-31

Anawrahta, King: 26-27

ancestor worship: 81, 83

Andaman Islands: 13

Andaman Sea: vii, 9, 12, 14, 15

Anglo-Burmese. *See* Eurasians

animals, domestic: 239-240, 241-243, 271

animism: viii, 2, 60, 82, 83, 84, 129, 142, 161, 181

Anti-Fascist Organization: 42, 43

Anti-fascist People's Freedom League (AFPFL): 43, 44, 45, 46, 47, 48, 49, 50, 51, 160, 165-166, 170; "Clean" AFPFL, 51, 53; "Stable" AFPFL, 51, 53

Arakan *(see also* Arakanese): Coast, vii, 11, 12, 13-14, 15-16, 202, 234, 269, 270; division, 11, 14-15, 145, 146, 185, 239; history, 28, 29, 32-34, 77; Mountains, 13, 14, 19

Arakanese: 53, 59, 60, 76, 77, 79, 185; history, 23, 25, 76, 77

archaeology: 26, 120

architecture *(see also* pagodas and temples): 90-91, 113

area and location (see also boundaries): vii, 1-2, 9, 10

ari: 27

armed forces *(see also* air force; army; coup; military navy): ix, 3, 47, 53, 55, 56, 61, 63, 152, 176, 178, 273, 276, 277, 282-284, Command, 276-277; training, 273, 279-280

army *(see also* armed forces): ix, 273, 276, 277, 279, 280-281, 283

Arts and Sciences University, Rangoon: 96, 109, 110, 111

Asian Development Bank: 206

Asian Youth Soccer Challenge Gold Cup: 99

Assam: xiv, 13; history, 25, 33, 83

Association of Southeast Asian Nations (ASEAN): 206

astrology: 26, 74, 92, 138, 142, 162

Atlee, Clement, prime minister of England: 44, 45, 201

Aung Gyi, Brigadier: 52, 169, 170

Aung San, Thakin: 40, 41, 42, 43, 44, 45, 46, 47, 61, 121, 144, 145, 149, 150, 162

Australia: 206

Auxiliary Union Police: 51

Ava: 26, 29, 30, 31, 32

Ava House: 126

Ayuthia, Kingdom: 29, 30, 32

Ba Maw: 40, 41-42
U Ba Swe: 51
Bagyidaw, King (1819): 33, 34
balance of payments: 6,229, 230
banditry *(see also* dacoits): 28, 44, 235, 248
banks and banking *(see also* People's Bank of the Union of Burma): 52, 193, 211, 213, 214, 222, 224-231, 238-239
Bassein: xiv, 21, 94, 96, 235, 270, 281; history, 30, 31
Bawdwin mines: 236, 251
Bay of Bengal: vii, xiv, 9, 12, 13, 14
Bayinnaung, King (1550-81): 30, 31
bell casting: 118
Bengal: 29, 33
births: 91
black market: 156, 179, 213, 234, 245, 257, 260, 267
"Blueprint for Free Burma": 150
Bodawpaya, King (1782): 32, 33
Bodhgaya, Benares, India: 27
bogyoke: 45, 47
boundaries, national: vii, xiv, 9, 10-11, 192, 193, 196; security, 164, 165, 192, 196, 197, 285; treaties *(see also* Communist China), 196
Brahmins: 26
British Broadcasting Corporation (BBC): 128
British Commonwealth *(see also* individual countries): 24, 44, 45, 200-201; aid, 50,200
British East India Company: 33, 34, 35
British minority group: 5, 7, 58
British rule (see also cultural influences: Great Britain and the British): vii, 1, 2, 7-8, 9, 11, 19, 23, 26, 35-45, 49, 56, 58, 62, 64, 76, 78, 83, 97, 106, 134, 156, 162, 193, 236, 237, 275, 285, 288; ethnic policies, 35-36, 47, 57, 61, 80, 81, 84, 145, 183, 195, 278; influence on present-day institutions, 3, 144-145, 273, 274, 276, 282, 283
Buddha. *See* Gautama
Buddha Sasana Council: 181
Buddhists and Buddhism *(see also* Gautama; missionaries and missionary activity; monasteries;

monks; pagodas; *sangha)*: vii, 1, 2, 6-7, 25, 26, 27, 34-35, 37, 38, 50, 55, 57, 58, 60, 62, 77, 78, 79, 80, 82, 83, 84, 129, 130-131, 139-141, 142, 162, 182, 184; education, 37, 38, 73, 105-106, 108, 140; literature and scriptures, 26, 27, 130, 133; and the state, 6, 53, 55, 60, 75, 79, 134-135, 147, 160-161, 180-181; values, 6-7, 88, 106, 140, 160, 241, 284-285
budget *(see also* public dept): 219-223, 277; deficit, viii-ix, 211, 219, 220, 223
Burma Army: 43, 46, 47, 78, 81, 83
Burma Broadcasting Service (BBS): 125
Burma Civil Police: 274, 285, 287
Burma Code: 290, 291
Burma Communist Party (White Flag party): 43, 44, 46, 185, 194, 195, 200, 285
Burma Defense Army: 42, 47
Burma Defense Services: 152, 153, 276
Burma Economic Development Corporation (BEDC): 247
Burma Five Star Line: 261, 262, 270
Burma Independence Army: 41, 42, 63
Burma Journalists Association: 122
Burma National Army: 275
Burma Rifles: 275
Burma Road: 41
Burma Socialist Program Party (BSPP) *(see also* Central Organizing Committee): vii, 3, 4, 55, 56, 63, 64, 67, 69, 143, 148, 151, 152, 163, 167, 169-182, 210, 214, 216, 217, 254; membership, 4, 175-177
Burma Surgeon. *See* Seagrave
Burma Workers and Peasants Party (BWPP, Red Socialist Party): 51, 170
Burmah Oil Company *(see also* Myanma Oil Corporation): 251
Burman language *(see also* literature): viii, 2, 27, 101, 102-103, 105, 108, 109; newspapers, 123, 124
Burmanization: 3, 5, 102, 106
Burmans *(see also* Burman language): vii, 1, 2, 7, 18, 23, 35, 36, 37, 41, 45, 47, 58, 59, 67-68, 76, 79, 80, 81, 183, 275, 276, 278; history,

English language: viii, 19, 38, 61, 66, 101, 105, 108, 109, 119, 125, 199; information, 5, 123, 124, 125, 128, 179

Enterprise Nationalization Law (1963): 5, 19, 20, 193, 195

ethnic groups (*see also* British rule; individual ethnic groups; minorities): vii, viii, 1, 2, 18, 23, 36, 55, 63, 81, 84, 85, 160; friction and insurrection, 2, 6, 19, 24, 41, 47, 53, 57, 59, 65, 77, 78, 81, 84, 141, 144, 164, 169, 176, 183-184, 185, 195, 197, 285; government policy, 75-76

Eurasians: 39, 41, 47, 49, 58, 66

European Economic Community (EEC): 266

European Free Trade Association (EFTA): 266

Executive Council: 44, 45

expenditure: ix, 219, 220, 277

export (*see also* rice): viii, 5, 6, 209, 210, 211, 217, 218, 230, 257, 261, 262, 263-265, 266, 270; licenses, 195

factionalism: 70-71, 160

family: 6, 63, 159, 255; Burman, 67-68

family planning: 219

fauna: 17

fertilizers: 239, 240, 241; production, 202, 205, 218, 246

Fifth Great Synod of Buddhism (1872): 34-35

films: 66, 99, 102, 125, 126, 128, 209, 213

finance (*see also* budget; capital investment; foreign exchange): viii-ix

First Four-Year Plan (1971/72-1974/75): 6, 210, 217

fishing and fisheries: 6, 15, 17, 89, 140, 209, 233, 243-244

flora. *See* vegetation

Flying Tigers of the Chinese Air Force: 41 folk art: 114

folk art: 114

folk medicine: viii, 91-92; practitioners, 96

food processing: viii, 233, 248

foreign exchange: 246, 257, 262; rate, viii, 227; reserves, viii, ix, 6, 50, 53, 188, 190, 211, 227, 230-231, 257

foreign policy: ix, 4, 50, 52-53, 98, 187-191, 198, 199; relations, 191-201

foreign relations. *See* foreign policy; trade

foreigners (*see also* capital investment): v, 5, 58, 65-66, 77, 102, 106, 156, 187-188, 238, 243, 286; business, 5, 49, 214

forests and forestry: 2, 6, 14, 16, 17, 209, 234

Forward: 127

France and the French: 31, 33, 34, 66, 123

freedom of expression (*see also* censorship): 127, 148, 164

Galons: 39-40

Gandhi, Indira, prime minister of India: 195

Gautama, the Buddha: 25, 27, 107, 114, 130, 132, 135, 136; images, 135, 136; relics, 25, 135

gems: 211, 251

General Council of Burmese Associations (GCBA): 39

General Council of Sangha Samaggis (GCSS): 39

geology (*see also* minerals; soils; topography): 236

Glass Palace Chronicle of the Kings of Burma: 34

government (*see also* administration; government policies; Revolutionary Government of the Union of Burma): vii, 1

Government of Burma Act (1935): 40

government policies (*see also* foreign policy): 149-150; cultural, 113; economic, 3-6, 209, 212, 213-216, 218, 220, 221, 238, 244-245; 246-248, 259; educational, 41, 101, 106, 108; ethnic, 75-76; information, v, 122, 126; religious, 6, 161-162, 181

government servants and service: 44, 55, 59, 63, 64, 144, 156-158, 165-166, 178; training, 158, 177, 185, 254

Great Britain and the British (*see also* British rule; cultural influences): 23, 31, 49, 123, 166, 193, 199, 200-201, 205-206, 273, 277-278, 281; entry into Burma, 7, 9, 32-35; trade, 211, 257, 265,

Japan and the Japanese: 197, 198, 258; aid, 198, 201-202, 206; trade, 211, 218, 257, 265, 266, 270; World War II, 8, 24, 38, 41-42, 56, 78, 87, 120, 275

Johnson, Lyndon B, president of the U.S.: 199

Journal of Burma Research Society: 121

journalists: v, 122, 180, 201

judiciary: 155-156

justice (*see also* courts; judiciary; legal system): viii

Justice Party: 51

jute: 240, 242

Kachin Independence Army: 84, 184

Kachin State: xiv, 11, 18, 78, 83, 145, 146, 147, 185, 221, 280

Kachins (*see also* ethnic groups; minorities): viii, 2, 18, 25, 36, 39, 41, 44, 45, 47, 57, 83-84, 103, 105, 125, 129, 140; separatism and rebellion, 53, 59, 185, 195, 285

Kaladan River: 15, 269

Karen National Defense Organization (KNDO): 47, 184, 285

Karenni (*see also* Kayahs): 35, 36, 46

Karenni State (*see also* Kayah State): 45, 46, 84

Karens: viii, 2, 18, 25, 35, 41, 44, 45, 47, 57, 59, 60, 79-81, 104-105, 129, 130, 278; language, 103, 104, 105, 125; separatism and rebellion, 39, 46-47, 53, 59, 81, 183, 185, 195, 197

karma: 131, 137, 140

Kaw-thu-lay Special Region: 46

Kawthule State: xiv, 11, 18, 80, 81, 84, 145, 146, 147, 185, 221

Kayah State (formerly Karenni State): xiv, 11, 18, 36, 46, 52, 84, 85, 145, 146, 147, 185, 221, 264

Kayahs (*see also* Karenni): viii, 18, 84, 125, 140; separatism, 59, 79, 84, 183

kinship (*see also* family): 7, 55, 67

Kittikachorn, Thanom, prime minister of Thailand: 197

Korea: 128, 198; war, 49, 50, 189, 198

Kublai Khan, Emperor of China: 28

Kuomintang (*see also* Nationalist China): 192

Kyansittha, King (1084-1112): 27

kyat: viii, 227

Kyaukse: 29, 235, 236

kyaung: See monasteries

U Kyaw Myint: 40

U Kyaw Nyein: 51

Kyaw Soe, Colonel: 177

labor (*see also* labor force; labor unions; personnel; working conditions: disputes, 210, 248, 254; recruitment, 253

labor force (*see also* labor; labor unions; working conditions): viii, 55, 209, 234, 246, 248, 252, 253; agriculture, viii, 252, 255; industrial, 250-251, 252; strike, 40

Labour Government, British: 44

labor unions: 51, 234, 254

lacquer ware: 117

lakes: 15

land (*see also* Land Nationalization Act): 234; grants, 28; nationalization and redistribution, 49, 55, 65, 67, 148, 218, 237, 238, 244; small holdings, 67, 68, 81; tenure, 36-37, 65, 67, 81, 213, 237-238

Land Nationalization Act (1948): 49

Land Tenancy Act (1963): 213

languages (*see also* Burman language): viii, 102-105, 122, 125

Lanzin Party. *See* Burma Socialist Program Party

Laos: vii, xiv, 9, 10, 12, 50, 130, 164, 192, 197; history, 25

Law of Fundamental Rights and Responsibilities of Workers (1964): 210, 254

Law to Protect National Solidarity (1964): 170, 254

U Law Yone: 197

Ledi Sayadaw: 119

legal system (*see also* Burma Code): 144, 155

Legislative Council: 39

leprosy: 92, 93

libraries: 121, 128

life expectancy: viii, 87

literacy: viii, 102, 133, 209

literature: 119-120

living standards (*see also* cost of living; diet; health; housing; sanitation): 1, 6, 87, 150, 255

local government. *See* administration

longyi: 89-90

Lower Burma: xiv, 16, 17, 36, 41, 47, 57, 129, 137, 185, 237, 238,

official language. *See* Burman language

oil, edible: 210, 240, 248-250, 257, 263, 264

opium: 262; cultivation, 83, 85, 89

Padaungs: 79, 85

Pagan: xiv; history, 26-28, 78, 113,

Pagan, King (1846): 34

pagodas and temples (*see also* individual pagodas): 27, 28, 38, 113, 114, 118, 129, 133, 135, 136, 137, 141, 142

Pakistan (*see also* East Pakistan): 196, 206, 218, 265, 270

Pakistanis, minority group: viii, 2, 5, 7, 18, 58, 65, 77, 123, 129, 141

Palaungs: 60, 79, 83, 84, 104, 105, 129

Pali: 27, 130

Panglong: 44, 45

Panthay: 65

Pa-o: 84, 129

Parliamentary Democratic Party: 168

parliamentary system. *See* Democracy

partisan politics (*see also* democracy): 1, 3, 148, 167, 168, 234

Patriotic Burmese Forces: 42, 43

Patriotic Volunteer Organization (PVO): 43, 46, 47

Patriot's Party: 40

U Pe Maun Tin: 119

peasants. *See* working classes

Pegu: 235; history, 29, 30, 31, 34-35; town, xiv

Pegu, division: xiv, 11, 16, 145, 146, 203

penal code and system (*see also* courts): 274, 290-291, 291-292

People's Bank of the Union of Burma: 153-154, 215, 222, 223, 224-227, 261, 262; Law (1967), 224, 225, 227, 230

People's Militia: 158

People's Peasants' Councils: 4, 56, 67, 174, 200, 212, 234, 245; Central, 177, 178, 214, 245

people's workers' councils 4, 56, 174-175, 200, 212, 234, 254; Central: 177, 179, 214, 254

personnel, trained (*see also* medical personnel; teachers): 279; managerial and technical, 234, 247, 248, 251, 258, 259; professionals,

42, 58, 64, 211.

petroleum: 42, 49, 202, 205, 210, 218, 236-237, 249, 251-252

Philippines: 197, 206, 218, 265

Pinya: 29

police (*see also* National People's Police): 154, 203, 274, 277; service, 287-288; training, 288

political indoctrination: 4, 56, 63, 101, 158, 176-177

pongyi. *See* monks

population (*see also* settlement patterns): vii, 1, 9-10, 17-21, 221, 252; growth rate, vii, 1, 19, 240

ports and harbours: ix, 9, 66, 258, 269-270; air, 271

Portuguese: 30, 31, 66

power. *See* electricity

precious stones. *See* gems

press (*see also* newspapers): 61, 122, 148, 213; editorials and reports, 63, 64, 66, 67, 76, 179, 193

prices: 212, 222, 233-234, 245

prisoners, political: 167, 168, 184

private enterprise (*see also* nationalization): ix, 3, 8, 49, 52, 63, 147, 169, 201, 210, 213, 214, 216, 218, 226, 248, 251, 257, 259, 260, 261, 262, 267

production: agricultural, 203, 209, 210, 241, 242, 245, 257; industrial, 248-252

Prome: xiv, 116, 237, 270; history, 26, 30

Public Administration Division: 152, 153, 158

public dept (*see also* budget): 223-224, 229

Public Law 480 (U.S.): 199, 203

Public Service Commission: 156, 158

Public Service Enquiry Commission: 157

public services: 49

publishing (see also newspapers; press): 126-127, 209

pwe: 75, 99, 115-116

Pyidaungsu Party: 53, 54, 170

Pyidawtha plan (1953-1960): 50, 87, 97

Pyu: 25, 26

radio: 122, 125, 128; receivers, 125, 249; stations, 102

Radio Peking: 128

railways: ix, 36, 258, 270-271

rainfall: vii, 15-16, 17, 234, 235, 239

Vietnam: 104, 124, 128, 198; North, 25, 185
villages (*see also* administration; rural society): vii, 7, 20–21, 37, 68–69, 80, 81, 90; headman, 55, 69–70, 81, 83
vocational training: 106, 107, 108, 109
Voice of America: 128
volunteers, army: ix, 63, 273, 279

wages: 157, 212, 254–255; the armed forces, 63, 282, 288
Wareru, Shan adventurer: 28
Was: 79, 85
weaving: 116, 215
welfare programs: 50, 53, 87–88, 97–99, 129
West Germany: 205, 236, 250
Western Mountain Belt: 11, 12, 13, 20, 269
westernization. *See* cultural influences
White Flag: ix
women: viii, 7, 17, 18, 28, 67, 68, 69, 71–72, 74, 87, 116; dress, 79, 80, 82, 84, 85, 90, 118
woodcarving: 117
Worker's Hospital, Rangoon: 94, 98
working classes (*see also* People's Peasants' Council; prople's workers' council): 164, 167, 170, 177, 178
working conditions: 254–255; armed forces, 282; police, 287–288
Working People's Daily: 5, 123, 124, 267, 268
World Health Organization (WHO): 94
World War I: 275
World War II: 3, 8, 24, 41–42, 56, 60, 78, 81, 87, 98, 105, 120, 121, 135, 202, 235, 258, 275; reparations, 198, 201

Young Men's Buddhist Association (YMBA): 38, 39, 98
youth (*see also* students): 64–65
Yunnan, China: 25, 28, 32, 34, 41, 65, 192
Yunnan Province Anti-Communist National Salvation Army: 192

PUBLISHED AREA HANDBOOKS

550-65	Afghanistan	550-41	Korea, Republic of
550-98	Albania	550-58	Laos
550-44	Algeria	550-24	Lebanon
550-59	Angola	550-38	Liberia
550-73	Argentina	550-85	Libya
550-20	Brazil	550-45	Malaysia
550-61	Burma	550-76	Mongolia
550-83	Burundi	550-49	Morocco
550-50	Cambodia	550-64	Mozambique
550-96	Ceylon	550-88	Nicaragua
550-26	Colombia	550-94	Oceania
550-60	Communist China	550-48	Pakistan
550-91	Congo (Brazzaville)	550-92	Peripheral States of the
550-67	Congo (Kinshasa)		Arabian Peninsula
550-90	Costa Rica	550-72	Philippines
		550-84	Rwanda
550-152	Cuba	550-51	Saudi Arabia
550-22	Cyprus	550-70	Senegal
550-54	Dominican Republic	550-86	Somalia
550-52	Ecuador	550-93	South Africa, Republic of
550-150	El Salvador	550-95	Soviet Union
550-28	Ethiopia	550-27	Sudan
550-29	Germany	550-47	Syria
550-153	Ghana	550-62	Tanzania
550-78	Guatemala	550-53	Thailand
550-82	Guyana	550-89	Tunisia
550-151	Honduras	550-80	Turkey
550-21	India	550-74	Uganda
550-39	Indonesia	550-43	United Arab Republic
550-68	Iran	550-97	Uruguay
550-31	Iraq	550-71	Venezuela
550-25	Israel	550-57	Vietnam, North
550-30	Japan	550-55	Vietnam, South
550-34	Jordan	550-75	Zambia
550-56	Kenya		
550-81	Korea, North